DOUBLE THREAT

p. 166

DOUBLE THREAT

Canadian Jews, the Military, and World War II

Ellin Bessner

NEW JEWISH PRESS

FIRST EDITION

This edition published in 2018 by
New Jewish Press
Anne Tanenbaum Centre for Jewish Studies
University of Toronto
170 St. George Street, Room 218
Toronto, Ontario M5R 2M8
www.newjewishpress.ca

Book design by Mark Goldstein
Cover design after Hubert Rogers' 1943 award-winning poster "Attack On All Fronts"

LIBRARY AND ARCHIVES CANADA CATALOGUING IN PUBLICATION

Bessner, Ellin, 1961–, author
Double threat: Canadian Jews, the military, and World War II / Ellin Bessner.

Issued in print and electronic formats.
ISBN 978-1-988326-04-7 (softcover). —ISBN 978-1-988326-05-4 (HTML)

1. World War, 1939–1945—Participation, Jewish. 2. World War, 1939–1945—Canada. 3. World War, 1939–1945—Canada—Biography. 4. Jewish soldiers—Canada—Biography. 5. Jews—Canada—Biography. I. Title.

D810.J4B467 2018 940.53089'924 C2017-908027-X
C2017-908028-8

PRINTED IN CANADA

For John, Alex, and Evan,
and for my late uncle Leo Guttman,
an RCAF veteran who served in WWII but didn't talk about it,
until he did, in 2014, with me

Contents

Acknowledgements

Normally, authors thank their family and support systems at the end of the acknowledgements. My husband, John Friedlan, and my sons, Alex and Evan, should be thanked at the beginning. Thank you for believing in me. This book is the third most important thing I will ever do, next to being your wife and mother.

Double Threat would not have been completed without these special people: Lois Lieff and Brenda Bessner, Ken Adessky and Morton Bessner. Special thanks also to Amy Langer, Rosalie Waller, Rhonda Kula, Terry Shatner, Sheryl Gencher, Linda Scales, Pat Walsh, Shannon Walsh-Moreau, Vita Kolodny, Naomi Krajden, Mark Kingstone, and Daphne Flatt for providing heartfelt encouragement.

To my cousin Judy Guttman, thank you for starting this journey by introducing me to Isabella Meltz, and then encouraging your father, Leo Guttman, to tell me his war story. To my cousin Gita Berman, thank you for finding the Nussbaums in Israel and for asking the right questions.

To Nellie Miller, thank you for telling me about your friend's brother Joe Gertel and then challenging me to write a book. To Elaine Archer and David Archer, thank you for sending me news clippings through your important project, Operation Picture Me. To Joel, Ross, and Aviva Lifschitz, thank you for hosting me on that fact-finding trip to Claresholm and Nanton, Alberta. To Elaine and Ray Feig, thank you for Ben Dunkelman's book *Dual Allegiance*, a gift from your parents' library. To Maylene and Rael Ludwig and Beth and Norman Shore, thank you for the kosher dinner and open houses in Winnipeg. To Stephen Glazer and the Glazer family, thank you for the connections in Canada and in

Israel. To William Wolfe-Wylie of CBC News, thank you for the database work.

To the Canadian author, broadcaster, and journalism professor extraordinaire Ted Barris, thank you not only for your idea to take my family to Normandy in 2011 but also for helping to guide my writing and sharing the joys and challenges of telling important untold stories. You have been a role model and mentor.

Thanks also to my colleagues in Centennial College's Journalism department in Toronto, including Lindy Oughtred, Eric McMillan, Tim Doyle, Steve Cogan, Malcolm Kelly, Rohan McLeish, and Jules Elder. And to my dean, Nate Horowitz, for a sabbatical in 2015–2016 so I could write the book. To Philip Alves for the website.

Special thanks to Shelley Rosen and the Royal Canadian Legion Wingate Branch #256 in Toronto for introducing me to some of the wonderful veterans whose stories populate the book and for entrusting me with your archives. A similar thank you to Harry Colt and Norman Gardner at the Jewish War Veterans of Canada Toronto branch, and also to David Chochinov of the Winnipeg Jewish branch of the Legion, for arranging interviews with Jewish veterans at the Shaftesbury Park Retirement Residence. To Sally Fur at Sunnybrook Hospital in Toronto, thank you for facilitating interviews with Manny Rubinoff, Jack Feldman, Norman Gulko, and Harold Fromstein.

Thanks to my crack transcribers Sean Pearce, Ryan Chatterjee, Fatima Texiwala, Daniel Mackenzie, Alex Boue, Alex Friedlan, Stephanie Hinds, Ariel Vered, Nicholas Misketi, Jaymee Gencher, Bogdan Stanciu, Bria John, Sandra Sukraj, Dileen Simms, Donstan Wilson, Sayada Nabi, Dillon Hiles, Trevor Goulding, Jonathan Costa, Christine Smith, Kate Paddison, and Arturo Chang.

Thanks, too, to my editors, Lara Hinchberger and Sarah Roger; to Alison Reid and Madeline Koch for painstaking copyediting; and to the New Jewish Press—Malcolm Lester, Andrea Knight, and Robin Roger — for taking a chance.

Special thanks to Janice Summerby, formerly at Veterans Affairs Canada; Dr. Stephen Harris at the Directorate of History and Heritage, Department of National Defence; the late Thelma Shapiro from the YMHA in Montreal; Stan Carbone and Ava Block-Super at the Jewish Heritage Centre of Western Canada in Winnipeg; Janice Rosen and Hélène Vallée at the Alex Dworkin Canadian Jewish Archives in Montreal;

Raymond Goodman in Cape Breton; Saundra Lipton and Agi Romer Segal at the Jewish Heritage Society of Southern Alberta; Dara Solomon and Donna Bernardo-Ceriz at the Ontario Jewish Archives; Shannon Hodge at the Jewish Public Library in Montreal; Saara Mortensen at the Ottawa Jewish Archives; Rosalie Waller of the Seneca College library in Toronto; Katherine Biggs-Craft of the Saint John Jewish Museum; Gail Alexander and the Story Arts Centre Library staff at Centennial College for help in finding esoteric books and journals; Francis Weil at Tiferes Israel Synagogue in Moncton; Ken Favrholdt at the Claresholm and District Museum; Sergeant Major Jack O'Brien (Ret'd) in Kingston; Charles Abelson; Eric Campbell at the Montreal Aviation Museum; Scott Masters and his Oral History project at Crestwood Academy; Doug Evans; the staff at the Reference Services Division of Library and Archives Canada, and also Paul Marsden, former head of Military Archives; Meaghan Dalby at Historica Canada for the interviews from the Memory Project; Daniel Byers, Peter Usher, Duff Crerar, D. Burke Penney, and Martin Sugarman for sharing their research; the Ontario Jewish Archives, Blankenstein Family Heritage Centre, for awarding me a Dr. Stephen Speisman Bursary to help support my research; and Warren Sheffer for the legal work.

And, finally, a debt of gratitude is owed to all the Canadian Jewish veterans and their families who shared their photos, mementoes, documents, and memories with me. I am honoured to be able to tell your stories. I only wish that I had started this work a decade ago, when many more of the Jewish Canadian World War II veterans were still alive.

Introduction

On July 8, 1944, on the outskirts of the French city of Caen, George Meltz was either hit by a German sniper's bullet or stepped on a mine.[1] He was taken to a Canadian Army hospital, where he died of his wounds. The Toronto-born gunner was twenty-five years old and had just married a British girl he had met in England. Meltz's parents had fled the religious persecution of Jews in Lithuania and immigrated to Canada. In 1941 George had left a job with a wallpaper company in Toronto to enlist in the Royal Canadian Artillery. Of course, the Germans knew none of this; Meltz was just another soldier killed in order to slow the 3rd Canadian Infantry Division's advance from the beaches of Normandy.

I didn't know any of this either when I visited the Bény-sur-Mer Canadian War Cemetery in Reviers, France, in July 2011. At first glance, Meltz's grave seemed the same as those of the 2,049 other casualties of World War II buried there. These soldiers died during the D-Day invasion in June 1944 and also during the breakout from the beaches over the following month.

My trip to the cemetery came on an overcast day at the end of a tour that I had taken with my husband and our boys. We went on the advice of Ted Barris, an author of books about Canada's veterans in wars from Vimy to Afghanistan. We had no guidebook to tell us where to visit, and the cemetery offered only a plastic folder containing brief references to who was buried where. We wandered around and spotted tombstones displaying Stars of David. As do many Jews, we picked up pebbles and placed them on top of the Jewish graves. It is an ancient tradition that honours the dead with a souvenir that doesn't wilt the way flowers would. My husband took photos of graves with names such as Freedman, Brownstone, Gertel, Mandel, and Silverberg.

At Section XI, Row C, Plot 11, the Portland limestone tombstone displays a few terse details:

B-11603 Bombardier
G. Meltz
Royal Canadian Artillery
8th July 1944 Age 25

Below the Star of David was an epitaph that took my breath away.

DEEPLY MOURNED BY HIS WIFE AND FAMILY
HE DIED SO JEWRY
SHALL SUFFER NO MORE

As I am both a journalist and a Canadian Jew, my interest was piqued: I had to find out who G. Meltz was and who had chosen the wording on his tombstone. I didn't have to look far. Googling turned up his namesake, a nephew, George Meltz, who lived in Richmond Hill, Ontario, and even attended my synagogue. I called and he gave me some of the story. A niece, Isabella Meltz, showed me some photos and also a pink handkerchief, which her uncle had sent to his family in Toronto while training in England. Isabella had been born too late to meet her uncle. She knew only what her father and his eight siblings had told her about their baby brother, the one who didn't come home from the war.

The Meltzes were no different from many other families who lived through those years. After 1945, most of the veterans and families of the conflict's casualties didn't talk much about the war. I had nearly a dozen relatives who served, but I knew next to nothing about their experiences. My great-uncle Al Singer apparently spoke Yiddish to some Germans he took as prisoners. My great-aunt Daisy Friedberg had been a military policewoman. My great-uncle Sam Hershon had served as a dentist overseas, and three of my grandfather's brothers had served in a Canadian uniform—Joe Lieff in the navy, Max Lieff in the army, and Hymie Lieff in the air force. My uncle, Leo Guttman, had served in the Royal Canadian Air Force, as had my father-in-law, Irving Friedlan, but I didn't know where or when. I discovered that the brother of my great-aunt Dorothy Lieff, Jack Brovender, was killed on his first training flight over England.

It was too late to find out more. My family, like so many others, has no one alive who can identify the faces or interpret the details on the backs of photos. I have a box of somebody's war medals, but no one knows whose they were.

The Meltz family is almost certain that George's twenty-year-old English widow submitted the epitaph for her husband's gravestone. Trudy (born Gertrude Shimalovitch) and George were married in a London synagogue on October 24, 1943. George was twenty-three and Trudy nineteen. The couple may have met while George was in a British military hospital recovering from knee surgery to repair an old football injury. The newlyweds would have just seven months together before George left for Normandy.

After the war, when tombstones were being erected, it was she who mailed the wording to the Commonwealth War Graves Commission. It is a stirring eulogy, a tribute to both loss and defiance. A cry of grief but also of pride. In those sixty-one characters, nearly the maximum allowed under the regulations, we see her husband's death as she saw it: giving his life in the fight to save the Jews of Europe from Hitler.

Like George Meltz, the nearly seventeen thousand Canadian Jews who donned a uniform in World War II came of age in a land where being Jewish meant facing antisemitism in personal and professional spheres. Some had been attacked by local gangs while swimming at Plage Laval, a popular summer spot north of Montreal, others while playing baseball at Toronto's Christie Pits. They lived in a country where some companies would not hire Jews, where there were quotas limiting the number of Jews enrolled in some university faculties, and where Jews were restricted from joining some private clubs. Canada's government was turning away thousands of Jewish refugees trying to outrun Europe's repressive racial laws. Yet despite the government's regrettable treatment of its Jewish citizens and refugees, many Canadian Jewish men rushed to the recruiting centres when the war broke out.

More than a million Canadians served in World War II. Among them, Canada's Jewish soldiers faced something unique: they were not only standing beside Britain against the dark forces of Nazism and dictatorship, but also fighting to save their own people from destruction. They did so while encountering widespread antisemitism at home, in the barracks, and even on the battlefield.

The title of this book, *Double Threat: Canadian Jews, the Military, and World War II*, comes from a letter that Prime Minister William Lyon

Mackenzie King sent to the Canadian Jewish Congress on March 20, 1947. King thanked Congress, the Jewish political and social action organization of the day, for the contribution of Jewish troops to the Allied victory. He called the war and Hitler a "double threat" to the country's Jewish servicemen: they had fought not only against "Nazi and Fascist aggression" but "also for the survival of the Jewish nation."[2]

After that, however, the contribution of Canada's Jewish community to the war effort received little attention. Although Veterans Affairs Canada's website honours other minority groups who served during World War II including Chinese Canadians, Black Canadians, and Indigenous Peoples, it did not acknowledge the involvement of Canada's Jews. I'm extremely pleased, therefore, that at the time of publication of this book, I was informed by VAC that they intend to use *Double Threat* as a source in order to rectify this omission.

In the lead-up to the seventieth anniversary of D-Day in 2014, I launched a campaign called "Kaddish for D-Day" to have synagogues hold memorial services for the seventy Jewish Canadian men in uniform who are buried in graveyards throughout Normandy. Meanwhile, my published news stories about Jewish Canadian soldiers, and about George Meltz in particular, prompted other veterans and their families to reach out to me. It became clear that I needed to put all this information into a book, one that was not only about the nearly 450 Canadian Jews who did not come home from the war but also about the thousands of young Jewish Canadians who donned a uniform and survived. More than seventy years after Meltz's death, *Double Threat* is an exploration of the experiences of this generation of Jewish fighters.

The book tells the stories of the men and women who served on the home front and overseas: from Alaska to Ortona, from the Gulf of St. Lawrence to the Murmansk Run, from the beaches of Normandy to the glaciers of Iceland, and from West Africa to Bergen-Belsen. It also tells the stories of those who were held prisoner by the Japanese and in German-occupied Europe.

These Canadian Jewish men and women speak to us in thousands of family letters, diaries, and photos; in hundreds of government records; and in troves of documents kept in archives and libraries. We were the victors, they are telling us, not the vanquished. Although we were too late to save the six million Jews killed in the Holocaust, we did help end the war, and helped save the remnants of the Jewish people.

1 Fighting Amalek

"Just remember I am fighting for our people"

There was no question in Prime Minister William Lyon Mackenzie King's mind that Canada was going to enter World War II. By the fall of 1938, the Canadian leader and his Cabinet had decided to join with Britain in a war against Germany should diplomatic efforts to appease Hitler fail. But unlike the Great War a generation earlier, when Canada was automatically involved in the conflict because it was a British Dominion, this time King was determined to hold out. Canada had been moving toward sovereignty since signing the Treaty of Versailles on its own behalf in 1919, and the 1931 Statute of Westminster had granted Canada more legal control over its affairs. King decided that a formal vote would be held in Parliament, as befitting a self-governing nation.

By September 1, 1939, while Hitler was ordering German tanks to invade Poland, Canada's army, navy and air force were mobilized to defend Canada, Ottawa having already invoked the War Measures Act on August 25. On Sunday, September 3, the day Britain and France formally declared war on Germany, King put Canadians on notice. "The people of Canada will, I know, face the days of stress and strain which lie ahead with calm and resolute courage," King said in his address on the radio that same day. "There is no home in Canada, no family, and no individual whose fortunes and freedom are not bound up in the present struggle."[1]

On September 7, lawmakers met in the House of Commons and the Senate. Only three politicians urged Canada to remain neutral, among them two Liberal members of Parliament from Quebec who represented the anti-British, anti-conscription sentiment of their province. By September 9, the decision was made. On September 10, the government's official newspaper, the Canada Gazette, issued a special edition proclaiming that Canada was officially at war with Germany.

At sundown on September 13, King's message was on the minds of Canada's Jews as they streamed into synagogues to mark Rosh Hashanah (Jewish New Year). Rabbis addressed their congregants with rousing speeches that mixed patriotism with historical memory. "Should Hitlerism win, the world will be plunged into utter darkness, in which case the Jews will be the greatest losers," said Rabbi Arthur Feldman at Temple Anshe Sholom in Hamilton. He told his flock the war was "the greatest hour of Jewish destiny in all our history rich in grim crises."[2] In Toronto, the New Year speech by Rabbi Maurice Eisendrath of Holy Blossom Temple received coverage in the *Globe and Mail*: "We of the household of Israel who have been so singularly blessed within this Empire, must do all in our power, with might and main and means and men, to help God to fulfill his ancient promise to bless those who bless us."[3]

For Canada's approximately one hundred and sixty-five thousand Jews, the declaration of war set in motion a massive mobilization effort encouraged from the pulpit and in the mainstream Jewish press, and financed and carried out mainly by the Canadian Jewish Congress. Although Jewish groups had been working since Hitler came to power in 1933 to bring European Jewish refugees to Canada and to raise money to send others to Palestine, the declaration of war provided them with an urgent mandate.

The board of the Canadian Jewish Congress met in Montreal on September 10 to put planning into high gear. The president, Samuel Bronfman, a Montreal industrialist in the distillery business, publicly pledged Congress's support of the war effort. William Abrams, Congress's War Efforts Committee's national executive director, declared, "The outbreak of war...found the Jewish Community of Canada ready and anxious to support to the fullest extent our country's struggle against Nazi Oppression."[4]

Congress set up War Efforts Committee regional offices, which, aside from encouraging enlistment and physically and spiritually supporting Jewish military personnel, also raised funds on behalf of the Red Cross, canvassed Jewish factory workers to buy war savings stamps, and carried out a massive effort to furnish fourteen hundred recreation halls at Canadian military bases across the country. Congress donated and shipped several thousand couches and chairs, 2,890 ashtrays, 406

Ping-Pong tables, and 215 pianos.[5] Their internal mandate was threefold: provide comfort to Jewish soldiers, stimulate enlistment, and create a Jewish chaplaincy. But the fourth and unspoken reason that Congress devoted millions of dollars and six years of volunteer efforts was that it saw victory as the best strategy to save the Jewish people overseas.

Historian and filmmaker Max Beer believes that Jewish leaders realized the King administration was not fighting particularly to stop the murder of millions of European Jews. After all, there was antisemitism in Canada, especially in Quebec. So rather than emphasizing the plight of Jews under Hitler, Congress and the Jewish community chose to focus on proclaiming their loyalty to Canada and on safeguarding freedom and democracy.[6]

An undated memo from Congress suggested talking points for a speakers' bureau. Jewish spokespersons were reminded of what was at stake once the war was over: "Finish by mentioning that the whole Jewish community is anxious to do its share and that all should pull together in every phase of the national war effort; so that the Jewish record, after the war, both in combatant and noncombatant activity, shall be excellent."[7] Rabbi Gershon Levi of Montreal's Shaar Hashomayim synagogue (later appointed the first Canadian Jewish army chaplain) referred to this as "the public relations aspect" of the war effort.[8] A rabbi in a Canadian military uniform could hold great symbolic and strategic value for both Jewish and non-Jewish Canadians, both during and after the war.

Congress's response to the call to arms was not the first time Jewish residents had seen war service. According to the historian Derek Penslar, Jews in Canada have a history of military service and even of seeing the military as a viable peacetime career. "Jewish valor was a function of emancipation and social acceptance," Penslar writes. "When Jews felt themselves to be part of the body politic, they willingly went forth to defend it."[9]

After Canada became a British colony in 1759, Jewish men were permitted to serve in the militia; under French rule, all non-Catholics had previously been banned. During the War of 1812, nearly all the eligible Jewish men in Upper and Lower Canada fought against American invaders.[10] The 1837 Rebellion also saw Jews help the Crown put down the Lower Canada uprising.

There is no clear picture of Jewish enlistment in World War I.

Sociologist Louis Rosenberg claimed that more than 38 per cent of eligible Jewish men served with the Canadian Expeditionary Force, a ratio that he said was higher than other ethnic groups. The Jewish Virtual Library counts more than a thousand Canadian Jewish officers and forty-six hundred Jewish soldiers who served. One hundred of these are reported to have died in service; eighty-four were decorated. The Canadian Senate counted 987 Jewish men who enlisted for overseas service by the end of June 1917.

Despite the patriotism that Canadian Jews displayed in previous wars, by the time World War II broke out, Canada's Jewish community had reason to feel anxious. Prejudice against Jews was ingrained at the highest levels in Canada, including the government itself. Immigration to Canada for Europe's Jews was all but closed; Canada famously turned away a boatload of German Jewish refugees in 1939 as part of the antisemitic policies espoused by immigration authorities.

During the 1930s and '40s, systemic antisemitism meant quotas for Jewish students in key programs at Canadian universities. Oscar Antel of Winnipeg, a veteran of the Royal Canadian Air Force, remembers being shut out of accounting because many local firms wouldn't take Jewish students on for apprenticeships. Estelle Aspler (née Tritt) applied to the Montreal General Hospital School of Nursing but was told it didn't accept Jewish students "because they get married too soon."[11] Many aspiring Canadian Jewish doctors faced entrenched quotas that kept them out of the medical schools. Some Jews went into dentistry instead, but rigid quotas existed there, too.

From 1932 to 1944, the Faculty of Medicine at the University of Manitoba applied a secret formula to limit the number of Jewish and other "non-desirable" students.[12] "Usually there were four or five Jews, two or three women, and five or six central Europeans accepted" out of seventy spots in the first-year class, according to a 1943 report compiled by the Avuka society of Jewish students, which lodged a formal complaint with the Manitoba legislature in 1944.[13]

Jews who finished medical school faced further hardship: many hospitals in Canada refused to accept Jewish staff for mandatory residencies. This was the case for the future major Joseph Minden of Hamilton. He had finished near the top of his class at medical school in Toronto but couldn't get hired. "Jewish graduates were not being welcomed" is what Sarah Minden, his daughter, remembers hearing. Non-Jewish interns at the Notre-Dame Hospital in Montreal went on strike in 1934 because they didn't want to work with a Jewish doctor. Regina's general hospital refused to hire two Jewish doctors as radiologists.[14]

Employment was often denied to Jews in subtle ways. Murray Jacobs, an army veteran, remembers being turned away from jobs in Toronto after prospective employers saw "Hebrew" on his application. The reception he received at one factory angered Jacobs: "'They're filled up,'" Jacobs recalled the manager saying. "So I said, 'You were just talking to me and you just told me you need watchmakers. I'm a watchmaker....' [They said,] 'Oh, no, no! Well, we just found out we got filled up.'"

A report in a 1939 American Jewish review summed up the position of Jews in the Canadian economy: "There is not and has not been for the past forty years a single Jewish director of a chartered bank, railway, ocean or air transportation company, telephone or telegraph company, public utility corporation, or pulp and paper corporation."[15]

In Quebec, anti-Jewish sentiment was widespread due to the influence of Catholic clergy as well as political leaders such as Adrien Arcand, who headed a number of fascist movements, and nationalist historian and priest Lionel Groulx. Their "Buy Local" campaign to boycott Jewish merchants took its toll, and their speeches and articles sparked what would today be considered hate crimes against Jews holidaying in the Laurentians. In August 1939, a bridge leading to a Jewish-owned resort on an island near Ste-Agathe-des-Monts was burned, and local Catholic priests delivered sermons urging French Canadians to remain masters of their own communities. In July 1943, a former Montreal Jewish Olympic boxing star, Moe Herscovitch, lost an eye after being beaten up by local French Canadian youths at Plage Laval. The ringleaders, including the son of the local police chief, were not punished. For years the Quebec City municipal council passed bylaws preventing the construction of a new synagogue. When the synagogue was finally built, arsonists torched it on its opening day.

Hitler's racial laws found favour among sectors of Canadian society, which led to violent confrontations. In the tense summer of 1933, local Hitler supporters who wore swastikas on their clothing tried to bar Jews from bathing at the beach clubs in Toronto. "On Sunday, the rabbi would take us through Kew Beach, of all places, for Sunday lunch. Soon as we got there, all these big guys with baseball bats, clubs, would come in and whack everybody," RCAF veteran Lieutenant Colonel Norman Cohen recalled.

Tensions erupted into riots at Willowvale Park (now known as Christie Pits) in Toronto's west end on August 13. A disturbance broke out after gang members unveiled a swastika symbol on a banner during a baseball game between the team from St. Peter's Protestant church and the predominantly Jewish team known as Harbord Playground. Six hours of street battles ensued as Jewish and Italian teens fought against Nazi sympathizers. Ten people were hospitalized, thirty more were injured, and it took three hundred Toronto policemen all night to stop the mobs. There were three arrests, but only one person was charged, for carrying a lead pipe.

Young Jews in Winnipeg had similar encounters with homegrown antisemitism. In the Market Square clashes on June 5, 1934, five hundred members of the Anti-Fascist League clashed with brown-shirted Nationalists. Eighteen men were injured and there were nine arrests. Manitoba army veteran Saul Cherniack remembers Nazi supporters being permitted to hold meetings and publish antisemitic literature until the provincial government changed the libel laws. Jews were considered "undesirables" in the wealthy Tuxedo neighbourhood of Winnipeg and also at Victoria Beach, a resort area north of the city, which meant that they could not register land titles to own property.[16]

Bill Walsh, an army veteran who served overseas, told a similar story. A labour organizer in Southern Ontario before the war, Walsh recalled seeing a sign in Fenelon Falls that said "No Jews or Dogs Allowed."[17] Nathan Isaacs, an RCAF navigator, remembered seeing a similar sign posted at the Manitou Hotel on Toronto's Centre Island during the summer of 1941, when his family moved from Winnipeg to Toronto. "We just walked by," he said.

When David (Tevy) Devor's family was closing the deal to buy a new house in Toronto, his mother brought him along, in his army private's uniform. They kept their mouths closed when the seller unabashedly, but mistakenly, explained why she thought they were the ideal buyers. "When the owner of the house...gave them the key, she said she was glad her house wasn't going to a Jew," according to Helen Feinstein, one of Devor's older sisters.[18]

Even where Jews were few in number, antisemitism was unavoidable. The farming community of Oxbow, Saskatchewan, had only five Jewish families when army veteran Morris Polansky was growing up, although he says there were few issues with the non-Jewish kids at his school. "It was the adults that could make snarky remarks, like 'The Lord said unto

Moses: All the Jews would have long noses,' and you had to laugh, because you were just a kid."

Eventually, according to historian Gerald Tulchinsky, over 39 per cent of the eligible Jewish male population of Canada would join the military in World War II, a figure only slightly lower than the government's post-war official data showing that 41.15 per cent of all eligible Canadian men between 18–45 years served[19]. At first, their motivations were the same: patriotism and duty. But as the war went on, and news of the plight of Europe's Jews began to trickle out, the stakes changed for the young Canadian Jews in uniform. They carried an extra burden: being a Jew in a war in which Jews were being murdered.

After the 1881 assassination of Czar Alexander II heralded the beginning of anti-Jewish laws and persecution in the Russian-controlled Pale of Settlement, some one hundred thousand Jews fled to Canada. The children of these emigrants now wanted to make sure the troubles that their parents' generation had faced didn't follow them into their new country. As the war went on, the overarching issue for Canada's Jewish military personnel became the fight against Hitler and the Nazis, an enemy whom Penslar later characterized as "the Amalek of the twentieth century," referring to the biblical enemy of the Israelites who attacked the Jews after their escape from Egypt.[20]

Oscar Antel and his family came to Canada from Poland in 1930. He was worried about his relatives who had stayed behind, as the war made communication with them impossible. Antel was only sixteen in 1939, but the Winnipeg teen and his friends spent a lot of time talking about joining up once they were old enough. When Antel turned nineteen in 1942, he enlisted as air force ground crew.[21]

Personal experience of living under Hitler's Nazi regime also motivated some Jews to enlist. In 1938, Nathan Dlusy arrived in Montreal from Berlin, where his family had lived since 1920, and where his father, Israel, had built a successful menswear business. As the restrictions against Jews in German society became more widespread, some of the non-Jewish neighbours in their apartment complex would no longer allow their children to play with Nat and his brother, Jon. By May 1938, a sympathetic former customer who had become a member of the Nazi party warned the Dlusys to flee. The family pretended they were going to Belgium on holiday and sneaked out of Germany, leaving everything behind.

Nat began thinking about joining the military in 1939. He wasn't yet a naturalized British subject, which was one of the requirements during the early years of the war. Through his father's business connections, however, Nat successfully enlisted. His motivation made a strong impression on the officer at the Montreal recruiting centre: "Very anxious to fly. Prefers WOAG [Wireless Operator Air Gunner]. Born in Berlin. Family are Hebrew. Parents not naturalized. Parents in Canada 3½ years. In Berlin before coming here. Hates Nazi doctrine. Family had to leave Berlin in a hurry."[22]

Recruiting officers at military depots heard similar explanations from other Canadian Jewish men and women. The army interviewer who met Montrealer Joe Gertel, 21, said there was no mistaking the young man's motivation: "He was merely anxious to get into the front line and settle a score which he felt that he, as a Jew, should be allowed to settle."[23] Many Jews clearly saw the war as their war. Toronto's Charles Krakauer, who was working as a physician in rural Saskatchewan before he enlisted, said, "Nobody's fighting for me." Krakauer told his family that he didn't want gentiles to be doing work that he felt as a Jew he ought to be responsible for.

It was seeing newspaper photos of European Jews being humiliated in the streets after Hitler took power that sent Arthur Pascal, a Montreal hardware retailer, to the local armoury. "The *Montreal Star*...and the *Gazette* would show a picture of old Jews, bearded, on their knees scrubbing the street, with German soldiers standing over them," Pascal said. "In those days, you had no idea [of] the bitterness and we felt, the Jewish community felt, so helpless. We weren't doing anything."[24]

In Toronto, Murray Jacobs also heard about the persecution of Europe's Jews. Despite his father's protests, Jacobs went to enlist. "I got myself all worked up and I heard that they were killing Jews...I thought to myself, I'm capable and I have a very good trade and I can be very useful."

That's also what motivated Maxwell Lerner to sign up. He served in Italy with the Royal Canadian Army Medical Corps. "The reason I enlisted was a strong feeling of my roots, my Jewish roots," Lerner would explain in *No Greater Honour*, a 1987 video documentary about Jewish war veterans. "While most Canadians were fighting to perpetuate a certain way of life, I was fighting for the very life of my nation, of my roots."[25]

David Devor landed in Italy in 1944, and on June 5 he wrote a letter home telling his mother exactly why he was there. "Just remember I'm fighting for are [*sic*] people." He described how another Jewish soldier in his outfit had been killed, but wrote, admiringly, that he'd "bagged more then twenty" before he got hit. "Ma, I promise you that I'll attempt [to] get five Gerrys for you. In fact, one for each one in the family, [because of] the way the German treated the Jew in Europe."[26]

2 Signing Up

"I don't think they're taking Jews"

Of the one hundred and sixty-five thousand Jews living in Canada when World War II began, the majority—one hundred and thirty thousand to one hundred and forty thousand, or nearly 85 per cent—lived in major urban centres: Montreal, Toronto, and Winnipeg.[1] Not surprisingly, therefore, it was the urban contingent who provided most of the Jewish staffing levels in the war and who would suffer the highest number of fatalities.

Murray Bleeman was eleven in 1926 when his family immigrated to Toronto from Drilz, Poland. They settled on Lippincott Street, in the heart of the city's Jewish immigrant district. When the war broke out, Bleeman owned a lunch counter on Spadina Avenue but sold it because he was determined to enlist. He went to a Toronto recruiting centre in the first weeks of September 1939 but was turned away.

His family suspects it was because of his religion. "I can't imagine why they didn't take him here [in Toronto]. He was physically fit. This couldn't have sprung up from nowhere," said Ferne Phillips, Bleeman's niece. "There were a lot of people in the recruitment office who didn't want that many Jews in the army, for whatever reason, so he went to Hamilton and was taken right away." Bleeman enlisted with the Royal Hamilton Light Infantry on September 29, 1939, and volunteered for overseas service.

It is true that during the first few weeks of the war the recruiting centres in the large cities were struggling to accommodate the crowds of men. Plenty of hopefuls were turned away because there were only two army divisions being mobilized at that time, one for home defence and one for overseas. After the initial rush brought Ottawa the sixty-five thousand men it needed, the government limited the further intake of recruits.[2] Prime Minister William Lyon Mackenzie King intended to follow a strategy of minimal losses during the war: Canada would provide munitions and food to help Britain and its allies but would not permit too much Canadian blood to be spilled.

In addition to the evidence from servicemen themselves, researchers have noted that Jewish men had difficulties enlisting in certain regiments and certain branches of the Canadian military, especially in the war's early years. One was the Royal Canadian Air Force, with its very high standards of education and physical fitness. The other was the Royal Canadian Navy, "where anti-Semitism was rampant."[3]

Enlisting in the navy was considered nearly impossible for Jews, especially as officers. Ben Dunkelman waited in vain for months to get his call back from the navy. He thought he was a good prospect. He had the right social status, being the son of the owner of Tip Top Tailors, the largest men's suit manufacturer and retailer in Canada. His childhood home was an estate in Toronto, Sunnybrook Farm, which boasted thirty-five acres of lawn and flower gardens. He had attended Upper Canada College, a private school for Toronto's Protestant elite.

Dunkelman also had plenty of sailing experience. He was captain of his own schooner, which he sailed every summer on Georgian Bay. Dunkelman would eventually learn from a friend that the navy's silence was no accident. "Many RCN officers were drawn from the exclusive yachting circles which were WASP-dominated and heavily tinged with racism," Dunkelman writes in his memoir. "With its heavily conservative tradition, the navy obviously considered that a Jew was not suitable company in the wardroom."[4] He eventually joined the army, serving with distinction overseas in the Queen's Own Rifles of Canada.

Unlike Dunkelman, Monty Hall (born Monte Halparin) was far from wealthy. The son of a Winnipeg kosher butcher, Hall had to leave university for a year because he couldn't afford the tuition. When the war broke out, the future host of television's *Let's Make a Deal* game show was enrolled again at the University of Manitoba. He was also serving with the Canadian Officers' Training Corps (COTC), which operated on university campuses and provided military training to students, and through which he saw a notice that read: "Wanted. Officer recruitment in Tank Corps." "I want to be one of those guys," Hall said. The officer in charge turned him away. "I don't think they're taking Jews."

Jacob Markowitz, a Toronto physician, was already renowned in his field when the war began. Markowitz had a PhD from the University of Toronto, where he also held a position in physiology and experimental medicine.[5] He'd worked with Charles Best—who had helped to discover insulin—doing experiments with insulin on dogs, and he had also pioneered the world's first heart transplant between warm-blooded animals. He wrote a textbook for veterinarians and published dozens of scholarly papers.

After his first wife, Cecile, also a doctor, died in May 1940, Markowitz tried to enlist in the army in Toronto but was turned away, according to his family.[6] Markowitz was told it was because he was born in Romania and didn't have Canadian naturalization papers. That was a common barrier to enlistment for many Canadian Jewish personnel, especially in the early months of the war: they had to be British subjects.[7] More than half of the Jewish population of Toronto at the time—some 24,077 of forty-three thousand—had been born outside Canada and not all had done the paperwork for naturalization.[8] Markowitz, however, wasn't buying the explanation. "Many years later, he declared that the most likely reason for the refusal was the typical prejudice against Jews in Canada during those years," according to his son, Thomas Markowitz.

Canada's loss was Britain's gain. After word began to circulate that the Canadian Army had turned the renowned doctor away, "the Man Called Intrepid" showed up at Markowitz's Toronto clinic. "Intrepid" was the code name of William Stephenson, the Winnipeg-born head of Winston Churchill's wartime intelligence operations in the Americas. "Instead of discussing his health, the intrepid Stephenson invited Jacob to become a spy, working for British Security Coordination, the famous BSC," Thomas Markowitz writes. The British considered the doctor's Romanian origins an asset because he spoke the language. Markowitz soon was posted to England. After Hitler invaded Russia in 1941, Markowitz joined the British Army as a medical officer. "They welcomed me immediately," the doctor said.[9] Although his naturalization papers arrived in 1941, Markowitz told his family he never forgave Canada for denying him the opportunity to wear the maple leaf on a military uniform. For the rest of his life, he carried only a British passport and referred to himself as British.

Markowitz was by no means the only highly trained, valuable Jewish medical personnel who faced obstacles in joining the Canadian forces. After finishing medical school, Joseph Minden had found hospital jobs closed to him in southern Ontario, so the fledgling physician went to

St. Louis, Missouri; he then took further surgical training in Baltimore, Maryland. After Canada entered the war, Minden came home to Hamilton and tried to enlist in the navy. He was not accepted. His family says he was told it was because they weren't taking any Jews. When he tried the army, they told him they weren't taking any Americans. "He turned around, angry [because] he had spent his last penny to go to Canada," said his daughter Sarah. Following the Japanese attack on Pearl Harbor in December 1941, Minden joined the U.S. Army as a combat surgeon.

Ironically, stereotyping and ingrained prejudice sometimes worked to the advantage of Jewish recruits, who were considered more educated than the general population.[10] Although RCAF regulations initially barred entry to air crew jobs to those volunteers who were not British subjects, or of pure European descent, later in the war, after the restrictive rules were lifted in June 1941, Jewish graduates who had earned good marks in math in high school were coveted as were those who took science and math courses in university.[11]

When Samuel Cohen went to enlist in Montreal at the end of 1940, he had both a BA and a law degree from McGill University, where he'd also been in the COTC. He spoke four languages, skied, and played tennis and golf. His RCAF interviewer waxed enthusiastic about the new recruit, in spite of, or perhaps because of, his religion. "Bachelor of Arts and Law Degree. Keen and intelligent and quite a student. Confident, deliberate and athletic type. A very good Jewish Canadian type."[12]

Notwithstanding these occasional positive responses to prospective Jewish service personnel, Congress's War Efforts Committee was aware of cases of discrimination at the enlistment stage and beyond. In a 1941 report to Congress, the authors said these mainly involved "enlistment in a specific unit," though the report didn't name names. The report suggested, however, that "such instances of prejudice were manifestations of the viewpoint of a few individuals and did not reflect the attitude of superior military officers who have given assurances that such manifestations of prejudice would not be permitted."[13] The official public position of Congress at the time—that everything was fine—may have been taken for political reasons. It is also possible that, in the early years of the war at least, officials were simply not aware of the extent of discrimination and anti-Jewish incidents concerning enlistment.

It would take a publicity stunt by arguably the highest-profile

Canadian Jew to enlist in the war, Mayor David A. Croll of Windsor, to break down the barriers for the Jewish men in his city who wanted to enlist in the local Essex Scottish Regiment. At the start of the war, the unit opened its armoury to volunteers, but Jewish men informed Croll that a certain colonel didn't want to take any of them. "He was furious about that," said Croll's daughter, Crystal Hawk. She remembers her father phoning the *Windsor Star*, telling them to send a photographer, and then marching down himself to enlist. "They couldn't refuse."

Croll's decision was partly to press the issue but also for another important reason: "To some I appeared to represent the Jewish element in Canada," Croll would later tell an Ottawa journalist. "I could not find anybody else to set the example, so I said, 'Croll, it is you.' I did it deliberately."[14]

It isn't surprising, then, that the Canadian Jewish Congress's public relations bureau in Toronto featured Croll on the cover of its glossy 1940 enlistment booklet. The publication received wide distribution in southern Ontario's Jewish communities. The rousing headline on the cover shouts "THEY answered Hitler's challenge."[15] Over four pages, Congress showcased the black-and-white portraits of 126 Jewish men from Ontario who had enlisted. Although there were many who came from modest backgrounds, there were also the scions of prominent Jewish families. There were doctors such as Samuel Mirsky, serving as a major in the Royal Canadian Army Medical Corps (RCAMC), the son of Ottawa's Rabbi Jacob Mirsky. Corporal Fred Harris was another who answered Hitler's challenge; he was the son of Willie Harris of Toronto, a family physician and World War I veteran who probably delivered most of the babies in the neighbourhood of his Beverley Street clinic during the inter-war years. One could speculate that it was in large part directly because of their own or their families' high profiles in the Jewish world and, in some cases, in the wider Canadian community that these individuals and others decided to set an example and enlist.

Jewish youth who were active in the community in their own right were also driven to enlist. In Ottawa, the Maccabean Athletic Association saw eighteen of the club's twenty-five members volunteer for active service. All but three members of the city's Jewish youth group known as Aleph Zadik Aleph—the junior wing of the B'nai Brith men's service organization—were in uniform by 1940.[16] They included Flight Sergeant Herbert Wolf, the son of a leather-goods retailer on Sparks Street. It was important to him that so many members of his group were in uniform.

"Frankly I get disgusted at times when I see a lot of kids of our faith bragging about letting the other fellow fight, etc.—about it is all volunteer and if some fool wants to fight, let him," Wolf wrote home after he arrived overseas. "To me this is more our fight than anyone else's and I pray to God before I die I will have the satisfaction of seeing some work of Nazism destroyed by my own hand."[17]

As in Ontario, enlistment was common for members of well-known families and engaged Jewish youth from across Canada. Morton Heinish in Halifax, a member of Young Judaea (a Zionist youth movement) and the son of the local War Efforts Committee leader, Noa Heinish, served in the RCAF.[18] Joseph H. Aronovitch of Winnipeg, a gunner, was wounded while serving with the Royal Canadian Artillery; his father, A.H. Aronovitch, a well-known real estate entrepreneur, was a Congress vice-president. From Calgary, the lawyer Morris C. Shumiatcher enlisted in the RCAF in 1943, when he was twenty-six. His father, A.I. (Abraham Isaac) Shumiatcher, also a lawyer, had helped to build many of the city's Jewish schools, synagogues, and social and charitable associations.

Like in families of all religions, some Jewish parents tried to keep their sons and daughters safe at home. Hymie Steinberg of Winnipeg had a hard time persuading his parents to let him join the RCAF. His father, Jacob (Yashe), was a rabbi who worked as a cantor at the Chevra Mishnayes Orthodox congregation in the city's North End. His parents had come to North America from Dubossary, formerly part of Romania. His mother, Ruth, had witnessed armed Cossacks kill her father during a pogrom. Hymie, fourteen when the war broke out, took home a copy of the extra edition of the *Winnipeg Free Press* to show his father. "I'm going to get into the war," Hymie declared.

"You're never going to get in because it isn't going to last long," Hymie's sister, Tammy Lazar, recalls her father replying. Hymie registered with the Winnipeg Light Infantry for militia training at the city's McGregor Armoury while still in Grade 11, but he was impatient to do the real thing, even though he wouldn't be eighteen until December 1943.[19] His mother did everything she could to talk him out of it, remembers his baby brother David Steinberg, the Hollywood comedian.

"He said he was going to make us all miserable if we didn't let him enlist," said Tammy. Hymie took to stomping up and down the steps of the family's home, making enough noise to disturb their tenants until his embarrassed father relented. He drafted a letter on official Jewish Community Council stationery, granting permission for seventeen-and-a-half-year-old Hymie to join the RCAF.[20]

Both David Heaps and his younger brother Leo enlisted in the army in 1942. They were the sons of A.A. Heaps, a Jewish Winnipeg member of Parliament who was one of the founders of the CCF (Co-operative Commonwealth Federation) party, a forerunner of the New Democratic Party. A.A. Heaps was defeated in the 1940 federal election, partly because CCF leadership opposed the war. He suggested to Leo that he quit the army and go work on an aunt's farm near Toronto. Ottawa granted official postponements of army duty to more than one hundred and ninety thousand men who had received call-up notices, either to work in essential services, including farming, or to continue their studies.[21] But Leo, who did so poorly at officers' training school that even his army superiors thought he should probably give up, wouldn't quit. "I rebelled at the idea of working in the manure and dirt," he writes in his 1976 memoir, *The Grey Goose of Arnhem*.[22] Instead, Leo joined the British Army, landed in France on D-Day, and later served as a spy in Holland.

When Ben Dunkelman's parents learned that their son wanted to enlist, they were outraged.[23] Despite the Toronto couple's deep ties to the local and world Jewish community—David was a top donor to the Zionist movement, and Rose had founded the Canadian women's arm of the Zionist Organization, which ran its famous Hadassah charity bazaars in Toronto—they wanted their son to stay home.[24] The family's menswear factories had a contract with the Canadian government to manufacture uniforms, and there was a chain of retail menswear clothing stores to supervise.

"Didn't I know I was in an essential industry?" Dunkelman recalls in his memoir. "Wasn't I going to help run it? Didn't I know how hard it would be on my father? The whole thing was 'the height of irresponsibility.'" But none of that was enough to keep Dunkelman at home. "As a Jew I had a special score to settle with the Nazis," he writes, although at the time he couldn't imagine the horrors that Hitler would perpetrate on the Jews. "As a loyal Canadian, it was my duty to volunteer to fight."[25]

Much was probably expected of Michael Stein Jacobs of Montreal.

He was the only son of S.W. (Sam) Jacobs, only the second Jew in Canadian history to be elected to the House of Commons. When the war broke out, Michael was a student at Yale University. His father had died suddenly the year before and left a void not only in the family's Côte-St-Antoine home in the tony Westmount district but also in the leadership of the Montreal Jewish community. Sam Jacobs had founded many important Quebec Jewish institutions, such as the *Jewish Times* and the Canadian Jewish Congress. Michael's mother, Amy, was head of the National Council of Jewish Women, a social action organization, and she also sat on Congress's Dominion Council.[26] She wrote directly to a federal Cabinet minister asking for special treatment for her son.

"No, the pressure was not as S.W. Jacobs's son," maintains Sue Ransohoff (née Westheimer), Michael's widow, describing a conversation they'd shared. Michael told her the RCAF would help him find his own path in life, away from his parents' enormous influence. "He once said, 'A lot of us don't know what we're going to do when we graduate—the war is a way of finding something to do.'" The American debutante married Michael Jacobs in Montreal in late July 1941. He went overseas in September, as an air observer.

The Hart family of Quebec was one of the original and most prominent Jewish families in Canada, so it shouldn't be surprising that they may have had as many as a dozen relatives in uniform during the war.[27] Their ancestor Aaron Hart is thought to have been the first Jew to put down roots in Canada, having arrived as far back as 1760 with the British military in conquest of New France. Almost two centuries later, John Lewis Michaels, whose mother was a Hart, would do his duty just like his ancestors. After graduation from Bishop's University, Michaels joined the British Army, with which he saw action in the Arab uprising in Palestine before World War II. After Britain declared war on Germany, he served in North Africa, where he was killed.

Miriam (Mimi) Hart (née Freedman), of another branch of the same Hart family, joined the London Ambulance Service in England, on September 27, 1939. She was the daughter of Mabel (Hart) and Albert Freedman, and was born in Montreal. A brother served with the RAF, a sister worked for Scotland Yard, and a third worked as a nurse during the hostilities. Mimi later enlisted with the Canadian Women's Army Corps and landed in Normandy in 1944.

Other large Jewish families in Canada also sent multiple children to war. Of the twelve siblings in the Shnier family from Emerson, Manitoba, and later of Winnipeg, three boys would serve overseas: Jack became a sergeant with the U.S. Army; Clifford and Norman both flew with the RCAF. Two other brothers, George and Irving, received exemptions because they provided essential services. "My brother Irving [age twenty-eight in 1939] was working for an auto supply company, Empire Radio and Auto Supply, in Regina. Irving didn't want to go to war but was conscripted. He went to Toronto and got a job for Canada Wire and Cable, a war supply company. You could work there and get away with not going into the army," Max, another brother, said.

There were six Weiss brothers from Montreal who served, as did six of the twelve Hurwitz siblings, also from Montreal, including daughter Esther.[28] However, the Maser family from Ottawa may hold the record for being the largest contingent of Jewish siblings to fight for Canada in World War II: seven came from their family.

Rabbi Max Maser and his wife, Bessie, were affiliated with Rideau Street's Agudath Achim synagogue, where he served as a cantor and ritual slaughterer. They had nine sons and a daughter. The *Ottawa Journal* called the family "military-minded" and referred to the boys as "among the most popular of the Ottawa Jewish Community."[29] Even the daughter, Dorothy, made headlines in the city in 1942 when she married an Ottawa airman, William Segal, who was in uniform at the wedding.

As in the Maser family's case where younger brothers followed older brothers, so it often was in smaller families, too. Zave Brown of North Bay was "obsessed" with joining the armed forces, his relatives say, in hopes of finding his missing brother.[30] Sydney Brown joined the RCAF in 1941. He was seven years older and had always taken it upon himself to set Zave on the right path, scolding Zave in a wartime letter from overseas for running around and neglecting his studies in high school. "I hope that this will be the first and last time that I will have to write you concerning this, as it is very hard for me to write to one who is my brother and my best friend."[31]

Sydney's Wellington bomber was shot down on April 15, 1943, after a raid over Stuttgart. A year went by. The government advised the family to consider Sydney dead. But Zave had other plans. He joined the army in 1944 in part to search for his older brother. He never did find him, and he was killed in the final weeks of the war, during the Canadians' push across the Rhine and into Germany in March 1945.[32]

Once the decision was made to enlist or the call-up notice arrived, Jewish personnel had to get their affairs in order, take medicals, and fill out the formal paperwork that bound them to serve, choosing either a posting in Canada or volunteering to go overseas on active service. It was at this point in the enlistment process that being Jewish posed a dilemma: deciding what religion to disclose on official forms was not simple. Religion was listed on documents such as hospital admission forms, and also on the two identity discs that servicemen and -women wore around their necks. Saying you were Jewish could open the door to a host of problems and sometimes closed the door to promotions, both in Canada and overseas.

During the early years of the war, Canadian Jewish Congress staff was having a hard time obtaining an accurate count of how many Jewish men were enlisting.[33] They discovered it was because of the identity discs. A number of Jews had not enlisted as Jews, a Congress report said, for fear of being captured by Nazi forces and found to be Jewish. An estimated two thousand Jewish men may have enlisted under other religions.[34] For example, Pilot Officer Edmond Fleishman came from a prominent Jewish family in Vancouver. His father, Arthur, a lawyer, was president of the Vancouver Schara Tzedeck synagogue. Yet Edmond told the RCAF recruiters in Longueuil, Quebec, that his religion was United Church.[35]

"Down doors!"[36] The shout came just before 8:15 a.m. from on board Fred Harris's landing craft off Bernières-sur-Mer, France. It was June 6, 1944, and the young Toronto infantry soldier, now a sergeant who everyone called Guts Harris, was about to lead his men in the first assault wave of the Allied invasion of Normandy. The infantrymen lined up to jump into the waist-deep water. Harris was the first man out. He was immediately killed by German fire from the beach.[37]

Five months later, Harris's personal effects arrived at the family home on Beverley Street in Toronto. Harris had enlisted as a Jew in 1940 with the Queen's Own Rifles of Canada. His mother, Tillie Harris, was shocked to see a wooden crucifix encased in silver in the parcel, attached to her late son's identity tag. For a long time, she refused to sign for the delivery. "I was very upset at its contents, which contained a pen, pencil, identification disc and a crucifix which certainly didn't belong to him, as he was a Jew," she told the army. She didn't say whether she'd noticed that Freddie had also scratched out his original entry of Hebrew in his

Soldier's Pay Book, which had to be carried at all times. Instead, the letters "C. of E." (Church of England) had been put there, in black ink.[38]

"I think he was just probably trying to bank on all the help...possible, as opposed to not being tracked [as a Jew]," said the soldier's nephew, Robert Harris. He thinks that his uncle, who had belonged to Toronto's Holy Blossom Temple, one of Canada's oldest synagogues, might have considered the crucifix a form of divine insurance during battle.

Fred Harris's reasoning for both the crucifix and the change of religion remains a mystery, but Congress decided that the mandatory religion disclosure posed a serious problem and lobbied Ottawa for a solution. As a result, the defence ministry permitted incoming personnel to use the designation "OD" (Other Denominations) where the religion was required. The option was welcomed by some Jewish personnel, including Norman Cohen, who didn't change his Jewish-sounding name when he enlisted in the RCAF in Toronto, although he did register as OD. Still, he felt the ambiguous designation wouldn't be much protection when he thought about what could happen to him overseas, and that feeling never went away, especially during his time as a navigator on fourteen bombing missions over Western Europe. "I didn't like being there at all, Germany. Over it, sideways, or whatever. It scared me. It frightened me to death, it really did, being shot down and put in a cage, and [the] Auschwitz...death camp," Cohen recalled.

Being Jewish would lead to fistfights for Murray Jacobs outside the barracks during the war, but he steadfastly refused to hide his religion. Having "Hebrew" or "Jewish" on his application forms and on his identity discs was a logical step for Jacobs, who as a teenager had taken part in the Christie Pits riot. "First of all, if you're not proud of who you are, you shouldn't be there. That's what this was all about," he insisted.

A sergeant with the Royal Canadian Electrical and Mechanical Engineers, Jacobs dismissed the idea that Jewish soldiers could stay safer if they hid their religion. "There's guys in our outfit that had different denominations [listed on their papers]," he said, gesturing as if he was holding up some dog tags from around his neck. "They think that they're not gonna find out that they were Jewish? If they were found out? Come on! This is *bubbe meises* [old wives' tales]!"

David Bindman, of Thetford Mines, Quebec, enlisted for active duty on September 5, 1939, with the Royal Canadian Engineers.[39] Bindman's family worked in the asbestos industry. Before the war, his father Carl's company had sold asbestos to the Germans, and he knew that country was stockpiling the material in order to rearm. Carl had got his wife's relatives out of Germany to London just in time. The Bindmans supported David's enlisting without question. They worried, however, about what would happen to him if he registered as a Jew.

"The only thing I ever learned from my father and my aunts was that he shouldn't put 'Jewish' down on the form when he didn't have to," said David's niece Bea Bindman. "And he said, 'That's not who I am. I'm not Catholic, I'm not Protestant, I'm not Other.'"

Bindman's attestation papers for active service did state his religion as Jewish. It remains a mystery why four years later in Italy, the Field Medical card for the fatally wounded explosives expert had his religion written as "C. of. E." Lieutenant Bindman was killed during an attack near the Moro River in December 1943. He'd been on the front lines for only ten days. Despite what the card said, his grave south of Ortona is marked with a Star of David.

Colonel (Hon.) David Lloyd Hart (no relation to the long-established Hart family, although David was also from Montreal) had proudly declared his Jewish background on the registration form when he enlisted in the Signals Corps. "I insisted on having 'Hebrew' on it. I said to them, '[If] the Jerries capture me, I want them to know I'm a Jew.'"

A review of military records belonging to some non-Jewish Canadians who died in World War II found that recruiting officers paid no extra attention to these men's religions.[40] Yet many Canadian Jewish servicemen and -women who declared their Jewishness had it noted and commented on in writing. Some of these reports would be considered racist and even illegal by contemporary standards. Consider the interview of Charles Males, a shipper from Toronto, at the RCAF No. 11 Recruiting Centre: "Intelligence slightly above average, co-operative, friendly—alert—has only a few racial mannerisms—quite well balanced—of average aircrew material."[41]

Jacob Silverstein of Windsor, Ontario, worked as a truck driver in his family's produce business before he enlisted with the RCAF. The interviewer's report noted that Silverstein was a "below average" candidate: "Jewish lad of nice enough appearance but pretty common in manner. Not grammatical. Education is minimum and post-school jobs no help."[42] Silverstein had finished four years of high school at Kennedy

Collegiate. He'd told the interviewers he wanted to further his education when the war was over.

After interviewing Hamilton's Alex Balinson in the spring of 1940, the RCAF recruiting officer wrote that the twenty-one-year-old man was Hebrew. And then, despite a glowing review of Balinson's character and potential as a pilot, the interviewer expressed his reservations: "Hebrew. Quite pleasant, self-assured ambitious good physique. Will be rather pushing. Polite, rather rough due to background."[43] It is hard to know what the officer meant by rough background. Balinson was a graduate of Westdale Collegiate High School in Hamilton. One brother was a doctor, already in the service. His father, Henry Balinson, spoke seven languages and was a prominent printer and community leader who published a Yiddish-language newspaper, *The Jewish Voice of Hamilton*.[44]

Although many Jews had changed their family names when they immigrated to Canada, some of the Jewish recruits who hadn't done so yet tried to avoid further discrimination when they signed up for war service. George Holidenke, of Montreal, had driven a truck for a fish wholesaler when he enlisted, and had put down "Hebrew" on his attestation papers in June 1942. However, he was George Holden when he drove a tank with the Grenadier Guards regiment.[45]

Nathan Isaacs served in the RCAF under his birth name, Isaacovitch. He acknowledged that he enjoyed going to synagogue and was proud to enlist as a Jew. But the rookie airman found that his superiors kept tripping over their tongues trying to pronounce his last name.

"So every time the corporal had to call my name, it was, 'Isa...,' I mean, he stumbled, stumbled, stumbled, so finally I went to the legal officer and said, 'You know, I'm having trouble with my name, can I change it to Isaacs?'" He was told he had to wait until he was twenty-one to do that, which rankled. "It was okay to fight for the air force, but I was too young to have my name changed."[46]

Aside from the external, institutional barriers that affected how and where Canadian Jews would serve, there were other factors—often close to home—that influenced enlisting. Many Jewish families were reluctant to see their sons and daughters sign up to go overseas and get in harm's way. Joe Gertel's father, Israel, had served in the kaiser's army in Germany during World War I. Father and son fought bitterly over Joe volunteering for the artillery. Joe's sister, Ruth Lande, who was six or seven at the time, remembers the constant bickering at the family's Montreal kitchen table. "My father was wounded three times," Lande said. "So he said to my brother things like 'Being in an army is not just wearing a uniform and looking like somebody or something. There are consequences to being in the army. People get killed.'"

By September 1943, with Joe already overseas, his father wrote to the army urging them to send his son home on medical grounds. Joe had a congenital birth defect: a fistula, or cyst, in his neck that constantly leaked fluid.[47] After a round of tests, the army doctors concluded that the condition wouldn't prevent him from soldiering. The younger Gertel was furious about his father's meddling.

Signalman Hymie Greenberg wished his mother, Sonya, had behaved more stoically after the Manitoba clerk enlisted for active service in March 1941. He suggested she copy the behaviour of his landlady. "Tonight the son of the lady with whom I stay is going away to war. This is his last leave and his mother knows that she won't see him again until the war is over," he wrote to Sonya. "Still they are all sitting in the next room laughing and joking. I sure wish all the Jewish mothers were like that."[48]

By the middle of 1940, all of Canada's able-bodied men over the age of sixteen appeared on the government's radar as part of a nationwide registration system. Canada passed the National Resources Mobilization Act in June of that year, bringing in mandatory call-ups for army duty for home defence only. Prime Minister King had promised no overseas conscription for the army unless it was necessary. It would take until November 1944, and manpower shortages on the front lines in Europe, for the prime minister to send Canadian army conscripts overseas and into battle.

The conscripts were despised. Canadians called them "zombies."[49] The zombie issue preoccupied Canadian Jewish Congress officials, who were anxious to dispel the public perception that a significant number of Canadian Jewish personnel had not signed up for active service, meaning they were not willing to serve outside Canada. Of the 150,000 Canadian conscripts in the general population, 3,479 were Canadian Jews.[50] This may have been "the highest percentage for any religious denomination."[51] However, it is more likely that the preferences of the Jewish conscripts were "at least roughly similar to those of other Canadians, and had as many reasons why they were not interested" in serving abroad.[52]

Gurston Allen, the chair of Congress's Toronto War Efforts branch, was an army officer in the military's motion picture branch. He ordered an internal investigation into the question of Jewish zombies: "I think that it is urgent and that immediate steps must be taken to rectify the impression that we have 2,900 zombies in the army," Allen wrote in a 1944 memo, adding that the number was likely lower, nearer to one thousand four hundred.[53]

Jack Tweyman of Toronto admits that he hadn't rushed to enlist. "I didn't have anything to do with politics.... We read things that were happening. Let's be honest: we didn't know how bad it was. A lot of Jewish boys signed up, but I didn't, and people around me didn't." Instead, he waited for his call-up notice for compulsory military service. It arrived during Passover 1941, when he was twenty-one. Trained in anti-aircraft artillery, Tweyman was posted to conduct home defence at army installations in Nova Scotia. By 1943, the Royal Canadian Navy sailors who took shore leave in the nearby town of Mulgrave were merciless in harassing the conscripts at the local restaurants. For Tweyman, that prompted his decision to switch to active service.

"I wasn't scared," Tweyman said. "I didn't want to go over, but I did it because I was sick and tired of fighting with these guys. We were fighting with the sailors...and because we weren't signed up, it would bug them...they called [us] zombies, so they were always giving us a hard time, so I said, 'Enough.'"

Before he could go overseas, Tweyman had to pass a medical. He says a sympathetic doctor in Sydney, Nova Scotia, pulled him out of the lineup and then had him sent to Halifax for surprise medical tests on his heart. His heart checked out fine, of course. Tweyman was assigned light duties and sent back to Mulgrave, where he remained until he was discharged in early 1945.

"I could swear up to this day that he must have been a Jewish doctor," Tweyman said, smiling. His twin brother, Albert, who was also called up, switched to active service in 1944 in order to be with a best friend, Mac Latner, already overseas. Sadly, Albert did not come home.

George Meltz was the only one of his nine siblings to be sent overseas. Two brothers, Al and Sam, served in Canada, but Jake, then twenty-seven, was rejected for medical reasons. More than one in every three Canadian conscripts, Jewish or otherwise, failed the army medical. They were rejected mainly for mental and nervous problems (39.5 per cent). Another 5 per cent were turned away for poor eyesight.[54] Plenty bore a sense of guilt about this. "I have a pin that says 'Registered for Enlistment,'" noted Jake's daughter Isabella Meltz, explaining that her father had to carry the pin to prove why he wasn't in uniform. She isn't sure if it was her father's heart murmur or his poor eyesight that kept him out of the war.

Still, the zombie issue rankled. Some Jewish personnel looked down on their zombie co-religionists. Esther Thorley (née Bubis) of Toronto was stationed in Vancouver as an office worker with the Canadian Women's Army Corps. Her older brother had been killed in Dieppe in 1942. So when her brother-in-law, a zombie, was on leave near her, Thorley gave him the cold shoulder. "He wanted to go to the Service Centre and I wouldn't go with him," Thorley said. "When he came to visit me, I was ashamed and wouldn't go outside with him."

Irving (Kappy) Kaplan of Montreal was serving on HMCS *Assiniboine* by the fall of 1944, on patrol in the English Channel. He had enlisted in 1939, at eighteen, one of the first in his group of friends to do so.[55] After spending five years at sea and surviving the sinking of his previous warship by a German submarine off the coast of Newfoundland just months earlier, Kaplan had a hardened opinion of those who avoided combat. "What do you think of the commotion they are creating, the yellow b———s. I've spoken to some of the men just back from France, wounded, and they convinced me that those 70,000 men can certainly be used," he wrote to a friend. "You can imagine what we fellows think of the zombies."[56]

In 1941, the Canadian Jewish Congress began to compile a list of Jews in the Canadian forces. Staff scoured synagogue bulletins, canvassed men's club lists, and clipped articles from Jewish and secular newspapers. Rabbi Gershon Levi, then an army captain serving as a Jewish chaplain, wrote to every military base in the country, asking officials to send him a list of Jewish personnel. Knowing how many Jewish Canadians were in the service had important applications; for one, Ottawa required proof that at least one thousand Jewish servicemen were in uniform before the government would appoint a dedicated Jewish chaplain to minister to them. But Congress also wanted the information because of claims in the press that, especially early in the war, Jews weren't pulling their weight. A confidential memo to Maurice Hartt, a Jewish member of the Quebec provincial legislature for Montreal, from H.M. Caiserman, the general secretary of Congress, acknowledged the issue and outlined a possible public relations strategy until it was fixed. "The actual number of Jewish enlistments for active service is not up to our percentage. I am thankful to the Government for refusing to publish figures; we can thus claim ignorance and maintain that we are doing our share."[57]

These concerns led to a push by Congress and others to encourage more Jewish enlistment. Rabbi David Monson of Toronto was sent out on recruiting campaigns to meet young people at the Brunswick Avenue YMHA athletic centre and to Jewish youth clubs around town.[58] Jewish newspapers published editorials urging the boys to sign up, including one by the founder of the influential Yiddish-language *Jewish Daily Eagle*, Hirsch Wolofsky: "It is not enough, we must do more, more than our share, more than is expected of us. And the responsibility of fulfilling this duty rests upon Jewish parents as well as upon their sons. They as well as the young men must answer this call and it must be answered immediately."[59]

By the summer of 1941, Congress had opened a Jewish recruiting bureau at 150 Beverley Street in Toronto. Sergeant Bennett Isaacs, a World War I veteran, was named the registrar. In an article in the *Daily Hebrew Journal* Isaacs laid on thick Jewish guilt to persuade his readers to sign up. "How can you sleep at night and why shouldn't your conscience bother you, when you, yourself, know you are not doing your duty as a man and as a Canadian. You cannot expect other citizens to shoulder your burden. You must do your part."[60] A similar recruiting bureau opened at 5054 Park Avenue in Montreal a few months later. The wooden sandwich board sign outside the doors was printed in English, French, and Yiddish; it urged men to "Enlist Here Now! Canada Needs You!"

Congress officials soon began to push the message that Jews were meeting or beating their expected enlistment rate. Sam Abrahamson, at Congress, crunched the numbers. "When one out of every 32 Canadians has enlisted, there should be 102 enlistments from the 3,400 Jews in Ottawa...On our nominal roll of August 25, there were, as an example, 166 Jewish boys from Ottawa who had enlisted in the various services."[61] Ben Ginsberg, a prominent Calgary lawyer, told a crowd that 107 local Jews had enlisted, 8 per cent of Calgary's Jewish population at the time.[62] By 1942, Congress was declaring, "There is not a single Jewish community in the country without its quota of men in uniform, and 31 of these cities and towns throughout Canada have all of their Jewish men of military age in the Services."[63]

Despite the best efforts of Congress, the issue of Jewish participation again blew up into a nasty public debate. In 1943, when Nathan Phillips, a Jewish Toronto alderman (later elected mayor), asked city council to express its sympathy with the Jewish victims of Nazi terror, Alderman Leslie Howard Saunders, whom historian Gerald Tulchinsky has called "a first-class bigot," said Jews should do more than just talk about fighting.[64] Saunders and the Canadian Jewish Congress then engaged in a war of words over numbers, with Congress insisting in the press that after a slow start, mobilization had turned around. The *Ottawa Citizen* printed Congress's response:

> *The Canadian Jewish Congress is prepared to show its records proving the above-mentioned figures to any reputable individual or organization desirous of knowing and disseminating the truth on this subject. Our enlistment ratio exceeds our population ratio. Our record in the war is one of which we can be proud.*[65]

A survey for the Canadian Jewish Congress in 1939 found 37,774 Jewish men living in Canada who were of eligible military age—that is, age eighteen to forty.[66] By the end of the war, the total estimated number of Jewish men and women in service was 16,883. Of these, 10,235 had served in the Canadian army, 5,889 in the RCAF, 596 in the navy, and 163 in other Allied forces.[67] Jews made up 1.5 per cent of Canada's population in 1940, and eventually provided 2.6 per cent of its airmen, 1.4 per cent of its soldiers, and 0.7 per cent of its sailors.[68] With the population of Canada's Jews by 1941 at over one hundred and sixty-eight thousand, it's clear that at least 10 per cent of the Jewish community served.[69]

Although the organized Jewish community devoted most of its energy to drumming up new recruits in big cities, the smaller Jewish communities actually sent a higher proportion of their young to war. The majority of Jewish men of eligible age from farming communities on the Prairies and in rural Quebec and from the paper mill towns in northern Ontario and the mining and steel towns across the Maritimes saw service or tried to.

Mitch Pechet's grandfather Simon was among the first 365 Jewish settlers from Romania to begin a new life as a colonist in Saskatchewan, having received 160 acres of land to farm near Lipton after fleeing czarist rule in 1901.[70] A profile of Simon in the *Winnipeg Free Press* somewhat naively described his mandatory army service in Romania, where Jews were discriminated against and anti-Jewish sentiment was part of the national psyche, as his "colourful career with the army before leaving his native land."[71] Simon's son Bill settled nearby in Cupar, Saskatchewan, and, with his wife, Sophie, had five sons. At the start of the war, Bill ordered Mitch and his two oldest brothers to come home for a meeting. "With tears in his eyes, he said, 'You boys know what you have to do,' so all three of us joined," Mitch Pechet told an interviewer in 2007.[72]

All three enlisted in the RCAF. Sam, then twenty-five, was working in Winnipeg at the Hudson's Bay Company. Morris, twenty-two, was studying at the University of California in Los Angeles, while Mitch, then twenty-one, had been drafted by the New York Rangers and was playing hockey at Madison Square Garden for their farm team. Mitch's widow, Judy Pechet, said that growing up in Cupar, which even today has fewer than seven hundred residents, goes a long way to explain why geography and memory played a big part in the strong Jewish enlistment from rural areas. "When you live in a small community with maybe four Jewish families, five Jewish families, there's a difference," she explained, adding that it has also to do with the unique immigration experience of the Jews who escaped from Cossacks and pogroms and made their journeys to settle in Western Canada. "I think that they were feeling very loyal and devoted to their adopted country and grateful to be in Canada and prepared to put their best foot forward in the name of Canada. Canada was their safe haven."

If rural Jews seemed to respond to the war in greater numbers than their city cousins, perhaps it was also because in small towns, young people couldn't remain anonymous the way they could in big cities.

In Morris Polansky's farming settlement of Oxbow, Saskatchewan, his immigrant parents raised cows and horses and farmed grain. "No pigs," said Polansky, with a smile. When the war broke out, Polansky was eighteen and wanted to enlist. He knew what happened to young able-bodied men who didn't. "During World War I, mothers would get envelopes with a white feather inside," he explained, saying the message meant that their boys were cowards.

Ironically, it was a Great War veteran in Oxbow who convinced Polansky to wait another year. "You get your ass back to school and get your Grade 12," the veteran advised. This new war wasn't going to end soon, the man reasoned, which meant Polansky had plenty of time to complete his education. Yet the decision to finish high school didn't sit well with other neighbours, who scolded Polansky's father.

"My father came home and told us about it. And some of them were drunk. It made him feel bad," Polansky said. "But that's the sort of thing that you get in a small town...where there's seven hundred people and you know every one of them. It's a different kind of an environment." The following year, Polansky enlisted after hearing a radio commercial that the army was looking for truck drivers. "My antennae went up. 'Oh! My God! Can you imagine me, Moe Polansky, driving a truck?' This was a big thing."

Even though Oxbow was somewhat better off than most Jewish farm colonies because the railway line serviced the community, Polansky said economic hardship was one factor that pushed him and his brothers to enlist. "It was the Dirty Thirties—you had nothing. People didn't have jobs, so you got room and board [in the service]," he said, noting that his own family had depended on government relief for a good part of the time before the war.

Polansky went overseas with the Royal Canadian Army Service Corps, fixing mobile dental clinic equipment. His youngest brother, David, was wounded in Belgium in late 1944, and died after the war from shrapnel in his lungs. Older brother Hymie joined up too but was discharged in 1940.

The Faibish family had moved to Markinch, Saskatchewan, from Romania in 1907 to farm but found it difficult to fit in, being the only Jewish family in the hamlet of ninety people, populated mainly by German Lutherans. Ben Faibish had tried to join up on the day the war broke out. Married with children, he was scraping out a living by helping his father sell cattle. They were so poor that their home had dirt floors. He came home from the army centre "quite crushed" because he'd been rejected for service, said his daughter June Claman. "He was 4-F because he had bad eyesight," she said, using the American term for being turned down for military service. Had her father been accepted, it might have helped the family afford a nicer house with indoor plumbing and clean drinking water. "He would've got a paycheque because we didn't have any money."

Ben's younger brother Jack ran the family's grocery and farm supply store in town, together with another sibling, Abe. When Canada declared war, Jack waited two weeks until after Yom Kippur (Day of Atonement) and then travelled to Regina to enlist. Jack told the military interviewers that his pro-Nazi German neighbours were his reason for joining, although police kept an eye on groups of fervent Hitler sympathizers in Saskatchewan.[73] Jack reported that he had "lived among a bunch of Nazis who made me mad."[74]

The army money helped support his aging parents. Overseas with the 2nd Canadian Anti-Tank Regiment, Jack sent home $10 each time he got paid. As he got promoted, he would send more to cover a life insurance policy and a Victory Bond. Faibish, a thirty-year-old bachelor, was killed in the fighting near Verrières in Normandy in 1944; his distraught mother told the government they couldn't even cover the cost of probating his will.

The Jews in Prairie villages might have been isolated, but they were also ardent consumers of news: about the war, the situation of the Jews in Europe, and the movement to build a national home for Jews in Palestine. The geography fostered a uniquely strong Jewish cultural experience. Rural families raised impressive sums of money for relief efforts for Jewish refugees and for settlements in Palestine.[75] That strong Jewish identity was especially evident in Kamsack, Saskatchewan, which had a significant Jewish minority of one hundred residents. Despite its small size, Kamsack supported a combined ritual slaughterer/teacher/rabbi and a synagogue on Fourth Street.[76]

Author Cherie Smith, the daughter of Iser Steiman, a Kamsack doctor, recalls how Main Street looked while she was growing up in the 1930s. Most of the local shops were Jewish owned, she writes in her memoir *Mendel's Children*, including Laimon's O.K. Confectionery, Olfman's Meats, Bay's Hardware and Furniture, and Rubin's Clothing Shoes and Boots. Out of a total of twenty-six young people, nineteen were members of Young Judaea.[77] When hostilities began, nearly all of them enlisted.

In August 1941, the *Canadian Jewish Chronicle* ran an editorial praising Kamsack's Jews and urging the rest of Canada's Jewish community to follow their example. The writers described Kamsack as "a hamlet, such as Bialik wrote about, where the spirit of our people remains unadulterated, unawakened, strong with its pristine vigor."[78] The Canadian Jewish Congress put out a news release, noting the local Olfman family's "proud record" with five sons in the military: Abe, Jack, Maurice, Hymie, and Shia. "Kamsack's Jewish community of fifteen families has furnished 13 men to the Army and Air Force. This represents every eligible man of military age in the community," the release said.[79] A provided photo of the Olfman siblings in their uniforms was reprinted in newspapers across the country, including the *Ottawa Journal*.[80]

The Canadian Jewish Congress even found it difficult to maintain a local branch in Kamsack to direct war efforts because the three top volunteers had themselves enlisted for active service in the RCAF: Iser Steiman, a doctor, A. Rabinovitch, a dentist, and Bernard Isman, a local lawyer.[81] Kamsack again came to national attention in 1943, when Flight Lieutenant Hector B. Rubin won the Distinguished Flying Cross. Rubin had two older brothers in the service: Mitchell with the RCAMC and Abe, a podiatrist, serving in the U.S. Army.

For Harold Laimon, a Kamsack native whose two older brothers served, it was clear why his small Jewish community sent so many men to war. First, it was a sense of duty and patriotism. "They wanted to serve," said the retired Vancouver physician, who was too young to go. "That was the thing to do." The second reason was that the town of Kamsack held narrow career prospects for its young people. Although Kamsack was on a railway line, Laimon and the other young men felt their futures lay elsewhere. "There was nothing really there to keep them there," he said.

Approximately twenty Kamsack Jews would put on a uniform by the end of the war. Two, Shia Olfman and Hector Rubin, would be killed.

For the Jewish boys in small towns and villages in central and eastern Canada, the war was a way to expand their horizons, including the boys from Ansonville, a northern Ontario paper mill town (now part of Iroquois Falls) that was a world away from life in the major Jewish centres of Winnipeg, Montreal, or Toronto.

"Like many of them, they didn't really know where they were going, they just wanted to get out, as an adventure," said Richard Nosov, whose grandfather Barney was Ansonville's long-serving mayor. Nosov feared the young men from the isolated community had very little idea of what they were getting themselves into by enlisting, or "what waited for them in Europe." Even though Barney tried his best to keep his son Nathan out of the military, he didn't succeed. "My uncle wanted to serve," Richard said.

Ansonville's Jews were immigrants from Lithuania who came to northern Ontario as farmers at the beginning of the century. Like the Jews of Western Canada, most Jews in Ansonville didn't remain in agriculture. By the 1920s, many had taken up peddling. By the 1940s, the more successful men were running stores and businesses supporting the workers of the mill.[82]

Sixteen Jewish families lived in Ansonville. At least ten local Jewish men put on a uniform, or tried to. Art and Walter Crotin served. Art's twin brother, Louis, was rejected for medical reasons. Louis says pressure to enlist came from the town's authority figures: the police and their high school teacher. "We didn't get involved in politics. We just knew that we had to sign up to put Hitler down," he said. "The boys at my age were signing up because it was sort of an honour to enlist voluntarily instead of waiting to be drafted and there was friction between volunteers and draftees."

Three Abramson brothers and their families lived in Ansonville. Alec, who ran a store, saw his oldest son, Albert, enlist in the RCAF. Louis Abramson and his wife ran the Union Hotel at the top of Railway Street. They had thirteen children, of whom at least three served. Harry was a second lieutenant with the Royal Canadian Artillery, and Sam went overseas with the Canadian Forestry Corps. The third son, David, had been working for eight years as a manager and bartender in his parents' hotel. When he enlisted, he was thirty-one. He wanted to join the RCAF, but they turned him down because he wore glasses. The interviewer described him as "rather phlegmatic." Nevertheless, they said he "should make [a] normally efficient soldier" because he "seems to be anxious to develop, co-operative, average stability. Has bright outlook." He was accepted into the Royal Canadian Corps of Signals, and sent overseas two months before D-Day.[83]

He never made it into combat. In England, he came down with appendicitis and underwent emergency surgery, and doctors then diagnosed inoperable bowel cancer. Shipped home, Abramson died on May 10, 1945, with his mother at his bedside at the Red Chevron Veterans Hospital in Toronto. It was two days after the war in Europe ended.

Congress didn't open a Jewish recruiting office in the Maritimes. It doesn't appear that it needed one. In August 1943, when the Congress held a meeting in Saint John, New Brunswick, the executive secretary,

H.M. Caiserman, made this startling claim: "The excellent record of enlistment of the Jewish population in the entire Dominion includes every able-bodied man of military age in the Maritimes."[84]

More than sixty Jewish men and women from Saint John served, out of a wartime population of approximately six hundred Jewish residents.[85] The estimates for Glace Bay, Nova Scotia, vary, but between seventy-five and a hundred Jewish personnel wore a uniform, including some who served in the U.S. military, out of a population of about eight hundred Jews.[86]

Steve Nathanson's father, Nate, left Glace Bay to serve as a rear gunner in the RCAF. Steve believes the tremendous participation rate was because the young Jewish men from Glace Bay—especially those who didn't leave before the war to go to university—thought joining up would let them escape the small-town milieu, see a bit of the world, and postpone their predetermined futures of joining the family's retail or wholesale business. Most of the boys also thought the war would be short, as did his own father. "Get away from the family, because if you'd stay in the store, you'd be stuck in the store," Nathanson said. "Some of these families, just about all the boys left town."

3 Jewish Communists in Uniform

"I was being followed"

On August 12, 1944, the 4th Canadian Armoured Division was in Normandy, their tanks rolling south from Caen to Falaise, chasing the retreating German front-line troops.[1] During a pause while their tanks were being reinforced with extra plating and having fuel and ammunition topped up, Lance Corporal Dick Steele of the 21st Armoured Regiment, formerly the Governor General's Foot Guards, wrote a letter to his wife, Esther, back home in Toronto. Steele couldn't wait to tell her about a heartfelt reunion he'd just had with a dear friend, an infantry soldier currently serving with the Stormont, Dundas, and Glengarry Highlanders. "Words can never express that meeting of two comrades on that field. Muni unshaven, black as night, covered with grime and dust, but eyes shining," he wrote. "Guess if we would have had time for more than a big hug and handclasp we'd have had a good Russian cry."[2]

Muni was Muni Erlick, born Morris Erlickman. Like Steele, he was a high-profile Canadian Jewish communist. Both had been active in the labour movement, and had been arrested and jailed as traitors by the King government in the early years of the war. Erlick was thirty-eight, Steele thirty-four.

Richard (Dick) Kenilworth Steele was born Moishe Kosowatsky in Montreal in 1909. His parents were Russian Jewish immigrants, and his father Sam (Shia) eked out a living driving a horse and wagon to collect empty bottles and potato sacks from back alleys. The six Kosowatsky children helped after school.[3]

Kosowatsky's high school, Baron Byng, was a breeding ground for the social justice values adopted by many of the pupils who later became communists, and then also served in uniform. The message of the Young Communist League, which was active in the 1920s and '30s, was very attractive to immigrant Jewish kids.[4] The group was closely affiliated with the trade union movement, calling for better working conditions and support for socialism.

For a time, though, Kosowatsky had belonged to the cadets, an extracurricular youth group in which they got to wear military uniforms. He'd liked the uniform, which, combined with his grey eyes and black curly hair, attracted girls. Eventually, he abandoned the after-school activity because, he said, "I realized what the uniform really represented—war, misery, death."[5]

At school, he hung around with Moishe Wolofsky, the son of the publisher of the city's influential Yiddish newspaper, the *Daily Jewish Eagle*, also known as the *Kaneder Adler*. Despite differences in their economic and social situations, the two Moishes became best friends. Their efforts to pursue a post-secondary education at Columbia University in New York ended after one year when the Depression hit. The pair ran out of money and decided to quit school to see the world.

The two Moishes arrived in Europe in time to witness the birth of National Socialism in Germany. In the city of Breslau (now part of Poland), they were present at a rally where a crowd of seventy thousand people wore brown shirts. "We turned away sick with the sight of this nationalistic ecstasy-Fascism," Kosowatsky wrote in his travel journal.[6]

The friends wound up in Minsk, which was then part of the USSR. They found jobs as metal workers, and it was there that they began a lifetime commitment to communism. They both joined the Soviet Young Communist League, known as the Komosol. After moving to Moscow in 1933, they found work at another factory, studied Marxism, and attended meetings of the party's local association. Although Kosowatsky would remain for another year, Wolofsky's father travelled to the Soviet Union, determined to bring his son's communist adventure to an end. Once back in Montreal, the younger Wolofsky found that the Communist Party's Canadian branch and the trade union movement were active, although the authorities were watching them closely. He attended meetings of the Young People's Socialist League and the Workers Unity League, a communist trade union organization.[7]

Muni Erlick was born in Bessarabia (now part of Moldova) in 1905.[8] He joined the communist movement in Paris, where he lived before moving to Montreal in 1927. Erlick spent several years working for Jewish communist organizations in the city and for *Der Kampf*, the Jewish labour weekly.[9]

By 1934, the Communist Party–affiliated Industrial Union of Needle Trades Workers had sent Moishe Wolofsky to Toronto as its educational director. Muni Erlick was already there, working for the Communist Party.[10] It was about this time that Wolofsky changed his name and began calling himself Bill Walsh. Moishe Kosowatsky returned from Russia and joined Walsh in Toronto. He also adopted a new name, Dick Steele. He took the name partly in homage to Stalin but also to protect his family in Quebec, who were being watched because of his support for communism.[11]

Steele went to work as a union organizer for the Steelworkers and did social justice work for the Communist Party on Toronto's east side. He also fell in love with one of Walsh's friends. Esther Slominsky (Silver) was a former leather factory worker, then serving as the office manager at Walsh's union's headquarters at Spadina and Grange Avenues. "I brought him down to the office and introduced him to Esther," said Walsh. "Boy, was that a mistake...! It wasn't too long after that that they got married."

Muni Erlick didn't change his name again but he did use an alias, Jack Taylor, and moved out west, where he began fighting for workers' rights and representing the Communist Party in British Columbia. The Vancouver police kept an eye on him, describing him in bulletins as "32 years, 5′11″ eyes brown, hair black and curly, wears no hat, blue overcoat, blue serge suit" and speaking a particular form of "Yiddish English."[12]

With the outbreak of the Spanish Civil War in 1936, some of the Canadian Jewish communist leaders turned their focus to helping the republicans battle the nationalists and General Francisco Franco. Although Canada made it illegal for anyone to travel to Spain to enlist, Steele's older brother, Mortimer Kosowatsky, joined the all-Canadian Mackenzie-Papineau Battalion of the International Brigade, using the name Jack Steele, and was killed in action. Dick also wanted to go but was persuaded to stay home and continue his union work.[13] Erlick, meanwhile, managed to get to Spain as a correspondent for his communist newspaper, renamed the *Daily Clarion*.

In Ontario, Steele and Walsh were rising stars in the Canadian labour movement. The pair organized strikes in their respective industries,

Walsh working with the rubber workers in Kitchener and with the auto workers in Windsor, and Steele organizing the first union actions among the steelworkers at plants in Toronto, Oshawa, and Hespeler.[14]

"It was Dick Steele more than any other single individual who planned that [Steelworkers] campaign, who wrote its inspiring literature, and whose voice rang in union halls and at steel mill gates throughout Ontario," wrote J.B. Salsberg in the *Canadian Tribune*.[15] Salsberg, a former union leader, went on to represent the Communist Party as a member of the Ontario legislature for twelve years. Aside from their union work, Steele and Walsh also lent their support to Communist Party candidates who ran for office at many levels of government.

Despite the ballot box success for some communists in Canada, the war would bring dramatic changes. Since 1935, the international arm of the communist movement had been opposing fascism and working with moderate and socialist allies in a number of countries, including Canada, to stop Hitler's rise. But on August 23, 1939, with war brewing, the Soviet leader, Joseph Stalin, turned his back on the West, and instead signed the Molotov-Ribbentrop Pact, a non-aggression pact with Germany. The two countries agreed not to attack each other for ten years, and to partition eastern Europe. All international branches of the party were under orders from Stalin to oppose their countries' war efforts.

The move stunned the Communist Party membership in Canada. "For all these years…, I was taught to fight antisemitism and I wanted to, and fascism, and all of the sudden they [Hitler and Stalin] had a pact and I couldn't understand it," army veteran Hy (Chud) Chudnovsky recalls. His family was active in Montreal's communist circles, and often hosted Muni Erlick, whom Chud idolized.

Despite discomfort with this turn of events, the Canadian communists complied with Moscow's orders. But Ottawa moved quickly to develop the Defence of Canada Regulations under the War Measures Act, which made it illegal to criticize the government's war efforts, especially in newspapers or periodicals. Over three hundred left-wing news outlets were banned, and by the summer of 1940 so was the Communist Party of Canada itself. Known communists were placed under heavy police surveillance, but they continued to do their work, living in hiding and relying on fake identity cards.

Now living in Toronto, Chud was working at Supreme Printing on Spadina Avenue. It handled some communist publications, including the *Vochenblatt,* edited by Joshua Gershman. Every day, Chud took circuitous routes on his bicycle from the printer to carry the paper's proofs to Gershman's apartment on Mutual Street. "I was being followed, and the police aren't so stupid as we liked to think, and every time they knew who I was in contact with," Chud said. Soon, security forces began to round up the communists and jail them.

Steele's house on Spadina Avenue was being watched. Although he was in hiding, the police had already raided the premises where his wife, Esther, heavily pregnant with twins, was living. "Esther knew the authorities were watching her because they knew he'd show up [for the birth]," said Ruth Lazare, Steele's niece. "He did show up when the babies were born [and] that's when they got him." The twins, Michael and Johnny, were born in August 1940. Steele spent five months in the Don Jail and then another year and a half at a Guelph reformatory.

The RCMP was watching Walsh, too. He continued to distribute communist publications and their anti-war message. He was arrested in London, Ontario, on New Year's Eve 1940. "I had to go to the printer to pick up leaflets I'd ordered," he recalled. "I'm being very cautious. I picked them up and started to put them in my trunk [when] about three hundred cops surrounded me." Walsh was carrying two identity cards that night. One bore the name of someone buried in a local graveyard. Unfortunately, he handed the police the other one, which had his real name.[16] He was jailed, then sent to an internment camp in Hull, Quebec. Canadian authorities jailed more than a hundred communists between 1940 and the fall of 1942, including Walsh, Steele, Erlick, and Gershman, as well as many non-Jews.

In June 1941, with Hitler's stunning reversal and subsequent invasion of Russia, the communists were ordered to resume the struggle against fascism. The Canadian communist internees who were of military age argued to be let out of prison so they could join the front lines in Canadian uniforms.

Steele's son Michael understands why his father and the others asked to enlist. "In my mind it was an absolute mission," he said. "If communism was the ideal for them, workers' rights, fairness, equality, all of those things couldn't have happened if Hitler would've won the war, so aside from any Jewish issues of antisemitism and everything else, those were obviously factors."

While their supporters worked for their release, the Canadian Communist Party—now called the Labour-Progressive Party—worked for conscription in a 1942 national plebiscite. The prime minister went to the country on April 27, 1942, asking for permission to renege on a 1939 promise not to send men overseas should the need become clear.[17] Quebec voted no, but the rest of Canada was in favour, as were the communists, who believed the King government wasn't doing enough to win the war. Walsh wrote to the government begging to be freed so he could enlist. Esther campaigned on behalf of her husband through letters to the editor and by writing directly to the minister of justice, Louis St. Laurent: "Dick Steele's every word and action proves and always have proved his sincerity in fighting the Fascist ideal. And a willingness to fight and bleed and die for his home and his country makes me proud of my husband."[18]

By late 1942, public sympathy for the jailed communists and union leaders had grown. Many of the inmates started filing appeals of their detentions to the government's advisory committees, which had replaced the court system for enemies of the state during the war. Some, including Steele, eventually agreed, at least publicly, to renounce their political work. Steele signed a sworn affidavit that he would be loyal to Canada and would stop criticizing the government.[19] He was released on October 3, 1942. Walsh got out a week later, but his union told him he was needed in Windsor.

Chud, then nineteen, and his brother Ben, twenty-one, enlisted about this time. They had no trouble being accepted. "I wasn't a big enough communist to attract any kind of attention," Chud said, adding that he actually didn't officially join the party until the war was over. His reasons for enlisting? "I had [a] double, triple reason to hate the German[s]: antisemitism, Hitler who had special treatment for the Jews, and even the antisemitism here and the injustice here. I was gonna clean up the whole works, in one shot."

After Steele was freed, he spent a few weeks at home in Toronto, where he built a wooden slide for his by then two-year-old toddlers. A newspaper photographer went to the Steele house to do a profile on the freshly paroled union leader. Dick and Esther are all smiles watching Michael and Johnny with their new toy.

The domestic bliss wouldn't last long. Steele was antsy to enlist. He did so in Toronto on October 29, 1942. His attestation papers say he apprenticed as a tool grinder, although he didn't mention that this had been in the Soviet Union. He also didn't explain where he had learned to "speak a little Russian." For employment, Steele put down "union organizer, 7 yrs, United Steelworkers of America Local 1111."[20]

Before he left for basic training, Steele made sure to take care of his young family's future. He made his friend Bill Walsh swear to look after Esther and the boys should anything happen to him. Walsh extracted the same promise from Steele. It was a promise each man hoped to never have to keep.

Steele thrived at the army base in Fort William, Ontario. When he wasn't learning about battlefield tactics, he was pressed into service to teach the men about Hitler and his policies. In a torrent of letters to Esther, he described being worried that Canada wasn't doing enough to teach soldiers to hate Nazism and fascism. "I joined the army to help and kill the Nazi vermin," he wrote and reminded her of his travel with Walsh in the early 1930s through Germany. "I have seen the murderous gangsters set out armed with hatchets, steel clubs, guns, and knives to hunt and maraud and kill Communists, Jews and Catholics."[21]

In early 1943, Steele was posted to Camp Borden, west of Barrie, Ontario, for advanced training as a loader operator in a tank. Despite being happy that he was closer to his family, he was frustrated with being far from the front.

While Steele, Erlick, and the Chudnovskys were in training, Walsh suffered an unexpected blow: his wife died from drinking unpasteurized milk. He was distraught, and although the conditions of his release stipulated that he not leave Windsor, he nevertheless succeeded in enlisting.

Erlick was released in November 1942. He, too, enlisted. They took him, despite his being thirty-seven and despite his renegade background. "He seems to be a keen soldier," the army interviewer at Camp Shilo wrote.[22]

Steele shipped out in June 1943. He wrote to Esther to share his excitement. "Never was I so conscious of my love of country, and my people," he told her. "Isn't it natural for one who has always tried to give leadership by example, to do so in this most deadly of all our struggles for a better life."[23]

Even though they'd sworn not to, some of the Canadian Jewish communists resumed their political work once they were in England, although they kept it low key. When Steele got leave, he would seek out likeminded comrades, such as Joe Levitt of Montreal, who was in the same regiment. The pair would visit the local recreation centres run by the British Jewish community, or see a movie. The left-wing Toronto artist Henry Orenstein joined them one time. They also met up with former fur worker Reuben Gorodetsky, who had enlisted in the Black Watch (Royal Highland Regiment) in 1942 in Montreal, where he had been vice president of his union local.[24]

Steele's letters from England were partly love letters to Esther, whom he called his "Darling Lassie," and to the boys, who knew him vaguely as their "Daddy Sojer." But they were also political treatises, which read as if Steele wanted them to be shared with an audience back home.

Steele was not an observant Jew. As a communist and trade union leader, he had more secular views—he and Esther would even put up a Christmas tree every year. Yet the mysterious disappearance of his Jewish head coverings (skullcaps) pained him. "I'm in tears—someone stole the yamelke. Could I get a couple more?" he asked Esther in a letter from Fort William.[25] For Steele, being a Jew and being a communist were not mutually exclusive. "The Nazis seek to destroy an idea—the idea of freedom and justice, progress that is richly symbolized in the Jewish tradition."[26]

By April 1944, Canadian soldiers stationed in England knew they would soon be sent to France to open a second front, which Stalin had been forcefully demanding. By then, Erlick had arrived in England as a reinforcement; Walsh, too, was based in Aldershot. Walsh knew that he was still under surveillance by Canadian police and military intelligence. He wasn't sure whether it was for violating his parole conditions or for suspicions that he might still be doing communist work to undermine the war effort.[27]

Chud says the military singled out Canadian communists and gave some of them the most dangerous jobs to do. "Some people would have said, 'Why don't you let them go get killed instead of us,' you know? 'Send them up into action and get killed,' and they did." At least nine of the higher-profile Canadian Jewish communists in uniform served overseas, and most saw action on the front lines. Several were wounded. Three died in France.

Likely the first of the previously interned Canadian Jewish communists to touch French soil was Harry Binder, landing with the Regina Rifles in Normandy on D-Day. He came from a Ukrainian family who had immigrated to Winnipeg's North End in 1916. Support for communism was strong in Winnipeg, and Harry attended a left-wing secular Jewish afternoon school run out of the Freiheit (Liberty) Temple. The curriculum supported radical Marxist theory.

Binder rose through the ranks of the Young Communist League, working in Saskatchewan and Hamilton before moving to Ottawa. There he became a parliamentary correspondent for the *Daily Clarion* and continued with party work, even after it was illegal. Binder was well aware that the police were watching him. He'd even registered at his Ottawa rooming house under a false name, but he was nonetheless arrested for disseminating anti-war materials. His subsequent trial for sedition was heavily covered in Canadian newspapers. Binder received a three-year sentence in Kingston Penitentiary. His younger brother, Louis, who had served with the Royal Canadian Engineers, was also convicted for helping him with the pamphlets. On his release, Harry went back to Winnipeg and enlisted in June 1943. He was sent overseas. The first time he was wounded was after D-Day, halfway between Caen and Falaise. He recovered, only to be wounded a second time, in October, in Belgium. He recovered that time, too.[28]

Chud went to France next, four days after D-Day, on June 10, with the 17th Duke of York Royal Canadian Hussars, which had been renamed the 7th Reconnaissance Regiment. For the first few days, before the beachhead was secure enough for the men to go out on patrol, Chud fought as a regular infantryman and slept in slit trenches. "Scared the life out of us," he said. "One of our guys dropped his mess tins, I'll never forget that. We thought that the whole German artillery and army would come in on us, but it didn't."[29]

Erlick landed in Normandy on June 13, with the infantry. Gorodetsky arrived with the Black Watch on July 5. It would be the end of July before Steele made it to France. Steele and Levitt crossed the English Channel on July 24.[30] By then, the Canadians had captured Caen. The ruins of Caen reminded Steele of photos he had seen showing what the Germans did to Stalingrad, Kharkov, and Minsk.

Levitt would be the next communist to make his mark on the war, as the Sherman tank wireless operator carried out not one but two courageous actions that would earn him the Military Medal. On August 8, the 21st Armoured's tanks were rooting out the German artillery hiding in Quesnay Wood.[31] When Levitt's crew commander was temporarily blinded by enemy fire, Levitt took over, gave his commander first aid, and kept their tank in action for an hour. Less than a week later, Levitt put himself in harm's way, when he clung to the outside of his tank to fix the wireless set while under heavy fire.[32]

On August 12, Steele and Erlick met by chance and exchanged that heartfelt hug on the battlefield. The meeting left Steele resolute but also for the first time somewhat doubtful whether he would make it home. He wrote to Esther, "So when you think of North Star Lassie, remember that. Me and you, and I have helped some to settle a big score against the Nazis. S."[33]

With Caen finally captured and the Canadians and British pushing southeast along the National Route 158 to Falaise, the next stage of the battle for France would be decisive, including for Steele. Now the main escape route for the Germans was between the strategic towns of Falaise, Argentan, and Trun, and the Allies eagerly hoped to take tens of thousands of prisoners and maybe even end the war sooner.[34] Less than a week later, on August 17, Steele's tank squadron was part of the fighting at the Falaise Gap.[35] The war diary of Steele's 21st Armoured Regiment records the story, and although it is full of military jargon, it leaves no doubt what happened.

> *At 0200 hrs., Major H.P. Baker A/O.C. of the Regt. gave orders for Operation "Smash", which had as its first objective the ground north of TRUN.... At 1100 the column was straffed by a Sqn of Focke Wulf aircraft and no casualties were reported within the Regt.*
>
> *The Regt crossed the river at MORTEAUX...during the early afternoon and advanced South by South East towards the woods along LA DIVES River. The C.O's tank was hit by an [anti-tank gun] and burned immediately. One of the crew failed to get out in time and was killed. The other four members managed to bail out.*[36]

The man who failed to get out was Dick Steele. He was buried beside his destroyed tank on August 18, with a wooden cross as a marker.

The next day, back in Toronto, a florist delivered a bouquet of roses, gladioli, and other cuttings to Esther Steele. It was from Dick, of course, for their anniversary. He'd arranged the gesture before he went to France. Esther immediately wrote to thank him for the beautiful gift, and she added a bit about the twins' birthday, which was also in August. She signed off, "Well good night my darling, here's to our next anniversary together."

An official telegram from Ottawa arrived August 27, saying that Steele was missing in action. The one telling her he had been killed came two days later. Dick's regiment sent a letter of condolence. Joe Levitt also wrote to Esther telling her what he knew about the loss of a man he called "a brother." "He helped to smash the once proud German 7th Army, and when Canadians knifed their way through to Falaise to close the ring around the Nazis, he was there fighting with his magnificent courage," Levitt told her. "And since this is real life, his tank was hit by an enemy shell and he died instantly. He never knew what hit him."[37]

News of Steele's death spread to the other regiments, including Hy Chud's, who remembers hearing about it from Rabbi David Monson, then one of the chaplains overseas.

"What do you do? What can you do? Nothing. You carry on, you maybe grit your teeth," Chud said.

Esther did not tell the twins what had happened right away. She was still coming to terms with Steele's death herself, especially after her thank-you letter for the flowers had been returned, stamped DECEASED. She broke the news to Johnny and Michael in a way she thought four-year-olds might understand. "I said, 'Some fathers did not come back but we hoped he would come back.'...They were still in their crib."[38]

Erlick was killed in action three days after Steele, on August 20, although details of his death are not known. Gorodetsky died of self-inflicted injuries on August 21.[39] An inquiry ruled he'd been careless while cleaning his gun. The military top brass were kind enough to tell Gorodetsky's widow, Rita, only that her husband had died "as a result of injuries received in action against the enemy."[40]

When news of Steele's and Erlick's deaths reached the communist leadership in Canada, it received front-page treatment in labour and left-wing newspapers. "We revere the memory of these two Jewish labour heroes," the communist *Vochenblatt* said.[41]

Bill Walsh arrived in France with the Essex Scottish Regiment a few days after Steele's death. When he was informed of what had happened, he too wrote to Esther. He vowed revenge. "Dick wrote to me that he got his quota of Nazis and mine too. That quota has gone way up now. I'll fulfill it."[42]

Six months later, as the war moved onto German soil, Walsh nearly became a casualty. The sergeant was pinned for nearly twenty-four hours in a cellar near Calcar, along with nineteen other men. Walsh's regiment lost fifty-one men in that skirmish, with another ninety-nine wounded. Fifty-four others were taken prisoner. The Canadian Press called Walsh and his cellar mates the "Heroes of Calcar."[43] The Jewish press would call Walsh one of the "Unkillable 20."[44]

When he thinks back now, Chud says the Jewish Canadian communists had even more obstacles to donning a uniform than did the rest of the country's Jews. In the early years, communists had to oppose the war because the Soviet Union did. They were considered traitors, rounded up, and jailed. When Ottawa did eventually release them, some remained under surveillance, even overseas in uniform. For these reasons, and because he believes his comrades acted out of a sense of what Chud calls *Gerechtigkeit*, which is Yiddish for a sense of social justice, he thinks they deserve recognition.

"I believe they were out to make life better for people like myself," he said. "All these guys were my heroes."

4 The Battle of Hong Kong

"If you meet Confucius, tell him I would like to talk to him"

While Dick Steele was in prison in Canada for his political activities, the communist newspaper *Canadian Tribune* published an update on his situation. The article came out in December 1941, just after the Japanese had overrun Hong Kong and attacked Pearl Harbor. "At Hong Kong two Canadian battalions were casualties. Now Steele wants to fill the breach," the paper said, blasting the government for keeping the labour leader locked up when he could be useful in the war effort.[1]

Steele would not see action for another two and a half years. Indeed, most Canadian soldiers did not see combat until the 1943 invasion of Sicily. But in 1941, Britain asked Ottawa for military aid in the form of troops to shore up the fourteen thousand–strong British garrison already present in the Pacific colony of Hong Kong. The result was two unlucky battalions known as Canada's "C" Force, made up of nearly two thousand men from the Winnipeg Grenadiers and the Royal Rifles of Canada, as well as a brigade headquarters including dentists, ordnance men, drivers, and signallers. The Canadian chief of the general staff, Harry Crerar, famously assured the King government that there would be "no military risk."[2]

The Canadians were only supposed to do guard duty. Instead, they were thrown into an impossible situation: defending Hong Kong from the Japanese invasion, an ill-fated mission that has been described as a "catastrophe."[3] Ten Canadian Jewish volunteers were in the thick of it.

When the war broke out, David Golden, the son of Russian immigrants, was studying law at the University of Manitoba. As he was underage, he stayed in school and spent weekends and summers taking militia training with the campus Canadian Officers' Training Corps. That's where Golden learned how to assemble and disassemble a Bren gun, but never actually fired the weapon. The Brens would become the main light machine gun used in the war, and normally required a crew of two: one to load it and one to fire it.

By 1941, after Golden obtained his law degree and won a Rhodes scholarship (although travelling to England to use it would have to be put on hold due to the war), he enlisted and became an intelligence officer with the Winnipeg Grenadiers.[4] They sent the unit to Jamaica to do garrison duty, where Lieutenant Golden taught himself to assemble a rifle and ride a motorcycle.

Max Berger, the son of Hungarian immigrants, had completed three years of high school at Sarnia Collegiate before quitting to go to work.[5] When the war broke out, Berger was nineteen, an assistant manager in a fish-and-chips shop in Toronto. After the fall of France in June 1940, Crerar issued an appeal on the radio for Canadians to join up. Berger may have been listening, for the next day he was at a recruiting office in London, Ontario, where he signed up as a reservist with the Elgin Regiment.[6] Eight months later, he switched to active service. In July 1941, the army sent Private Berger to train as an electrician.

The month of July 1941 was also a milestone for Sergeant Robert Macklin and his wife, Ursula. They became parents to a daughter named Bonita, Bonnie for short. Macklin was the youngest son of Russian-born immigrants, and, like the children of thousands of immigrants who lived on the east side of Mount Royal, attended Montreal's Baron Byng High School for a time, and also Strathcona Academy.[7] In 1928, he moved to New York to work as a bank clerk. After a romance there went sour, Macklin ran away to England. He joined the British Army and also met and married Ursula Carroll, whom he called Girlie. In 1937, Macklin was posted to Hong Kong as a sergeant instructor with the British Army Educational Corps, reporting to the Hong Kong Censor's Office.[8] Girlie went with him. Macklin was wiry, with blue eyes, dark brown hair, and a moustache. He had dimples when he smiled. The couple lived in Victoria, on Hong Kong Island, in the British Army's married quarters along Kennedy Road in the Mid-Levels, and that's where Bonnie was born.[9]

At thirty-seven, Toronto's David (Moishe) Schrage wasn't exactly in the age group that the Canadian Army recruiters usually looked for. He also had knock knees, slight varicose veins in both legs, and no bottom teeth.[10] But Schrage had language skills that the army could use. Although he had quit school in Poland at age eleven, Schrage spoke English and Yiddish, as well as German, Russian, and Polish. Three army doctors signed his medical clearance forms.

The Toronto mechanic was born and raised in Tarnopol, Poland. He served two years with the Polish army, where antisemitism and attacks against Jewish soldiers were common.[11] Arriving in Ontario in 1929, Schrage went to work as a shipper at the Acme Paper Products plant. His girlfriend, Helen Dressler, had sailed to Canada separately from Poland and was living in Winnipeg and working as a seamstress. Schrage's boss gave him the money to send for her. The couple married in Toronto in 1930 and had three children: Katie, Alvin, and Richard. Money was tight. Schrage had had to leave the paper factory because it aggravated his asthma and was eking out a living working for a chicken dealer.[12] After the Germans invaded Galicia, where Schrage was from, and local ethnic Ukrainians began rounding up and murdering Jews, Schrage enlisted on July 4, 1941. He immediately began sending $20 a month to his wife.

Hymie Greenberg was called up in March 1941. He had planned to enlist months before and had written home to ask his mother's permission. "I sure would like to join the army. But I wouldn't like to and then you should feel bad about it."[13]

Greenberg's parents were Russian immigrants. His father had been hit by lightning and killed while baling hay on a farm in Beausejour, near Winnipeg. His mother later married Moses Jampolsky, a schoolteacher, who adopted Hymie. Two half-brothers soon followed. The family settled in Spedden, Alberta, where Jampolsky taught school. Hymie's mother ran a trading post and grocery store.

Greenberg spoke Yiddish, English, Hebrew, German, and Ukrainian and could drive a car, but his job as a clerk in a store in Roblin, Manitoba, brought in just $50 a month.[14] After paying room and board, he was having trouble making his salary last. Greenberg applied to join the RCMP but was turned down. He told his mother that the police thought he was shirking his responsibility to go to war. After his call-up came, he chose the Signal Corps and was sent to train at the Barriefield base in Kingston.

It's not clear what motivated Greenberg to volunteer for active service in the summer of 1941 rather than continue to serve only in Canada as a conscript. Perhaps he, like Jack Tweyman, had felt the intense pressure from other soldiers already heading to England for duty with the Canadian Active Service Force. Perhaps he didn't like being labelled a zombie. What is clear from his letters is that that his motivation for joining the army was evolving from financial to patriotic. "I am proud of you," his stepfather, Moses Jampolsky, wrote. "No Jewish boy has a right to stay home while England bleeds. Mine won't."[15] In August 1941, Greenberg was sent to the massive Debert military base near Truro, Nova Scotia.[16]

William Allister hated Debert. Military life there was quite the assault on his artistic sensibilities. A month older than Greenberg, Allister was the son of Ukrainian immigrants who had settled in Benito, Manitoba, before moving to Montreal.[17] When the two Jewish signallers met in Debert in August 1941, Allister described the camp, dramatically, as a place where "hundreds of identical gray huts, humped and soggy under interminable rain, sat mired to their haunches in mud."[18] He had studied art at Baron Byng High School and was a noted actor, a member of the Montreal YMHA's Little Theatre. The year the war broke out, Allister had won the Quebec Regional Award in a national drama festival for his role in a one-act play titled *Road of Poplars*, portraying a veteran with shell shock.[19] He'd even lived in New York, where he took professional drama courses and worked as a successful commercial artist.

In Debert, Greenberg and Allister roomed together and became close friends. Allister called Hymie Hank. The two would spend their evenings drinking at a nearby tavern and comparing their lives. Greenberg told Allister he loved playing hockey and baseball and playing the violin.[20]

On October 9, 1941, the Canadian government sent word to the Royal Rifles and Grenadiers to get ready to deploy. The men were not told where they were being sent. The choice of these two infantry regiments would later prove to be controversial. Both outfits had spent time doing guard duties outside Canada—one group in Newfoundland and the other in Bermuda and Jamaica—but they weren't considered ready for field combat.[21] David Golden would later agree that he and his men weren't very well trained. "I spent a good part of my time telling people how to do things even though I didn't know how to do them myself," he said. "We never fired any Bren guns; we just assembled and disassembled them."[22]

The British governor in Hong Kong was asking for additional manpower, including a brigade headquarters. The word went out to selected Canadian bases seeking 440 more volunteers.[23] In Debert, Hymie Greenberg heard about the chance to sign up for the mysterious "C" Force expedition and tried to persuade Allister to go with him, as the actor would later recall in his memoir, *Where Life and Death Hold Hands.*[24] "I'm not sure which idea fired me up more, the secret mission or leaving Debert," Allister writes.

He would live to regret saying yes. Thinking they would be heading to England, they had medical exams, got their shots, and went on leave. They were told to be in Ottawa for October 21 at 1300 hours.[25] Greenberg dashed off a postcard home.

I am leaving for Ottawa to take special training. I will write you when I get there. Don't expect letter for a few days. Don't worry.
Love, Hymie.[26]

In Toronto, David Schrage was sure he was being sent somewhere warm. "He said he was going to go to Jamaica, that he would be on the beach, that he would be back soon. He got white gloves, flip-flops. He was very naive," his son Alvin said.

On October 23, a CNR troop train began picking up the "C" Force volunteers coming from the east coast.[27] It stopped in Valcartier, Quebec, on October 24, where Schrage got on. He was officially attached to the Royal Rifles of Canada. The train also stopped in Ottawa to pick up Greenberg, Allister, and Berger. All weekend the train rolled west. Sonya Jampolsky took her youngest son, Murray, down to Edmonton to say goodbye to her oldest son. "Murray and his mother went to see the train, and saw Hymie as that train came through Edmonton," said Murray's widow, Doreen Jampolsky. "And what I was told was that they had rifles from World War I."

The train arrived in Vancouver at eight o'clock on Monday morning, October 27. The converted New Zealand passenger liner HMS *Awatea* was waiting for them. The men were still not told their destination. Greenberg sent a final postcard home: "Just arrived in Vancouver. Everything is fine. Will write as soon as I can. Don't worry. Hymie."[28]

There was plenty for the servicemen to worry about, though. They soon discovered the elegant ship with its teak deck wasn't big enough to take all 1,973 Canadians and their equipment, which included vehicles.[29] The ship was so overcrowded that one company of the Rifles had to travel on the escort vessel, HMCS *Prince Robert*. Although the officers on *Awatea* had enough space in their quarters, some of the enlisted men felt their own sleeping arrangements were unfair.

One of the disgruntled soldiers was George Harrison, from Winnipeg's working-class Elmwood neighbourhood.[30] Harrison was born in 1920. His father died shortly after, and his mother put George and his older two siblings into a Jewish orphanage in Winnipeg for a while.[31] He finished Grade 9 and went to work for the Canadian Pacific Railway Telegraph Company.

Harrison had enlisted with the Winnipeg Grenadiers three days after Canada officially entered the war. Like Golden, Harrison saw duty in the West Indies, guarding Axis prisoners of war.[32] The regiment returned to Winnipeg in October and received new tropical uniforms, and more than nine hundred men joined "C" Force. Harrison, a sergeant by this time, became outraged when he got his first glimpse of where the army intended his men to sleep on board the ship. "Our hammocks are right over the eating tables," he recalled. "I said, 'This is terrible. I mean, suppose people get seasick and then we got to get up in the morning and eat a hot breakfast off this?'"[33]

An estimated fifty furious men, including Harrison, pushed their way off the ship without permission. The protest didn't change anything, and the men were escorted back under armed guard.[34] Harrison was punished and demoted a rank, back to corporal. His day got even worse, when the men discovered their lunch was going to be tripe and onions.

The first few days at sea were busy. There were some lectures on the Japanese and on keeping clear of the temptations of prostitutes. Soon, training started: the men carried out target practice with two-inch mortars and Bren guns.[35] Allister tried to improve his Morse code skills during the long voyage by using the Aldis lamp to signal *Prince Robert*.[36] When they weren't doing drills, the men were gambling at card games of crown and anchor or blackjack.[37] Allister and Greenberg were also getting to know the other men in the Headquarters Signal Corps who had been stationed at other Canadian bases. One of them was Jacob (Jack) Rose, who was born and raised in Vancouver. When he was in his teens, Rose had worked for a circus. After leaving Kitsilano High School, he delivered telegrams for the Canadian Pacific Railway. But he wanted a better-paying job, so he trained to be a telegraph operator, and in April 1940 those skills helped him get taken on by the Royal Canadian Corps of Signals.

Three days after *Awatea* left Canada, David Schrage turned up in sick bay. He was in such bad shape that two men had to carry him there. The doctor, Lieutenant J.G. Gray, couldn't get any coherent information from him, but the men said he had been fine until after breakfast, when he started throwing up. "Schrage said very little to anyone," Gray wrote in his report. "His only complaints were occasional mumblings for water, and at times he seemed to complain of some abdominal distress and pain in his knees."[38]

With Schrage breathing heavily and quickly through his mouth, the medical staff examined him. They took his blood pressure and pulse and listened to his chest. When they checked his tongue, it looked dry, with a dirty brown coating. Gray was baffled. Two other doctors examined his patient. They all agreed there was no reason for Schrage to be so sick. They chalked it up to seasickness. They gave him a sedative and prescribed fluids.

At three the next morning, Schrage took a turn for the worse and died. The doctors wrote it up as a heart attack and seasickness. Schrage became the first casualty of Hong Kong and the only "C" Force soldier to die en route. They stopped the ship to bury him at sea.[39]

A telegram from the army arrived at Schrage's Toronto home two days later, addressed to his widow, Helen. "Regret deeply B38365 Private David Morris Schrage officially reported died 31st October 1941 as result of heart failure. Further information follows when received."

The ship's doctors soon discovered what had really killed her husband. In Schrage's personal effects they found a dozen vials of protamine zinc insulin and a complete hypodermic kit. The senior medical officer, Major John N.B. Crawford, later emended the medical report. In red pencil he wrote that Schrage was presumably a diabetic and had died of hypoglycemia. The medical charts when Schrage enlisted said nothing about diabetes. The three medical officers who had signed his forms had given him an A rating.

Alvin Schrage is certain that his mother had been aware of her husband's medical condition.

"He was taking insulin every day," Schrage said, although he was just four and a half when his father died. "Apparently he was worried he'd not be accepted if they knew."

The ship stopped in Hawaii, after which the men were told their real destination: Hong Kong. The Canadians steamed into Hong Kong

Harbour early on November 16. Their arrival got good reviews back home. The *Winnipeg Free Press* ran a political cartoon titled "A Canadian Surprise." It shows a giant Canadian soldier holding a bayonet, towering over a tiny, fearful Japanese sailor who is frantically rowing his dragon-shaped boat away.[40] It would take several weeks before the Canadians would discover how misguided that cartoon was.

After *Awatea* and *Prince Robert* docked, the two Canadian battalions marched down Nathan Road in Kowloon, on the mainland, to the accompaniment of two bands. The soldiers wore their steel helmets and made quite a spectacle for the crowds lining the main street to watch. Some people cheered and waved small Union Jacks.[41] The Hong Kong that the Canadians encountered was crowded with refugees from northern and central China, which the Imperial Japanese forces had already captured. Disease and poverty afflicted the refugees, but life for most of the British garrison and for the British civilians living on Hong Kong Island continued nearly normally. Well-dressed shoppers strolled along the city of Victoria's arcaded sidewalks, and the Peak Tram carried passengers up the slopes of the island to reach luxury hillside homes.[42]

Back in Spedden, Hymie Greenberg's seventeen-year-old half-brother, Lyman Jampolsky, penned a letter to the Far East. Lyman was thinking about joining up but was still underage. In the meantime, he was busy with school, and his new project was building a skating rink in the community. "I suppose Hong Kong hasn't got a rink. How do you like China? Did you ever dream that you would one day walk upon China's soil?" Lyman asked. "If you meet Confucius tell him I would like to talk to him."[43]

Over the ten days following "C" Force's landing, the senior Canadian officers took stock of the colony's existing defences. They toured a rebuilt system of tunnels and pillboxes north of the city known as the Gin Drinker's Line. The soldiers were sent marching up and down Hong Kong's steep hills carrying full packs to get used to the terrain. As the diplomatic rhetoric heated up between Japan, the United States, and Britain, fifty thousand Japanese troops were massing along the northern outskirts of Hong Kong.[44] The British officer in charge of the Allied forces in Hong Kong, General Christopher Maltby, was aware of the threat. He intended to defend the mainland for as long as possible, then order a withdrawal to Hong Kong Island, where the Canadians would be deployed, the Grenadiers on the west and the Rifles on the south and east.[45]

On December 7, a church parade was under way at the Canadian barracks in Sham Shui Po near Kowloon on the mainland, and Sunday services were taking place on the island, inside Victoria's historic St. John's Cathedral. A messenger rushed in and whispered urgently into the ear of General Maltby. By four o'clock, the front-line troops in the Canadian battalions were in their assigned positions on Hong Kong Island.[46] David Golden remembers feeling ill prepared for what was to come. "We were given a briefing which was very, very inadequate and, you know, [it was] mentioned that there were possibilities of troop movements and so on but there wasn't really anything that you could put your finger on," he said.[47]

Just before five the next morning (it was still Sunday in Pearl Harbor, Hawaii, but already Monday in Asia), Japanese planes began their attack on an airfield near Sham Shui Po. About twenty bombs fell on the Canadian barracks.[48] Over the next four days, the Japanese overran the Gin Drinker's Line of defence and won control of the mainland side of Hong Kong. The Canadians joined civilians in a scramble across the harbour, commandeering whatever boats they could find. By December 12, the Japanese laid siege to the island. Twice the Japanese generals suggested to the British governor, Sir Mark Young, that he should surrender. Twice he refused. Missives from Churchill encouraged the colony to keep fighting.

On the night of December 18, Japanese soldiers crossed the narrowest part of the harbour and launched their assault on the island. The next day, the Japanese were poised to overrun the mansion known as Casa Bianca, where the Canadians in the signal outfit were operating. Hymie Greenberg and the other signallers were told to move their gear to a safer spot in the Wan Chai Gap. They set up their radio equipment in a house at 526 Coombe Road in the Peak district. Communication links were established, and then some of the men collapsed in exhaustion for a brief nap. A 9.2-inch artillery shell hit the front part of the house and exploded in the middle of the sleeping men. Greenberg and two others were killed instantly.[49]

William Allister wasn't there when it happened. He was with a British unit not far away. Someone came running down the road yelling that a shell had killed a whole bunch of Canadian signallers. Allister made for the site. He met four of the survivors. A British sergeant asked Allister to provide assistance with the burials. He took a swig of rum and started shovelling. As they were placing the bodies in gunnysacks, the British sergeant held up a respirator. It had the name Greenberg on it. Allister held out hope that it wasn't Hymie's.[50] He had sworn to Greenberg's mother that he'd look after her son. He then recognized a sweater on one of the bodies. They buried Greenberg and the others in a single grave.

Meanwhile, near the Hong Kong Police Station, George Harrison unexpectedly regained the rank that he had lost in the failed mutiny aboard *Awatea* just a few weeks earlier. His captain, R.W. Philip, delivered the news during the fighting with a terse "Corporal Harrison, two of our sergeants were just killed. So now you are a sergeant." The newly re-minted sergeant spent the rest of the day sheltering in an alcove to avoid being machine-gunned by the Japanese, who had captured the police building. When it was dark, Harrison and his men commandeered a car with four flat tires, squeezed in six or seven men, including a soldier whose jaw had been shot off, and drove for their lives downhill.[51]

Over on the Ridge, an elevated part of the main road leading south to the beaches of Repulse Bay, Sarnia's Max Berger was trying to hold that strategic geographical site. There were very few houses in the area, but whoever controlled the Ridge and the nearby Altamira House would control access to the southern part of the island.[52] Berger, a private, had driven a taxi in Sarnia and spent the first few days of the invasion using his pre-war transport skills for the Royal Canadian Army Service Corps to deliver supplies to the front-line units, scrounging whatever vehicles he could find, including local taxis. By December 19, with Japanese troops now swarming over the island, Berger's unit held the north end of the Ridge.[53]

For three days, the Japanese made several attempts to take the Ridge. Eventually the order came for the Canadians to pull back, but some troops who tried to get down to the south side of the island were ambushed.[54] Berger was killed sometime before December 22. It's not known if he was among the ninety-nine Allied soldiers the Japanese murdered as prisoners of war at the Ridge, at another house called Overbays, or at Eucliffe Castle.

While Canadian newspapers were still reporting how the defenders of Hong Kong were holding off the Japanese, the reality couldn't have been more different. Over 250 Canadians had already died. Hundreds more were wounded. The holdouts were still fighting, including Sergeant Harrison and his remaining men, who found themselves in possession of a Lewis machine gun, but because they'd trained only on a Vickers, they had trouble loading ammunition. They resorted to using hand grenades instead. "They told us all to get our grenades and more or less line up in a big sort of a line by this gap and everybody throw, count three and throw your grenade," Harrison recalled. "And from what I understand we took out a whole bunch of Japanese."[55]

Three days later, Christmas Day, in the face of overwhelming odds, mounting casualties, and a looming water and food shortage, Governor Young signed the surrender. Robert Macklin was officially listed as missing. Over sixteen hundred men of "C" Force became POWs, including David Golden, George Harrison, and a Jewish soldier from Toronto, Louis Brown, who served with the Royal Rifles of Canada.[56] Jacob Rose and William Allister joined them.

Some of Allister's fellow POWs knew that he was Jewish, but he asked them not to divulge the fact to his Japanese captors.[57] He was worried about what would happen to him if the guards discovered this information. Winnipeg's Frederick (Zeke) Zaidman could have told them what the Japanese were capable of. Zaidman had been wounded in his leg on December 22 and was also suffering from shrapnel wounds elsewhere on his body. He had made his way to St. Stephen's College, a building that had been converted into a hospital, near Stanley, on the island's south side. On the day of the surrender, Zaidman witnessed the Japanese massacring wounded patients, including some Canadians. Among the victims were local Chinese militia and some of the hospital medical staff. He told the *Toronto Daily Star* about his experience.

> *The Japs rushed in and bayoneted my wounded buddies, took many V.A.D.s [members of the Voluntary Aid Detachment] and the nurses and assaulted them. The rest of us crowded into a small room. Every hour a Jap would come in and pick out some poor wretch. His dead and mutilated body would be found later. I was beaten down by the flat of a sword.*[58]

Right after the surrender, the Japanese went on a spree of raping and looting while the captured Allied troops were left to their own devices. That meant no food or water or medical care for the wounded and no proper registration of the prisoners' names. None of the 1,683 men of "C" Force, including the Jewish Canadians among them, expected their captivity would last nearly four years and reduce them to skeletal wrecks from starvation, slave labour, and disease.

While waiting for his captors to figure out what to do with all of them, Harrison thought it best to be prepared. He scavenged some abandoned equipment and supplies, including a Gurkha knife and a scabbard. "I had two kit bags and a haversack...I was a pretty strong fellow, then—180 pounds and well equipped with muscle—and I had this all on my back." Eventually, the men were housed at a former refugee camp in North Point on the island, or taken across the harbour to their Sham Shui Po Barracks, now their prison.

Robert Macklin was one of the thousands of Allied prisoners held at Sham Shui Po. He died there a year later, on December 22, 1942, of what the records would later describe as acute enteritis and "mobague."[59] Macklin's British friend Staff Sergeant James O'Toole of the Royal Army Ordnance Corps noted the death in his camp diary that day, reporting also that the Japanese sent in two Christmas trees for the POW camp church. "Sgt. Makelin [*sic*], AEC [Army Educational Corps], died today of dysentery. His wife and baby are at Stanley. They used to live above us in Kennedy Road. Always thought of him quite a tough egg. But who can say?"[60]

Girlie Macklin and their new baby spent twenty-one months at the Stanley internment camp for civilians. Girlie got a card from her husband, around Christmastime, although he had already died.[61]

When news of the Hong Kong disaster began to reach Canada, Hymie Greenberg's mother kept hoping her son was alive as a POW. Lyman's letter with its reference to Confucius had been returned to sender. A stamp on it read, "It is regretted that circumstances have made it impossible to forward this letter to destination. As soon as contacts can be established information will be provided." All through 1942, Sonya Jampolsky continued to mail Red Cross parcels for Hymie. The Canadian military reassured her that everything was being done but that the Japanese weren't cooperating. Moses Jampolsky offered to personally cover the government's costs to make inquiries: "ATTENTION [in red]—we will deposit, if necessary, the amount of cost of such cable to be used as soon as news is obtained in Hong Kong," he wrote to the National Defence department.[62]

At the end of 1942, the Canadian government issued a casualty list. Hymie's name wasn't on it; however, the Allisters on Bernard Avenue West in Montreal were notified that their son was "alive and well in a

Japanese prison camp."[63] Months later, Allister received a letter from his relieved parents. "I opened the letter with trembling fingers and stared uncomprehendingly at the first sentence: 'We were overjoyed to know you are a prisoner of war,'" he writes in his memoir. "There I sat—in shit up to the eyeballs, half dead, crawling with lice, exhausted, starved, disease ridden, jolted by electric feet, a bloody walking skeleton—and they were overjoyed?"[64]

David Golden survived by eating whatever he could find, no matter how disgusting. "The basic ration was poor quality rice, which I guess in retrospect was good for us because it had some husks left and so on," he says, explaining that this was healthier than white rice. "[It was] filled with weevils. I guess that gave us our protein. Some people used to try and pick them out but that was hopeless." They also got tea and vegetable scraps. Once, the men were given fish heads.[65]

Jacob Rose endured his share of medical problems, including dysentery, which put him in the North Point hospital for a while. While recovering, he signed up for Japanese lessons and eventually became fluent. The new language skills came in handy later back in the barracks, where he carried out black market operations with a Japanese guard.[66] William Allister found that painting was a way to fill his rest periods. He fashioned his own rudimentary tools. His artwork was rolled up and hidden for safekeeping.[67]

On January 12, 1943, the *Winnipeg Tribune* published another military casualty list, this time with Hymie Greenberg's name on it. His mother refused to believe it. Lieutenant Colonel F.W. Clarke wrote back telling her to be prepared for the worst. He said that the three hundred Canadians who remained unaccounted for were probably "killed in action, or missing."[68]

After the casualty list was published, the Japanese gathered up a thousand POWs and transported them to Japan to be slave labourers. William Allister, Jacob Rose, and Louis Brown were among them. Rose and Allister were sent to Tsurumi, not far from Yokohama, to build warships.[69] Allister was put on ship-painting duty. Rose worked as an acetylene welder in the pipe workshop.[70] Brown was sent to the Omine coal mining camp in Fukuoka Prefecture on Kyushu Island. Frederick Zaidman was sent to Niigata, on the west coast of Honshu, the central island, where he spent two years. He was assigned to the coal docks. He called the site "about the worst camp under the Japs." He lost so much weight from beatings, starvation, and exhaustion that he weighed ninety-seven pounds.[71]

George Harrison would remain a POW in Hong Kong for another year, where he did his best to sabotage the Japanese war machine. One of his efforts was carried out while working on an extension to the Kai Tak airport on the Hong Kong mainland. "When the Japs weren't watching we'd put four or five buckets of sand into one bucket of cement so it wasn't very sturdy," he says.[72] "I can still remember the first plane that came down after it was supposed to be all finished, the plane came down and the runway just crumbled."

Harrison was plagued with medical problems due to malnutrition, including pellagra and beriberi. He lost his eyesight. At Christmastime 1943, it was his turn to be shipped to Japan as a slave labourer, arriving at the Omine camp where Louis Brown was. Harrison endured an excruciating bout of foot trouble that led to gangrene, but he narrowly avoided having his toes amputated.[73]

In the spring of 1945, Jacob Rose was transferred to yet another Japanese slave labour camp, a coal mining operation at Sendai, on Honshu's east coast. Rose was able to write letters home to his family then, and although these were heavily censored, he used a sort of code to let them know he was in a bad way. He described how his surroundings were like the notorious Oakalla prison in Burnaby, British Columbia. He also was given the opportunity to broadcast recorded messages that were heard back home, although the Japanese carefully checked his prepared script first.

With the world's attention focused on the war in Europe, most of the Canadian Jewish POWs in the Pacific likely thought they would die there. Over the three and a half years of their ordeal, some did long for death to end their suffering. Others clung to the hope, no matter how faint, that someday it might be their turn to be liberated, if only they could stay alive long enough.

5 Dieppe

"We're going on an exercise"

In August 1942, Maxwell London, who was training in England as a commando with the Royal Regiment of Canada, sent a letter home to his parents in Toronto. Choosing his words carefully so as not to invoke the scissors of the Canadian Army censors, London tried to warn his family that something big was about to happen. "I think I should tell you that we may be going into action any day now," he wrote. "When it comes, Mother, please don't worry about me. I can take care of myself. There isn't a German alive that I can't lick."[1]

London and the nearly five thousand other Canadians who participated in the raid on the French coastal resort town of Dieppe on August 19, 1942, would discover just how wrong those predictions were. Although London would survive, he would have the next two and a half years to regret his cocky attitude as one of 1,946 Canadians captured that day who spent the remainder of the war in German prisoner-of-war camps. Among the Canadian infantrymen, engineers, tank crews, sailors, signallers, and pilots who took part in the raid were about thirty Jews. Their failed mission, the largest amphibious landing undertaken in the war to that date, was a costly rehearsal for D-Day two years later.

While the Japanese forces were overrunning Hong Kong in December 1941, German troops were capturing huge swaths of territory in the Soviet Union after Hitler's decision to rip up the non-aggression treaty and his attempt to wipe out not just communism but also the Jews of the USSR. Moscow was under attack, and the Germans were winning the war. Hitler and his allies controlled land from the north of Europe to North Africa. Stalin was pressuring Churchill to open a second front against Hitler somewhere in Europe in order to make the German leader divert resources from the Eastern Front. Although the British and Americans weren't ready to do that—busy as they were fighting against the Nazis' commander Rommel in North Africa—they were open to smaller actions.

Initially Canada wasn't supposed to be involved in the Dieppe Raid, which was meant to be an all-British operation. Then Lieutenant General Harry Crerar, the same Canadian officer who had authorized the ill-fated deployment of "C" Force to Hong Kong, heard about the plan. He had been promoted and was now the senior general responsible for the Canadian Army in England, where tens of thousands of Canadian troops had been idling in bases. Some had been overseas for years without seeing action and were restless. "The reputation of the [Canadian] corps was at stake," Crerar wrote to Lieutenant General Bernard Montgomery, who was in charge of British operations in the south of England at the time.[2] It was because of Crerar that the Canadians came to be given the mission's largest and toughest jobs in one of the most controversial episodes in the country's World War II experience.

Planning for the raid began in late March 1942, and some Canadians got their feet wet by taking part in small commando raids along the French coast to probe or disable German naval installations, including operations in St-Nazaire, Brittany, and near Boulogne.

Morris Lozdon was a thirty-one-year-old married father of three who had worked as a printer at Easy Built Model Airplane in Toronto before enlisting in the Royal Regiment of Canada in the spring of 1941. After the raid on Boulogne, Lozdon, a private, boasted that he was now the owner of two pistols confiscated from German officers. "I had enough bombs on me to blow up Toronto's two largest department stores," he wrote home.[3]

By May, Canadian troops had moved onto the Isle of Wight, off the south coast of England, to practise amphibious landings. Two major rehearsals took place, each called Yukon. The raid itself, originally code-named Operation Rutter, was supposed to take place in June 1942, but British officials decided the men weren't ready. In early July, Montgomery again cancelled the raid at the last minute, after the men had already been loaded into the ships that were to take them across the Channel. The weather was poor, and the Germans knew something was afoot.

They bombed the men and boats at the assembly points in the Solent, the waterway between Portsmouth and the Isle of Wight, causing minor injuries to four men. Controversially, Montgomery wasn't in England when Operation Rutter was relaunched just six weeks later under a new name—Operation Jubilee—using a scaled-down version of the same plan, one without any pre-raid air force bombing.

At six o'clock in the morning on August 18, David Lloyd Hart from Montreal was asleep in an army billet in Swindon, England, when his captain shook him awake. "Sergeant Hart, wake all the men. We're going on an exercise. Movement at seven o'clock. It's called Exercise Ford. Make sure they take all their equipment and everything with them." The Jewish radio operator had participated in so many training exercises in the past few months that he yearned to roll over and go back to sleep. "Oh sure, another goddamn exercise," Hart remembers mumbling sleepily. Hart didn't take any extra food or clothing, although he did stuff a reminder of home in his backpack: a thousand cigarettes that he'd recently received from a Jewish businessman in Montreal, Gordon Brown, for whom Hart, an accountant, had done audits.

After eleven hours on the road, Hart's section arrived at the port of Newhaven, one of the main marshalling points. He and his signallers boarded a landing craft and were stunned to see three Churchill tanks already loaded. This raid would be the first time the Canadian Army tested the tanks in an amphibious landing. Hart also nearly blew himself and his men up. "I see these bags that I kick aside," he remembers, "and an engineer corporal comes over to me and he says 'Sergeant, I wouldn't do that if I were you—there's seventy pounds of high explosive in there.'"

The opening stages of the operation required a surprise silent attack. Some British commandos were to get to shore first and secure the outermost flanks of the beach town, while the 556 infantrymen of the Royal Regiment of Canada were to land east of the harbour, at Puys, at about five o'clock in the morning.[4] Their target was codenamed Blue Beach. They were supposed to take out the German gun positions at Pollet Cliff, which overlooked Dieppe Harbour. The Black Watch of Montreal was to follow them ashore.

At least eight Canadian Jews served with the Royals: Lionel Cohen, Morris Greenberg, Morris Lozdon, Jack Clausner, Maxwell London, Joseph Moskowitz (later Moscoe), Simon Green, and Meyer Bubis. Most had enlisted during first weeks of the war. All were from Toronto.

Green, the youngest at twenty-two, was the only one not born in North America, having emigrated from Poland with his family. Moskowitz was in his mid-thirties and married, from a family of seven. London, one of ten siblings, a Harbord Collegiate graduate, ran a brassiere factory with one of his brothers. "He used to say that women who worked for him came in flat [chested] and left with big boobs because they used to steal [the brassieres]," says his daughter, Sandra London-Rakita, with a smile.

Bubis was a stenographer, Green had worked as a tool grinder, and Greenberg had been a cutter in a tie factory but was also a well-known Yiddish poet.[5] The war brought out a different side of Greenberg's character. He had earned his sniper's designation and taught commando tactics at Rowland's Castle, near Portsmouth, where battle drill courses were given.[6] The army wanted him to take officers' training, but Greenberg demurred. He thought he needed a little practical experience first.[7]

Maurice Harold Waldman from Assiniboia, Saskatchewan, served with the South Saskatchewan Regiment, which was supposed to land on the west side of the town, at Pourville.[8] Their drop zone on the left bank of the Scie River was codenamed Green Beach. They were to cross the beach, climb the headlands, and capture the Luftwaffe-controlled airport and the German officers' quarters. The Queen's Own Cameron Highlanders of Winnipeg were also supposed to land at Green Beach, along with tanks from the 14th Canadian Army Tank Regiment of Calgary. The armoured crews had spent hours practising waterproofing techniques, and they'd also practised driving across pebbled beaches such as the ones they expected to face in Dieppe.[9]

Five Canadian Jewish men served in this part of the operation. Benjamin Brachman was forty-one and an internationally trained dermatologist from Regina serving as medical officer in the 10th Field Ambulance.[10] Louis Todros was from Ottawa, and Abram Arbour was born in Narcisse, Manitoba, and lived outside Winnipeg. Arbour had worked since 1934 as a transport driver and mechanic for Safety Freight Lines.[11] Twenty-four-year-old Michael Poplack of Vancouver was with the Calgary Tanks, as was Elly Raskin, twenty-two, from Rumsey, Alberta.[12]

The initial landings at Puys and Pourville had to succeed in order for the rest of the raid to work. The main frontal assault on the town of Dieppe was to start thirty minutes later, and two regiments of Canadians were to land directly in Dieppe harbour: the Royal Hamilton Light Infantry (RHLI) to the west and the Essex Scottish to the east.[13] Some of the 14th Army Tank Regiment (Calgary) would go in with them, as would a group of Royal Canadian Engineers. The Fusiliers Mont Royal (FMR) were to be held offshore, as reserves.

The RHLI had at least six Jewish men in their landing boats: Leon Paul Magner, Leizer Heifetz, Jack Gralick, William Korenblum, Murray Bleeman, and Arthur Liss. Liss was the son of a fruit peddler, and had to quit Westdale Collegiate to go out to work. Heifetz had worked for Imperial Tobacco in Delhi, Ontario, tying leaves into bundles.[14] He was the youngest in his family, as was Jack Gralick, the youngest of eight kids from Euclid Street in Toronto. Gralick was learning the printing business and played shortstop on a local baseball team. At least two, Magner and Korenblum, were married.[15]

When Murray Bleeman arrived in England, his army superiors originally had him pegged to be a quartermaster because of his experience owning a lunch counter in Toronto, but he wanted to see action. Bleeman's family considered him invincible, having already escaped death twice while on leave in London. Once, he dropped his watch during a blackout, and when he retraced his steps to try to find it, a German bomb fell on the spot where he had been standing. The second time, he was supposed to stay at the Beaver Club for Canadian servicemen but changed his mind. A bomb hit the popular locale that night.[16] His good luck held when he was sent as a commando in the March 1942 raid on the German-held dry dock at St-Nazaire, rendering it useless to repair the battleship *Tirpitz*.[17] Although there were many casualties—169 killed and over 200 taken prisoner—Bleeman returned safely.

The Essex Scottish Regiment's objective, meanwhile, was to get into the inner harbour and capture the dozens of German military barges and also the hotels housing the Germans' offices. Historian David O'Keefe believes the Dieppe Raid was staged as a cover for a secret intelligence pinch, in which the real objective was to steal a new model of the German Enigma encryption machine, its spare parts, and related codebooks, which the Allies thought were stored in Dieppe. The Germans used Enigmas to transmit orders to their submarines, selecting targets among vital Allied merchant ships crossing the Atlantic. According to O'Keefe, only the most senior people knew about the secret agenda. One of them was Commander Ian Fleming, the British author of the James

Bond novels, who was working for British Naval Intelligence at the time. Two Jewish men from Windsor were with the Essex Scottish: Sam Berger, who worked in the intelligence wing of his regimental headquarters in England and later took commando training, and Joseph Brenner.[18] It is unlikely that either of them knew about the Enigma pinch.

Major Bert Sucharov was second-in-command of the 350 Canadian Army engineers taking part in the raid. Sucharov, who managed his family's creamery business in Manitoba, had been in the militia since 1934 and went active when the war broke out.[19] One description of Sucharov noted his flamboyant personality, his moustache, and his habit of wearing two pistols in holsters. He was put in charge of the beach assault team. Sucharov and his men had to get the Canadians and their equipment off the landing craft and into the town. To get the tanks up to the town required ingenuity, and Sucharov is credited with inventing a portable wooden net that crews could roll out like a thin road. It was supposed to help the tanks ford seawalls of up to twenty-eight inches in height. For anything higher, Sucharov's unit had wooden ramps, which would take thirty men approximately five minutes to assemble.

The Montreal-based battalion of the Fusiliers Mont Royal was not scheduled to participate in the initial assault. They were to remain offshore to be placed where and when the commanders needed them, mainly to provide cover for the retreat. Two Jewish servicemen from Montreal were with the FMR: Louis Goldin and Manuel Manis.

After months of training and false starts, it was only when the flotilla of over 250 vessels had cast off from southern England to silently cross the English Channel that David Hart and his men learned the action was not a drill. "That's when the commanding officer said, 'This is it. We're going into Dieppe. Go brief your men,'" he remembers. Aiming to land at the pier of Dieppe's eastern harbour, Hart and his crew were supposed to get to work relaying communications to the troops on the beaches from the generals who would be running the raid from on board the British naval vessel HMS *Calpe*.

The Canadians had been told that the Germans were not expecting such a large invasion. They were also told that Dieppe was lightly defended. They were badly advised on both counts. Despite all their preparations and the silent approach without lights, a German patrol vessel spotted the Canadian flotilla at 3 a.m. and opened fire, alerting the defenders on shore.

The raiders were ordered to proceed with the operation. Maxwell London's landing craft missed its target. "On the boat going to Dieppe... they heard the gunshots and the cannons," said Sandra London-Rakita, recounting the stories her father had told her. "They were all told, 'Keep your head down.' The guy beside him went to see what was happening and got shot, so that was his first...experience with a dead person."

Hart calls the terrain "terrible" for the infantry. "They're coming from the beach trying to land, there's a cliff thirty feet high," not to mention the German machine guns that gave enfilade fire right along the sea wall. The men were trapped. "The sea wall was supposed to be four feet; it was seven feet. That's where our intelligence was bad."

Over the next four hours, bullets and shells rained down on the exposed Royal Rifles. Morris Greenberg was in charge of a company of Royals during the assault. He was last seen trying to get a landing craft unstuck so his men could retreat. Eyewitnesses told the *Toronto Star*'s correspondent Frederick Griffin that the boat capsized and they saw Greenberg, "now badly injured," helping several wounded men hold on to the top of the hull. "The last I saw of him, he was sinking through exhaustion," Private H.E. Wright said.[20]

The Royals lost 227 men that day. Greenberg was buried in the Hautot-sur-Mer cemetery, as were Morris Lozdon and Lionel Cohen. Meyer Bubis's body was found only in November, having washed up on shore near Dunkirk.[21] A further 264 Royals were captured. That's about an 88 per cent casualty rate.[22] There was no cover on the hundred metres of open beach, and although some of the commandos did make it up to the headlands, they had no reinforcements. Their commander eventually told them to surrender.

London was already thinking about what would come next. "When he got on the beach and he knew that he was going to die or be captured, he hid his dog tags because one said 'H' for Hebrew," his daughter says. At the prison camp Stalag VIII-B, in Lamsdorf (part of German-occupied Poland), London kept his Jewish identity a secret. When a Red Cross parcel with special Jewish food arrived at the camp, he refused to accept it.

Joseph Moskowitz (Moscoe), who was wounded, was also at Lamsdorf, but he wore his Jewishness openly with a tattoo of the Star of David on his arm. Moscoe later told the *Toronto Telegram* that he flaunted his religion. "I kept my sleeves rolled up and told them I was a Jew but they wouldn't believe me."[23] When he recovered from his wounds,

Moscoe worked in the *Lazarett*, or camp hospital. He served as an interpreter for one of the English doctors, also a POW, and as an orderly.

Jack Clausner was sent to Oflag VII-B (Oflag is an abbreviation of *Offizierslager*, officers' camp) in Eichstätt, Bavaria. In both Lamsdorf and Eichstätt, beginning in October 1942, hundreds of Canadian POWs were shackled during the workday—treatment that was in retaliation for information contained in some captured Allied documents, which suggested that any German POWs should be tied up.[24]

Simon Green died of wounds while in captivity, and he was originally buried near Boulogne.[25] He was later reinterred at the Calais Canadian War Cemetery.

The raid was proceeding better for the South Saskatchewan Regiment on Green Beach, by the village of Pourville, west of Dieppe. They'd landed successfully, albeit on the wrong side of the Scie River. Some captured a radar station but didn't reach the headlands from where the Germans were aiming their fire at the men below. Maurice Waldman was taken prisoner and sent to Lamsdorf.[26] Ben Brachman, the medical officer, nearly died. He was seen "floating face down in the water, but was recovered and returned with the other casualties to England."[27] He would later receive a Mention in Dispatches for gallantry.[28] Louis Todros was injured but survived, and Abram Arbour returned safely to England.[29]

Elly Raskin, with the Calgary Tanks, believed that of the 110 men in the unit, only 20 came back. His frantic British wife wouldn't learn whether he was alive until four days after the raid. "The day after the battle she went to the train station to find me. I wasn't there. So she came back the next day. I still didn't show up," Raskin recalled. She came back again on the third day and was told he was probably dead, or a prisoner of war.[30] She received the shock of her life when Raskin came home the next day.

The RHLI landed successfully in Dieppe and on schedule. A small raiding party, including Sergeant Arthur Liss, raced through town and headed for the taller buildings such as the casino and the cinema, which they knew the German defenders would be using as vantage points. "Captain [Anthony] Hill led us," Liss would later tell interviewers. "Machine-gun fire was heavy and I even saw the tracers passing in front of us," he said, describing dashing through the cinema and then through a gun battle out to a narrow street.[31] Liss suffered shrapnel wounds but made it back to the beach and quickly set up his Bren gun to engage the Germans while his men made their escape. He was one of the last Canadians to leave, swimming out to the vessels waiting offshore to collect survivors. He was repatriated to a hospital in England.

Of the remaining five Jewish RHLI members, one was taken prisoner. William Korenblum didn't even make it off his landing craft. Under fire from the casino, his lieutenant, Fred Woodcock, issued orders. "Take the Bren!" he shouted. Korenblum fired at the cliff. Then their boat was hit. The torpedoes, which they had brought to blow holes in any concertina wire, exploded. Woodcock and Korenblum were the only two men in the boat to survive, but they were captured.[32]

The remaining four Jewish RHLI members died at Dieppe: Jack Gralick was last seen getting into a landing craft during the retreat. "He was up against small arms and mortar fire from which there was no cover," said Private L. Lardie.[33] Leizer Heifetz was also trying to climb into an assault landing craft when a German plane flew overhead and machine-gunned him. He fell back into the water and disappeared.[34]

Murray Bleeman was one of the first casualties of the operation. He was on board a landing craft carrying infantry plus three tanks and a bulldozer. "As we approached the beach, our ship was hit, artillery or whatever it fired, come through the side of the ship, punched a good-sized hole in the side and ricocheted off the tanks," Fred Englebrecht, one of Bleeman's non-Jewish comrades, wrote. "I know this well because one fella that was in my company, died—was killed then—the shrapnel took half his head off—Murray Bleeman."[35] Bleeman didn't die right away. He was brought back to England sometime around midnight with the surviving Canadians and admitted to hospital, in Smallfield. Unconscious and in severe shock, Bleeman "went steadily downhill and died 0115 hours" on August 21.[36]

It is not known how Paul Magner died.

Major Bert Sucharov and his engineers would discover to their horror that they had been given faulty intelligence about the geology of Dieppe's beaches. They were covered in chert stones, which wreaked havoc on the tank treads, and many tanks got stuck when they rolled off the landing craft. Sucharov's own landing craft was hit before he could get ashore. He suffered a shrapnel wound in the neck, behind his left ear. Later, when receiving a bravery award at Buckingham Palace, he would tell reporters,

"I was lucky. It's remarkable the amount of stuff they can throw at you without hitting."[37]

The fate of one of Sucharov's men was not so happy. Saul Shusterman of Toronto was on a landing craft carrying some of the Calgary Tanks. He was blown off, fell off, or jumped off. He doesn't remember because he suffered a concussion. Somehow he made it to the sea wall but spent the next six or seven hours pinned down under fire. He knew he was going to be captured, so buried his dog tags, which had his real name and Jewish identity. When the Germans took him into custody, Shusterman lied. "He told them his parents were Jewish and he was Protestant," said Lorne Shusterman, his son.

According to his daughter, Barbara Fitchette, Shusterman never lost his sense of humour. "When captured and asked what he did in Canada, he told the Germans he had shaken hands with the pigs when they came into Canada Packers abattoir," she wrote.[38]

Rumours were rife that Jewish prisoners would be shot or sent to death camps, so Saul didn't take chances at Lamsdorf. He told the other captured prisoners to call him Sandy Chesterman. Toward the beginning of 1945, with the Russians closing in from the east, the Germans ordered many of the prisoners on a series of forced marches back through occupied Europe. It was the height of winter, and plenty would die en route of starvation or exposure. Shusterman came down with pneumonia. When he was liberated by the Russians in May, he had lost his hearing in one ear. He was also severely malnourished.[39]

David Lloyd Hart had a unique perspective on the Dieppe Raid. The twenty-five-year-old radio operator was manning a wireless radio set on board his tank-landing craft. He was waiting to go ashore, but just as the sailors were lowering the steel ramp to let the tanks off, the Germans hit the control mechanism for the ramp's cable. Everyone on board was trapped. Hart didn't think he would make it home that day. "People were being shot at; people were being killed all over. It was an absolute catastrophe and I could see and hear the disaster, taking place all around me."[40]

Although they didn't know exactly how badly things were going for their men, the Canadian senior commanders decided to abort the mission, opting to send in the rescue boats an hour earlier than planned. Hart heard the urgent retreat message broadcast for the men on shore, but the Camerons and the South Saskatchewans didn't acknowledge receiving the generals' message. Hart begged permission to try to contact the beach himself. Headquarters wasn't too happy about it: with only one working radio channel, Hart would have to cut the line in order to transmit the message, but they allowed it. He got through to the Canadians on shore and is credited with saving the lives of about a hundred men.

His own evacuation back to England was harrowing, as the disabled landing-craft vessel had to be towed slowly across the Channel. It came under attack from the Luftwaffe. "The Navy did a grand job in all that man-made chaos," Hart would later write to his family. "Even though we were dive bombed all the way back, their gunners got all the planes that did get through the RAF umbrella, which was really marvellous."[41]

Survivors started trickling back to England shortly around noon on August 19. As the landing craft and corvettes approached shore, *Maclean's* war correspondent Lionel Shapiro, a Canadian Jew embedded with the Canadian Army and wearing an army uniform, as correspondents did, was waiting to file his story to the world. He could see the vessels disgorging the men and the casualties.

No one asked how the battle had gone. There was no need when a[n] LCI [landing craft infantry] came in under tow, its steel sides twisted and holed, its decks almost awash, its passengers lying in grotesque positions, lying dead; or when battle-shocked soldiers, their faces blackened by terror, were led faltering like whipped children into the reception tent.[42]

Of the nearly three dozen Jewish Canadians who had gone to Dieppe, just seven returned to England physically unscathed. Four were seriously injured. Eleven had been killed. Eight more experienced captivity.

The Canadians held a mass funeral at the Brookwood Military Cemetery southwest of London on Sunday, August 23, for the first forty casualties brought back from Dieppe, including Murray Bleeman. Many newspapers in Canada and the United States ran a photo of the service on their front pages. It showed senior Canadian Army officers in attendance, including General Andrew McNaughton, Lieutenant General Harry Crerar, and the front-line commander of the raid, Major General John Hamilton Roberts.[43] The army had flown in some maple leaves from Canada especially for the ceremony. These were strewn over the coffins.

Sixteen months later, Hart was back in Canada taking officers' training. During a speech at the Montreal YMHA, he tried to make sense of what had happened to him at Dieppe.[44] He told the audience he believed the raid had been a necessary step in the Allied war effort.[45] Hart's opinion would mirror the rationale being used to justify the raid by the top generals responsible for Dieppe. They said Dieppe was a test of equipment and a rehearsal for the eventual D-Day invasion to come.

And what of the secret British plan to use Dieppe as a ruse to capture the German's valuable Enigma machine, parts, and codebooks? It failed. Nothing was recovered.

6 Jews in the Air Force

"Sometimes I get scared in those planes"

Just a few months after the Dieppe disaster, Lawrence Balfour (Duke) Abelson of Ottawa arrived in England. He had been impatient to start shooting at Germans, but first he had to finish an advanced radio operators' course at the Royal Air Force National Academy at Cranwell.[1] In the meantime, the twenty-year-old son of a prominent Ottawa Jewish family was quickly adapting to air force culture.

"'Sprogg' means 'rookie,'" he explained to his parents in a letter to their home in the city's Sandy Hill neighbourhood. Abelson sent them a list of twenty-one expressions together with their Canadian meanings. That way, his parents could more easily decipher future letters. For instance, he told them, "In the Soup" meant "In a Tough Position," "Pukka Gen" meant "Real McCoy," "Kite" meant "Aircraft," and "A Piece of Cake" meant "Easy Flight."[2]

Canadian Jewish airmen participated in all the major theatres of the war, seeing combat from the Battle of Britain to the Italian campaign to D-Day and the liberation of Europe. They hunted submarines off the Canadian coast, sank enemy ships in the Far East and the Mediterranean, and took part in the controversial firebombing of German cities.

Countless Jewish Canadians also served on the ground in some of the less glamorous branches of the RCAF. Melville Neuman of Regina was stationed in Sydney, Nova Scotia, in the "radio shack," as he called it, responsible for maintaining fourteen transmitters. Oscar Adler of Montreal did General Duties at CFB Claresholm, Alberta, which included taking care of the officers' dry cleaning. Israel Yamron of Winnipeg was an aircraft technician maintaining seaplanes at the RCAF Patricia Bay base on Vancouver Island.

Eli Ross of Winnipeg didn't fix planes or carry bombs, but his service helped raise the morale of Canada's fighting forces overseas and changed the course of long-distance aviation. Pilot Officer Ross flew the first 189 bags of Christmas mail from the home front to Scotland for the men and women in uniform, helping to inaugurate transatlantic airmail service.[3] Ross was one of the nearly six thousand Canadian Jewish men who volunteered for the Royal Canadian Air Force during the war. Jews represented 2.61 per cent of the total personnel in the RCAF, a percentage that was significantly higher than the Canadian Jewish presence in either the army or the navy.[4] Considering that service in the air force was strictly voluntary, and also very dangerous, especially for aircrew—94 per cent of the RCAF casualties—it is important to consider why so many Jewish Canadians signed up, especially when, as was true in Abelson's case, they usually had little to no previous flying experience.[5]

Perhaps some were influenced to follow in the footsteps of their aviation heroes. Moses Rabovsky of Owen Sound, Ontario, admired the World War I ace Billy Bishop, born in his hometown in 1894. Others like Nathan Isaacs felt the air force offered an easier life than being a foot soldier, provided that one could survive the dangers of raids over German territory. "I had a nice room, I had a batman who made my bed, started up my fire in the morning, did all that for me. It was great," he said. "We had an officer's mess where the meals were a little better than regular."

Toronto's Beryl (Bunny) Bergstein wanted to avoid the damp and muddy slit trenches at the front. "I thought air force life might be a little better than army life." Although he was tempted to become part of an aircrew, Bergstein, then only nineteen, asked for non-flying duties on compassionate grounds. "I didn't want to get killed and my mother be left without me, after losing my father."

Norman Cohen said everyone wanted to be in the RCAF, not just the Jewish boys. "It gave us a clean life. It looked like it was a clean life. [I] met some of the soldiers who were already under training, and there was a bit of romanticism in there," he said.

In 1941, Charles Power, the minister of national defence for air, described successful candidates for the RCAF as "the very cream of the youth of Canada...the future leaders of this country."[6] The air force required each candidate to submit at least three character references from employers, teachers, and community leaders, as well as proof of their high school or post-secondary achievements. It gave the air force an allure as home to the best, which is partly what motivated George Nashen to put his university studies on hold, interrupt his apprenticeship at a Montreal accounting firm, and enlist. When Nashen turned eighteen in 1941, he began to worry that he would be called up for compulsory army duty. To forestall that fate, he followed his best friend, Jay Singer, into the air force, which he expected would place him with a higher class of people. "Don't go into the army with riff-raff, [or] others, you don't know who," was Nashen's reasoning. "Pick where you want to go. And for the most part the Jewish boys joined the air force being, what, the elite part of the services."

Other volunteers thought the air force might be safer than being sent to the front with the infantry. Bill Novick was planning to attend McGill University after high school but couldn't afford the tuition. He knew that he would be conscripted into the army shortly, so he didn't wait for his call-up. "I enlisted, figuring that it would be better for me to choose what I could do if I had to go into the war...rather than be told what to do, which probably saved my life," Novick said.[7]

Some Jewish Canadians joined the air force because they loved flying, like Tommy Marshall of Glace Bay, who was an experienced pilot when he joined up. Gordon Steinberg of Toronto had spent all his spare time hanging around a city airfield, even though his parents wouldn't permit him to take lessons. Eddie Saslove couldn't afford flying lessons, so he contented himself with building model airplanes. "I remember as a kid, in our room there was a big string across the room with airplanes hanging," said his younger brother, Martin. Eddie couldn't wait to join the RCAF. For the Ottawa man, it was an opportunity to see the world or, as he used to say to his brother, "to let the world see me."

Although Norman Kendall of Toronto had done only three hours of flying in his life, strictly as a passenger, before applying to join the air force, he had his heart set on joining the RCAF. The son of a cabinetmaker from Poland, he, too, had built model airplanes during high school. He was already working at the De Havilland factory in Toronto, which was churning out warplanes, including the Tiger Moth, the Mosquito, and the Avro Anson, but Kendall wanted to fly planes, not fix them. When his call-up notice came for mandatory army service, he did his training in North Bay, Ontario, in the summer of 1941. Then he got married, took a two-week honeymoon, and immediately went to North Bay's RCAF recruiting centre, where he passed the interview. "Alert, keen individual, anxious to fly, should make excellent aircrew material. Fit, heavy handed type but otherwise good pilot material."[8]

It probably helped when Kendall told them his favourite subject in high school had been physics. Airmen needed to have completed Grade 11 at the minimum to meet the RCAF's high entrance standards. Airmen who were educated enough for the specialized aircrew jobs began training as pilots, observers, and engineers—jobs that all required excellent skills in math and sciences.

The air force would take plenty of Jews with impressive post-secondary education credentials. Sydney Shulemson applied while at McGill University, after having graduated from Montreal's Baron Byng High School with an over 85 per cent average.[9] He hoped to become an aeronautical engineer. Monty Berger had an honours degree in economics and political science from McGill, and a master's degree from Columbia University.[10] Edmond Fleishman of Vancouver took a master airplane mechanics course in Glendale, California, and then spent two years studying commerce at the University of British Columbia.[11] Lou Somers was not only a top varsity football player at the University of Toronto but also graduated with an honours degree in commerce and finance and won two undergraduate academic trophies.[12]

Top marks weren't always enough to guarantee acceptance, however. The RCAF also had tough medical standards. Doctors weeded out nearly one in every four applications for aircrew, mainly because of problems such as poor eyesight and colour-blindness.[13] One in six applicants for ground crew was rejected for similar reasons. Disorders such as stomach problems and hernias also disqualified many. After his medical, George Nashen learned, to his surprise, that he was colour-blind. He would serve in the accounting branch at RCAF Headquarters in London rather than as aircrew.

A similar thing happened when Leo Guttman, a clothing salesman in Montreal, took his RCAF medical in 1941. "I tried to get into the aircrew, but my eyes were not up to par," he said. The only flying he did during the war was unofficial, when one of his pilot friends took him up. Guttman was instead trained as an airplane mechanic and posted to a British Commonwealth Air Training Plan (BCATP) base in North Battleford, Saskatchewan, to maintain Harvards and Ansons. The Canadian government had created the BCATP program in 1939; it was a national system of training schools and airfields to meet the growing Allied demand for pilots, air observers, wireless operators, and air gunners. Over 130,000 airmen would graduate by the time the war was over, with candidates coming from Canada, Britain, Australia, and New Zealand. Most of the flight engineers, however, were trained in Britain.[14]

There were also some systemic regulations that directly barred entry to the air force.[15] From 1938 until these prohibitions were formally lifted in 1942, RCAF policy required its officers to be white, of pure European descent, and British subjects. Admittedly, it is easy to understand why RCAF recruiters in wartime would be wary of accepting recent immigrants, especially from Eastern Europe. Officials had to be sure they weren't taking on spies or other objectors to the war. But some historians and veterans think the restrictions on visible minorities and foreigners were inherited from long-standing colonial prejudices in England's class-conscious Royal Air Force.[16]

Norman Cohen remembers exactly where he was on Sunday, December 7, 1941—the day Japan attacked Pearl Harbor. He was in Toronto, playing cards with friends. The next day, the eighteen-year-old and his pals went to the RCAF recruiting centre. "Now my friend...big guy, black fella. They wouldn't let him in the air force. They don't take black people," Cohen said.

It is understandable why so many might have been keen to get into the air force. In 1941, it seemed that it was the only service having any success against a seemingly unstoppable enemy. In his memoir, the journalist turned navigator Ray Silver described himself and men like him as the last of the gladiators. "We were the warriors available in those desperate years between Dunkirk and Normandy," Silver writes. "While Europe lay captive and the Nazi forces raged across the Eastern frontiers killing Slavs and Jews and other *untermenchen*—soldiers and civilians alike—we were the only striking force on the Western Front."[17]

Frank Fainer certainly felt that way, having served as an air gunner with the Royal Air Force providing cover for one of most dramatic events of the early war. With the German invasion of France well under way in late May 1940, the son of a baker in Saint John, New Brunswick, helped hold off the enemy while the British Navy scrambled to ferry some three hundred thousand stranded Allied troops from Dunkirk back to England. Soon afterwards, Fainer wrote that he wanted vengeance for losing friends, casualties of the air war known as the Battle of Britain. "We'll lick hell out of him," the cocky twenty-one-year-old wrote from

England, referring to Hitler's plan to invade the country. "There are too many good fighters here. There are a number of Canadians in the Air Force and one Canadian is equivalent to six Jerries in a fight."[18]

Those Jewish men who made it as pilots shared some of Fainer's cockiness. It was a potent ingredient in the character of men such as Squadron Leader Philip Foster. He was the son of Kadish Fenster, a farmer from Edenbridge, Saskatchewan, but he'd changed his Jewish-sounding last name while at university in Regina so he could more easily join a plumbers' union. Foster earned the moniker "the Flying Plumber of Flin Flon" because he would travel by air to provide service to customers in northern Manitoba, where he had opened a business.[19] Foster was famous around Flin Flon for always wearing a white hat, and for romancing a local schoolteacher.

He originally enlisted with the RCAF but was impatient to get overseas. He wound up his financial affairs, took private flying lessons in Winnipeg and Trenton, then headed to England looking for an audition with the RAF.[20] "He made a friend, also staying at the Regent Palace Hotel, who just happened to be from the Air Ministry," his sister Freeda Baron said, describing her brother's careful approach. "Phil said little, drank little, and kept refilling the other fellow's glass until he finally extracted a promise that the RAF would give him a tryout to discover if he really could fly."[21] They did, and he was in. Before leaving Canada, Foster stopped in at the family farm in Edenbridge to say goodbye. His sister remembers crying as she prepared a hearty breakfast for him, but he seemed fearless. "Don't worry," he told her. "I will bring you Hitler's moustache."

In his early days at flying school, Clifford Shnier's overconfident personality didn't impress his instructors. They once described the former electronics salesman as a "problem child." Indeed, his attitude earned him a reprimand while he was in England for flying underneath a bridge just to show off. Later, however, that same confidence would impress the RAF enough to put Shnier, then an experienced pilot and the only Jew in his crew, in the elite RAF Pathfinder bomber squadron, No. 97. The Pathfinders went in first during bombing raids over German territory, marking the targets with coloured flares for those who followed.

Although Foster and Shnier were successful in their quests to become pilots, approximately three of every four candidates in the RCAF failed to secure that much-sought position. Historian Peter J. Usher has suggested that an additional reason accounts for why so many Jewish airmen became observers or navigators instead of pilots. Usher's examination of Canadian Jews in the air force found that the top brass at the RCAF and the RAF believed pilots should be selected from only Anglo backgrounds. It came from the widely held view that men of this ethnicity had the right character to be leaders in a stressful cockpit setting. Another theory had it that lower-ranked crewmen wouldn't follow orders from officers of diverse ethnic backgrounds. "The preponderance of Jews selected for training as air observers, in comparison to the general population, seems too striking to be mere coincidence," writes Usher.[22]

Nathan Isaacs originally wanted to be a pilot. At the recruiting office in Toronto, when he said he was good at math, Isaacs was told, "Okay, young man, you are going to be a navigator." It's a refrain many others would hear. "Most Jewish boys were navigators because they were smart," Isaacs said. (After June 1942, the RCAF discontinued the designation of air observer and created two classifications: navigator and bomb aimer. The former calculated the route, while the latter handled the payload.[23]) In his case, Isaacs thinks the air force made the right decision. Being a pilot required good mechanical skills, and his early rocky landings at flight school didn't impress the instructors. "I'd get to thirty feet and plop." He was sent to No. 4 Air Observer School, near London, Ontario, eventually serving with the RCAF's No. 427 Squadron on a remarkable thirty-five bombing missions.

Dave Waterman of Calgary was also redirected to train as a navigator and, after receiving his wings, was sent to England. He liked to tell the story of the time he was being courted to join a bomber crew. Pilots often chose crews in a way similar to that of Canadian kids' sizing up potential players for road hockey teams. "My pilot thought because I was Jewish, I was smart. So he chose me," Waterman said. On one of the crew's first flights, Waterman mistakenly directed the pilot to fly over a restricted British Navy base. Immediately the friendly guns in Plymouth Harbour opened fire at the shocked air force sprogs. "The pilot wouldn't talk to me for months," Waterman said.[24]

A class photo taken in 1942 at the No. 7 Air Observer School in Portage la Prairie, Manitoba, shows twenty-four smiling student navigators-in-training posing in front of a hangar. At least three of the airmen were Jewish: Reuben Bricker of Lavoy, Alberta, and Charles Green and David Dworkin, both of Calgary.[25] Dworkin had wanted to be a pilot but, like Isaacs, was advised to go the navigator's route. In his case, it was because of his size. "I was small. They questioned my ability to reach the pedals and do other things that required height."[26]

It must have been quite a blow to Lawrence Abelson's self-esteem to be remustered out of pilot training and into observer school. But the air force didn't like his attitude or work ethic. They did like his book smarts, which soon rocketed the young observer to the top of his classes. At the No. 3 Air Observer School in Regina, Abelson finished ahead of all the other candidates, with an 88 per cent score.[27] He sent a report home about it, signing one of his letters "Duke the Great." Doing so well on his tests would keep Abelson in Canada for a further fifteen months. The RCAF liked to hold on to its top graduates, putting them to work as instructors. That likely suited Abelson's nervous parents just fine, as it would keep him away from combat.

But being on this side of the Atlantic had risks for rookie airmen. In fact, during the early years of the war, Canada was considered "the most dangerous place a pilot could be."[28] About 460 Canadians were killed in flying accidents while progressing through the BCATP system of schools, including twenty Jews.[29] The Department of National Defence blamed most of the accidents on student "escapades" such as unauthorized low flying and performing aerobatics. Changes to the curriculum in 1942 were supposed to reduce fatalities.[30] But they didn't help Norman Kendall, who was training at the No. 14 Secondary Flying Training School, in Aylmer, Ontario. Kendall was learning to fly single-engine Harvard trainers. After six weeks, Kendall's reviews remained mixed. "Very forgetful of small details but flying is improving satisfactorily."

On a hazy Friday afternoon in June 1942, Kendall and his co-pilot took off and headed east to practice instrument flying. When they were just outside Tillsonburg, a mere twenty minutes away by car, something went wrong. Their plane crashed into a barn, killing both airmen. Kendall was twenty-three. Both students left behind young widows. The official inquiry blamed the trainees. "Primary—disobedience of flying orders in performing aerobatics while on mutual instrument flight. Secondary—structural failure of the aircraft while pulling out of a steep power dive at excessive speed."[31]

Many graduates of the BCATP schools eventually got to England, where they were given more training before going operational. Another nineteen Canadian Jewish airmen met their deaths in training accidents there.[32] Flying small aircraft above prairie wheat fields in Canada was a "piece of cake" compared with what the aircrews faced in England. Many of the squadrons were located on bases near the mountainous areas and fells of Yorkshire and the Lake District, and the weather was often foggy and rainy.

In September 1942, Jack Brovender and his crew were killed on a cross-country night training exercise in their Wellington bomber. It crashed into a mountainside called Johnny Wood near Keswick, south of the Scottish border. Brovender, "one of the most popular Jewish youths of Timmins [Ontario]" had been studying business in Montreal.[33]

A test flight also killed Lawrence Abelson, after his extended term as an instructor was finished and he had shipped overseas to England. After a couple of weeks of training on fighter planes as a navigator, his pilot was killed during a solo flight. Abelson received two weeks off, to get over the shock, then was put back to work.[34] He and his new pilot, Al Horn, went for a test flight. Their Mosquito crashed into the rolling, hilly countryside thirty kilometres southwest of the base, at Bearn Bridge, in Shropshire.[35] Both men died. The subsequent inquiry blamed the pilot. Officials also suggested it might have been because he was working with a new navigator. The inquiry recommended giving all Canadian Mosquito crews a refresher in night dual flying. Abelson had written this note to his parents shortly before his death. "Be assured Mom that I, too, share your hopes for me. As regards returning soon, not before I have done my share."[36]

Michael Stein Jacobs was killed on a training flight near Stratford-upon-Avon on February 13, 1943.[37] Mechanical issues with the Wellington bomber caused the crash. Jacobs had been on board as a navigation instructor, training a plane full of rookies. That position was meant as a reward for surviving seven months of attacking targets in Germany with the RCAF's famous No. 419 Moose Squadron. He had even flown in the famous thousand-bomber raid on Cologne in May 1942, in which the Allies hit German cities with massive quantities of incendiary bombs that destroyed tens of thousands of homes and businesses, killed hundreds, and terrorized the civilians. During his "tour," Jacobs once wrote to his wife, Sue, an admission that she never expected to hear. "'God, sometimes I get scared in those planes,'" his letter said. "This was very strong, heavy-duty stuff, not just being scared of, well, spiders, as I am," she said.

For a bomber crew, a tour could be as many as thirty or more raids over enemy territory. In 1943 and 1944, only one of every four crews survived that long.[38] It was no wonder that fear was a constant companion. The Canadian and British crews often flew at night and had to evade the Luftwaffe. Powerful enemy anti-aircraft guns shot at them from below across northwestern Europe. Added to all that, there were often mechanical problems and bad weather. Nearly eighteen thousand airmen lost their lives with the RCAF during World War II, including about 250 Jewish Canadians, a figure that accounts for more than half of the 450 Canadian Jews who died during the war.[39]

Eddie Saslove usually didn't tell his family the specifics of what he was doing when he was flying bombing missions in his Lancaster. He kept his letters light and pretended he wasn't busy. But after one too many close calls, his family received a hint that Eddie was afraid. Brother Martin Saslove remembers what Eddie had written. "He said to my mother, 'Remember I once told you that I would travel the world so I was ready to crawl home? I'm ready to crawl home now, but I got to have somewhere to crawl to.'"

To cope with stress, Canadian Jewish airmen reported doing things that provided more immediate relief, including everything from urinating on the wheels of their aircraft for good luck to carrying talismans and even writing jokes on the bombs. On May 16, 1943, Hamilton's Abe Garshowitz chalked the caption "Never has so much been expected of so few" on the special bouncing nine-thousand-pound bomb that his Lancaster crew was planning to drop on a German hydroelectric power dam later that night.[40] Garshowitz was trying to get his crewmates to relax, and it's no wonder they were nervous: they had been handpicked to carry out a daring, top-secret mission across the English Channel that, if it worked, would make them all famous as the Dambusters. The squadron's nineteen bombers flew stealthily into Germany at just eighteen metres above the ground, then turned on their lights and headed straight into the gunsights protecting three important Ruhr valley dams. They blew up two, but at great cost. Fifty-three of the 113 crewmen were lost, including Garshowitz, the only Canadian Jew in the Dambusters operation. The twenty-two-year-old wireless operator's plane hit some powerlines and crashed—and his autographed bomb exploded, killing all seven airmen on board.

Meyer Greenstein of Toronto was a University of Toronto English major and working as a journalist at the Canadian Press when he enlisted. Before he went overseas in May 1944, his best friend, a Catholic, presented him with a St. Christopher medal, the patron saint of travellers.[41] Although Greenstein's parents didn't object to the gift, they were concerned that it shouldn't find its way on board any of his airplanes once he was operational over Europe. "Because if anything happened to him, they didn't want people to think he was a Catholic," said his nephew Hersh Gross, who couldn't be sure his uncle kept that promise.

Some airmen were superstitious and liked to fly the same model and serial number aircraft. Arthur Hiller, the future director of the 1970 Hollywood film *Love Story*, served as a navigator for one such crew. The Edmonton native flew seventeen missions in the exact same Halifax bomber, which they'd nicknamed Li'l Abner. The plane's luck ran out but Hiller's didn't. One day, another crew flying Li'l Abner had a tire blow out on takeoff. "The wing then hit the ground, half the bomb load exploded, and everybody on board except the rear gunner was killed," Hiller told a reporter after the war.[42]

For some time afterwards, Hiller had nightmares, waking up in a cold sweat. He coped by keeping busy during subsequent bombing operations. "I was always crawling on the floor, picking up my pencils and compass and all the things that fell off my table during these manoeuvres," Hiller said.

Many men suffered from emotional or mental strain. After forty-three operational trips and over 530 hours of flying, Samuel Cohen had to be shipped home to Canada for counselling. The former Montreal lawyer had been serving as a navigator in England, Scotland, and North Africa until nervous anxiety and debilitating stomach cramps rendered him unfit to fly. It took a full year, until after D-Day, before Cohen was considered recovered enough to go back into combat.

The RAF set up hospitals across England to handle stressed-out airmen suffering from what today is post-traumatic stress disorder (PTSD). Being sent for treatment was humiliating for the men because their superiors put down the official reason as LMF, for lack of moral fibre.

The special white scarf from his mother that Norman Isaacs wore on every mission didn't make him feel safe on the day when a flare fell out of his Halifax aircraft during takeoff, then exploded. His crew wanted to abort the mission. "We said, 'That's a bad omen, we don't want to go.'"

When the commanding officer drove out to meet the rattled men, he told them to get back in their plane, and threatened to charge them all with LMF. "So we got back into the plane and went."

Norman Cohen completed fourteen missions over Europe as a navigator and admits that he vomited before each one. After a while, many airmen accepted the idea that fate and luck would play a key role in their survival. But sometimes, concrete action had to be taken to improve the odds. Cohen asked his commanding officer to send him somewhere a little warmer than northern Europe. "I wanted a hot climate," he said, explaining that he was hoping for Jamaica, where he could have fun. In a case of "be careful what you wish for," the air force posted Cohen to the RCAF's No. 436 Dakota transport squadron, in Burma. There, instead of Germans, he had to combat the Japanese and monsoons, as well as tropical diseases, scorpions, and pythons.

Cohen avoided his worst nightmare of going to a German prison camp, but dozens of Canadian Jewish airmen would suffer that fate after being shot down and captured. Forty-nine out of eighty-five Canadian Jewish POWs were airmen.[43]

Joseph Sonshine, from Toronto, kept his religion a secret after he was captured in June 1944 and shipped to Buchenwald. The Germans had thought he was a spy.[44] At least fifty-six thousand prisoners were murdered there, including eleven thousand Jews.[45] Sonshine was sure he wouldn't survive the forced marches and transfers to other camps.[46] Only after enduring all that did he break his silence. "Although he knew the consequences could be dire, Joe had told a guard that he was a Jew, because he wanted a Jewish burial," Ruth Pike, whose daughter married Sonshine's son, told the *Globe and Mail* in a 2006 tribute. "Despite everything, emaciated and ill, Joe outlived the war."[47]

Other POWs owed their lives to righteous non-Jews who helped them survive or escape. At the Stalag Luft VI camp at Heydekrug (now Silute, Lithuania), nearly two hundred Jewish Commonwealth POWs, including Simon (Sam) Shapiro, a native of St. Catharines, Ontario, were told one day to be packed and ready to leave the next morning for an unknown destination. They thought they were being sent to a death camp. A non-Jewish POW, a British RAF sergeant, James (Dixie) Deans, intervened on their behalf with the commandant.[48]

Flying Officer Manuel Rabinovitch (later known as Manny Raber) of

Medicine Hat, Alberta, credits the Hoebke family in Ciney, Belgium, for rescuing, feeding and clothing him after he was shot down over Belgium on November 26, 1943. Raber was just twenty and serving as the mid-upper gunner on a Halifax bomber on a mission to Frankfurt. The Hoebkes agreed to help Raber try to make his way back to England and called on their Catholic priest for assistance. But before the clergyman decided whether to get involved, he wanted to see the Canadian's wounded left arm, which had been hit by shrapnel in the dogfight. Raber's command of French was poor and he panicked. "I hesitated as I thought he was asking to see my circumcision!" Raber writes in his memoir, *Manny Goes to War*.[49]

The religion question came next, and Raber answered honestly, pointing to the word "juif" in the priest's English-French dictionary. "He was genuinely astonished," Raber writes. "I'm quite sure that like most Europeans he had been told all this life that Jews were craven cowards, cheats, Christ killers and international bankers who controlled all the money in the world for their own nefarious purposes." The clergyman took Raber into his home, arranged for medical care, and then invited some other religious men to meet him, including one who spoke English. "Does that create some sort of a problem?" Raber asked them. "If Jesus came to you for help in a similar situation, would you hesitate to help him?"

The Alberta airman's rescuer gave Raber some clothes and false papers then personally accompanied him by train to the next Resistance cell. As a parting gift, the priest gave Raber a black rosary. "He said that he knew I was not a believer but he would like me to carry it with me, just for 'Bon Chance' [*sic*] good luck," Raber writes. "I thanked him, we shook hands again, and he even embraced me, much to my embarrassment."

The rosary came in handy when Raber, later hiding in a factory in Brussels, was arrested and taken to the local Gestapo headquarters, on February 1, 1944. Thanks to the rosary, the Germans decided that he was a Catholic. They also thought he was a spy because he wore civilian clothes. After his interrogation Raber was jailed at Brussels' notorious St-Gilles military prison, through which some thirty thousand people, including Jews, members of the Belgian Resistance, and captured Allied airmen, would pass on their way to POW or concentration camps or to execution. He was kept there for two months, mainly in solitary confinement.

While in prison, Raber again relied on the goodwill of a clergyman, this time the prison's Catholic chaplain, to deliver a letter for him. He wrote to a senior German general, whose name he had read in the local newspapers, decrying the injustice of keeping him, a downed Canadian air force officer, as a spy, which he said was a violation of the Geneva Conventions. It worked. Raber spent the remainder of the war as POW #3614, mostly at Stalag Luft III in the town of Sagan, 160 kilometres southeast of Berlin. Arriving in March 1944, Raber found the camp in mourning. Just two days earlier, nearly eighty prisoners had carried out what has become arguably the most famous breakout from a prison camp in World War II, known as the Great Escape. The episode would inspire bestselling books and the classic 1963 Hollywood movie starring Steve McQueen. The Germans had caught most of the escapees and shot fifty of them.

Calgary's David (Pappy) Rosenthal, who had been a navigator in a Halifax bomber with No. 158 Squadron and had been shot down over Holland a couple of months earlier, played a small part in the preparations for the escape.[50] He acted as a lookout for the tunnel diggers, including Simon Shapiro, the downed pilot from St. Catharines, who was not chosen to go when the time came.

Very few Canadian Jewish airmen managed to escape once they were POWs. Percy (Pinky) Gaum got free, once. The Sydney, Nova Scotia, air gunner had been shot down over Denmark in 1942 while laying mines. On a forced march out of the Fallingbostel camp in northwestern Germany, he ran away but his escape was short-lived. After six days on the run, he blundered into a house full of German soldiers.[51]

However, at least one downed Canadian Jewish airman, David Goldberg, succeeded in returning safely to England. Abandoning his Spitfire near Lille, France, in March 1944, the Hamilton pilot tossed away the identity discs that would have revealed his religion. By "some fluke," as Goldberg later told the *Hamilton Jewish News,* he managed to make contact with the French Resistance, who hid him for weeks in German-occupied Paris. "No matter where you went, you'd go to the movies and they would have a lot of propaganda about people who were Jewish, and of course it was a great fear," Goldberg said.[52]

He set out on a trek across the Pyrenees through to Spain, which was neutral, and when he arrived in Barcelona, Goldberg contacted the British consul, who helped him return to England.

Although bomber pilots and crews probably come first to mind when the air war is mentioned, many flew in other divisions and suffered as dramatically as their more high-profile colleagues. Some of them flew in Ferry Command (later known as Transport Command), which carried mail, men, and equipment into battle zones but received barely any attention.

Bill Zelikovitz's hair turned white after a year of flying in Ferry Command. The Ottawa wireless operator delivered all kinds of new North American–built military aircraft overseas, including Baltimores, Bostons, Liberators, Douglas DC-3 Dakotas, Flying Fortresses, and Marauders. The new airplanes were fresh off the assembly lines and needed in battle but not refitted for the long transatlantic air journey east. That made for uncomfortable trips for Zelikovitz.

"Most of these aircraft had not had auxiliary gas tanks [installed], which gave us a maximum of 15 to 20 minutes of spare gas to cross the ocean and land at our destination," he wrote in a letter home. "I can tell you a few good stories about some trips across the north [Atlantic], 68 below zero, with oxygen masks, at 32,000 feet retching [into our] Balaclava masks [and] electrically heated boots."[53]

Although Ferry Command flights from North America via the southern Atlantic across to Africa and then to points northeast seemed a piece of cake by comparison, the southern skies were full of dangers. One trip in February 1943 nearly meant curtains for Zelikovitz. A regular stop on Ascension Island, some sixteen hundred kilometres off the west coast of Africa, was home to a flock of notoriously aggressive birds called wideawakes (also known as sooty terns), which launched themselves en masse against planes coming in to land.[54] "We had to land before dark as they had wideawake birds that are attracted to light," Zelikovitz wrote. "They are very large and I saw one hit an aircraft on takeoff, which was the end of them [an American combat crew], poor chaps."

After a year of this, Zelikovitz was posted to an RAF Transport Command squadron in England just as the Allies were preparing for the invasion of Normandy. At RAF Broadwell in Oxfordshire, his four-man Dakota crew would learn to carry paratroopers over drop zones and to tow Horsa gliders full of equipment and men.

On the eve of D-Day, June 5, Zelikovitz was airborne before midnight. He was the radio operator and was also in charge of making sure that the heavily armed British and Canadian paratroopers got out the door and dropped safely into German-occupied Normandy. The parachutists were to capture strategic targets and pave the way for the sunrise D-Day infantry landings. "I knew every blade of grass, every fence, every mud path, every tree, every barn house, every shed. The moon was out and we did our job properly and correctly despite the German opposition and defences," he recalled. When the Dakota returned to base, Zelikovitz received a terrible shock. He was informed that all the paratroopers who'd jumped from his plane had been "wiped out." "I ran to the washroom and retched and retched."

For the rest of the summer, Zelikovitz shuttled between England and the new forward bases in liberated France carrying mail, supplies, and the wounded. Then in September 1944, another handwritten entry in Zelikovitz's flight logbook placed him in the forefront, literally, of the storied but controversial Operation Market Garden. This was the failed attempt by British Field Marshal Bernard Montgomery to end the war early, dramatized in the 1977 movie *A Bridge Too Far*. The plan was to drop thousands of Allied airborne troops into Holland to capture strategic bridges over the Rhine. According to Zelikovitz's logbook, "September 17, 1944: First Drop Glider at Arnhem. Co-pilot of Glider killed 15 minutes before Arnhem."[55]

The Americans succeeded in capturing some of the bridges, but the Germans soon surrounded the outnumbered British paratroopers. The German siege lasted for more than a week. Zelikovitz flew into Arnhem—"that hellhole"—every day through deadly anti-aircraft fire, dropping supplies. "One day we lost half our squadron in five minutes," he noted. "About 50 Messerschmitt and Focke-Wulf sprang up. We were unarmed and no fighters turned up to protect us. Talk about lucky to get out of it."[56]

Being lucky was frequently the explanation given by the airmen who made it through a complete tour. Some earned Distinguished Flying Crosses (DFCs) for doing so. Bill Novick won his DFC for completing thirty-five sorties with the RCAF No. 433 Squadron.[57] Novick continuously drilled his crew in safety procedures because he wanted them to survive. "Because of his insistence on practice, instead of going to a pub when [they] stood down, his crew hated him," according to Novick's colleague David Sinclair, a Montreal physician. "But on landing after their last flight, they lined up to individually express their gratitude for getting all of them home safely."[58]

Other airmen won their DFCs for saving their crews when their aircraft was shot up or suffered mechanical problems. Harry Knobovitch completed twenty-five missions as a pilot with the RCAF No. 415 Swordfish Squadron. He was involved in several close calls, including a landing accident after a raid to Holland aboard a Halifax bomber nicknamed "Eddie's Nightmare."[59] Knobovitch won his DFC after a mission to Duisburg, in northwest Germany, when one engine failed and then a fire broke out. He calmly had the men put out the flames, and then cleared the smoke by turning on the heater.[60]

Nathan Isaacs survived thirty-five operational missions. Isaacs considered it "a miracle" that his crew made it through alive, despite being shot up more than once and losing engines from time to time. Although a DFC would have been nice, for Isaacs living was reward enough.

During the battle for Arnhem, Bill Zelikovitz's commanding officer, RAF Wing Commander T.A. Jefferson, promised to nominate him for a DFC. He never put the paperwork through, and Zelikovitz accepted a transfer to a Canadian transport squadron. He continued to fly into European battle hotspots until the end of the war, completing his tour on July 11, 1945, having logged 1,566 hours in the air. Zelikovitz's family still marvels at the role he played in so many pivotal moments in history. "We used to tell him that he won the war," Judi Zelikovitz, his daughter-in-law, said.

7 The Navy and Merchant Navy

"If you hit the water you had six or seven minutes to live"

Petty Officer Irv (Kappy) Kaplan wasn't the type of person who would be comfortable serving as a role model for anyone. The sailor had declined the chance to take officers' training because he thought his modest family background—the twenty-three-year-old Montrealer's father was a tailor—wouldn't measure up in a naval wardroom. Even in his private life, Kaplan wouldn't accept invitations to deliver the priestly blessing in synagogue, although he was permitted to do so as a descendant of the Cohen tribe. But on May 6, 1944, the unassuming signals officer serving aboard HMCS *Valleyfield* was flung into the national spotlight.

Kaplan had just finished taking a late-night shower and lain down for a short nap in the Petty Officers' mess, due to go on watch at dawn.[1] *Valleyfield* was heading into St. John's, Newfoundland, after a ten-day journey escorting a convoy across the Atlantic from Londonderry, Northern Ireland, and the men were looking forward to some shore leave.

"He chose the navy because he figured, 'If I come back, I'll come back in one piece,'" said his daughter Joyce Kaplan. Her father thought army or air force men were more likely to suffer permanent disfiguring wounds if they survived.

Before his nap, Kaplan had put on all his clothes, including the wool-lined waterproof double-zippered survival suit nicknamed the zoot suit. A life jacket went under his head as a pillow. Twenty minutes later, with the frigate just fifty nautical miles south of Cape Race, a German submarine took aim and fired a torpedo. It split *Valleyfield* in two. The ship sank within minutes, but not before Kaplan managed to get out from below deck and jump into the freezing ocean. He swam to one of his ship's emergency Carley life rafts, towing another sailor who was holding on to Kaplan's leg for dear life. The other Canadian warships in the convoy didn't notice anything was amiss, although Kaplan later said he remained confident that someone would come back to their rescue.[2] An hour later HMCS *Giffard* returned to pick up the survivors, as well as five bodies.[3]

In relatively good shape because of his survival suit and life jacket, Kaplan remained in the water to help the other men clamber up nets lowered from the side of *Giffard*. He nearly didn't join them. At one point, he became tangled in one of the life raft's cables and had to cut himself free with a knife. Safely on board *Giffard*, he started counting.[4] "They asked me to identify the bodies. That was tough," Kaplan told the Montreal *Gazette*.[5] Only thirty-eight men survived out of a crew of 164.[6] He won a Mention in Dispatches for "brave rescue work" that night.[7]

After recovering from the ordeal, Kaplan could have taken a posting to Bermuda, which was the usual routine for survivors of torpedoed ships. Instead, he wanted payback for what had happened to him. Being in action in Europe was better therapy, as he told his best friend, Corporal Abe Goldbloom. "I am sort of looking forward to it, because I figure lightning won't strike twice in the same place (I hope) and besides I really have something to hit back with this time," he wrote. "A destroyer isn't as comfortable as other types of ships but at least one can have confidence in their fighting ability."[8]

Kaplan would win another Mention in Dispatches when his new ship, HMCS *Assiniboine*, destroyed three armed German trawlers near Brest, France, in August 1944. "We returned to base by the light of dawn, tired but happy. I was especially pleased to have been a part of striking a visible blow against Nazi Germany," Kaplan wrote in his memoir.[9]

Fewer than six hundred Jews served in the Royal Canadian Navy in World War II, a miniscule 0.53 per cent of the nearly ninety-seven thousand men in that service.[10] The navy attracted only 3.5 per cent of the total overall Jewish enlistment in the war.[11] One reason for this figure was that, at the outset of the war, the Royal Canadian Navy was tiny, with just six fighting ships and thirty-five hundred men.[12] Most of their officers were professional British-trained sailors, who wore the same uniforms as the Royal Navy and had the same rank system.

Then, in the winter of 1940, the Canadian government embarked on a massive shipbuilding program and opened up the navy to civilian volunteers, most with no sailing experience. As was the case in the Royal Canadian Air Force, British traditions and class prejudices also kept some Canadian Jews out of the Navy. Historian Jack Granatstein says prevailing attitudes against racially diverse recruits discouraged "all but the most ardent sailors" amongst Jewish Canadian men.[13] A 1946 honour roll of Calgary's Jewish servicemen contains just thirteen names from the navy; the rest of the nearly two hundred men and women had served in the army or the air force.[14]

Edwin (Eddie) Goodman grew up in Forest Hill, a wealthy enclave of Toronto. His father was a prominent lawyer, David B. Goodman, K.C., and Eddie had himself been studying law at the University of Toronto when he interrupted his semester in 1941 to apply to the navy's recruiting office at HMCS *York*. He was advised point blank that an application would be futile. "I doubt that anyone who is Jewish will be an officer in this man's navy," Goodman was told.[15]

David Rubin, an Ottawa engineer, also experienced discrimination when he tried to enlist, even if he was finally accepted. He certainly had a respectable résumé. With a science degree from a university in Michigan, Rubin had built a career designing projectors for the cinema industry. Like Kaplan, he chose the navy because he thought it would be safer. "I already had two brothers in the air force," Rubin told the *Calgary Sun* in 1992. "I told them I'd sooner swim a mile then fall one."[16]

His religion initially raised doubts for the navy enlistment officer who interviewed him. Rubin would later describe the environment in the navy as "very, very, very, very British and very, very Church of England." Rubin served on patrol in corvettes and also launched a film society for the fleet.[17]

David Hart of Toronto (not the same David Lloyd Hart of Montreal who landed at Dieppe) joined the navy in the fall of 1942. He enlisted because one of his school friends was joining, and also because the navy was a less conventional branch of the services. He recalls only fifteen Jewish men in the navy during his time. A half-dozen of his friends had applied but were rejected, although Hart found no obstacles because he had a skill that the navy needed. "I was [working] as an apprentice as a tool and die maker, and I had gone to Central Tech [Toronto's Central Technical School] instead of high school, and they were desperate for tradesmen," said Hart, who served keeping the engine room machines running. He also had no trouble when he reported for duty in September and immediately asked for leave to celebrate the Jewish holidays. "It wasn't the boys, it was higher up. They [the top brass] didn't want us."[18] "I personally can say, once [I was] in the navy, the Jewish element never entered into it. I've never run into any antisemitic incidents in the entire time," said Hart.

Like the RCAF, the RCN had policies in place to effectively bar entry to people not British subjects and not of white European Christian descent, especially in the officer corps.[19] These policies delayed the application of Harold Chizy. He was born in Wysock, Poland, and his family came to Montreal when he was a baby. When he enlisted in December 1942, the navy asked the RCMP to investigate the accountant's political loyalties. "Discreet inquiries" were made to the Montreal police, the Quebec provincial police, to Chizy's employers, to his neighbours, and even to the local anti-communist squad. In the end, the Mounties found no evidence "that Harold Irving Chizy had ever been brought to their attention."[20]

While Chizy was a landlubber before the war, at least one Jewish volunteer had amassed an impressive seagoing background long before hostilities broke out. Max Abramson was the son of a furrier who had emigrated from Romania. Despite a typical Jewish immigrant upbringing on the Prairies and in northern Ontario, and despite living nowhere near the ocean, he joined the Royal Canadian Naval Reserves a good dozen years before the war broke out. As early as 1927, he would spend thirty nights of each year in a drill hall and two weeks each summer training on the water.[21] Abramson worked on fuel tankers out of Vancouver and had obtained the rank of able seaman by the time Canada went to war.

Abramson probably didn't get seasick much anymore, but many Jewish volunteers took a while to find their sea legs. The Royal Canadian Navy had actually been the last resort for Harry Hurwitz. In 1940, the Montrealer had tried to enlist in several army regiments in his hometown. At the Black Watch, the lineup was too long. The Grenadier Guards tanks came next, but at only five feet five inches tall, he was too short. So Hurwitz and a school chum hopped onto a train, hid in an empty box car, got off in Picton, Ontario, and joined the army's Hastings and Prince Edward Regiment. He had a tough time during training. "I had boils on my back, pimples, and every time I'd put my pack on, my back would bleed," Hurwitz said.

After a year, he received an honourable discharge. He tried the RCAF next but was politely turned away because he had only a Grade 7 education. The navy took him in 1941 as an able seaman. Instead of a sore back, he had to cope with seasickness. "When we left Halifax, we hit rough water and I was throwing up," Hurwitz admitted, explaining that his inaugural bout of queasiness hit him en route to Scotland.

It was worse on convoy duty in the Barents Sea after Hurwitz joined the crew of HMCS *Athabaskan*. The Allies were sending ammunition and supplies to the Russians from ports in Scotland and Iceland. These famous Murmansk runs were brutal. "We hit a storm and the ship would go about ten feet off the water and come bouncing down," he said. "I was throwing up and I remember even the captain was throwing up, too."

Canada's navy played a vital role in the war, particularly in the early years when Canada was tasked with protecting the North Atlantic shipping lanes, the cargo vessels, and troopships carrying supplies and men across to England. During the Battle of the Atlantic, from 1939 to 1945, convoy duty often meant the ever-present threat of running into German "wolf packs," groups of enemy submarines.

There were other dangers as well. For warships on the so-called Triangle Run between Halifax, Newfoundland, and New York or Boston, icing of the vessel was a serious and frequent hazard. David Rubin remembers the frantic efforts to remove the frozen white coating that threatened his ships. "We'd have to chop away the ice to prevent it capsizing," he told the *Calgary Sun*.

The sailors themselves also struggled to keep from freezing during winter crossings. Hurwitz remembers a resupply mission to the northern Norwegian coal-mining island of Spitsbergen in 1943. He was manning the lookout position high above his destroyer, checking for enemy targets and for icebergs. "I was up in the masthead. It was about, oh, I'd say about twenty-five below and they'd hoist me up a cup of Kai, better known as coffee," he said. "By the time it got to me—it took about maybe fifteen or eighteen seconds—it was already cold."

If the elements weren't a big enough challenge for the men, living arrangements were certainly an issue. Israel (Ichy) Glassman remembers the food being terrible during basic training at the naval base known as HMCS *Cornwallis*, located in Deep Brook, Nova Scotia. But the hungry eighteen-year-old ate everything anyway, even the bacon, which broke the dietary laws of his Jewish faith. "Except when the cooks smothered it with tomatoes," he said, which he couldn't stomach.[22]

The close quarters on board the corvettes where he eventually served also took some getting used to, especially for a boy who grew up exposed to the sweet aromas in his mother's Montreal candy store. "You slept with your clothes on in your hammock, and you had your boots and your life jacket and you never took your clothes off," Glassman said. "But you had to make sure that you took three to four showers a week or you smelled."

In order to live and work in those foul spaces for months at sea, Glassman and his crewmates had to develop a certain level of tolerance for smelly uniforms and smelly bodies. The same was true, in Glassman's case, for religious diversity. Like most Canadian Jewish sailors, Glassman was often the only Jew on his ship's roster. He found himself between Christian mates who wanted him to attend their regular religious services. "Every morning they called, 'RCs, Fall out! Roman Catholics, fall out for prayers.' They would grab me and pull me," Glassman said, who went by the nickname Ichy. "The Protestant guys on this side would say, 'Hey!' They grabbed me. 'You let Ichy alone.'" Glassman had to explain that he was unable to join either prayer service because he was Jewish.

Other Jewish sailors encountered antisemitism, and some chose to deal with it using their fists. Harry Hurwitz punched a crewmate in the face and knocked out one of the man's teeth after the other sailor asked, "How come Hitler missed you?" At a subsequent navy disciplinary hearing for both men, the non-Jewish sailor told the judge it had just been a joke. He was demoted. Although Hurwitz was a short man, he had been a boxing champion at the YMHA. "You don't mess with a Hurwitz," said daughter Debbie Cooper. Hurwitz was put in the ship's prison and lost a month's pay.

Before Ed Rasky went to sea, he spent three months training to be a sick-berth attendant at a hospital in Sydney, Nova Scotia, where he was constantly having run-ins with one of the pharmacists. Rasky bore the brunt of insults such as "What can you expect from somebody Jewish?" and "You're too loud." Eventually, the Toronto resident and his tormentor participated in a sanctioned duel. The boxing match, he claims, was condoned by the navy. "I got hurt pretty badly because the guy was bigger and stronger," Rasky admitted.

Gerald Rosenberg, from Hamilton, said that he didn't encounter any antisemitism while he was at sea but, like Rasky, endured harassment while still in training in Halifax. One fellow kept "agitating me," as Rosenberg called it, until one day, he had had enough. "I was on the wireless, and he was beside me and I just tore off the set, and picked him up and hit him as hard as I could, and threw him across the room." Rosenberg blamed his actions on the fact that he had just come down with scarlet fever and wasn't thinking clearly. He spent the next six weeks recovering in hospital. The pair would eventually become best friends.

Rosenberg wasn't so forgiving to a group of German seamen whom he encountered while on board the corvette HMCS *Battleford* in 1942. Rosenberg was serving in the ship's communications room when *Battleford* left Ireland on December 19, as part of a slow convoy of forty-five freighters headed for St. John's; his friend Petty Officer Louis Cohen—a Jewish officer originally from Argentina—was on board as an engineer.[23]

When the convoy approached the stretch of ocean between Iceland and the Azores, a group of eighteen German submarines was lying in wait. Sailors had nicknamed the zone the "Black Pit" because Allied anti-submarine planes couldn't reach it and get back safely without running out of fuel.[24] In the early hours of December 27, the submarines pounced. One of them, U-356, fired off torpedoes that quickly sank three freighters and damaged a fourth. *Battleford* and three other Canadian warships mounted a counterattack and hit the submarine. Official reports say it had forty-six crew members on board; there were no reported survivors.[25] Rosenberg takes credit for some of the statistics, saying he and Cohen exacted some private revenge of their own. "We knew that the Germans were pretty ruthless, even for survivors at sea. They used to machine-gun the lifeboats," Rosenberg said.[26] There were eight German sailors who didn't die in the initial attack. "We picked them up on one side, tore their life jackets off, and threw them over on the other side." Rosenberg and Cohen were never charged for their vigilante actions.

Dying of exposure was a common and deadly consequence for seamen who found themselves unexpectedly thrown into the North Atlantic. If rescue didn't come quickly, it would usually mean the end for the drenched, oil-covered, and often lightly dressed sailors. "In the North Atlantic, if you hit the water you had six or seven minutes to live," Israel Glassman pointed out.

He might have been describing the fate of Ralph Zbarsky of Saskatoon, who had enlisted in the navy when he was seventeen. On April 16, 1945,

Zbarsky's minesweeper, HMCS *Esquimalt*, was doing anti-submarine patrol in the Halifax area. Germany had already lost the battle at sea, but its navy was doing what it could to sink cargo ships and still had some submarines hiding along Canada's east coast.

A lone German vessel, U-190, torpedoed *Esquimalt* right outside Halifax Harbour. The ship sank before a distress call could be made. Zbarsky managed to get on to one of the Carley floats, but it would be six hours until another Canadian warship came to investigate. Able Seaman Zbarsky, twenty years old, was one of at least sixteen *Esquimalt* men who died of exposure while waiting for help.[27]

About this same time, Harry Hurwitz was preparing to mark the one-year anniversary of his own ship's loss. HMCS *Athabaskan* had been sunk off the coast of France on April 29, 1944. Hurwitz had been manning one of the anti-aircraft guns when a torpedo hit.[28] Another explosion from inside sealed the ship's fate. "When the whole ship was ablaze, Captain Stubbs yelled out, 'B-gun,' which was us—me and four other guys—'Man the hoses, see if you can do something.' We couldn't do anything."

It became clear they would have to abandon ship. Hurwitz started stripping off his heavy clothing, but he kept on his watch, which had been a present from his mother. He jumped off the port side into the English Channel.[29] He spent the next four hours in the water, clinging to floating debris. He heard some of his wounded crewmates begging in vain for rescue. "Some of them had their legs blown off. The doctor had both legs blown off. One guy had a big hole in his stomach."

The sinking of *Athabaskan* has been described as "the most significant naval warship loss" in the history of the Royal Canadian Navy.[30] The death toll was 127 men. HMCS *Haida* came back to pick up a few dozen survivors, but had to leave the scene after just twenty minutes, because dawn was breaking and the ship was dangerously close to the German-occupied French coast. The German navy sent out one of the destroyers involved in the attack, and some smaller vessels, to look for survivors. About eighty-seven Canadian sailors were taken prisoner when they climbed aboard the German lifeboats. Hurwitz was one of them. He quickly got rid of anything that would divulge his identity as a Jew, including the small Star of David pendant he wore around his neck.

On reaching dry land in France, Hurwitz was interrogated. He told the Germans his last name was spelled Hurwitt, "with two *t*'s." It seemed to work, even when one of the German guards recognized him—in a strange coincidence, the German had been employed in Lachine, Quebec, before the war.

Hurwitz spent D-Day in the Marlag und Milag Nord POW camp, but several other Canadian Jewish naval men played roles in the Normandy invasion. Maurice Novek, of Montreal, had been trained as a cook because his eyesight wasn't good enough for other naval duties.[31] In the weeks leading up to the invasion, Novek and the crew of HMCS *Prescott* were in England, protecting the dismantled sections of giant floating docks known as Mulberry Harbours. The Allies towed these docks in pieces across the English Channel for D-Day.[32] They were assembled off the Normandy coast to allow offloading of supplies rather than risk the booby-trapped and clogged beaches at Arromanches.

"Our excitement was intense," Novek would later write in his memoir, describing waiting on board *Prescott* until midnight June 5. *Prescott* soon took up anchor and headed to France, escorting the tugs carrying the Mulberry. "I had the impression of a pre-fabricated bridge being pushed out from the English Coast across the Channel towards the French Coast as if in one massive, long, endless structure. The sight was incredible," he wrote.[33]

Despite all the attention that was being accorded to the Royal Canadian Navy, John Lazarus was content to be where he was. When the war broke out, the Montreal photographer was pushing thirty. His long interest in electronics led Lazarus to take a radio operator course, before joining the Merchant Navy. "It's pretty grand to be a part of it and I pity the Canadians who've been digging frosted trenches for a place to lie in," he wrote to his sister Sylvia, assuring the family he was "as safe as if I was at home."[34]

Considered by many as the fourth service, the Merchant Navy of Canada comprised the crews of the cargo freighters and oil tankers and passenger ships that kept the Allies fighting during the war. The pay was a bit better than for the enlisted men. Some twelve thousand Canadians served in this vital service. The Canadian Jewish Congress did not collect statistics on Jewish men in the Merchant Navy during the war, and historians, including Martin Sugarman, have only recently collected the names of more than ninety Canadian Jews who served in the Merchant Navy, mostly on Canadian vessels but also on board some British cargo ships.[35]

"Most merchant seamen were too old or too disabled to get into the [regular navy] service or too young, age fifteen, sixteen, seventeen," explained Leslie Kemp of Oshawa, a veteran who volunteered with the League of Merchant Mariner Veterans in Canada.

John Lazarus completed his first Merchant Navy contract working in the communications room on a freighter to England in July 1940. The sailors in the Merchant Navy did not have to enlist for the duration of the war, as Royal Canadian Navy volunteers did, but signed contracts for the length of the voyage, which could last weeks or months. Lazarus's first crossing had gone well, although he made some rookie mistakes. "I've done some dumb things, including completely discharging my batteries under the impression that I was charging them," Lazarus wrote.

While still in England, he decided to upgrade his skills, taking a week-long radio operator course at a Marconi training school in South Shields, near Newcastle upon Tyne.[36] Lazarus then signed up as second radio officer for SS *City of Benares*, a passenger liner under the command of the British Navy. On board were ninety British children being evacuated across the Atlantic to safety in Canada. They were part of the Children's Overseas Reception Board (CORB), a wartime program that shipped more than three thousand British children to other Commonwealth countries. *Benares* left Liverpool on Friday, September 13, 1940, with three escort ships. These remained on patrol only for the first few days of the journey because no one expected the Germans would bother with a civilian ship. On September 17, during a gale off Ireland, a German submarine torpedoed *Benares*.[37] Of the ninety CORB children, just fourteen survived.[38] In all, 250 passengers and crew died.

Lazarus's family heard about the sinking on the radio but wouldn't learn their son's fate until a Montreal radio station broadcast an interview with a local woman who had been on board. She later met the Lazaruses and told them their son had stayed at his post to transmit distress signals. "I will always remember there was a very brave young man in the wireless station," the woman told them, according to an account published in the Montreal *Gazette*. "He could have saved himself, but stayed there after we had all left the ship."[39]

The *Montreal Standard* called Lazarus one of the "knights of the key," referring to the key of the Morse code machines used at the time.[40] Lazarus is one of at least nineteen Canadian Jewish men in the Merchant Navy who died during the war. The fact that he was a radio operator working in his ship's communications room is significant. The trade seems to have been a popular choice for Canadian Jewish volunteers in both the regular navy and the Merchant Navy. It also put them at a greater risk than other crew, as German submarines purposely tried to disable their quarry's radio rooms first.[41] Moses Greenblatt of Montreal and Sidney Shinewald of Winnipeg both served as telegraphists on Canadian warships, and both died at sea when their ships were torpedoed.[42]

Some Canadian Jewish merchant mariners received wartime medals for their heroism, although, disgracefully, Ottawa did not recognize members of the Merchant Navy as war veterans until forty-seven years later. Somer Oscar James of Toronto was working as a stevedore in Montreal when the war started. He joined the Merchant Navy in 1941, choosing it because he was a pacifist. The Harbord Collegiate student wanted to avoid conscription but still make a contribution to the war effort; he "didn't want to get involved with killing people, shooting them with guns from far away, and getting involved with anything like that."[43]

James served on no fewer than a dozen freighters. In November 1943, he was on SS *Empire Lightning* in Naples, Italy. The cargo ship carried high explosives for the Allied invasion of the Italian mainland. An enemy attack on the port on November 5 ignited an ammunition dump in the dockyard. The explosions damaged James's ship and set fire to the dock. He jumped down onto the burning dock, where he helped release the mooring lines so *Empire Lightning*—itself a floating bomb—could move away from the flames. Then he did the same for other ships. James earned both the British Empire Medal and the Lloyd's Medal of Bravery.[44]

8 Jewish Women in Uniform

"It's a queer job for a girl"

Sue Jacobs had nowhere to hide when her corporal caught her having a beer with a handsome Canadian air force officer at the Château Laurier Hotel in Ottawa. But instead of punishing her on the spot, her superior waited until the twenty-two-year-old widow, freshly enlisted in the Royal Canadian Air Force Women's Division, had returned to the barracks. "At least don't choose the most public spot in all of Ottawa," the kindly corporal warned Jacobs. "One of our officers might be there, and then I'd have to put you on charge. Fair enough?"[1]

Jacobs's nail polish got her into further trouble during mandatory parade the next morning, leaving the American-born Smith College graduate certain that she was going to be kicked out of basic training. How would she explain this to her parents, she wondered? Luckily, Jacobs was again only admonished. "Nail polish. That's much too bright. Take it off right after parade," she was ordered.

These rules for women concerning behaviour and personal grooming were just some of the conditions Jacobs had to get used to when she and approximately 280 other Jewish women volunteered to put on a military uniform for Canada during World War II.[2] At the outbreak of the war, women had been welcome to volunteer as civilians doing Red Cross work, selling Victory Bonds, salvaging recyclables, and working on the farms or in factories. Some four thousand and five hundred nurses enlisted, but it wasn't until after 1941 that the Canadian military took in civilian women. More than twenty-one thousand women served with the Canadian Women's Army Corps (CWAC), some seventeen thousand joined the RCAF Women's Division (WD), while seventy-one hundred

"Wrens" served with the Women's Royal Canadian Naval Service. At first, Wrens had to be over eighteen, have no small children, and possess at least a Grade 8 education. They also had to be white and British subjects. Officers had to be over twenty-one and with some university training. The goal of accepting women into the various services was to free up men for combat duty. "We serve that men may fly" was the WD slogan.

For Sue Jacobs, enlisting was a direct result of the death of her husband, Pilot Officer Michael Jacobs, in England, in February 1943. "I passionately made up my mind to join it. It seemed to me what I wanted to do, in memory of Michael, or to follow in his footsteps," she said. Her parents, who lived in Baltimore, were against her decision. They feared she might lose her American citizenship, plus they worried she'd be sent far away from Montreal. Jacobs enlisted anyway, in July 1943. "I wanted to wear the uniform Michael wore, to do what he did as much as was possible, for a girl," she said. "You couldn't join the aircrew, of course."

For Toronto's Esther Thorley, it was losing her brother, Meyer Bubis, at Dieppe that motivated her to sign up. She went down to the CWAC recruiting centre to enlist on June 13, 1943, the day she turned eighteen. Esther had been working in a factory sewing uniforms but wanted to wear one herself as soon as she came of age. With a house full of sisters, and two half-brothers both rejected by the military for medical reasons, she felt she had to represent the family. "My brother was a soldier, so I thought I should be taking his place since he was no longer there," she said.

There are many stories of Canadian Jewish women following their brothers already in the war. When Estelle Aspler joined the medical corps as a nursing sister, her older brother Jack Tritt had already been in the RCAF for two years. He would be killed while she was in basic training.

Harry Hurwitz's sister Esther (whose married name was Zion) of Lachine, Quebec, also served as a CWAC.[3] She had five brothers in the service: Max and Ike Hurwitz were with the Engineers, while Archie was in the RCAF. Samuel Moses (Moe) Hurwitz was a tank crew leader with the Grenadier Guards in France and Holland. A sixth brother, George, was rejected with a bad back.

In at least one case, two sisters joined together. Montrealer Evelyn Bloom (née Bernstein) joined as a CWAC with her oldest sister, Betty. Their father had served in the United States Cavalry overseas in the last war, and Evelyn looked up to him as an example. She recalls that the war was not going well for the Allies when she volunteered. London, England—where her father had been raised and still had family—was suffering under the relentless German bombing campaign. "It was a very rough time in 1942. We almost lost the war," she recalled. The Bernstein sisters roomed together in Ottawa after completing their training in Ste-Anne-de-Bellevue, west of Montreal.

Patriotism was what motivated Mildred Richmond of Napanee, Ontario, to become a CWAC. She served in London, England, as a medical secretary. She always claimed to be the first Canadian Jewish woman to enlist in the army and the first one to volunteer to go overseas.

"I felt it was part of my duty," she says in the *No Greater Honour* video.[4]

The desire to stop Hitler sent one unnamed, relatively new arrival to Canada into uniform. Her enlistment even made the papers in Ottawa, although the editors agreed not to name the Polish immigrant or her hometown for fear of endangering any relatives who might still be alive in the Lublin area. The woman had worked in a garment factory in Montreal and as a teacher. She joined the WD to protect her new homeland. "I am now a Canadian citizen and saw enough of Fascist government in Poland that I wouldn't want to see it here," she said. "After all, I'm not sacrificing anything, for if I had stayed in Poland, I would be dead already."[5]

It's not clear whether the unexpected death of her oldest sister Edith in the summer of 1941 sent Rose Jette Goodman of New Glasgow, Nova Scotia, to be among the first women in the RCAF. The daughter of Austrian immigrants, Rose graduated from Dalhousie University that spring, where her yearbook entry predicted a nursing career. It also hinted at her immediate plans.

"Many of our boys have entered the service of our country," she wrote. "Their absence makes us all realize the gravity of the situation in which the world is involved at present." After the thirty days of mourning had ended for her sister, Goodman surprised her family by going to Halifax in September 1941 to join the Women's Auxiliary Air Force, as the WD was originally called.

Most women in the Canadian military served in the more traditional female roles such as nurses, laundresses, cooks, secretaries, clerks, and typists, freeing up men who could then be posted elsewhere. Evelyn Bloom served as a typist. Once she was posted to Ottawa, her job involved inputting information into rudimentary databases of supplies as varied as socks and tanks. Her toughest assignments were processing the lists of the names of the young men who had been killed. "Sixteen years, eighteen years, twenty years [old]," she said, remembering meeting some of boys and men who later became casualties. "I [had been] in registration in Longueuil, [Quebec,] and I put people in the army…and I said, 'That's the kids that went into the army, they died.' And that was very upsetting for me and I think about it constantly."

Some of the Jewish women also chose to serve overseas. Evelyn Miller's family had immigrated to the Prairies to become homesteaders in the farming community of Alliance, Alberta. Before enlisting, Miller had gone to business school and was working in Edmonton for a well-known Jewish wholesaler, Hy Weisler. While serving in uniform, Miller did four years as a clerical worker, including serving in Belgium and France.[6]

Evelyn Robson (née Fainer) was working as a shoe store clerk in Saint John, New Brunswick, where she met a soldier from Fort William, Ontario. After Clarence Robson left for England, she joined up. The CWAC Personnel Selection Board form describes their new recruit as "eager for overseas service; prefers cooking to other work."[7] Even today, their daughter finds that funny. "I laughed when I read she was eager to go overseas," said Shirley Ellis. "She was following my dad!" Her mom arrived in England as a cook in 1943.

Women also served in more technically advanced positions during the war, performing aircraft maintenance, packing parachutes, conducting aerial surveys, and driving transports. Some of these jobs were dangerous. Esther Mager (née Mendelson) of Montreal was stationed at the RCAF Bombing and Gunnery School at Mont-Joli, Quebec, at the edge of the Gaspé Peninsula, where winter was colder and snowier than anything the former jewellery store manager had ever experienced. She learned to handle the station car on icy roads. Occasionally she had to race to the site of a flying accident. "Many times we had to go from the station to where the plane crashed and nine times out of ten, there were bodies there when they crashed," she recalled. "Because these [students] were learning, you see. So we had to go to pick up the pieces."[8]

Mager's work at Mont-Joli once put her into the hospital, suffering from exposure, but like other women at that time she did not serve in direct combat roles. Nevertheless, several Canadian Jewish women in uniform did come under enemy fire overseas. Medical secretary Mildred Richmond was sent flying when a bus exploded right beside her on a London street. Eve Daniels (née Keller) of Regina served in Belgium. She typed and filed health records of the front-line troops. When the shelling came too close to her location behind the lines, Keller had to pack up her work, jump into a Jeep, and flee to safety. "One time, she was working, and she left her desk, and the windows were open," said her daughter Leslie Kinrys. "She came back and there was a bullet in the back of her chair."

At least one Canadian Jewish woman worked overseas in top-secret intelligence operations.[9] Theodora Ginsburg (née Schatz) served as a Wren for nearly three years, including at Bletchley Park, the famous estate outside London where the British cracked Axis communications codes.[10] Her job was tracking Japanese merchant shipping.

The Montreal *Gazette* said Miriam (Mimi) Freedman (later Hart) saw more excitement in her "six years and eight months in uniform" than "many Canadian men in uniform."[11] Freedman was born in Montreal before World War I, but her family relocated to Belgium in 1920. In 1933, when her father realized that Hitler was rearming Germany, the family moved to London, England. After the war broke out, Freedman served as an ambulance driver for three years including during the Blitz (September 7, 1940 to May 10, 1941). Then she joined the CWACs in 1943 as a driver attached to Canadian Military Headquarters. Two months after D-Day, in August 1944, she became one of the first forty Royal Canadian Army women to land in liberated Normandy with the 2nd Echelon, 21st Army Group. They were stationed just a few kilometres from the fighting near Le Havre. As the Canadians pushed toward Belgium, Freedman went with them.

Her long and valuable service in uniform was profiled in the *Gazette*. The story mentioned her duties behind the lines and it also noted her talent for languages made her a sought-after soldier in northwestern Europe. She spoke French, Dutch, German, and Flemish and was called in as an interpreter with captured enemy prisoners of war when the Canadian forces liberated Belgium and, later, in western Germany.[12] Disappointingly, however, the story about her wartime experiences was relegated to the fashion section, beside a photo of the Princesses Royal, Elizabeth and Margaret, sporting the latest style in kerchiefs.[13]

Freedman was the only Canadian Jewish woman in uniform to win a bravery award in World War II, but she was not the only Jewish woman whose contributions were publicly diminished. Daisy Friedberg (née Lazarovitz, but who went by the name Lazare) enlisted in Ottawa in 1942 and was a graduate of the first class of army women to be trained as military police.[14] Although she didn't carry a weapon, she was trained in jiu-jitsu and wrestling techniques. Her duties included checking passes at the city's train station and making sure other women in uniform didn't disgrace themselves or go AWOL—absent without leave, meaning not returning to duty after sanctioned days off.

Friedberg was tough, but sometimes that wasn't enough to get people to take the thirty-four-year-old corporal seriously, not least because she was a woman. She made the front page of the paper once, but as part of a large group photo of women in uniform, with the cutline "Girl M.P.'s Check Passes at Ottawa Station." The full story appeared on the social page, under the banner "For and about Women."[15] This pattern repeated itself when Friedberg won another brief mention in July 1944, after she and another female military police officer, both corporals, stood at attention and saluted the prime minister and his guests, the prime minister of New Zealand and his wife. The politicians "were so impressed by the smartness of their appearance" that they stopped for a chat and "to shake hands with the two girls and Corporal Wylie." In the newspaper article, only the male military policeman was referred to by rank, although both women were also corporals.

"It's a queer job, for a girl," Friedberg acknowledged at the time. "But nobody can say it's not interesting."

Even some of the military's own female recruiting officers used language in their official interview reports that today would cause a storm of condemnation. Evelyn Fainer Robson was described as a "jolly woman" and also as a "girl," despite the fact that she was twenty-nine at the time.[16] The selection board in Halifax commented on Rose Goodman's looks first, then her religion, then her age, and, last, her brain: "Attractive Hebrew, 22, intelligent. A very capable girl full of ideas and initiative. Will make a good NCO [non-commissioned officer] and later, perhaps an officer."[17]

The chauvinism of the period posed a challenge for women on bases, who regularly had to confront behaviour that today would qualify as harassment. When Evelyn Bloom was posted to the No. 4 District Depot south of Montreal, she was immediately assigned to sort out the books in the canteen, even though she was supposed to work in ordnance. That rankled, but even more humiliating was how the commanding officer of the base, Colonel Sam Echenberg, assumed she would deliver his coffee and salute while she did it. "He knew I was very young and had a little game," Bloom recalled. "It was awkward."

His rule was that anyone who was wearing his or her army hat had to salute. If you left it on your desk, no salute was required. Bloom didn't wear hers because she didn't want to spill his hot drink. But Echenberg always insisted. "Soldier, why don't you wear your hat? Why don't you salute?" he asked her. "In the future, wear your hat and salute."

Manny Raber's sister Esther Nobelman (née Rabinovitch) of Medicine Hat, Alberta, was able to stand up for herself a little better when she was assigned to a chain-smoking officer at air force headquarters in Ottawa, for whom she had to take dictation full of top-secret technical language. Although she didn't know much about radar, Nobelman knew her grammar. Her boss would stand behind her chair, hover over her steno pad, and tell her to add commas. "I had been very good in English in high school and after a few months I swung around in my little chair and I said, 'Sir?…I can punctuate, you know.' He says, 'Oh, to be sure, to be sure.' So that took care of that problem," she recalled.[18]

Women in Canada's military were paid less than the men. New privates in the army earned $1.30 a day; Esther Thorley received a little more than half of that rate. "Try 70 cents. For the first six months," she said with a laugh.

Evelyn Bloom said the lower pay was not an issue; it was normal for the times they lived in. "We expected it, you know," she said. "I'm mad about it now, but I was not mad about it then, because I thought that… I was very young and very inexperienced in life."

Aside from the financial inequality, some Canadian women in uniform also had to deal with the social stigma of leaving home to serve their country. Disapproval came not just from society at large but their families as well. Bloom felt that their community was judging them. "The parents didn't want it. It was considered not a Jewish thing to do, you know?… For the girls," she said.

When enlisted Wrens were posted to the navy signal school in Ste-Hyacinthe, Quebec, Irv Kaplan noted his mixed reaction in a letter to a friend. "We have quite a few Wrens here and as yet I haven't quite decided whether it is for the better or worse," wrote the then petty officer. "In some ways yes and others no but they do brighten the place up."[19]

Bloom says she was propositioned all the time during her army service. "I don't know why it didn't upset me. It would upset me now, because I'm a feminist, but I thought men were like that and you had to handle yourself," she said. "And I did." She did let one fellow's advances progress. It turned into a memorable wartime romance. It started when she took a trip to New York City. "I was on leave. I liked to go to the museums, so I went alone," she recalled. She didn't stay that way for very long. Also on the train to New York was a Canadian Jewish paratrooper from Winnipeg. They dated but broke up when he went overseas.

The sexual innuendos were a part of the working conditions for army cook Evelyn Fainer Robson who also had to serve meals to the servicemen. "They were considered whores," said her daughter, Shirley Ellis, adding that being engaged to a soldier helped protect her mother from more serious forms of sexual harassment overseas. "There were always people flirting with them but they knew who she was; she was Robby's girl [Clarence Robson, her eventual husband]."

Esther Thorley learned to look after herself while in the army. She wouldn't go to bed with her dates, and she had a method for finding out the background of the men who asked her out. Her duties included processing Part Two Orders. These had to do with personnel movements and next of kin, among other things. "I'd look it up and see if he was married or not. I had an advantage," she said. If they were married? "I just broke the date or didn't show up."

While working in the Flying Control office at Gander airport, Sue Jacobs initially welcomed the uneven ratio of men to women. It was "about ten to one; a girl wouldn't be human not to admit that was grand for the ego while it lasted." The leading aircraftwoman doesn't remember hearing anyone call her "loose." She does, however, remember having to wear a skirt to work, even in the middle of winter, including in the busy Bomber Operations Room. It was an underground area with a huge map of the Atlantic Ocean on one wall. The women had to plot the position of Allied ships and German U-boats for the flight crews' pre-patrol briefings. "We used a ladder on wheels to reach the northern parts of the map," she said. "The joke about this situation was 'Either put trousers on those WDs or move the convoy to the South Atlantic.'"[20]

Just as their faith was important to many of the Canadian Jewish men who served in World War II, it played an important role in the war experiences of some of their female colleagues. For both sexes, being Jewish could be a good thing but also a potential problem.

Evelyn Bloom describes herself as more secular than religious. Yet she made it a point to put Jewish down as her religion on her attestation papers when she enlisted. Her identity discs also said she was Hebrew. Once, when an army friend asked her for a small loan of money in order to go home for Christmas, she agreed even though none of the CWACs had much to spare. Months passed and the woman did not pay the loan back. When it was Bloom's turn for leave, she approached her friend for the money. Instead, she got a dose of antisemitism. "'Oh, you're…a Jew,' [the other soldier retorted]. I was hurt, very hurt, and particularly because I was a very good friend of hers."

Esther Nobelman's encounter with antisemitism left her a little regretful of how she reacted. She had been collecting signatures in the office on behalf of the Ottawa Jewish community's refugee work. The petition was going to be presented to the government. An "officer came out of his office and said, 'What is this?' Well, I explained to him and he was immediately so insulting. He said, 'I wouldn't sign to have one Jew come into this country.' It was a shock to me." She ran to the bathroom and burst into tears. Someone reported the racist remark to her superiors, and the offender was "called on the carpet," Nobelman said. Although he did apologize to her directly, she wasn't ready to forgive and forget. "I'm sorry to say I was quite cool," she said.[21]

Esther Thorley grew up in a kosher home on Gerrard Street in Toronto. Her Yiddish-speaking father had come from a religious family in Russia, although in Canada he chose to work on the Jewish Sabbath for financial reasons. Thorley's background was important to her. "I always made it very clear at the first opportunity I could get to let people know that I was a Jew and if they didn't like it, that's too bad," she said.

Observing her faith landed Thorley in trouble when her father died. She went home from Vancouver on leave. Rabbi David Monson, one of the Jewish chaplains, reassured her that nothing would happen if she remained in Toronto for the first seven days of the traditional Jewish mourning period, when the family receives visitors and refrains from work or daily duties. "So when I got [back], I told them where I was," she said. They weren't happy about her going AWOL. "I had a week confined to barracks for extra duties."

Incidents of antisemitism aside, being in uniform and serving in World War II brought women tremendous benefits, both personally and professionally. They got to see some of the world, they learned to get along with groups from many different walks of life, and they were proud of their contribution to Canada's war effort—even if they couldn't actually drop bombs on the enemy.

For Esther Thorley, serving in the army formed her character: "I became more demanding, more [outspoken]; I became more honest, too. If I found a nickel or a dime or a dollar and no one was around, I'd take it. I would never do that after I got into the army."

Rose Goodman's wholesome good looks caught the recruiting officers' attention when she enlisted, but her personality and brains earned her a promotion in 1942, while posted to the No. 15 Service Flying Training School in Claresholm, Alberta. "This officer has brought a lot of enthusiasm and energy to her work," wrote Claresholm's Wing Commander W.E. Kennedy in recommending her.[22]

Within two months, Goodman was serving as adjutant for the base's flying wing, including about fifteen hundred officers, pilots, trainees, and civilians.[23] Wartime photos of her in uniform always show her smiling, whether she was on leave in Calgary or in the formal photo of the station staff at Claresholm. In that shot, she is surrounded by male officers wearing serious expressions on their faces. Goodman has her right foot primly crossed over her left, with her gloved hands resting on the skirt of her uniform. She is the only woman on that side of photo, and she is the only person smiling.

Goodman's sister, Anetta Chernin, said Rose was happy being in the RCAF. "She loved everything of it. She was a really up person."

9 Life in the Barracks

"Don't let that goddamn Jew in!"

David Croll earned his law school tuition shining shoes and selling newspapers in Windsor, Ontario, where his family had settled after emigrating from Russia. He subsequently set up his legal practice in Windsor in the late 1920s. When the Depression began, the city's workers were hit hard, especially those who had lost jobs in Detroit. Croll successfully ran for mayor in 1930, pledging to give struggling citizens the necessities. His opponents hurled accusations of corruption against him and attacked him for being Jewish—opposition he also confronted in provincial politics and in the war.

Croll was in his second term as mayor of Windsor when the war broke out. When he enlisted as a private in September 1939, it was front-page news across Canada.[1] Iconic photos show Croll wearing his Essex Scottish uniform while on city council business. The newspapers covered many aspects of his early military career in Canada, but Croll's daughter says they left out an important part of story: the antisemitism he faced after enlisting. Crystal Hawk blames her father's former political rival, Lieutenant Colonel Ernest S. Wigle, for making Croll's early army life miserable.

"Colonel Wigle assigned my father to clean the latrines," said Hawk, who remembers having to "chalk the white squares" in her father's regimental hat to make his uniform look fresh before he left for the barracks every day. Wigle had been mayor of Windsor between 1905 and 1909, then commanded an area battalion during World War I. He served again as mayor in the 1930s before losing an election to Croll in 1938.

Although antisemitism may have been to blame for the fact that

Croll was not immediately offered the rank of officer, he played down the issue. It was, he would later explain, his own decision to start at the bottom as a private.[2] "Well, I wasn't any kind of soldier; I didn't know anything about soldiering. The army did everything they possibly could to get me out of that private grade," Croll told the Multicultural History Society of Ontario in 1977.

Of the close to three hundred veterans or their next of kin interviewed for this book, the majority experienced antisemitism not just in their efforts to enlist but also during their war service. Incidents ranged from minor examples, such as hearing anti-Jewish jokes and racist talk in their barracks, to more extreme cases, including fistfights away from the eyes of commanding officers.

Walter Crotin was born in Russia and came to Canada as a child. He had been working as a milkman and fuel dealer with his father in Ansonville, Ontario, before he enlisted.[3] One evening, while he was taking basic training in Brampton, someone started talking about "the G.D. [goddamn] Jews."

Crotin heard this and said, "I'm a Jew. I'm Jewish."

"No you're not, you're Swedish or Norwegian," the other soldier reportedly replied.

"People used to call him Clark Gable, he was so handsome," said his brother Louis. Walter had blond hair and fair skin and he was tough. At five foot eight and 186 pounds, Crotin had collected many sports trophies. Louis said that particular situation in his brother's hut ended without a fight. Instead, the other soldier backed down, sort of, saying, "I'm not including you in my statement."

But Crotin's harassment didn't end there. He was posted to Petawawa, Ontario, for training on a six-inch Howitzer, where his gun crew was involved in an accident on the firing ranges. Someone didn't close the gun breech properly and the shell exploded inside the gun. The accident sent Crotin to hospital with a ruptured eardrum that left him deaf, but the doctors ruled it a pre-enlistment lesion. Soon Walter began to be plagued by headaches and ear infections.[4] He endured taunts from both a superior officer and some of the men. "When he was sick and couldn't function there was a lot of antisemitism that he was faking it," said his cousin Abraham (Manny) Crotin, a Toronto physician who also grew up in Ansonville.

Leo Guttman's religion would cause some problems for him soon after he enlisted in the Royal Canadian Air Force in July 1941. He was the youngest son of Romanian immigrants to Trochu, Alberta, who eventually abandoned their attempts at farming on the Prairies and moved to Montreal. Guttman was posted to the RCAF's Manning Depot, which was on the grounds of the Canadian National Exhibition in Toronto. Guttman remembers being called "the Jew boy" by a couple of guys. He chose to ignore it rather than fight back. "Because they were all bigger than me," he said with a laugh. Nevertheless, he made sure to claim a safe spot to sleep in his temporary living quarters. "You fought to get the upper bunk, you know," said Guttman, a retired salesman. "If you got the lower [bunk], some guy comes in, in the night time, drunk, or knows that you're Jewish... [Well,] there was some antisemitism."

While some Jewish personnel chose to find ways to avoid conflict, others stood up for themselves using their fists. Charles Krakauer's family likes to tell the story of the way he came to the defence of a short Jewish soldier who was being pushed around on the troop train taking them to Halifax for overseas deployment. Krakauer, a doctor, was an amateur boxer, and at five foot nine and 166 pounds he was no pushover. "He went up to these guys...there might've been two or three of them... and basically knocked the crap [out of them]," said Howard Tenenbaum, Krakauer's nephew. His uncle warned the bullies: "Next time pick on somebody your own size."

Ruben Ostfield wasn't a boxer, but he still used force to teach one of his bunkmates a lesson. In late 1940, the Winnipegger was posted to England, where he got along well with most of the men in the Saskatoon Light Infantry. However, he once had to get physical with a fellow who was calling him names and berating him for being a Jew. "My dad just said, 'I'd had enough,'" Ostfield's son Michael explained. "He said, 'I picked up a small bench and I rammed it under his chin and pushed him up against the wall and told him something like "You son of a bitch, if you say one more thing, I'll beat you to a pulp".' And he said the guy just sort of shrank."

Ostfield also had run-ins with a sergeant who made him do latrine duty—an unpleasant task that involved emptying pails of human waste down a hole—more often than most of the other guys. This kind of harassment was also part of Murray Jacobs's induction into the army. A lance corporal made Jacobs and another Jewish private get on their hands and knees and clean the toilets with toothbrushes, among other punishments. A "miserable son of a bitch," Jacobs said, remembering the officer decades later.

Nathan Dlusy's family thought that a posting as a wireless operator and air gunner at the Royal Air Force base at Alness, on the northern tip of Scotland, would be a relatively safe place for him to contribute to the fight against Hitler. The Dlusys had fled antisemitism and racial laws in Berlin only a few years earlier. Now Nathan was back in Europe as part of a Coastal Command crew, flying submarine hunting missions over the North Sea in a Canso flying boat.

On August 15, 1944, fifteen airmen including Dlusy were on a night radar exercise when the weather turned bad. The RAF Alness control tower ordered them to come home. En route back to the base, the aircraft crashed into a mountain and exploded.[5] Jon Dlusy says his brother had never flown with those particular men until that fateful night but had joined them after he appealed to the base chaplain for an urgent transfer: he'd wanted to get away from the men in his regular Canso plane who were Polish volunteers and antisemitic. Nathan was the only Jewish airman among the casualties that night.

For Toronto's Lorne Winer, brushes with antisemitism also happened overseas. One was relatively minor. In early 1944, he was training in England with the Second Survey Regiment of the Royal Canadian Artillery, preparing to serve on the front lines in Normandy. One day, a lower-ranked man, a gunner from another battery, came over to look at him. The man was from a small town in Ontario. "He said, 'I was told there was a Jewish sergeant up at the regimental headquarters and I can't believe it,'" Winer recounted. The man, who had never seen a Jew, had expected the "hooked nose and horns" he thought all Jews had.[6]

But that incident would pale in comparison with an episode that Winer witnessed involving a senior officer in his regiment. It has haunted the retired real estate executive ever since. By early August 1944, Winer's unit was in Normandy. As a sergeant, Winer wasn't allowed in the Officers' Mess at Colombelles, near Caen. But every time he walked by for breakfast that week, he'd hear Captain Leslie Gilbert Briscoe bellowing, "Ginsburg, Ginsburg, Ginsburg!" whenever Captain Fred Pascal, an engineer by training and Arthur Pascal's younger brother, was present. "'Ginsburg' was his way of saying, 'Jew, Jew, Jew!'" Winer believes.

Winer couldn't bear it when he heard Briscoe behaving that way with

Pascal, especially because the two officers held the same rank. One day, Winer had had enough. He waited outside on the wooden walkways and confronted Pascal. "I stopped him and I said, 'Sir, I've been walking by for the last two days and I hear Captain Briscoe...I hear him reviling you. Making antisemitic barbs and calling you 'Ginsburg' and I don't know why you are not retaliating. I can't stand it, sir."

Pascal only said, "Sergeant, step aside."

Winer would never find out if the Jewish officer was going to continue to ignore Briscoe or do something. Two days later, on the afternoon of August 8, 1944, the regiment was on the starting line for the second phase of Operation Totalize, a large-scale Canadian action to break through the German lines south of Caen en route to capture Falaise. It was to begin with hundreds of Allied bombers flying over to soften up the German positions. Around 1300 hours, 678 American bombers entered the area. Some crews mistakenly dropped their bomb loads directly on the Allied troops below. "I was only ten, twenty feet away, and a piece of shrapnel came across and disemboweled [Pascal]," Winer said. "And it kills me, to this day, to see him there.... Here we are, Jews fighting in Normandy, a common enemy, and there is this antisemitic bastard casting antisemitic barbs in a theatre of war," Winer said.

Briscoe survived the war, returned to Montreal, and resumed his career in banking. His daughter Lee Thompson says her father had a lot of Jewish customers from the clothing business and got along well with them. She has never heard of any of these allegations but acknowledged that Briscoe hardly ever talked about his war experiences. Her father had grown up in Cartierville, a working-class suburb of Montreal, where the population was multicultural. As for the tragic error that killed Pascal, Thompson says her father remained traumatized by his experiences in Europe. "He did say he'd lost many good men," she noted.

Fred Pascal's brother Arthur, the Montreal hardware retailer, did not face the same kind of reception as his late brother had; perhaps it was because he took pains to establish good relations with the non-Jews in his regiment. At the outbreak of the war, while still in training in Montreal, Arthur was the senior Jewish non-commissioned officer of a regiment in which most of the men were Catholic. "We [the few Jewish boys] took over the guarding duties during the Christmas holidays so that the whole regiment could...all have Christmas holidays," he said.[7]

Other Jews in service found that food was the key to fostering goodwill with non-Jewish coworkers. Hy Chud and his older brother Ben served in the same reconnaissance unit. Their parents would send them Chicago Kosher No. 58 brand beef salamis, also known as voorsht, from the Union Kosher Sausage Company on Lippincott Street in Toronto—a treat they would share with their non-Jewish friends. "We were the most popular guys in the troop when we got voorsht," Chud said.

Leo Guttman remembers being jealous of another Jewish fellow who was stationed with him at the Exhibition Grounds in Toronto. That airman would receive a voorsht once a week and used it to curry favour with the higher-ups. "Every Friday night there'd be a parcel arrive for him, and he'd share it with us and, of course, with the officers," Guttman said. "Consequently, he didn't get any dirty jobs to do; he got an office job."

Herbert Reiter from Winnipeg was performing across Italy and England with one of the Canadian Army shows as part of the variety act known as the Tin Hats, which included two men who performed in drag.[8] Reiter shared his food parcels from home, including the voorsht, with the non-Jewish singers, dancers, and musicians. "I am going to enjoy everything you sent me, but the biggest pleasure I shall have is to eat the salami sausage. The boys…stood around while I opened the parcel, and suddenly everybody was running for their knives to cut themselves a slice," he wrote to thank the Canadian Jewish Congress's War Efforts Committee in Winnipeg, which had sent the parcel.[9]

Rabbi David Monson of Toronto, one of the best-known Jewish military chaplains in eastern Canada, didn't hesitate to include non-Jewish men when he was handing out treats at Camp Borden, near Barrie, Ontario. Jack Tweyman remembers that Monson would visit the giant army base loaded with voorsht and fruit. When Morris Polansky was training to be an electrician at Camp Borden, he remembers attending one of Monson's Sunday Jewish prayer services (they were held at the same time as church parade) at the local YMCA facility.

"Everybody got a 'salami-ette' and an orange. When I got back to the billet, the guys were saying, 'Hey, where did *you* get *that*?'" Polansky said. He told them he'd got them from his rabbi.

"So one [Sunday] morning there's some guys coming in [to the service] here, three of them, [and] they're all gentlemen [so] they take their hats off."

Polansky smiles at the memory of the dead giveaway that the visitors were not Jewish. The trio apparently thought that they should act the way they did in church, where they were supposed to uncover their heads. In Jewish religious services, male worshippers keep their heads covered. "Quick!" Polansky whispered to the men. "Put your hat on!"

In the end, the guests did "cash in," as Polansky calls it, and received salamis and oranges.

"The rabbi never discriminated," Polansky said, impressed.

Not everyone was as willing to share the booty. When two New York–style kosher salamis arrived for Joe Greenberg at his air force base in Torbay, Newfoundland, the Toronto RCAF flight sergeant decided he'd have to take drastic measures to hide them from the men in his 5th Bomber Reconnaissance Squadron. "My brother-in-law, who married my older sister, had a sister in New York and she was married to a butcher, and he took great pride in handmaking salami. You can imagine the quality of it," Greenberg noted. "I said, 'There's no way these guys are going to get it,' so I used to take it and hang it up with my clothes," he explained.

Groups ranging from synagogues and labour councils to Jewish social action groups like B'nai Brith all sent parcels to Canadian Jews stationed abroad, but the so-called comfort boxes project operated by the Canadian Jewish Congress during the war was an especially large-scale undertaking. By the end of the war, Congress had sent an impressive twelve thousand comfort boxes and four million cigarettes to Jewish servicemen and -women overseas.[10] Organizers felt that sending food to the Jewish personnel provided more than sustenance—it also boosted the Jewish soul.

"The comfort, welfare and maintenance of morale of our fighting forces are our joint responsibility, yours and mine," urged E.E. Workman, the national chair of Congress's fundraising campaign for the comfort box project. He hoped to raise $150,000 (more than $2.5 million in today's dollars) for the parcel operation.[11]

Congress tasked its War Efforts Committees in each region with collecting and packing the donations. The contents of the boxes varied. Every month, for example, Manitoba's Jewish servicemen overseas would get a pound of salami, plus cheese, crackers, fruitcake, biscuits, chocolate bars, chewing gum, shaving cream, and packets to make hot chocolate.[12] For Ontario servicemen, the boxes contained:

> 1 1-lb. package Fruit Cake
> 2 large Neilson's chocolate bars, 1 French, 1 Milk
> 1 jar jam
> 2 packages cheese
> 1 package raisins
> 1 package figs
> 1 1-lb. package Asstd. Fruit Drops
> 4 packages Asstd. Neilson Fruit Drops
> 2 packages Chiclets
> 2 packages razor blades
> 1 toothbrush
> 1 shaving stick
> 1 small Colgate Tooth Powder
> 1 pr. socks
> 2 handkerchiefs[13]

When the parcels arrived, they must have provided respite from the ever-present reminders of the death of friends and colleagues in action. The food from home and the familiar brands of Canadian cigarettes helped servicemen cope, as is evident in a letter from gunner William Rosenthal, a young Montreal journalist who was serving in the artillery. After receiving a comfort box full of Sweet Caporal cigarettes, the grateful twenty-year-old wrote a three-page thank-you letter to Congress. "I, or rather we, wonder sometimes whether you people realize how much receipt of your gifts mean to us. Getting a letter from home and from you people, and ditto parcels, is to us here as a 'bit of hope,'" he wrote. "Getting mail from you is like seeing that kosher stamp again. Your letters and gifts warm us as no sun has ever warmed the heart of a man. Hearing from you folks is like a breath of spring or a kiss from a Red-head."[14]

Although some Jewish personnel found that sharing the contents of their comfort boxes was a good way to build bridges with non-Jewish comrades, Congress was still receiving reports of antisemitism. An official study was commissioned into the overall relationship between Jews and non-Jews in the military. "On the whole a splendid relationship exists between Jewish and non-Jewish men and officers in the armed forces and very few instances of personal friction resulting from religious prejudice have been brought to our attention," the authors of the report wrote in 1941.[15] Some historians have also reported "negligible" and even "rare" levels of antisemitism among men in the same platoons.[16]

This was certainly true for the soldiers in Lieutenant Mitchell Sterlin's platoon in Italy. Ron Barkley, who was not Jewish, was a private in D Company, 16th Platoon, of the Royal Canadian Regiment (RCR) and Sterlin, of Montreal, was his platoon commander. Barkley says everyone knew Sterlin was Jewish. "It didn't cause any problem at all," Barkley would later tell members of his regiment in 1992. Sterlin was liked, he added, because "he looked after his men."[17]

Some personnel in a different company, however, had a harsher opinion, according to Ian Hodson, an officer who had sailed for Italy with Sterlin and the Royals in July 1943. He recalled an incident on a transport ship from Scotland, when several junior officers urged him to get rid of Sterlin and one or two other Jewish lieutenants. "Listen, if I ever hear that stuff again, you'll be on your way back home so damn fast your head will spin," Hodson rebuked them. The incident remained with Hodson even half a century later. "He was a very good officer," said Hodson, who had befriended Sterlin at officer's training school in British Columbia. "It was the small minds of the people who were criticizing him that were at fault."[18]

Nathan Isaacs says this sort of experience was also true for him. Despite being the only Jew in his Halifax bomber crew, he never experienced any prejudice from them. He did, however, witness one incident that he will never forget. Isaacs was having a few drinks in the officers' wet mess at RAF Leeming in Yorkshire, England. He heard an officer, whom he didn't know, say, "You know what we'll do? After the war we're gonna take Hitler back to Canada with us so he could clean out Jews in Canada."

"I was shocked," Isaacs admits, and to this day he regrets that he didn't do anything. "He was twice as big as me, so I just felt bad that I wasn't big enough to hit him over the head with a bottle or something. I've never ever mentioned that to anybody."

Ben Dunkelman also claimed he never felt any hostility from his men. Indeed, he felt that they would follow him anywhere because he treated them so well. He does, however, recount one incident of antisemitism in his autobiography. A mumps epidemic had spread through the crowded troopship RMS *Queen Elizabeth* as he was making the Atlantic crossing from Canada in March 1943. Not long after Dunkelman disembarked and began training at Aldershot, he came down with the illness and was sent to a military hospital. The patients were listening to the radio. The announcer was reading a news story about large-scale massacres of Jews in Europe. According to Dunkelman, a patient in the next ward yelled out his support for Hitler and said he wished the same fate for Toronto's Jews.

"I hurled myself out of bed and stormed into the next ward," Dunkelman writes, saying he intended to kill the man. As he reached for the man's throat, he stopped, realizing he could be court-martialled for murder, or worse. "'No', I told him, through clenched teeth. 'You're not worth my while. I've got a job to do and if I kill you—or a lot of Nazi bastards like you—I won't be allowed to do it.'" He left "shaking with rage."[19]

Although Dunkelman would rise through the ranks to become a major, a significant number of Canadian Jews experienced obstacles when being considered for promotion during their service. Harry Niznick of Winnipeg was a McGill University engineering student whose parents had left the Ukrainian area of Russia and come as farmers to southern Manitoba in 1912. They took the name Niznick because they thought it didn't sound as Jewish as their original last name, which was Kraines. Harry joined the Canadian Officers' Training Corps at university, then joined the army in March 1943. He told the interviewer he spoke not just English, but also Jewish (Yiddish). His interviewer noted Niznick's ethnic origin: "This officer is of Russian Jewish descent."[20] Later when he was in officers' school in Gordon Head, British Columbia, an army captain decided he didn't like the way Niznick talked. His rather contradictory report reads, "Intelligent, alert, and ambitious. Speaks with a rather heavy accent. Does not seem to possess very much spirit and potentialities for leadership seem doubtful. Infantry. Not a good prospect."[21]

Niznick's niece Sharon Glass says it is clear to her what was really going on. "All [the recommendations] were good save from one officer. He reported that he did not think Harry was officer material because he was of 'East European origin and did not speak English well' —read, antisemitic," Glass says. "Harry was born in Winnipeg and attended school there, so if he did not speak English well, it would be an indictment of the Winnipeg School Division."

Niznick's one bad review wasn't enough to counter the praise he received from other officers, and he earned his commission as a lieutenant in July 1943. He was sent on further training courses at Shilo and at Brockville before volunteering for the CANLOAN program, which sent Canadian infantry officers into battle with units of the British Army.[22] Niznick went to England in May 1944 and served with several British regiments. He fought, and died, in the liberation of Belgium in September 1944.

By the time Jacob Silverstein was posted to wireless school in Montreal in the winter of 1941, he'd applied to formally change his last name. He told the RCAF to call him "Silverstien," with the *i* before the *e*.[23] He may have come up against what the author Stephen Franklin explains were "regimental recruiting officers [who] sought to dissuade qualified Jews from seeking to become officers on the grounds that Christian troops would not follow them into battle."[24] Whether changing the spelling of his name would have smoothed his way through the ranks of the air force is open to debate.

Silverstein went on to become a respected wireless operator and air gunner, flying anti-submarine patrols off Newfoundland against German U-boat "wolf packs." He was recommended for a promotion in early 1943 while he was with No. 10 Squadron, but he didn't get it. Instead he was formally called up in front of his superior officer, informed of his deficiencies, and told to work harder for the next three months. There is no evidence in Silverstein's service files of any discipline problems or any charge sheets that would have prevented him from receiving timely promotions. A non-Jewish airman who was recommended for a promotion at the same time received one.[25] When the commanding officer of the Gander air base, Group Captain Larry E. Wray, discovered what had happened, he demanded an explanation. His staff couldn't account for why they had treated Silverstein differently. Wray called it "embarrassing" and ordered the man promoted retroactively to warrant officer second class.

Winnipeg's Earl Braemer always felt that he did not get the promotion he deserved. Braemer served with the tanks of the Fort Garry Horse Regiment between 1942 and 1946. Born Israel Abramovitch, he served using his birth name.[26] Despite praise from his platoon commander, who said that he "was an outstanding soldier and with experience may become a [non-commissioned officer] prospect," Braemer was never promoted higher than a corporal, not even after he helped liberate Holland.

After he died in 2003, his widow, Laya, told the author Allan Levine, who was writing a book about the history of the Jews of Manitoba, that her husband always "felt it was because he was Jewish."[27]

Even the most highly decorated Canadian Jewish serviceman in World War II, Sydney Shulemson of Montreal, remained at the rank of flight lieutenant during the war despite a stellar career that included being awarded both a Distinguished Service Order and a Distinguished Flying Cross. His last name seems to have raised concerns for at least one senior British officer. While overseas, Shulemson was supposed to be seconded to the Royal Navy to lead a weeklong course in airborne rocket attack techniques. Just two days into the training session, Shulemson's RCAF squadron received a strange telephone call.

"An Admiral called 404 Squadron and asked 'What kind of a name is Shulemson?'" wrote Joe King, an aviation expert and former RCAF pilot officer. Even though whoever answered the phone didn't take the caller's antisemitic bait, replying instead that Shulemson was a Canadian from Montreal, the gig was cancelled.

Although Shulemson didn't lack for medals, controversy surrounds his lack of a promotion.[28] The group captain at RAF Banff, Max Aitken, son of Lord Beaverbrook, a Canadian-born financier and politician living in England, had promised Shulemson a promotion, but no one ever followed through. Stéphane Guevremont, a Calgary aviation historian, sees discrimination as the reason. "He served two years and got two medals of bravery, yet he only went up in rank once? Come on! That is a shame," Guevremont said. "POWs who came back from the camps got an instant promotion of one or two ranks retroactively depending on their number of years in captivity, and Shulemson who fought and did real combat on the Norwegian coast and in the Channel, got nothing?"

There are those who argue that Shulemson wasn't bothered by the rank controversy, and that he actually preferred to remain where he was. Eric Campbell of the Canadian Aviation Heritage Centre believes that Shulemson felt it was safer to be at the lower rank, since all the wing commanders above him kept getting killed in combat. When asked to describe his treatment as a Jew, Shulemson was careful to say that as far as his colleagues in the Royal Canadian Air Force were concerned, he got along just fine. "The guys on my squadron would follow me into hell and back, they had a lot of faith in what I would do," he told author Wayne Ralph.[29]

To be sure, it wasn't as if Jewish personnel were the only ones who faced discrimination when it came to promotions and advancement during the war. Rabbi Gershon Levi, a chaplain, wrote about a quota system for promotions, particularly for Protestants and other Christian denominations, who were permitted to receive only 20 per cent of the promotions for a certain officer rank during a specified period.[30] In spite of limitations such as these, plenty of Canadian Jews in uniform advanced through the ranks.

Esther Thorley was offered the chance to get on the track to promotion from being a private, but she turned it down. She had her reasons. "I wouldn't take it because I thought that if I did that I wouldn't be with my friends, and I didn't want that."

David Croll's earlier troubles with antisemitism did not hold him back once he got overseas. He trained first in reconnaissance, then was sent to become an officer. It was big news back home in Canada and in Detroit when Croll received his commission from the Royal Military Academy at Sandhurst in January 1941.[31] As a lieutenant, Croll wrote a highly regarded training manual for dispatch motorcycle riders on how to read maps, including a suggestion about what riders should do with the classified messages they were carrying, should the enemy capture them.[32] "Swallow the message" was how the *Ottawa Journal* book reviewer described Croll's advice. "Don't be afraid; your stomach has digested much worse if you have been in the Army any length of time."[33]

Croll would eventually become a major, then the commanding officer of the Oxford Rifles, with the rank of lieutenant colonel. There are those who have suggested that the promotion didn't sit well back home in Windsor and went "against the wishes of some people who had even been opposed to his getting into the regiment," as the Honourable Paul Martin Sr., a former Windsor lawyer who was part of the King government during the war, was quoted as saying. But Croll's rise from the rank of private certainly gave him credibility at home and abroad. "That made him a worthy and strong man and gave him a stature that was quite unique," said Martin.[34]

Croll wasn't the only Canadian Jew to attain a senior rank in the wartime Canadian military. Major General Robert P. Rothschild rose from being a lieutenant to become the highest-ranked Jew in the Canadian Army in World War II, and for a long time after the war he was the most senior Jewish army officer in Canada.[35] Rothschild was a son of

Ben Rothschild, the long-serving postmaster and mayor of Cochrane, Ontario, and had graduated from Kingston's Royal Military College in 1936—possibly the first Canadian Jew to do so.[36] Lieutenant Rothschild was in Dunkirk after the evacuation of the British Expeditionary Force in 1940 and made it back safely to England a week later, at which point he was promoted to the rank of captain. He was made a major by November 1941 and landed with the 2nd Canadian Armoured Brigade in the invasion of Normandy on D-Day. Rothschild, who isn't related to the wealthy European-Jewish family of the same name, was wounded in action in France in August 1944. It happened while he was already a lieutenant colonel in charge of the 2nd Canadian Corps during the advance to Falaise. He won a Member of the Order of the British Empire four months later.[37]

Jewish men also held top positions in the RCAF during the war. Maurice Lipton used to fly model airplanes in the streets of his Nova Scotia hometown and later studied aeronautics at Dalhousie University. Lipton enlisted in the RCAF in 1938 and soon qualified as a pilot. After the war broke out, he became one of the first flying instructors in 1940, until being sent overseas in 1941—by then a wing commander—to run a Canadian night fighter squadron in Scotland. Lipton would win an Air Force Cross and eventually run all air training for Canada during the war.[38]

Ed Ryan of Kingston rose through the service to become one of the highest-ranking Jews in the Royal Canadian Navy.[39] According to his family, he was also one of the first Jews to be accepted into Queen's University's engineering faculty. The son of an immigrant grocer from Sislovitch (Svislach), in what is now Belarus, Ryan graduated in 1929. After working in a series of engineering jobs in Saskatchewan and Ontario, he taught high school in his hometown. Upon joining the navy, he served in the Works and Services Branch of the Department of National Defence, which built naval installations on bases.[40] He attained the rank of commander.

There is evidence that at least a few Jewish personnel got help from fair-minded non-Jewish enlisted men and senior officers. When Montrealer Israel Pervin, known as Issie, joined the RCAF, he was working for his older brother Joseph, who ran a sportswear factory. Pervin was the youngest of six children born to immigrants from Odessa.[41] The family kept a kosher home, observed Jewish holidays, and belonged to the

Shomrim Laboker congregation. A commanding officer suggested that Pervin might want to find a less Jewish-sounding first name, especially if he was going to be a fighter pilot over Germany. "He was told by his CO that being a pilot, it really wouldn't be to his advantage to be known as Israel Pervin," said his nephew Tim Pervin. In April 1941, his uncle went before a justice of the peace in Montreal and legally changed his name to Tim Issie Pervin. Pervin flew Typhoons in Europe and was shot down on his thirtieth operation, near Eindhoven, Holland, on September 22, 1944.

A non-Jew also came to the aid of Sam Boroditsky. The Winnipeg-born soldier had been living in Palestine but returned home when the war began and enlisted. Boroditsky volunteered for a top-secret commando unit assembling in Fort Harrison, Montana. They were the joint Canadian–U.S. First Special Service Force, later to be immortalized in a 1968 Hollywood movie, *The Devil's Brigade.*

On December 2, 1943, the Devil's Brigade scaled Italy's Monte la Difensa in one of the most dramatic feats of the war. Monte la Difensa was a vital German holdout southeast of Rome. Serving as a medic, Boroditsky raced up and down the 960-metre mountain to attend to casualties.[42] The next day, as the German defenders were firing down the slopes while the commandos climbed, the exhausted Boroditsky looked for shelter near the command post. "[I] asked if there was room for me in their bunker. It was the 2nd Regt. Supply Section. I heard someone say, 'Don't let that God-damned Jew in,'" Boroditsky wrote in his memoir.

What happened next did not make it into Boroditsky's memoir, but he told his family. A senior non-commissioned officer stood up for him. "His friend said, 'The Jew boy doesn't go in, I don't go in,'" said Boroditsky's sister, Rivka Selchen of Winnipeg.

The man was likely Battery Sergeant Major Douglas Libby of Brome, Quebec. Libby's widow, Julia, had never heard this story, although she knew the two friends spent a lot of time together in foxholes. She isn't surprised by her late husband's gesture. "It sounds like him," she said.

Boroditsky was promoted from corporal to the rank of acting sergeant on April 7, 1943. He would lose and regain that rank twice during the war, but the demotions were not due to antisemitism: Boroditsky had a habit of returning late from leave, including once from a visit to his fiancée in Montreal.

10 Off-Duty Activities

"Was drink involved?"

There wasn't an empty seat in the hall at the Jewish servicemen's centre on Halifax's Quinpool Road as the Stadacona Band put on their show on July 28, 1943. The stage was decorated with a backdrop of British and Nova Scotia flags. The performers included four men wearing straw hats, shiny vests, white gloves, and black-painted faces portraying African American minstrels. "Laughter re-echoed throughout the hall when the company's black-faced comedians gave their jokes and cracks in their own style," declared the *Evening Mail* newspaper's reviewer.[1]

The entertainment didn't have a particularly Jewish theme and the centre was open to everyone in uniform, regardless of race or nationality. With nearly three hundred and sixty thousand Canadian troops embarking from "an East Coast Port" on their way to England during the war, the Halifax Jewish servicemen's centre was likely one of the busiest in the country.[2] But for Jewish personnel who dropped in, it felt like home. While Nathan Isaacs waited to sail overseas in the winter of 1943, he found the Jewish centre a haven: "It was just going someplace where you could get a bite to eat, or something that you couldn't get in a restaurant, and just socialize with Jewish people."

Women from the city's Beth Israel Synagogue on Robie Street volunteered to serve up two thousand traditional Jewish meals each month, and Isaacs enjoyed mingling with female co-religionists. "There were girls there; we spoke to them," he said. For him, the centre was the one place where Jewish servicemen could find people who understood what it was like to serve within the predominantly Christian atmosphere of the Canadian forces.

The Halifax centre was one of sixteen Jewish servicemen's clubs opened and funded by the Canadian Jewish Congress during the war and run by local Jewish organizations in cities across the country, including Victoria, Brandon, Moncton and Montreal.[3] There were also centres set up and supported by other Jewish organizations, such as the YMHA. The Canadian Jewish community threw itself into offering recreation and hospitality for the Jewish men and women who were serving, and for troops who began their military service in Canada before heading overseas.

Some of the official Congress "canteens" were inside existing Jewish community buildings, such as Vancouver's Oak Street site, but the centre in Montreal was operated out of the stately home belonging to the Ballon family. The three-storey sandstone-and-granite mansion on Bishop Street was donated by one of their daughters, the concert pianist Ellen Ballon, and it opened as a servicemen's centre in 1943.[4] Distinguished guests paid visits. On his way to perform in England, the American Jewish violinist Yehudi Menuhin stopped by in 1943; he met some of the Jewish servicewomen, as well as some of the society women in charge, and signed autographs.[5]

It's not clear if Menuhin was required to sign the guest register but all the service personnel certainly were. Troops from many countries passed through the Montreal canteen, and many were not Jewish; the canteen was open to all. There were sailors from the United States and airmen from New Zealand. It was a place where off-duty personnel could relax, read a newspaper, write a letter home, play bingo, catch a show, or even perform in one.

Abe Ferstman made his first visit to the Montreal canteen on June 10, 1945. The flight lieutenant showed up with his army buddy, Martin Standard, who signed them both in.[6] Ferstman was a navigator with the Royal Canadian Air Force who had survived thirty-three missions over Europe, won a Distinguished Flying Cross (DFC), and been repatriated to work as an instructor at Ancienne Lorette, Quebec, for the last months of the war. Standard, a private, appears to have been a bit of a practical joker. In the centre's registry book, he put a DFC beside his own name. It's a bravery medal that he certainly couldn't have won because the honour was issued only to airmen. To be fair, he also awarded his friend Ferstman the highest bravery award you could win, the rare Victoria Cross.

"So I'm guessing that Standard [wrote] my father's name and added the extra medals as a joke to posterity," said Brian Ferstman, Abe's son, a Toronto lawyer who owes his existence to his father's friend, as Standard introduced his father to his mother about the same time the men visited Montreal.

In Toronto, a city famous for being reserved, especially on Sundays, the opening of the Jewish Servicemen's Club was heartily welcomed. It operated seven days a week at 44 St. George Street in a building that had originally housed the headquarters of the National Council of Jewish Women. It was turned into a canteen in 1942 and would welcome six hundred thousand visitors by the time it closed in early December 1945.[7] "You go there, all the Jewish girls were there, you could dance with them, they had food," recalled RCAF veteran Mitch Pechet. "It was great!"[8]

With so many young and mainly single service personnel passing through, the servicemen's canteen in Toronto provided a venue for Jewish and non-Jewish personnel to look for love. The *Evening Telegram* reported that "more than 500 boys have married girls they met through the [Jewish servicemen's] club's parties and functions."[9] A canteen official called the spot "a beehive of romance" after sixty-four members of the 48th Highlanders married servicewomen they met at the club.[10] An estimated two hundred hostesses married their uniformed guests.

Ruth Friedlan (née Bogan) was among those who volunteered at the Toronto canteen as a "pinafore girl"—the label given to the twelve hundred hostesses, because they wore a full-length frilly apron over their blouse and skirt while on duty. During the two years that Friedlan volunteered at the canteen, she served cookies and helped stage musical shows and skits. She also posed for many snapshots with uniformed men. In the end, though, her husband was not one of them. She met Irving Friedlan, a Montrealer, after he returned to Canada from serving overseas with the RCAF. They married in 1947.

Winnipeg's YMHA opened its doors to members of the service during the war and saw eighteen thousand visitors in 1941 alone.[11] The sports venue wasn't restricted to Jewish servicemen, nor was the YMHA at 265 Mount Royal Avenue West in Montreal, which welcomed sixteen thousand servicemen during the first year of the war.[12] In 1940, the Montreal Y opened a spot off the main lobby "with a radio, magazines, writing tables, and organized to act as a club room for the Jewish men in the armed forces." The Y's sports facilities were soon filled with enlisted men.

Any Y members who volunteered for active duty received free admission for the duration of the war.[13]

According to Thelma Shapiro, a former communications director at the Y, the institution played a big part in the war experience of many Jewish Canadians in uniform. "It was right in their neighbourhood, you know, Mont Royal...and Park Avenue, with about three military regiments around it, including the Grenadier Guards and the Mount Royal Regiment," Shapiro said. "And when you needed to go to the gym or just get a shower or get a *shvitz* [sauna] or get a good meal, the Y...was open to you now, for free, during that period."

The YMHA on Mt. Pleasant Street in Sydney, Nova Scotia, was open only to Jewish personnel, which made it the ideal place for Cape Breton women who were looking for Jewish husbands "from away." "All the local girls from Glace Bay, New Waterford, and Sydney and everybody would get to the Y on Saturday nights," said Evelyn Davis, who grew up in the Whitney Pier section of town and attended some of the dances. "Most of them [the local Jewish girls] married these fellows."

Some Jewish men in uniform made other arrangements to meet girls while on leave. Mitch Pechet starred on RCAF hockey and baseball teams while also serving as an instructor on air bases in Canada; he could not be sent oversees because of an eye injury he suffered while playing hockey for the New York Rangers' farm team. "The major battles I served in were mostly on weekends," the veteran admitted to an interviewer, referring to his beer-soaked weekends at luxury hotels in the cities where his sports teams were playing.[14] His widow, Judy Pechet, swears she was not one of the rotating cast of female visitors at one particular hotel. "When he was stationed in Calgary, he won the Battle of the Palliser: he and whoever were on leave would get a suite at the hotel, four to six airmen, and they'd fill the bathtub with beer and they'd revel."

The war also brought together Jewish couples in which the person wearing the uniform was female. Esther Mager had enlisted in 1941 and worked in motor transport at several flying school training bases. Her husband, Saul Mager, was a civilian: he was in the dress manufacturing business in Toronto. They met on a blind date while Esther was on leave and were married in 1945.[15]

Despite the Jewish taboo against marrying out of the faith, some personnel ignored their parents' wishes and dated non-Jews in Canada and overseas. Yet the wartime loosening of social mores couldn't overcome all the roadblocks that differences in religion might cause. Irv Kaplan had as lively a social life as his navy pay and occasional gifts from his parents would allow, but he sometimes found that religion got in the way of romance. Kaplan was in a military hospital in Quebec City recuperating from twisting his knee when he wrote to his friend Harry Abelson, training with the air force in Summerside, Prince Edward Island, for advice. "I never get invited to farms with adjoining rooms. I never meet the captain's daughter. I don't get invitations to dinner every day and then am the honoured guest. How do you do it, Harry?" Kaplan wrote. "Do you ever get to talking about religion? Do you tell them you are a Heb?"[16]

Yude Brownstone, the son of Ukrainian Jews from Winnipeg, arrived at Debert, Nova Scotia, in December 1943 expecting to ship out to England within weeks.[17] Before his troopship left, Brownstone, a soldier originally with the Lake Superior Regiment, met a Cape Breton girl, Nellie Clarke. She had rosy cheeks and a mischievous smile, and wore her hair pinned up in a stylish wave. She gave Brownstone a photo of herself with her home address scrawled on the back. But she either didn't want to take the relationship further or didn't want her family to know about the dark-complexioned Jewish infantryman because she also wrote on the back of the photo that it would be best to contact her only care of a local coffee shop known as the Victory Café.

It doesn't appear that the Ottawa airman Cy Torontow let the religion of the women he chased become an issue while he was training in Canada. Torontow, who would become a wing commander with the RCAF and also serve in the Korean War, didn't see a girl's faith or the colour of her skin as an obstacle when he was on leave from Mont-Joli and looking to find a willing bedmate. "Each time I've gone to Sydney I've run into a lot of 'trouble,'" he wrote to his friend Bill Zelikovitz, the RCAF radio operator. "Liquor is too easy to get down there and the women look too nice after being in Gaspé for two or three weeks."[18]

Off-duty carousing brought even the most straitlaced afoul of the military's regulations, and Jewish personnel could be confined to barracks, lose pay, or both, for a host of infractions. The most common of these was being absent without leave. Often, romance was the reason. Michael Stein Jacobs's service record shows he was severely reprimanded and fined four days' pay after going AWOL in late July 1941.[19] Sue Jacobs was the reason—it was the weekend of their wedding.

Clifford Shnier was tall and handsome, and girls in Winnipeg were crazy about him. When he was training at the RCAF Elementary Flying Training School in Prince Albert, Saskatchewan, he learned that a girl he fancied had married someone else. His family says he was very upset. That could explain why Shnier went AWOL for more than eight hours one day in June 1941.[20] "Maybe he just had to go walk about for a while," mused Mitchell Shnier, a nephew.[21] Shnier was confined to barracks for two weeks and lost a day's pay, the only entry on his otherwise exemplary military charge sheet.

More serious infractions could result in the offender being demoted. When Sam Boroditsky received his promotion to acting sergeant with pay on April 7, 1943, he decided it was cause for a family celebration. But with just a forty-eight-hour pass in hand from the training base in Norfolk, Virginia, Boroditsky knew full well that he wouldn't make it to Toronto, where his sister Sarah was living, and return in time.[22] He went anyway. En route back to base, the highly trained commando decided that he might as well make a side trip to the Big Apple. "I suppose I drank a little too much and had a fight with a couple of sailors who probably wished I had not taken unarmed combat training," Boroditsky wrote in his memoir. "I feel guilty when I think about using our 'Force' kick." The army demoted Boroditsky to acting corporal again for an entire month.

Of course, servicemen weren't alone in being at risk of punishment for infractions. Esther Nobleman nearly lost her sergeant's stripe because of creamed eggs on toast. It was her least favourite meal at the military cafeteria in Ottawa. One night it was on the menu and Nobleman couldn't bear the thought of eating the dish, so she left her barracks and treated herself to a decent restaurant meal. While she was at it, she took in a movie. When she got back, she was surprised to discover that her absence had become a serious incident. "Where have you been?" her friends asked, alarmed. "Everyone has been looking for you! Tomorrow you are going to be demoted!"[23] The next morning, she meekly explained to the officer in charge that her unauthorized leave was due to dietary distress. He could barely stop chuckling. She got away with just a warning.

While Esther Nobleman, based in a city, was able to spontaneously take in a movie, others remember the travelling entertainment shows produced by the various forces' in-house entertainment units. Personnel at bases across western Canada may have seen the variety shows hosted by Monte Halparin—Monty Hall—who served in the militia a couple of times a week, on weekends, and during the summers while still at university in Winnipeg. As part of the Canadian Army Entertainment units in Manitoba, Hall was the master of ceremonies, told jokes, and sang patriotic songs. "We went to the camps all around, [including] Portage la Prairie, the air force base. We'd go out there on a Sunday, we'd take a bus with our troupe and we'd perform for the officers. Then we'd perform for the enlisted men and then we'd take the bus back at one o'clock in the morning and go to college the next day," Hall said.

Two of the highest-profile Jewish men in Canadian show business also entertained the troops while in uniform themselves. The wildly popular comedy duo of Johnny Wayne (born Lou Weingarten) and Frank Shuster got their start performing on radio. The pair met as Boy Scouts, and then teamed up at Harbord Collegiate's drama club in Toronto. They continued performing together at the University of Toronto, where they studied for their English degrees and were in the Canadian Officers' Training Corps (COTC).[24] Both men interrupted their postgraduate English studies in 1941 to enlist.

Their backgrounds in show business saw them assigned to the *Canadian Army Radio Show*.[25] The weekly musical review was broadcast for nine months on the Canadian Broadcasting Corporation, out of Montreal, between 1942 and the fall of 1943.[26] It had an orchestra and skits, and the cast included talented performers including singers and musicians in uniform. The military decided to turn this radio show into a stage version, and Wayne and Shuster plus a cast of 135 actors, dancers, and musicians criss-crossed the country to perform for the armed forces and the general public. Military personnel got in free, and the proceeds from the civilian tickets went to a soldiers' welfare fund.

In December 1943 Wayne and Shuster took their show to England. They played the length and breadth of Britain, and after the successful invasion of Normandy in June 1944, Staff Sergeant Frank Shuster and Sergeant Johnny Wayne wrote a brand-new act called *Invasion Review*. Just forty days later, they were sent across the English Channel to debut it on liberated French territory.[27] "We were in France…the first unit to play overseas, in Normandy," Shuster told the historian Laurel Halladay in 2000, describing the astonished faces of the soldiers in the audiences. "We'd see guys coming over to us and saying, 'What the hell are you doing here? There's a war going on.' 'Well, this is where they told us to play.' And they'd say, 'Well, you're welcome but keep your head down.'"[28]

Canadian Army newsreel footage from July 1944 shows large crowds of off-duty soldiers sitting or lying on a grassy hill in Banville, France, clearly enjoying one of these shows.[29] It was their chance to put the terrors of the battlefield behind them, if only for a short time. Shuster always felt that the men on the front lines appreciated his form of war service, whether he dressed up like a Nazi or as a cowboy, even though he never had to fire his army-issued rifle.[30] "Let me tell you the truth. They were so overjoyed to see us and hear somebody talk about Toronto or Montreal," Shuster told Halladay. "It made them forget the war for a minute."[31]

Of course, it was much easier for Canadians stationed in England and in other Allied territories to enjoy some time off than it would be later when they were sent into the theatres of war. There were Jewish servicemen's centres in England where they could socialize and even find a place to sleep. Many men and women used their leaves for sightseeing. Lawrence Abelson took in a greyhound dog race at a stadium in Leeds, England, in November 1942.[32] Bill Zelikovitz enjoyed the ice cream at the Grand Central Hotel in Nassau, Bahamas. William Rosenthal from Montreal liked taking his leaves in Scotland.[33]

The uniquely Jewish attitude toward and flavour of some leisure time activities sometimes set Jewish servicemen and women apart from their gentile comrades. "I shall probably have more news for you in my next letter. I am going *shpatzirin* [Yiddish for 'walking around'] in London tomorrow for the weekend," artillery Sergeant Norman C. Newman wrote home to Harvey Golden, the director of the Montreal YMHA, from Aldershot, England, in 1940.[34]

In the spring of 1944, David Devor was trying to come to terms with the wealth of Renaissance artwork in Italy's famed churches and museums. He wrote home to tell his mother that it was strange for him to get used to seeing "Old Yosky on every wall and ceiling," referring to images and sculptures of Jesus.[35]

Gordon (Johnny) Udashkin from Montreal served with the Royal Air Force's Middle East Command for three years and thus had plenty of opportunity to visit Palestine. In early 1944, he went to "the all Jewish city of Haifa," according to the *YMHA Beacon*.[36] In April 1944 Udashkin posed for a photo in Jerusalem standing beside a man dressed in traditional religious Jewish garb, including a broad-brimmed hat: "Guess which one is me?" Udashkin, who was in uniform, scribbled on the back of the snapshot.[37] Udashkin would do more than sightsee while he was in the country; he married Hannah Faigin of Tel Aviv in July 1944.

Alex Balinson was undergoing flight training with a bomber squadron in the Cotswolds while his older brother Robert was a doctor with the Royal Canadian Army Medical Corps.[38] Their October 1941 weekend reunion in England was spent, in part, gorging on traditional Jewish cuisine. "Right now, Bob is passed out on the bed beside [me] and I'm trying to finish this little note off to you," Alex wrote to his parents, describing how he, too, needed a nap after "having gut ungefressen with herring."[39]

While Jewish Canadians in uniform in Canada certainly didn't lack opportunities for off-hours fun, personnel who served overseas were often involved in escapades that were more intense. Perhaps they felt the need to live life to its fullest because each leave could well be their last. Liquor often played a prominent role in these adventures.

Although he was supposed to be responsible for handing out discipline for the RCAF's famous No. 427 "Lion" Squadron in England, Flight Lieutenant Joseph (Chas) Chasanoff had the reputation for being "the most colourful, the most dynamic" adjutant.[40] Chasanoff, a lawyer from Selkirk, Manitoba, earned the nickname "the Mad Adjit" for his antics, which included pretending to be an important Russian pilot while on leave in London in order to persuade the receptionist to find him a room at the fully booked Savoy hotel. It was also Chas who demonstrated his squadron's requisite alcohol-fuelled initiation ritual, known as the "Flarepath":

> *During the course of the festivities, more uniforms were saturated with the brew than was actually consumed. In the forefront again came "Chas the Adjit," who in his own inimitable style showed the sprogs how simple it was to balance a mug of beer on the noggin while at the same time coordinating with mind, body, and battling against inebriation to proceed through a "flarepath" of beer glasses. What a man, our adjit.*[41]

Chasanoff would be immortalized on film after he decided to find a real lion to be the squadron's mascot. Metro-Goldwyn-Mayer Studios in Hollywood had already come to a marketing agreement with the RCAF to sponsor the 427 "Lion" Squadron, including providing the unit with a bronze sculpture of a lion and giving each man a lion medallion that was good for a lifetime of free movies.[42] The crews were duly encouraged to paint likenesses of MGM's wartime film stars, including Lana Turner, on their airplanes. Chasanoff arranged for the squadron to adopt a six-month-old lion cub named Mareth from the London Zoo. News cameras captured the moment in November 1943 when Chasanoff's boss, the squadron commander, climbed gingerly inside the lion cage to bring his personal greetings to the new pet. In the British Pathé newsreel of the zoo ceremony, Chasanoff can be seen in the crowd with a huge grin on his face.[43]

Irving Friedlan did a lot of grinning when he spent his leaves visiting his mother's relatives, the Hardmans, in Manchester. On St. Patrick's Day 1943, Friedlan brought a friend along, another Jewish Montrealer named Sam Davidson. The two Canadians and cousin David Hardman decided to put their own stamp on Manchester's raucous Irish festivities. The way the family tells it, the uniformed trio had already downed a few drinks by the time they walked past the landmark Lewis's department store on Market Street. Inside the display window, a clerk was arranging clothes. With military precision, Davidson went into the store and took over the undressing of the mannequins. Outside, Friedlan signalled instructions, while Hardman waved at the naked plastic figures and encouraged passersby to watch the impromptu show. "The lads were in excellent spirits when they arrived home and, for some reason, they all had sticks of celery behind their ears," said Denise Stallman, Hardman's daughter. She thinks it might have been during that same booze-soaked leave that Friedlan introduced his Canadian friend to David's sister, Sylvia Hardman. "Sylvia and Sam seemed to hit it off immediately," she said. Sylvia, now Mrs. Sam Davidson, came to Canada as a war bride, one of over forty-eight thousand European women with Canadian servicemen husbands to immigrate during or after World War II.[44]

Barney Danson, who served with the Queen's Own Rifles of Canada, had had plenty of opportunities to meet eligible young Jewish women back home: his father, Joseph, founded and ran a popular co-ed Jewish summer camp, Camp Winnebagoe in Utterson, Ontario, in the 1930s. Yet, like so many others, Barney also met his wife, Isobel Bull, while serving in England.[45] Actually, Danson's closest friends in the regiment, Gerry Rayner and Freddy Harris, met Isobel first when her parents opened their home to visiting Canadian servicemen. "Gerry and Freddy told me of their smashing daughter Isobel who was a serious musician and an aspiring concert pianist," Danson, who went on to be a Liberal Cabinet minister, writes in his memoir. "I thought the situation was worthy of further investigation and called the Bulls' home, an initial contact that resulted in lunch in London's West End, many more subsequent lunches, dinners, and ultimately, breakfast."[46]

England served as the backdrop to plenty of wartime romances. Joe Gertel was training with the artillery near Guildford, Surrey. He didn't socialize much with the other men, preferring to spend his spare time reading books about politics and even the occasional Shakespeare play. Gertel also loved classical music, which is why he found himself in a servicemen's canteen one night, listening to a pretty blonde perform a classical melody. "So he went over to the piano just to watch her play, watch her technique and listen to the music up close and that's how they met," said Gertel's sister Ruth Lande.

The pianist was Hedwig (Hedy) Neumann, a music student and a Jewish refugee from Austria whose worried parents had sent her and a brother to safety in England when Neumann was fifteen. "It was kind of love at first sight," she said. "He was a very good-looking man, six foot two, and very handsome." Their romance blossomed. "We used to walk, do some hiking," she said. "He had a Jeep occasionally, and we used to go to...classical concerts and we used to go to plays and we went to London a couple of times...nothing terribly exciting."

Gertel's letters to Neumann beginning in February 1944 reflected his frustration at not being in action yet, his pride in the Jews who were building a new homeland in Palestine, and even his own regret at breaking his mother's heart by enlisting. Although Gertel personally considered himself an atheist, he happily described to Neumann the time he brought a touch of Yiddishkeit (Jewish culture) to the small southern English town near his base.[47] Gertel had met up with three other Jewish soldiers in mid-March 1944, and the group went to a teashop in town, ate and drank, laughed, told jokes, and sang songs—all in Yiddish. "All the people around stared at us in amazement and thought we were crazy," Gertel wrote to Neumann. The other customers probably didn't understand a word.

The couple planned for a future, even though all indications pointed to an imminent Allied invasion of France. That same month, on Neumann's twenty-first birthday, Gertel proposed. He began writing to Gertel's family in Montreal. She confided in them about her fiancé's plans to make their home in Palestine. "Hedy was an assimilated Jew, but, as she wrote to my mother, 'If he wants to go to a Jewish homeland after the war, that will be my homeland,'" Ruth Lande said.

Gertel arranged to have Neumann's name and address officially added to his military documents so the army would notify her should anything happen to him.[48] As preparations began in earnest in England for Operation Overlord (the codename for the invasion of Normandy), his letters to her sounded more fatalistic. "Look, Darling, you probably know now that I'm in the infantry," he wrote, explaining that he had been sent from the artillery to the Queen's Own Rifles of Canada. "A person does not have to be a military strategist to realize that this isn't by any means the healthiest position for a chap to be in."[49]

On June 6, when the D-Day invasion started, he scribbled a short letter to Neumann, breaking off the relationship and begging her to forget about him. "I am now most definitely no longer the master of my fate," he wrote, assuring her that his feelings for her had not changed. But the circumstances had: "In times such as these, our affair is an anachronism, tragically out of place."[50]

On June 8, Gertel was among those who crossed the English Channel. A month later, on July 8, his regiment was involved in the "furious battle" known as Operation Charnwood, fighting to capture the town of Authie, on the northwestern outskirts of Caen. By the afternoon, when the town was in Canadian hands, the casualty toll was nine officers and nearly two hundred men in lower ranks. Gertel died on that day. He was twenty-two. Neumann was officially notified of her fiancé's death, just as Gertel had arranged. "She told me the Queen sent a sympathy note, but that was no consolation," according to Hedy's daughter, Susan Ellman.

After the war, Hedy would meet and marry an American soldier, James Reeds II. He was with the famous Monuments Men team—their exploits were made into a 2014 movie starring George Clooney and Matt Damon—that rescued stolen European art treasures from Nazi hideouts. The couple moved to the United States when the war ended.

Not all Jewish personnel overseas were looking for a trip to the altar. George Nashen had barely arrived in England in 1943 when the air force issued him a pass from his airbase in Yorkshire to celebrate Rosh Hashanah. Nashen went down to London but admits he never set foot inside a synagogue. Instead, he and about twenty other servicemen rented a hotel room and took turns exploring Piccadilly Circus. When the boys discovered that one of the famous prostitutes known as the Piccadilly Commandos was actually a British Jew, Nashen's friend yelled, "Hey, guys! A Jewish whore! Look what I found."

Although Nashen didn't reveal what arrangements, if any, were made with the girl, he did pursue a romance with a more respectable young lady. They met at the Paramount Dance Hall on Tottenham Court Road. Her name was Anita. Nashen became a regular guest at her family's home in London's Stoke Newington borough. "During the years I was there, I had Friday night [meals] or Yontiff [High Holidays and Passover] with her mother and stepfather." The romance didn't last, but they remained friends.

Invitations like the ones Anita's parents extended were common both in Canada and overseas, and they were not only for the benefit of the lonely servicemen. Some Jewish families helped the matchmaking process along by appealing to a serviceman's yearning for hospitality among people of the same religion and a home-cooked Jewish-style meal, despite the wartime rationing. Harry Hurwitz was confronted with a choice of eligible girls after he met one of his father's boyhood friends at a synagogue while on leave in Sunderland, England. "He had five daughters, he tried to get me to marry one," Hurwitz said. "He was telling me how nice Sunderland is and he has a nice business. If I decide I want to stay in England, he said, 'You don't have to worry about a job, I'll find you a job.'" Hurwitz politely declined.

Bill Zelikovitz's own encounter with a British girl would have graced the gossip magazines had anyone snapped photos of it. He told his family after the war that he met Princess Elizabeth on a dance floor in England. "When he was overseas they had some function and she came to it, before she was the queen," said his son Joel Zelikovitz. "And he cut in for a moment, and someone else cut in on him after that, so everyone had a little twirl, I guess."

Although Zelikovitz often talked about that escapade, the parents of Canadian Jewish personnel weren't always aware of what their children were doing in the romance department. When a Canadian serviceman was killed, the military conducted an inventory of the personal effects and then sent them back to the next of kin. The families sometimes received a "sanitized" parcel, as senior men destroyed problematic personal letters and snapshots before the package was mailed, presumably wishing to avoid upsetting the grieving families any more than necessary.

"I'd have to go through some of their things," agreed Joe Greenberg, who was a sergeant in charge of an RCAF Coastal Command squadron patrolling off Torbay, Newfoundland. When there were accidents, it was up to him to collect the crews' personal belongings and return them to the next of kin. "If I found letters from girlfriends, and they [the men] were married; I would destroy them."

If religion didn't always matter while dating, it sometimes did when biology intervened. Mimi Freeman's family says that while still single and serving as an ambulance driver in London, England, she might have been having an affair with a British officer, who might or might not have been married, and might or might not have been Jewish. "At some point, she got pregnant," her niece Ruth Elias said, adding that her aunt was thirty-two or thirty-three at the time. "A lot of the suggestions around Mimi and the baby was that she didn't want to disappoint the Harts," Elias said, referring to the status of Mimi's mother's family as one of the founding Jewish families in British North America. The family does not know what happened to the baby, although it seems Mimi gave up her ambulance job, came back to Canada to give birth—some think Mimi delivered in Halifax—and put the child up for adoption. She then returned to England, and joined the Canadian Women's Army Corps in 1943.

Before he went overseas, Toronto's Murray Bleeman had dated a Jewish girl named Lil. She would write to him and send him gifts and Valentine's cards. But after he got to England in August 1940, Bleeman had other interests, as he wrote to his sister, Diana: "I'm a rough and ready young man of 26, am 5′8″ tall, weight 170 pounds (no fat). Big head brown eyes nice teeth (my own) charming smile, brown hair, pretty nose heart shaped face, that's what the girls tell me."[51]

Bleeman's charm captured the attention of a pretty Welsh nurse. She became pregnant and gave birth to a baby girl on September 10, 1941. Bleeman's family thinks he was probably present for the delivery because his military service records show he was AWOL at the time. When he returned to camp two days later, he received a week's detention and lost a week's pay.[52] Bleeman would die in a military hospital in England a year later, after the Dieppe Raid. His family would receive some of his personal effects, but they knew nothing about the Welsh nurse or the baby.

In 1997, Bleeman's family received an unusual telephone call from

England. An agency searching for the birth father of a woman in England located Bleeman's family in Canada. She was Murray Bleeman's daughter. Her mother had given her up for adoption, as she and Bleeman had not married. The woman, in her fifties, would make the trip to Toronto to meet her new-found family. She brought her own children with her.

"She does look like Murray, she's a mix," said niece Ferne Phillips, who met her English relatives at the airport and even brought them to worship at Beth Tikvah synagogue for the High Holidays. For Bleeman's daughter, attending a Jewish prayer service felt right, Phillips said, even though "she didn't know her father was a Jew."

Some Jewish servicemen came away from their wartime affairs with a less permanent souvenir. By 1945, nearly one in ten men in the Canadian Army overseas had contracted some form of venereal disease.[53] The RCAF was reporting close to fifteen thousand cases of sexually transmitted illnesses, mostly gonorrhea.

Trooper David Cramer of Winnipeg was the youngest boy in a family of nine children. The son of Russian immigrants, he earned a good-conduct badge while overseas in England. He sent $23 every month home to his mother. In early 1944, Cramer, then twenty-four, got a chance to sample the pleasures of London. He came back to his base complaining of a "funny" feeling at the tip of his penis. He was hospitalized for nine days. "Exposure 8 February 1944, London, name unknown, used no prophylaxis, was drunk. No previous VD [venereal disease]."[54]

When doctors in England treated the artilleryman Jack Faibish in October 1942, he had just come off a week's leave in Leeds. The medical team asked him whether he'd got it from a professional or an amateur, and whether alcohol was involved. "Amateur," Faibish answered, adding "Yes."[55]

Even a chaplain couldn't avoid a brief, if unsolicited, encounter with some of the most famous sex workers in the war. When Nathan Isaacs went on leave in England, he used to visit Squadron Leader Jacob Eisen, one of the Canadian Jewish rabbis appointed as chaplains. Eisen, who had held a pulpit in Edmonton and would later also work at Toronto's Holy Blossom Temple, was the first Jewish chaplain appointed to the RCAF overseas. One day, Eisen and some Jewish airmen—all in uniform—went to Piccadilly Circus.

"Piccadilly Circus was a place where all the hookers walked their dogs, so Rabbi Eisen, myself and Archie [Levine]—there was about five of us—this hooker stops us and says, 'Would you like to come and have a good time?'" Isaacs said, chortling. "[Eisen] wasn't embarrassed. I was more embarrassed for him than he was. He just said, 'No, thank you!'"

For married or engaged personnel, the war often meant months or years of separation and long lapses between mail delivery, and therefore, unsurprisingly, infidelity.[56] Lorne Winer was going steady before he enlisted. He was a heavy smoker—two packs a day—and once he was overseas with the artillery, his girl would send him parcels of cigarettes. But being away for five years ended both those parcels and the relationship. "I had a girlfriend that sent me a 'Dear John' letter. She met someone who was 4-F [unfit for service]," Winer said, although he insists that being dumped didn't bother him because he had become hardened by military life and the carnage he saw on the battlefield.

Lionel Cohen had been in the army for two months when he married Rose Bender in November 1939. The Toronto insurance salesman went overseas seven months later. While he was there, his wife started to worry that Cohen was forgetting his wedding vows. "The sense I got from looking through some of the old correspondence…I tend to doubt her first husband was faithful to her," said Jerry Richmond, Rose's son by her second husband, whom she married after the war. "She knew that [he was cheating], but, you know, back in those days, there were no long-distance phone calls, there was no long-distance travel, the only means…of communication was through letters that were censored or, if something serious happened, you would get a telegram." Rose Cohen would never confirm her suspicions, and in 1942 she received one of the dreaded telegrams notifying her that Lionel had died at Dieppe.

For the Canadians who were posted overseas to England, the long years of training until they finally saw action in 1943 or 1944 caused well-documented morale problems and discipline issues.[57] Private Louis Goldin, who joined up in the first week of the war, didn't take to army life all that easily. His charge sheet lists over a half-dozen incidents and punishments including for insubordination, for arguing with an order, for missing parade, and for being AWOL. He had two incidents while stationed in Iceland, and five more while in England before he was killed in the Dieppe Raid. Despite being docked about a month's pay during the two years he was overseas, Goldin was still a dutiful son, sending $20 a month home to his family in Montreal.[58]

Israel Freedman of Winnipeg had an unusually lengthy military conduct sheet.[59] The rifleman was considered a major offender for being AWOL at least ten times. He was also labelled a minor offender for drunkenness. His troubles had begun while still in training at Camp Shilo, near Brandon, Manitoba, and accelerated once he got to England. On one of his unauthorized jaunts to London, the Canadian Provost Corps officers picked him up just after midnight on April 1, 1943. Freedman had been gone for six days, eighteen hours, and forty minutes. Not only did the military send him for field punishment for two weeks and deduct three weeks' pay, but he also had to pay back the costs for the police to catch him—three pounds and ten pence. The last entry on his charge sheet, from May 1944, showed he had lost a piece of his gear worth $4.16. In total, Freedman's fines cost him $600, the equivalent of half of his annual pay.

Freedman was eight years old when his family immigrated to Canada from Poland in 1930 and settled in Winnipeg. His youngest sister, Esther Zajdeman, said that her brother "didn't have much guidance," calling him "a tough cookie." Freedman graduated from Grade 8 at David Livingstone School, and found a job as a tubing and sheet metal worker for a bed-making company. He earned $21 a week until he was laid off shortly before his nineteenth birthday. He joined the army because he was broke.

Zajdeman wasn't aware of her brother's run-ins with military authorities, but she remains sorry that he had such a hard time. She remembers him as a drinker but questions why he was singled out for punishment by his superior officers. "Was it antisemitism?" she wondered.

Jim Parks was in Freedman's class in Winnipeg's North End. The two would sometimes get into trouble with the local police. Parks, who is not Jewish, says they would be fined for riding their bicycles side by side—"50 cents"—or for riding on the handlebars—"a buck." But in Parks's opinion, Freedman wasn't a serious troublemaker. "Not any more than the rest of us," he says.

When Freedman and Parks reunited in July 1944 in Normandy, they were both serving with the Royal Winnipeg Rifles. Parks believes his friend became bitter about military life. "Once you get in a rut like that," Parks said, it was hard for some soldiers to snap out of it.

A more serious case in the history of Canadian World War II military justice involved Murray Steiner, a private with the Royal Canadian Army Medical Corps in Aldershot, England. The former Toronto druggist was put to work in the medical stores section. In May 1941, the thirty-five-year-old was caught in a police sting operation. He was arrested while in the process of selling forty-five hundred capsules of codeine and phenobarbital and other sedatives to another soldier. Steiner was sentenced to two years of hard labour, some of which he had to do as an inmate at the military's Wandsworth Prison in London. The army stopped his pay for those two years and froze the spousal allowance to his wife, Fay, back home. Steiner would petition for a reduced sentence in order to "carry out my desire for which I came to this country," namely "to take my part in the Empire's critical fight."[60] The army agreed, and he was eventually allowed to go back to work as field ambulance staff.

Some Canadian Jews in uniform found another way to enhance their pay—gambling. While fighting in the Italian campaign in 1944, David Devor politely refused his mother's offers to send him some money. He didn't need money, he wrote to her, "as I can pick tons of the stough [*sic*] up at cards and dice."[61]

Nathan Isaacs played the dice game known as craps on the troopship taking him across the Atlantic to Liverpool in March 1943. It helped take his mind off being seasick. "Craps, that was the big game, non-stop, and unfortunately I didn't have enough money to play with, because I was very lucky. I ended up with a big sock full of coins," Isaacs said.

Harry Hurwitz tossed his wallet into the depths in an effort to conceal his religion (it contained some printed Jewish prayers) when he had to jump into the English Channel after his ship HMCS *Athabaskan* was torpedoed off the coast of France. Losing the wallet has remained a sore point for Hurwitz to this day; it cost him his winnings from a night of gambling, along with his $60 monthly salary. "We were in Plymouth Harbour; we got paid that day and we rolled the old bones and I won $40 and I had to throw it," Hurwitz said with a rueful smile. "It killed me."

Misadventure, bad luck, and poor judgement contributed to the death of some of the 450 Canadian Jews who were off duty when their end came. Nearly five thousand Canadian army personnel died in accidents, of illness, and by suicide.[62] One hundred fifty-seven people in the navy died "due to misadventure." The air force tallied 833 fatalities not due to flying accidents, training, or the enemy.

The relatives of Morris Miller of Winnipeg, the only Canadian Jew buried in the Rome War Cemetery, long believed the soldier had been poisoned by tainted water while he was on duty. "They were marching from place [to place]. They stopped for a drink, a lot of them," according to Frank Zipursky, a nephew. The real story, though, was buried in his uncle's military service records. Miller, a former metal worker, was serving with the Royal Canadian Army Service Corps during the Italian Campaign. On the first Sunday in February 1945, the thirty-year-old private was on leave and en route to Rome. He was riding in a truck, heading south from Morciano, near San Marino, with some other men. They stopped at Chiaravalle, near Ancona, hoping to shop at the U.S. military store known as the NAAFI, but it was closed. So they found an Italian man who sold them six bottles of rum and a bottle of Cognac. During the seven-hour drive to Rome, the men ate pork sandwiches and oranges. They also got stinking drunk. Miller was "one of the most jovial" of the group, according to one of his army friends. The driver, Captain K.E. Slade, remembers the men "drinking fairly heavily" until the merrymakers eventually dozed off. As the party approached the outskirts of Rome, Miller was the only passenger who never woke up.

"I touched Private Miller's forehead, it was cold," said Lance Corporal Roland Barnabé, who later testified that Miller had also turned blue. "I felt for his pulse and could find none."[63]

An autopsy discovered large amounts of ethyl alcohol (drinking alcohol) in Miller's system; it also found methyl alcohol, which is poisonous. The court of inquiry ruled that Miller had been poisoned by contaminated alcohol. It has been known to occur with improperly bottled homemade gin and other spirits, especially rum. Miller's friends were asked to identify the Italian bootlegger, but the final report doesn't say whether the suspect was ever found.

The Canadian Jewish chaplain in Italy, Captain Isaac Rose, didn't tell Miller's family the details of the private's death; perhaps he did not know it himself. His condolence letter to his mother called Miller a hero. "Morris knew why he was ready to die. He would have told you that he gave his life so you might live. Life—happy, free and full cannot be without the death of Morris who made the supreme sacrifice."[64]

Missing his ship played a big role in the high-profile death of Charles Abelson of Montreal. In October 1942, Abelson, a well-known baseball and basketball star, was scheduled to take a troopship to Newfoundland. But the twenty-four-year-old overstayed his pre-embarkation leave in Halifax, a mistake his nephew, Charles P. Abelson, is convinced was because of a woman. "I met so many women in their nineties who claimed to have gone out with him," he said.

Abelson decided to get himself to his posting on board the civilian passenger ferry SS *Caribou*. It was leaving from Sydney, Nova Scotia, on October 13, making the night crossing to Port aux Basques, Newfoundland, with civilians and nearly 120 Allied personnel aboard.[65] U-boats had been sinking Allied ships in the area, and the navy sent a minesweeper along to serve as escort.[66] In the early hours of the next morning, U-69 torpedoed *Caribou* about sixty-five kilometres away from Newfoundland. One hundred thirty-seven people were killed, including thirty-five Canadians. Another hundred were rescued. Abelson's body was never found.

It wasn't the Germans who caused the drowning of nineteen-year-old Solomon Lavine in early June 1944 but rather the negligence of the skipper of an overcrowded excursion boat on Lake Erie.[67] Solly, as he was called, had worked in the mailroom of the *Calgary Albertan* newspaper before enlisting. He was studying to be an airframe mechanic at the RCAF Technical Training School in St. Thomas, Ontario.

The motor launch *Olga* offered hourly tours from the pier in Port Stanley on the lake's north shore about 15 kilometres from the base, and Lavine and some friends booked a 4 p.m. Sunday sailing. Local reports say the water was a bit rough, and *Olga* was having some engine problems. A kilometre and a half from shore, a wave capsized the boat, tossing the passengers into the cold water.[68] Seventeen people died, including Lavine. It took the RCAF's marine unit and the local fire department more than two weeks to recover his body.

A royal commission blamed co-owner Ted Vining for "gross negligence and incompetence"; the other co-owner had drowned in the sinking. The two had repeatedly ignored citations for overcrowding the vessel.[69] Vining was charged with manslaughter but was acquitted, although he was convicted for running afoul of wartime gas rationing regulations, for which he was fined $50.

No one was ever charged with the horrendous fire that killed ninety-nine people at the Knights of Columbus hostel in St. John's on December 12, 1942. St. John's was headquarters for the Royal Canadian Navy during the war, as well as home to a big United States military base, and the rec centre had an attached hostel with beds for off-duty personnel. The popular Harvey Road locale was packed that Saturday night when Toronto sergeant Max Goldstein turned up.

At 11 p.m., Newfoundlanders listening to the live broadcast of the show on VOCM Radio heard a singer performing "The Moonlight Trail," and then they heard screaming. A fire had broken out. Panic spread through the crowd when the discovery was made that the hostel had nailed plywood over the windows to comply with wartime blackout regulations. Also, the doors had inexplicably been installed to open inward, contrary to the building code. The frantic crowd could not escape.

Goldstein, a champion weightlifter and bodybuilder, and some other servicemen threw themselves against one of the locked doors. "He kept on slamming into the door until he finally broke it down," said Joe Greenberg, who had been sharing a bunk bed with Goldstein at the RCAF base in Torbay.

Ninety-nine people died, including Able Seaman Irving Epstein of Montreal. Epstein, formerly a well-known wrestler at the Montreal YMHA, was serving with HMCS *Orillia,* on convoy duty between Newfoundland and Ireland. At least a hundred people were injured in the fire. Goldstein stayed on the scene guarding the bodies of the victims at a local armoury until their next of kin arrived to identify them. The twenty-three-year-old cabled his own worried parents in Toronto to reassure them that they wouldn't have to confront the same wrenching experience. "Don't worry about me, folks, I'm feeling fine," he told them.

A subsequent judicial inquiry into the fire pointed the finger at German saboteurs who were thought to have lit it using toilet paper, although this has never been proven.[70] The judge also blamed shoddy construction.

A faulty bicycle led to the death of one of the Olfman brothers of Kamsack, Saskatchewan. The family had come to national attention in 1941, after newspapers across the country published a story describing the five siblings in uniform, including Solomon (Shia) Olfman, who was stationed in England with the Royal Canadian Artillery. His base was at Burton Rough, near Petworth, in the woodlands of South Downs National Park in West Sussex. The steep section of the road between Petworth and Chichester is known locally as the dangerous Duncton Down. It is thought to be the hill where the automaker Sir Henry Royce, co-founder of Rolls-Royce, once tested out his new cars.

In late July 1942, while most of the regiment was away on a training exercise, Olfman went for a ride on a friend's bicycle.[71] Witnesses say he was going very fast. The bicycle started wobbling, and Olfman tried to slow down. He smashed into the back of an army truck on a narrow section of Duncton Down. Olfman was thrown into a ditch, with the bike landing on top of him. Early the next morning, he died in a Canadian military hospital in Horsham of a fractured skull.

The Duncton police determined that only one front brake was working. "It is, in my opinion, unsafe to come down this hill on a cycle, without very efficient brakes," the investigator said. The army ruled Olfman's death "purely accidental." He was buried in the military cemetery at Brookwood, in Surrey.[72]

One hundred seventy-four Canadian airmen, including several Canadian Jews, died due to accidents involving motorcycles, cars, or trucks. Harry Ratner had done two years in the militia in Winnipeg before he enlisted with the RCAF.[73] In May 1944, having completed a full tour of operations in England as a bombardier in a bomber crew, Ratner and his friend, a pilot, decided that it was time to celebrate with a motorcycle ride. They found themselves south of Londonderry, in Yorkshire.[74] The pilot was driving; Ratner was on the back. The bike swerved to avoid an animal but hit an army truck parked on the road. Ratner fell off and hit his head. He died five hours later in a military hospital.[75] He was buried in Stonefall Jewish Cemetery in Harrogate, England, just south of the squadron's base.

A wedding celebration, bad weather, and bad judgement all combined to take the life of the only Canadian Jewish woman in uniform to die during the war. On the wintry evening of January 26, 1943, the Officers' Mess at the air base at Claresholm, Alberta, was hosting the nuptials of a pilot and a nursing sister. The wedding was big news; the local paper ran a story because it was the first marriage at the base between two officers.[76] The groom was Pilot Officer Charles A. Rainsforth, and the bride was Harriett Edith Broad. Section Officer Rose Goodman was the maid of honour.

After the strains of the song "Because" filled the room, the Protestant chaplain, Flight Lieutenant J.M. Roe, conducted the wedding ceremony. The newlyweds didn't get much time to enjoy the reception because a schedule change by Trans Canada Airlines (TCA) meant the couple had to scramble to catch their honeymoon flight to Vancouver.[77] The best man, Peter Douglas Meyers, volunteered to fly them to Lethbridge airport to catch a connecting flight. Rose Goodman went along to keep her friends company.[78]

Meyers had been a pilot in the RCAF for two years. He had graduated near the top of his class and was currently serving as an instructor. As they headed out in one of the base's Cessnas, Meyers experienced some mechanical trouble, but it cleared up and the plane landed safely in Lethbridge. "We stayed until P/O Rainsforth and Mrs. Rainsforth boarded the TCA aircraft and took off for Vancouver," Meyers would later tell an air force inquiry.

On the return trip to Claresholm, a cold front came in and blotted out visibility. "I decided to let down, with the intention of descending so far, and if I did not break through, return to Lethbridge," Meyers testified. After two or three minutes, something went wrong. The plane spiralled downward at 120 miles per hour. When he had plummeted to twelve hundred feet, Meyers "realized it was getting pretty serious, and told S/O Goodman to jump." He yelled at her for a second time to jump. She didn't. When he finally came out of the clouds, the Cessna's dive was "pretty bad." He saw some lights but didn't know where he was. He may have also run out of fuel. They crashed into a farmer's snow-covered field. Meyers passed out in the minus-twenty-degree Fahrenheit darkness. "The next thing I remembered, which must have been ten or fifteen minutes later, I got up. My ears were frozen. I'm not quite sure what I was doing," Meyers said. He checked the airplane. He called Rose's name a few times. There was no sign of her. Then he remembered the lights. He headed to get help, limping on a broken leg.

Hector Rose, a farmer, was at home with his family in Woodhouse, south of Claresholm. He had been listening to the eight o'clock radio newscast. "I heard the roar of an aeroplane, which seemed to be above the house," he would tell the local RCMP officer, Corporal F.J. Brailsford, who conducted the police investigation.[79] The family's German shepherd dog, Prince, started to bark. "I went outside and saw an RCAF officer coming across the yard from the east. He came in and said that he had crashed and asked to use the telephone," Hector said.

His daughter, Eleanor Sherman, was nine at the time. "He knocked on the door and my dad went and it scared us kids because [the pilot] broke his leg and he had blood on his face," said Sherman, who still lives near Claresholm. Meyers told the farmer there was "a lady travelling with him in the plane but he did not know what had happened to her." Sherman clearly recalls the injured pilot referring to Goodman as his "girlfriend."

The search party took about three hours to find the wreckage.[80] To this day, Sherman can't understand why it took so long. One of the other children told the men that their dog had been pointing east when Meyers showed up. "They wouldn't listen to my sister and they scanned every direction and east was the last place they looked, where the plane was," she said.

It was about "a half mile straight east of my house," her father later confirmed.

Goodman's body was brought back to base. The local coroner's office did an autopsy. The official RCAF court of inquiry interviewed twelve witnesses, including Meyers, who maintained that he'd had permission to take Rose with him. Although the final report wouldn't be finished until the end of February, Group Captain W.E. Kennedy didn't wait for it. Two days after the crash, Kennedy, the same senior officer who had praised Goodman and had recommended her for promotion, sent a telex to Ottawa. It said Goodman was on that plane without authorization. The RCMP concluded that the cause of the accident was bad weather.[81] The *Claresholm Local Press* reported that "[the plane] encountered severe icing conditions and became uncontrollable."[82]

Eleanor Sherman was told that Meyers was sent packing. "It was pretty bad because he took the plane without asking and he was let out of the service immediately," she said.

Another Nova Scotia mother would never be told the truth about her child's death in the war. Carl Fried from Glace Bay, a former carpet salesman, was serving in England as a dispatch rider with the Black Watch. He had a habit of going AWOL, but it was a legitimate leave in the summer of 1942 that made him seem—and probably feel—lucky.[83]

"Just came back from leave in Cardiff, Wales," he wrote home. "And while I was away my company saw action, you must have read about it, they are all missing."[84] His comrades had participated in the raid on Dieppe.

Fried went AWOL at least three times while in England, presumably spending the time with Miss Iris Emery of Cardiff. He lost a couple of weeks' worth of pay and was confined to barracks.[85] He told his sister Nina Cohen that he was "thinking of getting married but have not taken the plunge yet."[86]

He left a kitbag at Emery's house when he was sent to Italy in July 1943 with the twenty-five thousand Canadian troops involved in the invasion of Sicily. The mosquitoes were bad, and Fried came down with malaria, which kept him out of action for three months, missing big battles such as that for Ortona. In January 1944, then attached to the Seaforth Highlanders, Fried went AWOL again. After three weeks, he surrendered in Bari. It isn't clear if he was caught or came back of his own accord. He was court-martialled. The sentence was eighteen months in a military prison in Italy, with hard labour.

What happened in the next six weeks reads like the screenplay for a movie. While in prison, Fried pretended to sprain his ankle. They gave him a cane and then, on May 17, 1944, escorted him to hospital in Andria, near Bari, to have X-rays done. When the guard wasn't looking, Fried dropped the cane, made a break for it, and escaped in a truck that was heading west to Naples.[87]

A week later, on May 23, the Canadians broke through the so-called Hitler Line across the Liri Valley to open the road to Rome. The assault started at dawn with a creeping artillery barrage. By day's end the Seaforths were on their objective despite suffering the regiment's worst losses in a single day: fifty-two dead, the same number taken prisoner, and over a hundred wounded.[88] After the smoke and dust had cleared, Canadian patrols went out to collect the dead. That's when Lieutenant K.W. Reed discovered Fried's body. The regiment buried Fried with the other fallen Seaforths. A court of inquiry never did sort out how or why the Jewish soldier's body came to be on the front lines. The family was told nothing about Fried's troubled army history; they were told only that he had been killed in action.

In the end, the final report from Canada's top commander in Italy, Major General Chris Vokes, exonerated Fried and maintained the soldier's reputation: "I consider from the evidence that D-82925 Pte. Fried, C.M. was killed in action with his company and that his death was not due to improper conduct."[89]

11 Jewish Heroes

"I am on the objective. I'll hold her until you can come up"

The enterprising publicists at the Canadian Jewish Congress in Montreal must have been fans of the muscle-bound, square-jawed comic-book heroes gracing newsstands during the war years. Canadian teenagers couldn't get American comic books because of import restrictions, so they devoured stories about the exploits of homegrown characters including Nelvana of the Northern Lights, Johnny Canuck, Iron Man, and Canada Jack.[1] Nelvana, who debuted even before Wonder Woman did south of the border, is based on Inuit legends. She uses the power of the northern lights to defend Canada's north.[2] Iron Man came out in the spring of 1941; this Canadian original lived in the South Seas and surfaced to fight the Nazis and other villains.[3]

While Johnny Canuck fought against the Axis abroad, Canada Jack was a hero on the home front, fighting against saboteurs and German submarines.[4] Canada Jack was one of the most popular creations of a Montreal publishing house called Educational Projects, run by the Jewish businessman Harry J. Halperin. Halperin was already putting out *Canadian Heroes*, true-life comics profiling Canadian historical icons; *Canada Jack* was his first fictional series. The first issue appeared in the fall of 1943 and cost 10 cents. Soon, Canada Jack Clubs sprang up, inviting young readers to participate by helping the animators create the hero's next adventure.[5]

The War Efforts Committee at Congress headquarters in Montreal decided to launch a series of its own, called *Jewish War Heroes*. Officials hired two of the same graphic artists who had worked on *Canada Jack* and *Canadian Heroes*.[6] Between 1944 and 1945, Congress produced three black-and-white eight-page issues.[7] The aim was both to appeal to a young audience and to demonstrate to the wider Canadian public that Jews were serving with distinction and were doing their part to win the war.[8]

It was an unorthodox strategy but in keeping with Congress's overall marketing efforts. From Winnipeg to Toronto to Montreal, Congress publicists regularly collected stories about the exploits of Jewish men in uniform, and then issued press releases and photos that were subsequently picked up by both Jewish and the mainstream media.

The first *Jewish War Heroes* comic was published in February 1944. It introduced half a dozen Jewish heroes, but only one was a Canadian serving in a Canadian uniform. Squadron Leader Alfred Brenner of Toronto was credited with destroying a five-thousand-ton German merchant ship near the Frisian Islands off the coast the Netherlands in 1943. Brenner's own Hampden bomber was so badly shot up in the encounter that he and the crew had to ditch it into the North Sea. They spent forty-three hours in a dinghy, with no paddles and very little food and water, before being rescued.[9] Brenner won the Distinguished Flying Cross (DFC).

The other hero with a Canadian connection in the first issue was Sergeant Morris (Two Gun) Cohen, a veteran of World War I who had been serving in Hong Kong as a British military spy when he was captured by the Japanese in 1941. British-born Cohen spent seventeen years in Saskatchewan and Alberta after his parents sent him to Canada at the age of sixteen. He had been a juvenile delinquent back home, and although he continued his shady ways in Canada, he also became wealthy through real estate speculation. Cohen moved to China after World War I, where he worked as an adviser to the revolutionary leader Sun Yat-sen. When the Japanese invaded Hong Kong in the fall of 1941, Cohen was captured, tortured, and interned.[10] He spent nearly two years as a prisoner of war in the same Stanley internment camp as Ursula (Girlie) Macklin and her daughter, Bonita, and like them, he was released in the same prisoner exchange and sent to North America by ship on September 23, 1943.[11]

The second issue depicted five more Jewish war heroes, and again only one was serving in a Canadian uniform. This time, it was the most highly decorated Canadian Jew of World War II: Flight Lieutenant Sydney Shulemson, who had won the Distinguished Service Order

(DSO) in 1944, which is the medal just below a Victoria Cross, and would win a DFC in 1945.

Shulemson, the son of a Montreal dry cleaner, began his overseas combat career in July 1943 with a Royal Canadian Air Force Coastal Command squadron strategically based in northeastern Scotland. Five hundred kilometres across the North Sea was Norway—its high-walled fjords perfect hiding places for German merchant ships carrying valuable cargo to the Reich. Shulemson's No. 404 Squadron patrolled the air over the North Sea, looking for German naval convoys below. He shot down a German flying boat on his very first operational mission.[12]

The citation for his DSO praised him for displaying "inspiring leadership, great skill and courage."[13] He won it after a mission on January 26, 1944, at the controls of a Beaufighter leading a dozen Allied fighter planes off the coast of Norway. They sank a minesweeper and damaged four other German vessels while under intense fire from shore-based anti-aircraft batteries and Messerschmitt pilots. Shulemson could have made it safely back to Scotland but turned around to help one of the other Beaufighters, which was being chased by the enemy. The Germans went after Shulemson instead, as he had hoped, and Shulemson fought for his life, swooping in and out of clouds for twenty minutes trying to escape.[14] Eventually the German gave up. "Many congratulations and drinks to a badly scared crew" was the entry in Shulemson's logbook after their return to base.

Shulemson became famous not only for his bravery but also for perfecting a new method of attacking enemy ships. Until then, Coastal Command had relied on Beaufighters equipped with single torpedoes, but firing them gave the pilots only one chance to sink a ship.[15] Shulemson switched to multiple unguided rockets that were mounted to the underside of his aircraft's wings. His technique of aiming and firing by calculating exact angles and speeds at which crews could release the rockets in sequence proved to be deadly. The rockets would hit the enemy ship below the waterline, piercing the hull, causing it to sink. Other rockets would hit the deck and explode. Shulemson is credited with sinking at least a dozen enemy ships, although he maintained it was a lucky thirteen.[16]

The last issue of Congress's *Jewish War Heroes* comic series was an all-Canadian edition. It featured some men who had been awarded medals and others who had not, including Lieutenant Colonel David Croll, the former Windsor mayor and Ontario Cabinet minister, who graced the cover and was profiled in the first two pages.

The two downed airmen honoured in the comic's middle spread didn't win medals either. Flying Officer Max Shvemar, a Montreal accountant, was a navigator. His pilot, Flying Officer Lou Somers, was a business writer with the *Financial Post* in Toronto. The Jewish duo flew in a crew of seven on a Halifax bomber attached to the RCAF No. 427 "Lion" Squadron out of Leeming, North Yorkshire.

Somers and Shvemar were crewed up in the spring of 1943, at the start of the Royal Air Force's strategic four-month-long heavy bombing campaign against the industrial cities in Germany's Ruhr Valley.[17] On one mission that June, Somers and his crew accidentally went off course and wound up alone over Essen, where German searchlights "coned" them and German anti-aircraft guns tore into their plane from below.[18] Somers later described to a Toronto *Evening Telegram* war correspondent—in air force slang—how he saved himself and the crew. "I sure weaved that kite all over the sky. The Halifax was holed twenty times. Both inboard motors were hit but luckily they didn't conk, while the starboard rudder, fuselage and mainplane also took a severe beating," he said.[19]

Somers's flying skills, however, wouldn't be enough to save his entire crew on what would be its final mission just a few weeks later. On June 24, 1943, ten Halifax crews from their squadron bombed Wuppertal, east of Dusseldorf, destroying 171 factories and three thousand homes and killing eighteen hundred people.[20] Somers's plane was hit, but he kept flying north toward the coast, even upside down, to give the others time to bail out. The plane crashed into the sea off the coast of Holland.[21] Two crewmen survived and were taken prisoner.[22] The bodies of Shvemar and the British flight engineer were recovered and buried in Rotterdam. Somers's body and that of another missing crewman were not found until 1967.[23]

The comic ends with three decorated Jewish Canadian war heroes. On the back page is Petty Officer Max Abramson of Calgary, who served as the senior enlisted man in the torpedo room of HMCS *St. Croix*. In mid-July 1942, *St. Croix* was escorting a convoy of merchant ships from Londonderry to St. John's. The thirty-three freighters had delivered their vital cargo to the British war effort and were making the trip home across the North Atlantic.[24] About 475 nautical miles east of Newfoundland lurked a pack of eleven German submarines.[25] The Canadian escorts knew they were there thanks to Allied shore-based intelligence operators who had intercepted the German radio transmissions using HF/DF equipment.[26] On July 23, the crew of *St. Croix* spotted a submarine that had closed in on the convoy and gave chase.[27] Abramson's ship attacked, dropping depth charges on three separate confrontations with the U-boat. It was the third salvo that crushed the submarine.[28] It was the Royal Canadian Navy's third "kill" of the Battle of the Atlantic.[29] The remaining wolf pack hunted the convoy for the rest of the voyage west and sank five of the thirty-three cargo vessels before orders came from German headquarters to abandon the chase. For sinking the sub, Abramson received a Mention in Dispatches in the *London Gazette* in December 1942.[30]

Page 6 is devoted to Major Ben Dunkelman of the Queen's Own Rifles. The Toronto clothing manufacturer had already distinguished himself in the invasion of Normandy.[31] Dunkelman earned the nicknames "Mr. Mortar" and "Shoot a Million" for having his mortar crews shoot as many as twenty shells each at an enemy position. Dunkelman's DSO came in the spring of 1945, during Operation Blockbuster and the battle to capture the Balberger forest near the Rhine. According to his citation, the officer destroyed two enemy machine guns by firing his anti-tank gun and then led his men forward: "Dunkelman personally killed 10 of the enemy with his pistol and with his bare hands, all the time shouting to his men to press forward and to the enemy to 'Come out and fight.'"[32]

The final hero of the comic book, Flight Lieutenant William Henry Nelson of Montreal, didn't wear a Canadian uniform, although he had tried to. Of the three thousand Commonwealth airmen to serve in the RAF during the Battle of Britain, Nelson was the only Jewish Canadian, although British government records have him down as Church of England.[33] He was also the first Jewish Canadian to win a DFC in World War II.[34]

After he graduated from Strathcona Academy, where he was known by his nickname Orville Wright, his parents—who operated a small grocery store—couldn't afford to send him to university. So Nelson went to work as a draftsman at the Fairchild aircraft plant in Longueuil; he also took flying lessons there. His application to join the RCAF in 1936 was unsuccessful. His family says it was due to colour-blindness, but the aviation historian Hugh Halliday says it was more likely because the RCAF was so tiny in the interwar years that it barely accepted any new personnel.[35] By the fall of 1939, however, with England poised for war, Nelson worked his way overseas on a merchant ship and the RAF took him as a pilot.

He flew Whitley bombers from RAF Dishforth, near Leeds, and the crew participated in some of the RAF's earliest air operations against Germany. By 1940, after Hitler had invaded Norway and Denmark and captured Holland and France, Nelson bombed German-held railway yards, seaplane bases, and airport runways. A mission in April of that year won him his DFC. He had seen a German barrage balloon west of Stavanger, Norway. His radioed warning is credited with saving the lives of the other British aircrews in the vicinity; they were able to avoid the deadly metal cable that could be hazardous to attacking or strafing airplanes.[36]

After the RAF put out an urgent call for fighter pilots in June 1940, Nelson volunteered to fly Spitfires. He joined the Battle of Britain at the end of July 1940, and by October, Nelson was battling Messerschmitt 109s (known as Me109s) in dogfights over the skies of southern England, sometimes taking off several times a day. Nelson would be credited with shooting down or damaging seven enemy aircraft during that tense summer and fall. That made him an Ace, as five kills were considered the threshold for the title.[37]

On November 1, Nelson's squadron was scrambled to meet a large wave of incoming German fighters over Dover. Although he was supposed to be on extended leave, Nelson had come back to lend a hand. By then he was the highest-scoring Canadian Spitfire pilot in the campaign.[38]

"At the time, all of his buddies were being killed, and I think it's like being on a football team and you're playing a game and you're exhausted and you buggered your knee, but you still got to win the game so you don't think about your own well-being," his son Bill McAlister said.

Nelson's Spitfire was shot up. It went down into the English Channel. His English wife, Marjorie, waited for news at her mother's home in Cotherstone, north of Leeds. "His plane got hit and a friend who saw him go into the water—'into the drink,' as they call it—thought that maybe he would have managed to get out and swim to shore," McAlister said. "He was a very good swimmer and she lived in hope of that for a few days."

Nelson's body was never recovered. Back in Montreal, his mother, Sarafina, would receive a letter that her son had written before his death.

It remains a powerful testament to the role he would fulfill in the Battle of Britain. "I thank God that I shall be able to help to destroy the regime that persecutes the Jews," he said. "I have never had such a great desire to live as I do now; nevertheless if I leave whilst flying, I am happy in the thought that I am helping to crush Hitler."[39]

A fourth comic in the series was supposed to be called "Some Never Die."[40] The entire issue was going to be devoted to Sergeant Samuel Moses (Moe) Hurwitz, of Lachine, Quebec. Despite his low rank, he became the most highly decorated non-commissioned Jewish Canadian soldier in the Royal Canadian Armoured Corps. For his gallantry in France, Belgium, and Holland in 1944, Hurwitz won the Military Medal and the Distinguished Conduct Medal, which is just below the Victoria Cross for non-commissioned men.[41] Although the proofs for the comic book are in the Alex Dworkin Canadian Jewish Congress Archives in Montreal, there is no evidence that that issue of *Jewish War Heroes* was ever published.

Moe Hurwitz was one of thirteen children born to an immigrant from England, Chaim Hurwitz, and his Latvian-born wife, Bella.[42] The family observed Jewish laws and customs, although the boys would sneak out to watch cricket and football and hockey games on Saturday afternoons after synagogue. The children experienced antisemitism in Lachine, where bullies chased the girls off a tennis court for being Jewish. Chaim was once arrested for assaulting a man who made pro-Hitler remarks. The judge sided with Hurwitz but fined him $2.

Moe quit high school after one year to go out to work. Later he and another brother tried to get jobs at the Dominion Bridge Company, but their Jewish-sounding last name was a problem at first. "So they get up at six o'clock Monday morning. My mother says to my brothers Moe and Max, 'Maybe you'll get lucky, go there,'" Harry Hurwitz recalled. At the hiring office, they took men named Cutty, then Smith, then Johnson, but when it came to Hurwitz, his brothers were told, "We'll let you know."

Moe Hurwitz was, however, a well-known athlete—a Golden Glove boxing champion at the YMHA and a very good hockey right-winger who also played defence. A Dominion Bridge company executive was the coach of the Lachine Rapides, a team in the Quebec Provincial Hockey League, so Moe was hired and also given a spot on the company's hockey team. In the 1939–40 season, he helped the team make the finals, which Lachine lost to Sherbrooke.[43] "They practised like the

[Montreal] Canadiens do during the season," Harry Hurwitz remembers, although he says Moe didn't get much ice time.

Moe even caught the eye of a Canadian star on the Boston Bruins, Milt Schmidt, and was invited to Boston for a tryout. The family says Moe gave up his shot at a professional NHL career. "There's no time to play hockey when millions of my brothers are getting killed in Europe," Moe reportedly told Schmidt.

Moe enlisted in the army after the end of the hockey season in June 1940. He told the Grenadier Guards in Montreal that "patriotism" was his reason for joining.[44] After two years of training in Canada and two more in England, Hurwitz and his tank troop were eager to see action. By the end of April 1944, Moe had an even more personal reason for wanting to get to Germany; his brother Harry was a prisoner of war. "He tried to fight the whole German army to get to me," Harry Hurwitz said.

Moe Hurwitz's legend grew along with a fierce-looking moustache. His feats of courage were on full display from the day his regiment landed in France in July 1944.[45] As the 22nd Armoured (formerly known as the Grenadier Guards) tanks broke out of Caen and began the push south toward Falaise in mid-August, Hurwitz's men saw their sergeant leap out of his tank to flush out German snipers hiding in a village and take them prisoner.[46] That earned Moe a nomination for his first bravery award.

The second one came out of his actions six weeks later during the fighting to capture the area around Breskens, at the mouth of Holland's Western Scheldt estuary. The Allies needed to oust the Germans from the approaches to Antwerp in order to use the vital port, and when Hurwitz and his men came under attack at a town called Sluiskil, he wiped out a machine-gun crew that was hiding in a farmhouse. An officer who was there says Hurwitz gave "a great shout," jumped up, kicked in the door, and sprayed the interior. "Forcing the Germans to go back with him, he turns [twenty-three prisoners] over to the infantry." Later that day, the Germans shelled Hurwitz's tank—which he had named Geraldine—and it caught fire. Despite suffering from burns, Hurwitz scrambled into another tank, fired back, and put a German gun out of action. Then he carried out two rescues, including pulling a soldier out of another burning tank.

Hurwitz's luck ran out a month later. It was the day the commanding officer told him that he had won the Military Medal. "Well, sir," Hurwitz had reportedly replied modestly, "I'm mighty glad because the boys will know that their work has been appreciated."

The target was Wouwse Plantage, about forty kilometres north of Antwerp. After several unsuccessful attacks, the Canadian tank squadrons tried again at night. Hurwitz's was the first tank to make it through. Five hundred yards behind enemy lines, he sent his final radio transmission at 5:15 in the morning of October 24. "I am on the objective. I'll hold her until you can come up."[47]

After sunup, the Canadians went to look for Hurwitz's tank. A second tank crew was also missing. Hurwitz's pay book was recovered about sixteen kilometres to the north.[48]

"He was shot through the right lung after getting out of his tank," Guardsman Herb Poole reported after the war. Poole was one of the nine men captured with Hurwitz. "His tank was hit two or three times before they bailed out. He was delirious."

The Germans took Hurwitz across the Moerdijk Bridge to a German-run hospital at Dordrecht, south of Rotterdam, where he died two days later. His family was devastated but not surprised. Before Moe had left Canada, he'd bade them goodbye. "He told my brother, 'I won't be coming back, I'm going to get killed,'" Harry said.

Major Ivan Phelan recalled a similar conversation with Moe back in England, when the sergeant vowed that he would never let himself be taken prisoner because he feared what they would do to a Jew. It appears that the sergeant kept that promise. Hurwitz died before the Germans could register his name on an official POW list. Phelan called Hurwitz a man of "courage and steadfastness and human-ness (to coin a word) that put to shame the tinsel heroes of the silver screen."[49]

When the war ended, the Canadian Jewish Congress stopped issuing the comic books. Instead, in 1947 they published a catalogue listing the awards and citations won by nearly two hundred Canadian Jews who had served. Most were awards from the United Kingdom, but some came from Allied governments including the Netherlands and the United States. Moe Hurwitz received more ink than anyone else in that catalogue, including Shulemson and Dunkelman combined.

Like Moe Hurwitz, nearly a dozen of the Canadian Jewish medal winners didn't survive long enough to receive their hardware. One Canadian who was able attend his award ceremony, however, was David Lloyd Hart of Montreal. In November 1942, he was honoured with a medal for transmitting the retreat orders that saved many Canadians on the beaches of Dieppe. Hart admits his military training was no help for his nerves at Buckingham Palace. He messed up during his brief time with King George VI, a man who had had to overcome a debilitating speech impediment. "He pinned a medal on my chest. He talked to me for about five minutes. The only thing I remember, instead of saying 'Your Majesty' I said 'Sir,' which was okay since he was an officer in the army. I was stuttering, and not him," Hart admitted.

Although there were no photographs allowed during the ceremony, news cameras show a still-nervous and unsmiling Hart leaving the royal palace with his brothers Paul and Edwin, both also in uniform.[50] Captain Paul Hart, an army officer with the Royal 22nd Regiment, later received a Mention in Dispatches for his actions in Italy.[51]

The Hart brothers were among eight Canadian Jewish families in which two sons won honours. Captain Leo and Lieutenant David Heaps were the only Jewish brothers in Canada to both win the Military Cross.[52] David won his medal for action on the Goch–Calcar Road inside Germany in February 1945, in the same battle in which Bill Walsh and his men were trapped in the cellar of a German farmhouse.[53] Lieutenant Heaps and his artillery unit's self-propelled guns were credited with knocking out seven German Panther tanks.[54]

Captain Leo Heaps would take command of a British paratroop unit, even before the twenty-two-year-old Canadian had the opportunity to jump out of an airplane.[55] His first chance came during Operation Market Garden in September 1944. The Germans captured him a week later, along with six thousand British, American, and Polish troops.[56] Heaps escaped with the help of the Dutch underground, then accepted a job rescuing 150 of the men left behind, in what is now known as Operation Pegasus I and II.[57] He was recognized at a ceremony at Rideau Hall in Ottawa in December 1946.[58]

At least thirty-five Canadian Jewish doctors and medical specialists earned a spot on the King's honour lists or won medals from other Allied countries. Maxwell Lerner had come to Winnipeg in 1920 from Yednitz, Bessarabia.[59] After graduating from the University of Winnipeg in 1934, during the Depression Lerner worked as a doctor at government-run work camps for single unemployed men, where living conditions were poor and the men earned just 20 cents a day for clearing brush and building roads.[60] Then Lerner worked as a public health physician until 1942, when he enlisted in the Royal Canadian Army Medical Corps.

He was attached to the Hastings and Prince Edward Regiment, or Hasty Ps, who were in Italy struggling to cross a series of canals and ditches between the Lamone and Senio Rivers, in the winter of 1943. On December 12, the regiment was ordered to capture Canale Naviglio in Bagnacavallo; to get there, they had to cross a large ditch known as the Fosso Vecchio. There were no bridges in place, rendering Captain Lerner's field ambulances useless. "[Lerner] therefore quickly reorganized his regimental aid post, and moved off on foot with the battalion, man-packing his equipment. The whole advance was made under intermittent but heavy shelling," said the citation for Lerner's Mention in Dispatches. He set up his makeshift clinic in an Italian house just a football field and a half away from the shooting. "Captain Lerner's decision to establish his post forward of the Fosso meant the difference between life and death to many of the wounded men."[61]

Joe Minden of Hamilton received the Silver Star for bravery from the American president Franklin D. Roosevelt himself, for service with a medical battalion of a U.S. infantry unit during the storming of the Alaskan island of Attu in 1943. The eighteen-day-long battle ended with a surprise Japanese counterattack at dawn on May 29 that left hundreds of American troops wounded or dead. Minden had tried to warn his superiors the night before not to bivouac on an exposed plateau near the Japanese camp. He kept some of the men farther below with him for the night.

"We were wakened by yelling and screaming.... Our men got up on the plateau and their job was to bind up the wounds of the men who got shot in headquarters company and to evacuate to the sea shore where we had a hospital ship," Minden told his family later. "So we began binding up the wounds, I remember my best friend had a bullet hole, right through his forehead."[62] Minden worked for thirty-six straight hours supervising the evacuation of casualties.

The Aleutian events are only a part of the intense war journey that Minden described in the handwritten diary he kept through the major American battles of the Pacific. He was wounded in action in the Kwajalein Atoll in the Marshall Islands, and he was in the invasion of the Leyte Gulf in the Philippines, and at Okinawa. Minden carried out more than 780 surgeries, including twenty-six amputations, and was responsible for nearly ten thousand patients.[63] According to his family, Minden is also credited with inventing a new kind of battlefield stretcher.

He won a Purple Heart and a Bronze Star and earned two Presidential Citations.

Although he did not receive any medals, the family of the former watchmaker Murray Jacobs considered him a hero. When the commanding officer of the Second Canadian Corps, Lieutenant General Guy Simonds, wanted to make it safer for Canadian infantrymen in Normandy to travel into battle, Jacobs helped made it happen. For three days in August 1944, under the blazing sun in a French orchard near Bayeux, Jacobs and the men of the division's engineering repair workshop invented the prototype of today's armoured personnel carriers. They took the gun turrets off seventy-five tanks, removed the aiming devices—Jacobs's particular specialty—and then reinforced the sides. They nicknamed the new vehicles Kangaroos, for the protection they offered the infantry who rode inside.[64] Each one had enough room to transport ten soldiers safely. The Kangaroos took part in Operation Totalize, south of Caen, hours later, and their crews suffered significantly fewer battle casualties than the infantry who walked.[65]

Countless other acts of valour have gone unrecorded. Veterans Affairs Canada points out that it wasn't possible to track every gallant action. "While individual acts of great courage occur frequently during war, only a few are seen and recorded," the department acknowledges, explaining why only sixteen Victoria Crosses were awarded to Canadians during World War II.[66]

Charles Krakauer didn't get a medal for his efforts on the battlefield in Italy, but he was honoured in Canadian author Farley Mowat's wartime memoir, *And No Birds Sang*.[67] Krakauer grew up in an Orthodox Jewish home in Toronto, and his siblings worked to help put him through medical school. Like Maxwell Lerner, Krakauer ran a regimental aid post for the Hasty Ps in Italy, where one of his patients was Lieutenant Mowat. In his book, Mowat says that Krakauer purposely positioned the medical station close to the battlefield. "They helped me to the Regimental Aid Post which the medical officer Captain Charlie Krakauer had pushed forward to the doubtful shelter of a ruined hovel on the very lip of the valley," Mowat writes.[68]

"If you can get to them within the first hour, the likelihood of your being able to save their life is much higher," Krakauer's nephew, Howard Tenenbaum, explained. "He wouldn't have known about that, per se, at least in those terms, but he knew the closer they were to the front, the better it was."

During the Battle for the Moro River in December 1943, the Hasty Ps came under heavy fire, slipping in the muck along the banks of the rain-swollen waterway near Bagnacavallo. They lost about 150 men in 36 hours and had many wounded. Krakauer treated Mowat on December 6 for an injury to his foot.

"You lucky little prick! Shell cut your boot open from end to end and hardly creased the skin," Krakauer told Mowat with a "lopsided" grin. "Wait till we get a Band-Aid on it and you can go right back to work."

When Mowat tried to sit up, he remembered feeling a terrific pain shoot up his rear end. Krakauer took a closer look. "Then a bellow of raucous laughter burst from him," as the doctor pulled a piece of steel casing out from the fleshy part of his patient's behind. "Keep this in memory of me," Krakauer told Mowat, handing him the bloody souvenir.

The unit moved into the area known as the Gully. Soon it was December 22; Mowat was looking forward to Christmas. "Only three more shooting days to Christmas," the men joked. Then a German eight-inch shell flew over the bivouac area and landed on the aid post.[69] There was nothing left of Krakauer or his staff. Krakauer's family later arranged for the Latin motto *Pro Utilitate Hominum* to be engraved on his tombstone in the Moro River Canadian War Cemetery. It means "For the Service of Mankind."

British military tradition likely played a role in who received what kind of awards. Some medals were reserved for officers; some went just to enlisted men. Most could only be awarded if the person was alive.

Joseph Bodnoff of Ottawa probably wasn't thinking about whether he would win a medal when he was trying to revive his stricken pilot. They were in a dinghy in rough swells more than three hundred kilometres off the coast of Norway. Bodnoff was a wireless operator and air gunner on a Catalina flying boat, and he spotted a German U-boat during a patrol on June 24, 1944. His pilot, David Hornell, went in for the attack.[70] Bodnoff blasted away from his portside gun position. They sank the sub, but the Catalina was also fatally hit.[71] Hornell managed to crash-land on the water, and the eight-man crew found themselves adrift with only one useable raft. They had to take turns sitting in it while the others clung to the sides in the rough, cold water. As the hours ticked by, some of the men died of exposure.

When they were rescued the following evening, Bodnoff was tending to the pilot, but Hornell didn't make it.[72] For his "unsparing…efforts to assist others in spite of his own distressed condition," Bodnoff received a Distinguished Flying Medal. Hornell, a flight lieutenant, and thus two ranks higher than Bodnoff, would get the Victoria Cross, which could be awarded posthumously.[73]

Only one rank separated two Canadians who won medals from the famous Battle for Ortona in Italy in December 1943. Captain Paul Triquet won a Victoria Cross for capturing the farm hamlet known as Casa Berardi on December 14, 1943. Lieutenant Mitchell Sterlin, meanwhile, didn't live to receive the bravery medal he had been promised for a similar feat days earlier.

Sterlin grew up in Montreal, where his parents ran a grocery store on Décarie Boulevard. As a biochemistry student at McGill University he joined the Canadian Officers' Training Corps; he was later offered a spot in medical school, despite the quota system in place, but he deferred his acceptance and enlisted. When the Canadians landed in Sicily in July 1943, Sterlin was with them, attached to the Royal Canadian Regiment (RCR).[74] Although his fellow officers liked him, some were less than flattering in their evaluation of his military appearance. He was "stocky, perpetually overweight, and renowned for his clumsiness."[75] Indeed, Sterlin had done poorly at officers' school on the obstacle course and always came last in long-distance running.

On the night in question, he and some of his men were holed up in a two-storey farmhouse situated just south of Ortona at San Donato-Moro. They hadn't heard the order to retreat, and all night, German Panzergrenadiers fired machine guns at their shelter; one enemy officer even came right up to the windows to toss in grenades.[76] Although they were seriously outnumbered, Sterlin and the ten men with him fought back until morning. The German attackers ran out of ammunition and moved off, leaving the bodies of their dead piled up around the outside of the house.[77] Hours later, Sterlin and the survivors of his platoon were able to leave the farmhouse, renamed Sterlin Castle by the military, and reunite with their unit.[78]

Sterlin's superiors in the RCR immediately nominated him for a Military Cross, which can be awarded to officers with the rank of captain and below. Due to the ongoing fighting, the paperwork wasn't sent out right away, and ten days later a German sniper killed Sterlin while the Canadians were trying to secure a key junction outside Ortona.

Back home in Canada, Sterlin's parents learned their son was up for a prestigious medal.

"Our adjutant has asked me to pass on to you that he feels sure that in this case the award will be made without any difficulty," Captain Philip Dagnall told them, although he did advise them Sterlin's death complicated things, because the medal wasn't usually awarded posthumously.[79] The well-meaning officer's prediction came to pass. The historian Jack Granatstein writes that Sterlin was "shamefully awarded only a Mention in Dispatches" in January 1945.[80]

A retired Royal Canadian Regiment career soldier, Jack O'Brien of Kingston, Ontario, has spent years working to keep Sterlin's heroism in the public eye. O'Brien and other veterans raised $15,000 in the early 1990s to commission a painting showing the defence of Sterlin Castle. The artwork, by a Calgary-based artist, now hangs in an officers' mess at the Canadian Forces Base at Petawawa, Ontario, the current home of the RCR's 1st Battalion. A copy is in the Canadian War Museum. A memorial plaque in English and Italian was also commissioned and sent to the current owners of the Italian farmhouse outside of Ortona, who installed it on a cairn outside their building. O'Brien says that Sterlin deserved the Victoria Cross, which he could have won posthumously, and blames the culture of the Royal Canadian Regiment at the time. "The RCR were very stingy giving the medals," O'Brien said, explaining that in the minds of senior officers, bravery during wartime was expected. He calls it a "they were just doing their job" attitude.

A similar thing happened to Warrant Officer Jacob Silverstein in September 1943. He'd earned front-page newspaper headlines across Canada for participating in a two-day air-sea battle. Six Liberator long-range patrol aircraft from Gander, Newfoundland, had spent tense hours protecting a naval convoy making its way to Europe. Silverstein's plane carried a high-ranking visitor with them into action: Air Vice-Marshall A.E. Godfrey, who was in Gander for an inspection, had decided to join in as an extra gunner. He liked the way Silverstein handled himself during the action, and the Jewish airman was recommended for an Air Force Medal.

"This NCO [non-commissioned officer] has been an inspiration to the Junior Air Gunners in his squadron over a long period, and his action in this engagement is worthy of the highest praise," the award document read, citing Silverstein's 114 operational sorties.[81] Although he was certainly eligible for the medal, and the paperwork was marked "IMMEDIATE," it wasn't processed.

A few weeks later, on October 23, 1943, Silverstein and twenty-three others, all highly experienced airmen going on leave, took off from Gander on a flight to Ottawa. They never made it. After Silverstein went missing, someone in Gander pushed through the old paperwork for his medal. The new station commander, Group Captain Clare Annis, said that although Silverstein certainly deserved a decoration, it would be downgraded to a Mention in Dispatches.[82] He said it wasn't policy to award the medal to someone who was missing. The wreckage of their Liberator wasn't discovered for three years; it had hit a mountain near St-Donat, Quebec, in bad weather.[83]

While military tradition was the cause of some heroes receiving lesser awards or none at all, there was the lingering suspicion that antisemitism often played a role, too. Rubin Bider of the South Saskatchewan Regiment (SSR) was always convinced that is why he never won a bravery medal. In mid-July 1944, the Winnipegger landed in Normandy, where he took part as a private in Operation Atlantic, the Canadian portion of Montgomery's much larger Operation Goodwood, south of Caen. "I guess if my name had been James M. Smith, I would have got a ribbon," Bider is quoted as saying in Alexander McKee's *Caen: Anvil of Victory.*

The operation began July 18. Bider's regiment was sent to capture the ninety-metre-high Verrières Ridge.[84] The attack went ahead despite a heavy downpour in which the air force couldn't fly. The artillery remained idle, and there were no tanks to help out. Although the SSR had gone to ground in trenches dug into fields of peas and potatoes, German tanks and infantry were soon causing havoc.[85] There were over two hundred casualties, including some sixty men killed. The order came to bring out the wounded and retreat. Bider, whose nickname was Beansy, was asked to fend off the advancing Germans while the rest of his company escaped. He collected a Bren gun, two Thompson submachine guns, and two rifles. He used them all.

"He was kind of caught behind in a raid," explained the veteran Oscar Antel, who knew Bider from Winnipeg and had heard about his exploits.

"He really didn't know what he was doing and he jumped into a trench and as he jumped in [the Germans] all gave up, so he got decorated and marched them all into a camp."

Bider was convinced that his regiment had nominated him for the Distinguished Conduct Medal for his Johnny Canuck-style heroics. Unfortunately, a gushing mention by the *Winnipeg Free Press* was all the praise he would get. The story described Bider as "the only Jewish lad in his outfit" who could "dish it out to anything Hitler's 272 division has to offer."[86] After Bider's death in 1982, a book about Jewish veterans described him as "A Hero Without a Medal."[87]

Conversely, Harold Fromstein thinks of his gallantry hardware as a medal without a hero. The Toronto veteran was one of the few soldiers in the Black Watch to survive the assault on the same Verrières Ridge just one week later, on July 25, 1944, which left 315 casualties.[88] Fromstein, a private, was seriously wounded in the head and chest by machine-gun fire, captured, and held at a German military hospital for POWs in Rennes, France, where he was afraid the medical staff would discover he was Jewish. Within ten days, the Americans liberated Rennes, and Fromstein was sent to England for medical treatment.

He was sent back into action in January 1945, and earned a Military Medal for his bravery in the Battle for the Hochwald Forest. He carried stretchers back from the front lines, while under fire himself.[89] "Everybody was a stretcher bearer when somebody got hurt," he said modestly.

When the military announced it was awarding the medal to the Canadian private named Albert Fromstein, Harold didn't tell them they'd given it to the wrong person. He had used his older brother's Albert's identification papers to enlist in 1940, because Harold was only seventeen at the time. He'd even travelled to Montreal, where no one knew him, to sign up, answering as Albert all through the war in Europe, and again when he volunteered to serve in Japan.[90]

Fromstein would eventually enjoy some public recognition for his bravery, first in Congress's 1947 book of decorations, and again nearly seventy years later in a 2014 article in the *National Post*.[91] But the hero, who has been called an "Angel of the Battlefield," has never asked to have the official record corrected. "You know, you were so lucky to have two legs and two arms and two eyes," Fromstein said. "I felt the same way there, that if I can get through here, I'm not going to look for anything, any pat on the back. I was one of the lucky ones, I think."

12 Keeping the Faith

"I always had a Bible with me"

In May 1944, David Molot was a sergeant working at the 5th Casualty Clearing Station near Ceprano, Italy, when an ambulance brought in a gravely wounded Canadian Jewish signaller.[1] Private Simon Isenstein had stepped on a mine.[2] "He asked me to write a letter to his family to tell them he was OK," Molot writes in his memoir. "However, I looked up his history file which explained his condition and I knew at once that he wasn't going to make it."[3]

A few days later, Isenstein died in Molot's arms. The thirty-two-year-old medic commandeered a Jeep, found a Jewish chaplain, and brought him back to officiate at Isenstein's burial. After the war, Molot contacted his own relatives in Western Canada to ask them to let the boy's grieving parents in Calgary know that their son had been buried as a Jew. "[Molot] was like Radar O'Reilly looking for things to do to help," according to his son, John Molot, referring to a character in the 1970s American television show *M*A*S*H*, about a mobile army field hospital in Korea. Molot was doing more than just helping. The Ottawa druggist was performing a sacred final act of Jewish loving-kindness for Isenstein, known as *Chesed Shel Emeth*, or giving a loved one a Jewish burial. That Molot would go to significant lengths to carry out the rituals of his faith while in a battle zone speaks to the deeply held values that many Jews in uniform carried with them into the war.

At the time in Canada, most Jewish residents were first- or second-generation Canadians whose parents or grandparents had come from Eastern Europe and still kept observant homes.[4] For most veterans and their relatives interviewed for this book, that meant regular attendance at synagogue—if not every Sabbath, then at least on the major Jewish holidays of Rosh Hashanah, Yom Kippur, and Passover. At home, there would be kosher kitchens with two sets of dishes: one for dairy foods, the other for meat. And most of the young men had had bar mitzvahs when they turned thirteen.

Most Jewish servicemen and some servicewomen reported having received some form of supplementary Jewish religious education: either learning with independent Jewish teachers who would come to their homes or attending the formal religious schools known as Cheders, such as the Talmud Torah in Montreal where Royal Canadian Air Force Flying Officer Harry Knobovitch studied, or the Euclid Avenue Talmud Torah in Toronto where Army veteran Manny Rubinoff took his religious studies after school. Even the more secular Jewish families, including those from the socialist and communist circles, sent their children to supplementary schools such as Calgary's I.L. Peretz School, where they learned about Jewish culture.

There were certainly variations in how strictly the uniformed personnel had adhered to the rituals of their faith while growing up, but being Jews in the military put them in a unique position, as they either had to compromise their religious, cultural, and family values to serve their country or they had to find ways to fulfill multiple obligations at once.

Leaving Montreal to serve in the Canadian Army was Harry Kaushansky's first shock. Coping with the menu when he got to the army base in Huntingdon, Quebec, was the second. Kaushansky had grown up in a family of Russian immigrants, and his mother, Zissel, faithfully washed and salted her own meats to adhere to the biblical Jewish dietary laws. When Harry was called up in 1941, mealtime at the basic training camp posed a challenge. "When I first got into the army, I spent all my time eating [packages of store-bought] Dad's Cookies. I wouldn't eat [unkosher food]," said Kaushansky, a retired accountant. "When we would line up for mess...I'd pull my plate away."

Murray Jacobs also grew up in a strictly kosher home in Toronto. A few days after he enlisted, Jacobs suffered an adverse reaction to the inoculations he'd received in preparation for going overseas, and his arm swelled up to twice its normal size. When he went to see the army doctor at the camp hospital, he experienced a different kind of adverse reaction. "It was the smell of bacon. Thousands of pieces of bacon cooking, and the smell was driving me crazy," Jacobs said. "So the second day [in the military sick ward] I phoned my father out of desperation and said to him, 'Pa, I'm in trouble. I can't eat. I'm on bread and water. It's not enough to keep me going. What do I do?'"

His father paused on the line for a moment. "When you're in Rome, you have to do as the Romans do," Charles Jacobs advised him. "God will forgive you. Try it. You've got to keep strong." Murray took his father's advice and started eating bacon.

Manny Rubinoff claims it was a rabbi who absolved him for eating bacon in the army. The retired Toronto plumber remembers confronting his moral dilemma during basic training at Simcoe, Ontario. The nineteen-year-old spent the first few days in the army trading his bacon rashers with the other men for extra eggs. "I went to a rabbi and told him, 'What shall I do?' He said, 'You're in the army, eat what they give you.'"

Rubinoff decided to break his kosher diet at his next posting with the Canadian army at CFB Petawawa, although he insists that he did so only because the bacon reminded him of a Jewish treat from home. "The cook was better, and the bacon, they made it like *grimminkes* [also known as *gribenes*, or fried chicken skin with onions, rather like pork rinds]," Rubinoff said. "It tasted very good so I ate it."

However, Rubinoff insisted that he did not violate his Jewish traditions completely. For the rest of the war, if other forms of the forbidden animal were on the menu, he would trade them. "They served ham once in a while, maybe once a month, and they served pork once or twice a month, [but] to this day I have never eaten ham or pork."

For David Golden, imprisoned in a Japanese prisoner-of-war camp in Hong Kong, a decent meal was only a dream for the longest time. When his captors would sometimes trade cigarettes for extra food, Golden was grateful for anything, regardless of what dietary laws were violated. "I think we bought a pig once," Golden said. "Since I'm Jewish and you're not supposed to eat pig, they said it was turkey for me and pig for everybody else."

For those Jewish personnel who didn't feel as strongly about dietary prohibitions, it was still an exciting event when they could eat something kosher, even if that meant some unusual combinations. Jack Tweyman was training at an Ontario army base in the spring of 1941. He did his best to get used to the army's cuisine, including on one of the most important Jewish holidays of the calendar, the festival of Passover, when Jews are prohibited from eating leavened foods. "I went to Kitchener... it was Pesach...and the Jewish people of Kitchener sent over matzos, so we ate bacon and eggs and matzos," Tweyman recalled, chuckling at the memory of a holiday meal he described as "interracial."

At the outset of the war, the War Efforts Committee of the Canadian Jewish Congress created a religious affairs bureau with a mandate to look after the spiritual needs of Jewish personnel in uniform. Providing kosher food when possible was part of the committee's responsibilities. While there were no regular kosher mess halls in the Canadian military bases at home or abroad, Congress paid to ensure that kosher food was available on Jewish holidays. One year, every Jewish serviceman posted to Alaska, Newfoundland, Labrador, and in isolated areas in Canada, as well as patients in military hospitals, received a Passover hamper. It contained kosher salami, matzos, a Jewish calendar, and "other little luxuries not contained in official rations and issues."[5] Wives of Jewish servicemen living near the bases received special provisions for the holiday, including matzos, matzo meal, and Passover cooking oil. The Vancouver office of Congress paid $273.39 to send wine, schmaltz (chicken fat), horseradish, meat, matzos, matzo meal, and matzo farfel, as well as paper dishes, to nine military camps around British Columbia so the servicemen could "at least have a semblance of Passover," wrote Lottie Levinson, the secretary of the Congress War Efforts branch in British Columbia.[6]

In locations where there was no Canadian Jewish organization to provide a kosher holiday meal, some Canadian Jews in uniform were able to observe their annual rituals through the auspices of other Allied country's units. Joe Greenberg still remembers attending a Passover seder in Torbay, Newfoundland, put on by the United Service Organizations, a welfare and recreation operation for the American military personnel stationed there.[7] "They had some gefilte fish and I could not believe that quality of gefilte fish could be obtained at an airbase," he told an interviewer in 2013. "That was amazing to me." Greenberg said that he liked the chopped and spiced fish ball even more because it was different from the kind he'd eaten growing up in Toronto. "I hate sweet gefilte fish!"

It wasn't only official institutions that provided opportunities for Canadian Jewish personnel to observe their religious dietary needs. Local Jewish families in Canada offered hospitality for those far away from home. Every Friday night during the war, the dining room in Jerry Grafstein's home in London, Ontario, was full of Jewish soldiers eating a traditional Sabbath meal. His father, Solomon, was a veteran of the Polish Army and had fought in World War I. After moving to Canada, the elder Grafstein became a caterer at the Orthodox synagogue in London. He would routinely invite visiting servicemen from the base at nearby St. Thomas to his home to light the candles, bless the bread and wine, and observe the Sabbath. His father served homemade gefilte fish and chopped liver, then there would be chicken soup, either chicken or flanken (beef ribs), and then sweet cakes for desserts. "And we'd always make them little packages for them to take back to the barracks."

The lawyer Abraham I. Shumiatcher acted as an official liaison between the Jewish community of Calgary and Jewish men in the service who were looking for a place to celebrate the holidays. For the Jewish New Year in 1943, he found hosts for a dozen Jewish men who were posted to the army's base in Red Deer.

Pte. C. Krieger,
Military Camp,
Red Deer, Alberta September 27, 1943

Dear Sir,

This is to advise that Mr. and Mrs. Ben Sheftel of 308 Superior Avenue, this city, phone W 1958, will be your hosts for the coming High Holidays. You may attend services at the House of Jacob, 323 5th Avenue East, where your hosts will be, if you so desire to do so.

Wishing you a happy and prosperous New Year, and many of them, I remain,

Yours very truly,
A.I. Shumiatcher

After Harry Kaushansky finished his signals training in Kingston, Ontario, he was posted to Esquimalt, on Vancouver Island. By now, the Montrealer who had existed for a while eating nothing but Dad's Cookies had begun to adapt to the military's non-kosher food. Still, he was always yearning for a Jewish meal. While on leave in Victoria, Kaushansky went into the synagogue where he met a Jewish woman named Alice Mallek who ran a ladieswear store.[8] "She gave me a royal welcome, those people were very hospitable, you know, to the troops," Kaushansky said. "When I came into town I used to go into her store, [and] the first thing she did was to say, 'I'll call up my housekeeper to make another meal [since]... I'm gonna be there for supper.' It was very nice."

The Feder family of Whitney Pier, Nova Scotia, had an open-door policy when it came to hosting visiting Jewish servicemen stationed nearby. Jack Tweyman would often spend his leaves at the four-bedroom home of Bella Feder and her husband, Efraim, and their two children, Arnold and Frances. Efraim ran a jewellery and watch repair store on Victoria Street in Sydney. All these years later, Tweyman still can't get over their hospitality. "One Pesach time she [Bella] had twenty-three people at a seder, all strangers, you know, servicemen, and a couple had their wives there. So who would do that, eh?"

Evelyn Davis remembers Jack Tweyman distinctly. Davis lived a few doors down from her Feder relatives, and her parents also hosted large Passover holiday meals for servicemen. Her family would buy chickens—sometimes enough for forty—and have them ritually slaughtered, then Evelyn and her four younger sisters would pluck and clean the chickens and prepare them in large roasting pans. "They [the servicemen] used to love it, they'd come and have a really good time, and we [made up] packages...for them to take back, when they were going back to the barracks," she said.

Davis said the Sydney Jewish community extended such hospitality during the war years because they knew many of these men would be going overseas to stop Hitler. "We took care of them because we knew what was going on in Europe; we were not ignorant of what was happening to our families abroad," she explained. "We knew that that was their job."

When Canadian Jews in uniform arrived overseas, they were routinely hosted at the tables of local Jewish families, even though the United Kingdom was under strict rationing. The military visitors tried to do what they could to supplement their hosts' pantry. When he was stationed at the Royal Air Force base in Middleton–St. George, Sydney Brown of North Bay was invited to spend Passover with the Ash family, as he had done the year before.[9] He asked his mother to slip an extra voorsht in his next parcel for his hosts. "I believe they would greatly appreciate it," Brown wrote, as it was considered a luxury at the time.

When Oscar Antel was servicing Typhoons and Hurricanes returning from reconnaissance runs over German-occupied territory, his squadron moved every night to avoid the enemy's spy planes. Consequently, his parcels of food from home did not always reach him in a timely manner. Antel remembers receiving three parcels at once. To be sure, the salamis arrived with the outside layers a little worse for wear. "But that didn't matter because you peeled it off," Antel explained.

The three salamis soon found new homes when Antel went on leave to stay with a local Jewish family. He also brought hardboiled eggs packed in flour from Eaton's, the former Canadian department store chain. "You couldn't get eggs overseas, so we'd give those away to various families. And chocolates. Lots of chocolate. This is all rationed stuff," he said.

Finding a Jewish table was much harder for Canadians stationed in East and Southeast Asia, but it wasn't impossible. And it meant a lot to Norman Cohen while he was stationed with the RCAF in Akyab, Burma (now known as Sittwe, in Myanmar). A British chaplain arranged for the Jewish men to be transported across the Bay of Bengal and taken to one of the synagogues in Kolkata (then Calcutta), India. "They took Protestants to Calcutta and brought us to a shul. And we had a meeting, a whole event, in a shul, and gave us dinner. Jewish dinner," Cohen recalled.

In Europe, Jewish chaplains in both the RCAF and the Canadian Army went to great lengths to help their flock observe Jewish traditions. In London in the spring of 1945, Squadron Leader Jacob Eisen booked a famous Jewish-style restaurant called Isow's, in Soho, to hold a Passover seder for the Canadian airmen and -women who were in town. It was an invitation-only event, according to Nathan Isaacs. The tables were filled with glasses of red wine and plates of matzos and other Jewish delicacies. "They had food on the table that I hadn't seen since Canada. They had everything, we were shocked," said Isaacs, convinced that the owner must have bought the food illegally on the black market. "Where else he would have got the chickens and the wine?"

Among the Canadian airmen at the seder were Albert Glazer of Toronto, Bill Zelikovitz of Ottawa, George Nashen and Gil Mogil of Montreal, and a strong representation from Winnipeg including Jack Hershfield, Sid Slonim, Oscar Nerman, Archie Levine, and Isaacs. There were three uniformed chaplains at the head table. Eisen, who led the prayer service before the meal, had also invited a Protestant minister and a Roman Catholic priest as a goodwill gesture.[10] Isow's owners were so impressed with the event that for years after the war they displayed photos from the dinner on the walls alongside those of visiting celebrities such as the singer Frank Sinatra and the boxer Muhammad Ali.[11]

When Canadian Jews in uniform eventually found themselves on the front lines, observing the Jewish dietary laws was probably far from their minds. Survival was foremost. Yet just as the Canadian Army served its front-line soldiers the now famous Christmas meal in the ruins of a bombed church during the battle for Ortona in Italy in 1943, so too did Jewish chaplains work to procure traditional foods for their fighting men during important Jewish holidays. Rabbi Gershon Levi cabled Congress headquarters in January 1943 about purchasing cases of Passover matzos, although the holiday was still four months away.[12] He requested five hundred pounds of matzos; the S. Manischewitz factory in New Jersey sent double that amount directly to England.

Max Clement was serving with the 48th Highlanders in Italy. The Toronto soldier fought his way through the Italian campaign until a piece of shrapnel cost him his left eye and ended his war in 1944. But before Clement was hit, he was one of five Jewish men in his unit taken temporarily out of the fighting to attend a Passover seder. Clement remained amazed by the lengths to which the Canadian military went to ensure that its Jewish servicemen could take part. He remembers being in a slit trench when someone yelled his name and told him that he was wanted. He heard them call other Jewish names, too, including Roher and Goldberg. When Clement climbed out, he discovered that a truck and driver were waiting to take the Jewish boys from his outfit about thirty kilometres behind the lines. The group arrived at a large Nissen hut, and he saw about three or four hundred men inside having a Passover service. "We had a very, very fine meal and we had wine and everything else," he recalled. "That was something I suppose we'll never forget."[13]

While Clement recalled the culinary aspect of the Passover observance in Italy, for the Canadian Jewish soldiers who were part of the Allied push into Germany two years later, in February and March 1945, the Passover rites that spring left a deep spiritual imprint on them. Once established in the liberated German town of Kleve on the west bank of the Rhine on February 12, Captain Samuel Cass, the Canadian Jewish chaplain, had mere weeks to get the holiday organized. There was food, but more important was likely the satisfaction of participating in a Jewish ritual that had been all but wiped out by Germany during the six years of war. Lawrence Levy, an artillery spotter from Toronto, attended one of Cass's battlefield religious services that March. It seemed to Levy that the crowd of Jewish servicemen numbered in the thousands. There were Poles, Americans, and Brits as well as Canadians.[14] The service lasted several hours, Levy said, but that was fine with him. "They built a platform in Germany and I remember them saying this is the first Jewish service in Germany of the Allied forces," Levy said. "It was amazing and it made me feel good."

Cass assembled kosher food and utensils to feed hundreds of Jewish front-line personnel at a series of four Passover meals held in Kleve, as well as in the liberated Dutch communities of Grave and Nijmegen, on March 28, 29, and 30. "The recitation of the Haggadah took on new meaning, for in truth, the struggle they were engaged in was the freeing of the whole world from the threat of enslavement and bondage," Cass wrote, referring to the special Passover book telling the biblical story of Moses leading the Israelites out of Egypt.[15]

Lionel Mernick of Toronto and his older brother Gerald attended one of the seders in Kleve.[16] Mernick was an army medic and his brother was an ambulance driver. When Rabbi Cass made it known that he needed a minyan, the minimum of ten Jewish men required to hold a formal service, the Mernicks went on a mission to gather enough people. "He was really angry at the Nazis," said Lionel's granddaughter Melany Eli, describing how the former pattern cutter felt about attending that service. He saw the religious service as a way to "stick it to them."

To be sure, he probably also appreciated the effort Cass put in to provide the festive meals, including wine, matzos, bitter herbs, green vegetables, and the other symbolic foods required for the event.[17] Cass obtained "a kosher tinned meat preparation, tinned vegetables, fruit, tea and sugar from formation supply points," and somehow the rabbi was even able to buy new pots, cutlery, wine cups, and paper plates from liberated Brussels.[18]

Of the 250 soldiers who were able to attend the first of the seders in Kleve, one young Canadian Jewish private might have been too nervous to enjoy the experience. Nineteen-year-old Alfred Cohene of Montreal, the youngest present, had been picked to ask the traditional four questions in front of the large crowd, which included official Canadian army photographers.[19]

These organized expressions of Judaism were one way that Canadian

Jews in uniform could express their faith during the war, but some personnel also fulfilled their religious commitments in a more private, everyday way. When Manny Rubinoff was called up in 1942, his grandparents wove two Tallit Katans, weekday prayer shawls, for him. They believed that wearing the garment under his uniform would protect the young plumber's apprentice who had joined the Royal Canadian Electrical and Mechanical Engineers as a sapper. His family were observant Jews from what is now Belarus. Unlike the larger prayer shawls that Jews wear over their clothes during religious services, his grandparents' gifts, also known as *Arba' kanfot*, were to be worn twenty-four hours a day. The custom of wearing these small rectangular pieces of cloth with fringes at each of the four corners dates back to the fourteenth century.

"I promised them I would always wear them," Rubinoff said, and he did, although it wasn't easy. It made him the butt of jokes in his barracks, where he was the only Jew. "They'd say, 'Hey! Look at this guy! He took a dishtowel, cut a hole in it, put it over his head...put these fancy fringes on the corner, ha ha.'"

Although Rubinoff's grandparents likely thought the prayer shawls would go with him overseas, it was in Canada that they played a role in one of the most significant experiences of his war. Every Sunday morning at Canadian Forces Base Petawawa in Ontario, as at the other bases at home and overseas, the troops were required at church parade, where they had to march off to attend religious services. There were services for Catholics, while the Protestants would have theirs. In many cases, early in the war, anyone who refused to attend was punished, usually with kitchen duties. One Sunday, Rubinoff balked.

The next day he was marched up to headquarters to be disciplined by the colonel. That's when Rubinoff unbuttoned his uniform to reveal his grandparents' prayer shawl. He also took out a pocket-sized Hebrew Bible. "I always had a Bible with me," Rubinoff said. "I told him, 'Look, sir, we are fighting for freedom—freedom of religion is a basic freedom. The Catholics have their church parade, the Protestants have their church parade, I should not be discriminated [against].'"

The colonel agreed. When the next Sunday rolled around, Rubinoff was put in charge of organizing what the colonel called a Hebrew church parade. He was the only one to line up. Undaunted, he marched smartly off to the base's library. "It didn't take me long to pray. I do it fast," he said.

One Sunday morning, a group of five Jewish officers from western

Canada turned up. Rubinoff assumed that one of them would conduct the services, but they placed him in charge. "Four of them were doctors, one was a dentist. As soon as we got in [the library], one of them said, 'In here, we're all Jewish boys. Don't you dare use the word 'Sir.'"

When the service was done, Rubinoff told the group he wanted them to march back in style. "I said, 'Okay, guys, we have to impress the goyim [non-Jews].'" They shoved all the desks aside in the library and practised. When the Catholics and Protestants began passing by the library, Rubinoff's tiny Hebrew church parade platoon fell into line. "And everybody's looking because I'm a private ordering a bunch of officers around," Rubinoff said, chuckling at the memory.

Kitchen duty for refusing to attend a church parade was not unique to Petawawa. When Lorne Winer arrived in England, he was posted to the artillery school in Larkhill, near Salisbury. For the first two Sundays, Winer and another Jewish soldier attended the Protestant services. Winer says it didn't bother him at first. He had once attended a church service in Canada, although having to genuflect had scared him so much that he'd run out. When the third Sunday came around, Winer decided not to comply, whereupon he and another Jewish soldier were marched to the cookhouse to peel potatoes.

"I was humiliated and embarrassed to be singled out like this," Winer said. They were the only two Jews in a group of about 250 men. Although he'd been in the army a scant two and a half months, Winer decided to lodge a complaint with his senior officer. The man quoted something from the King's Regulations and Orders. Winer blurted out, "Sir! Are you saying that you are equating one hour of worship with one hour of KP [kitchen punishment]?" His complaint went nowhere.

Other Jewish servicemen report resignedly following orders and sitting through the services of other religious groups. When Barney Danson was stationed in Aldershot, England, with the Queen's Own Rifles, the Toronto soldier said there was a "significant" number of Jews in his regiment but nowhere for them to pray. Although he knew some soldiers who refused to enter church each week, Danson and his best friend, Fred Harris, went along to the Anglican services. They were uncomfortable, especially when reciting passages from the Book of Common Prayer. So they did some editing. "We worked our way through the hymns by dropping a few words not applicable to us such as Jesus Christ, Holy Trinity, or Holy Ghost," Danson writes in his memoir.[20]

Despite the obstacles that military life posed, Canadian Jews in uniform did their best to navigate the traditions of both worlds. Four Devor brothers, originally from St. Catharines, served in the war. John, the oldest, was stationed in Kingston as a radar instructor.[21] His letters home were written on sheets of stationery belonging to the Jewish youth group known as Young Judaea.[22] In April 1944, he wrote home to let his mother know that his schedule was being changed, leaving him the opportunity to be more observant. "Starting this week I work Sunday instead of Saturday," he wrote, referring to the Saturday as the traditional day of rest for Jews. "The army is making a good Jew of me. Just imagine!"

Younger brother Sydney Devor was posted to the Pacific with the U.S. Army. He served in New Guinea and the Philippines, building mobile water purification systems. Despite being far from home, he remembered the important dates on the Jewish calendar. He sent a V-mail aerogram to his mother on September 18, 1944: "As this is the first Day of Rosh Hashanah I want to wish you and all the family a very Happy New Year. May the year see our whole family reunited and happy."[23]

From Italy, David Devor apologized for sending home Chanukah greetings using the army's Christmas airmail paper. "Dear Ma, This is a Xmas card but it's the only paper I have at the time. But it's in time for Chanicka."[24] In another letter, David reported that he had attended an official Passover event in Naples in 1944.[25] He was thrilled to discover that he was one of hundreds of Allied Jewish personnel serving in Italy, and meeting with the Canadian Jewish chaplain, Captain Isaac Rose, was a highlight. Whether David Devor knew it or not, his encounter with Rose was a significant achievement for Canada's Jews, as it was the first time that the military sent Canadian rabbis overseas in uniform.[26]

Congress officials had begun lobbying Ottawa on the issue very early in the war. Just as Canada was in this war as an independent dominion for the first time, they argued, so too should Canadian Jewish servicemen have their own clergy and not rely on British chaplains, as had been the case in the last war.

There was some pushback to the idea of permitting a Canadian Jewish chaplaincy. An Anglican bishop, George Wells, who was in charge of the military's chaplaincy service, kept saying no. At the end of August 1940, Congress sent Ottawa a list of eight hundred Jews who had signed up for active service. The military agreed that number was enough to warrant action on the chaplaincy file, although Wells remained "skeptical," and a month later, the official appointment of the first Jewish chaplain was cancelled without an explanation. Internal Jewish community politics may have been part of the problem. A federal Liberal member of Parliament, Peter Bercovitch, wanted Rabbi Harry Stern of Montreal's Reform Temple Emanu-El to be appointed. Louis Fitch, a member of the Quebec legislature, championed Rabbi Julius Berger of the Conservative synagogue Shaare Zion.[27] It would take another six months until a third candidate emerged.[28] Rabbi Gershon Levi was educational director at Montreal's Orthodox synagogue Shaar Hashomayim. He was appointed effective March 21, 1941.

Eventually there would be sixteen Jewish clergymen serving the growing number of Jews in the forces in Canada and abroad.[29] Congress expected them to help their countrymen in uniform feel connected to their Jewish heritage and also inspire them to see their participation in the war effort as fulfilling a sacred duty. "The rabbi in uniform personified Jewish ideals," said Chaplain Isaac Rose, describing Levi. He "was, often, the sole link between the soldier and his wife and family, and between the Jewish people struggling to regain its homeland and the Jewish soldier fighting against the most bitter enemy in Jewish history."[30]

As the chaplains began to pay regular visits to Canadian military installations, the military eventually moved to accommodate the religious needs of Jewish Canadians in uniform. By June 1941, regular Jewish services were being held at military bases in Ontario, including Petawawa, Camp Borden, and Long Branch, near Toronto. The same was true at Farnham and Mount St. Bruno, south of Montreal.[31] The Canadian Jewish Congress allotted $12,000 in 1942 to provide synagogue huts at some bases. "No officer or soldier of the Jewish faith will be obligated to attend services of any religious body other than his own," proclaimed the army's new regulation.[32]

Rabbi David Monson of Toronto ministered at CFB Borden, near Barrie. Monson's services weren't to everybody's taste. Lance Corporal Dick Steele went but didn't like singing "Hatikvah," a nineteenth-century song about the return of Jews to their homeland that would later be adopted as the national anthem of Israel. Steele, a communist, thought it was disloyal. "Inasmuch as Canada is very much my homeland, I feel even more reluctant about attending a service which seeks to find Jewish National Expressions in an unreal Zionist ambition," he wrote to his wife.[33]

Religious services were held even in remote stations, although not always with the presence of a chaplain. In the fall of 1943, two Winnipeg officers, Captain Joseph Ludwig and Lieutenant A. Steinberg, conducted the High Holiday services on Alaska's Kiska Island in the Aleutians.[34] The pair was among the fifty-three hundred Canadians attached to the Green Light Force sent to recapture the island from the Japanese.[35] Since there were no Jewish chaplains, Ludwig, as the senior ranking Jewish officer, was asked to conduct services. "Dad did not consider himself to be religious, although he did have a lifelong love of cantorial music," says his son Rael Ludwig. Uncertain of his ability, Ludwig's father asked his friend Steinberg to help him prepare for the sacred duty. "He believed that he didn't do a good job, not that any of the soldiers cared."

Sometimes, especially in centres with a sizable Jewish civilian population, Jewish servicemen left the base to attend services in local synagogues. Israel Yamron enlisted with the RCAF in July 1942 and found himself posted to the No. 1 Technical Training School at St. Thomas in Ontario. Yamron and the other Jewish airmen would worship in nearby London, where he remembers being surprised at the style of Jewish services there. "I walked into the synagogue and there was an organ playing and I thought I was in a church. Coming from an Orthodox family in the North End of Winnipeg, I couldn't figure," Yamron recalled, although he couldn't have known that London's two Conservative synagogues, B'nai Israel and also B'nai Moses ben Judah, had been established inside former church properties.

Later, when Yamron was posted to Vancouver Island, he would attend High Holiday services on the mainland. Obtaining permission for the trip to Vancouver wasn't difficult. Canadian Jewish personnel serving in Canada often asked for leave for the major Jewish holidays and it was usually granted. Later in the war, the Canadian Jewish Congress was able to arrange Passover leaves for Jewish military personnel serving in Canada, as well as in the Netherlands and Belgium, and for Polish Forces stationed in Canada.

In March 1944 Yashe Steinberg wrote to the colonel at Calgary's No. 2 Bombing and Gunnery School. "We are of extreme Orthodox faith and the presence of our son at this religious ritual would mean so much to his mother and myself," he wrote, using official Jewish Community Council stationery for effect, just as he had done to get his son Hymie into the RCAF early.[36] Unfortunately, Hymie had been in a bit of trouble since enlisting and been punished once for going absent without leave. He'd also been caught putting used tickets into a Calgary streetcar fare box. Because of this, Squadron Leader O. Lawrence wrote back informing the Steinbergs that their request would not be granted, although he would make sure Hymie found Passover services to attend in Calgary.

Norman Gulko nearly wasn't permitted to attend Jewish services when he was posted to a base in Saint John, New Brunswick, but in this case, it wasn't the military's decision. When the Toronto soldier found the building where services were supposed to be taking place, he politely asked an older couple in the vestibule to direct him to the right room. Gulko soon heard them whispering to each other in Yiddish. "*Shaygetz*," they said, meaning, "He's probably not Jewish."

"*Nein, ich bin a Yid!*" Gulko replied. "No, I am Jewish!" and followed them up the stairs. The skeptical couple met the twenty-two-year-old soldier at the top of the landing, gave him a yarmulke, and placed a Siddur, or Jewish prayer book, in his hand. After services, the welcome got even warmer. He was invited downstairs for the Kiddush, the ceremonial meal. "News had gone all over the congregation about this [couple's] experience with me and they were laughing like hell, you know," he said.

If the Jews of Saint John didn't know what to make of a lone Canadian Jewish soldier in uniform looking for a place to pray, imagine the reaction that two-dozen Canadian and British Jewish soldiers received in Iceland when they held one of the most remarkable Yom Kippur services in history. It was a milestone not only for the Canadian Jewish servicemen stationed in Iceland at the time but also for the country itself, being the first Jewish religious services ever held in the country.[37]

The Canadians were stationed in Iceland as part of the twenty-five-hundred-strong contingent known as "Z" Force. When Hitler took France during the summer of 1940, Canada sent troops to Iceland to bolster the British military garrison on the island in case of a German invasion. In October, a British Jewish soldier approached his superiors for permission to mark the Jewish Day of Atonement. He was offered space in a building at Reykjavik's old cemetery, but a more dignified location was soon found at the Good Templar hall.[38] He could collect only two prayer shawls, one yarmulke, and a Torah borrowed from a local library. A committee of local Jewish civilians helped decorate the hall to make it look more like a synagogue. They covered a table with a pretty cloth embroidered with flowers to create a makeshift pulpit. A banner was affixed to the wall with the Hebrew phrase "Hear, O Israel, the Lord Our God Is One."

Abraham Cohen, from Leeds, England, served as the cantor. Meyer Bubis, Lionel Cohen, Maxwell London, Harry Yaros, and other Toronto Jewish men of the Royal Regiment of Canada participated. There was no rabbi available, so the senior British Anglican chaplain, the Reverend Canon John C.F. Hood, conducted the service using a Jewish prayer book. He apparently talked about soccer and long jump.[39] His sermon was not well received. After a full day of fasting and prayer, photos were taken at sundown. Meyer Bubis, then twenty-six, sent a copy of the photo home to his father, with this handwritten instruction on the back: "Pop, This is the first time in the history of Iceland that such a service has been held, Meyer. P.S. Take care of this for me, please. B66596 Pvt. M. Bubis, Royal Regiment of Canada."[40]

When the holiday was over, the group adjourned to a nearby hotel to break their twenty-five-hour fast. The worshippers decided to establish a formal Jewish community organization for Iceland. It lasted throughout the war years and beyond, although the Canadian servicemen did not stay in the country long enough to participate. Just a few weeks after Yom Kippur the Royal Regiment embarked for England.

The opening of the Balfour Service Club in London in June 1943 gave Canadian Jewish personnel and the chaplains more regular opportunities to practise their faith. Personnel on leave could rent a bed on the upper two floors, have a haircut, and take in a dance, and the Georgian-style mansion was also where Jewish chaplains held religious celebrations, including Passover seders one year that attracted 550 men.[41] In the fall of 1943, the club hosted a New Year's meal with Rabbi Gershon Levi leading prayers over the bread, while a senior American army chaplain, Rabbi Judah Nadich, led the prayers over the wine.[42] Levi also rented a larger hall on Red Lion Square to hold religious prayer services off site.[43]

Even those personnel who were not in London could, and did, get the opportunity to keep the Jewish holidays. While HMCS *Athabaskan* was docked for two weeks at Plymouth for repairs, it didn't even cross Harry Hurwitz's mind to apply for leave to observe the Jewish holidays. It was his captain, Lieutenant Commander John Stubbs, who reminded Hurwitz to do his Jewish duty. "You're of the Jewish faith?" Stubbs asked him. "You know what tomorrow is?"

Hurwitz didn't.

"It's your Yom Kippur. How would you like a twenty-four-hour fast?"

Hurwitz told the officer he would "Love it, sir!" and left the ship in time to find a synagogue.

Murray Bleeman was so eager to observe Passover in the spring of 1941 that he threatened to break curfew and risk yet another charge appearing on his record. Bleeman was already serving time in the guardhouse in England for coming back late from leave. "I hope to be out Monday and see the Major about Passover leave April 11–19," Bleeman told his sister in a letter. "Wish I was with you home for Passover. I will really miss it. Remember the way we used to try to rush Dad through the Saidurs [*sic*]?"[44] He got the leave.

Operational requirements didn't permit Flight Sergeant Meyer Greenstein to observe the Yom Kippur fast in 1944. Greenstein was in England, attached to Bomber Command at the time. The sheepish airman wrote home to his parents to apologize. He'd had to fly a mission. "You just can't be in the air for all those hours and not eat," he explained.

Perhaps Meyer Greenstein was able to make up for it the next day, after he had returned to base to get some sleep. He might even have prayed. He certainly wouldn't have been the only Canadian Jew in uniform to look to prayer as a source of forgiveness, solace, or strength. Lawrence Levy acknowledges praying when under fire. "I just dreamt that 'Please, God, save me,'" Levy recalled, after surviving four direct hits to his vehicle and watching two of his five-man crew get killed soon after they landed in Normandy.

Leo Guttman felt less vulnerable when praying while moving though France, Holland, and Germany: "I believed that being Jewish, I believed in something, and somebody up there is going to help me," he said.

Sam Boroditsky was pretty sure he wasn't going to survive the German machine-gun bullets whizzing over his head on a mountain trail high above the road to Cassino, Italy. The Winnipegger was trapped on the snow-covered Mount Majo in January 1944. His mother's lucky hand-knitted khaki scarf was snug around his neck, but Boroditsky feared its powers had run out. "Behind me I heard the voice of our old first Sgt. Marvin Yell. 'Oh God,' he was saying. I was saying, '*Shema Yisrael, Adonai Eloheinu, Adonai Echad!*'" Boroditsky said. "I often think of each of us, scared to death and praying."[45] The Shema is a fundamental Jewish prayer that praises but also beseeches God and is traditionally recited in moments of imminent peril.

Ed Rasky, of Toronto, served as a navy sick-berth attendant, and invoked the Shema one day in early November 1944. His ship, HMCS *Antigonish*, was on alert: a submarine that had been following the frigate for a week had come into range. Rasky, the son of a part-time cantor and full-time ritual slaughterer, ran to his assigned battle station and recited the Shema on behalf of the weapons. "I felt the sweat of fear on my forehead. When I saw our depth charges in mid-air, I said a prayer in Hebrew that might help them to their destination," he said. It might have made a good scene in one the films his brother Harry Rasky would later direct. But the submarine got away.

Two of Barney Danson's closest friends had already been killed in France when he himself was wounded in Normandy in August 1944 and sent to hospital. It was there he received more bad news, about the loss of a third friend, Earl Stoll. "I fell to my knees, not a Jewish practice, in the hospital chapel reciting some religious mantra from my childhood as tears streamed down my cheeks," Danson recalled, explaining that thinking about some higher power helped him cope with the unending deaths of the people closest to him. "We didn't understand God but we lived with his constant presence, a lifeline to sanity amidst the insanity of war."[46]

Danson also felt it was important to keep an army-issued Hebrew Bible in his left breast pocket, although whether he did so for spiritual reasons or to block bullets is not known. A significant number of Canadian military personnel kept Jewish religious artifacts during the war. Arthur Cherkinsky of Windsor brought his Sabbath prayer shawl and his tefillin (leather phylacteries containing prayers on parchment paper) overseas, where he served as a flight engineer with the RCAF's No. 419 Squadron.[47] Bill Zelikovitz carried with him a Jewish religious calendar listing the addresses of synagogues in England, should he wish to find a service to attend. Fred Pascal had four Jewish prayer books and his prayer shawl with him in England.[48] When he was preparing to depart for Normandy in the summer of 1944, he sent them for safekeeping to a massive military warehouse in Aldershot, England, called the No. 1 Canadian Kit Storage Depot. That was also where the RCAF navigator Harry Bloch, about to start flying bombing missions over Germany, sent his Jewish prayer book, a book of Jewish thoughts, and what the depot tersely described on the inventory list as "1 Red velvet bag Religious articles."[49] "My grandmother made three of them. One for my grandfather, and one each for Harry and [his brother] Norman for their bar mitzvahs," said Norman's son Gerry Bloch, referring to the red tallit bags that held their prayer shawls.

Mitchell Sterlin's shelf at the storage depot contained his Zeta Beta Tau fraternity pin from McGill and an item that the depot staff would recognize as a set of "phyllacteries in a cloth bag."[50] When the air force collected Flying Officer Max Sucharov's personal effects after he was killed in 1944, they drew up a list to send to his family. A blue velvet bag containing "leather strips and material" was on the list. So were three Jewish religious books.[51] Before it was his turn to land in Normandy in July 1944, Private Samuel Nichols (Nikolaevsky) put several items in storage, including a rabbit's foot and two prayer books.[52]

That so many Canadian Jewish personnel had prayer books is not an accident. Early in the war, Rabbi Levi had ordered three thousand copies of the *Prayer Book for Jewish Members of H.M. Forces*, originally produced for British members of the armed services. But the shipment was lost to enemy action. A subsequent order of five thousand copies got through, and Levi mailed one to every Jewish man on his list. The prayers it contained were stirring and humbling at the same time, as they reminded the Jewish servicemen why they were fighting and what was at stake.[53]

Unto thee, Heavenly Father, I lift up my heart in this hour of trial and danger. Pardon all my sins and transgressions before thee and, I beseech thee, extend the loving care over the lives of those near and dear unto me. Give me the strength to do my duty this day, as a true and loyal Israelite in this War for Freedom and Righteousness. Fill me with the faith and courage of those who put their trust in thine everlasting mercy and lead us through victory unto peace.[54]

The Canadian Jewish Congress and B'nai Brith teamed up to produce Canadian versions of the prayer books. *Readings from the Holy Scriptures for Jewish Soldiers, Sailors and Airmen* was popular.[55] David Croll, back in Canada as a training officer in Prince George, wrote the chaplains in July 1942 to ask for another ten copies of the book for "Jewish boys in British Columbia," particularly the Oxford Rifles. Even non-Jewish clergymen asked Levi for a supply. The Protestant chaplain at RCAF Claresholm,

J.M. Roe, needed six copies: as he had only one left for personal use and had already given it to a Jewish leading aircraftman named Lorencz.[56]

Many personnel would have also received a small *Book of Jewish Thoughts*. Readers could look for courage and inspiration in the quotations from famous contemporary personalities including Churchill, Albert Einstein, and Pope Pius XI, and from biblical sources such as the Book of Job.[57] Some servicemen who received these books wrote to thank Levi. Even non-practising Jews, such as the sailor Abe Halpern of Ottawa, found motivation in the pages. "So long as conditions exist which breed antisemitism—I am a Jew," he declared.[58]

A large number of Canadian Jews in uniform were also strong believers in the more modern political movement known as Zionism, which endorsed the creation of a Jewish state in what was then British-controlled Palestine. Although civilian Jews including refugees could not legally immigrate there, the British has a large force stationed in the historic land of the Jewish people, enabling some Canadian Jews in the service to fulfill a centuries-old dream to make the pilgrimage.

John Lewis Michaels had already developed a deep love for the Jewish colony when he first spent some time there right after college, in 1935.[59] He felt the longing of his people for a Jewish homeland, even penning an ode to Judaism's ancient capital city.

City of God, who calls for love and peace
When all around men talk of arms and strife,
Jerusalem shout out, demand your fate:
The Jews, who loved me, made me great of yore—
All others failed to keep my holy state—
May they again succeed to make me pure.[60]

His connection to the land prompted the Montrealer, who was living in England before the war broke out, to join the British Army, because he thought he could be posted to Palestine. That is what happened, when his regiment was sent in 1937, during the height of the Arab Revolt, an uprising by local Arabs against the British Mandate. When World War II started, his infantry unit, the Worcester Regiment's 1st Battalion, found itself in Sudan fighting against the Italians to oust them from their neighbouring colony, Eritrea. Michaels died on April 7, 1941, a week after the end of the battles to liberate Keren and the Eritrean capital, Asmara.[61]

He is buried in a war cemetery in Khartoum, twenty-five hundred kilometres away from his beloved Jerusalem.

Visiting Palestine left Irving Feldman of St. Catharines speechless and also angry. The airman took his leave in Jerusalem while he was posted to Cairo with the RCAF. His first sight of the precious symbol of Jewish survival, Jerusalem's Western Wall, was a shock. "The Wall was buried under garbage and [the trash] was ten or fifteen feet up," said his niece, Wendy Feldman. Her uncle told her that "it was a garbage dump." The majority Palestinian Arab population was pro-Nazi during World War II.

Some Jewish Canadians were sent to Palestine not for religious reasons but for medical ones, posted there in order to recover from malaria, a common problem for those flying in and out of Africa. RCAF Warrant Officer Ira Kliman of Regina was a law student when he enlisted in 1939, and he belonged to several Jewish youth groups including Young Judaea, whose mission was to strengthen its members' Jewish identity and love for Israel.[62] In late October 1942, Kliman dragged himself to the sick quarters of a British air force station at Almaza, Cairo. He was admitted, shivering, with a fever and aching joints. They sent him to Palestine to recover. It was good for his health and, as it turned out, for his Jewish soul. "During his stay in Egypt, he visited Palestine frequently and became deeply interested in what he saw there," according to a 1948 obituary.[63]

Gordon Steinberg also found himself transformed by his trips to Palestine. A former truck driver from Toronto, he was flying Hurricanes over the Mediterranean. Malaria was what first sent him to Palestine, and the beaches in Tel Aviv later offered him a soothing respite from the stress of combat patrols out of Alexandria, Egypt.[64] But what really stirred the airman's Jewish soul was meeting a group of German Jewish orphans in Palestine. Soon, Steinberg's fighter plane sported an iconic symbol on the nose: "The other airmen would put Mae West (a movie star) on their planes, and he was so impressed by the Holy Land that he put the Star of David on his plane," said his brother Lawrence Steinberg, a retired New York doctor.[65]

The Star of David was also on the distinctive patch worn by some Canadian Jews who volunteered for the famous Jewish Brigade, formed in Palestine in late 1944. The combined infantry and artillery regiment was commanded by Brigadier Ernest Frank Benjamin, whose father had been president of Holy Blossom Temple in Toronto until the family moved back to England. The Zionist Organization of Canada began receiving inquiries from Canadian Jewish men already in uniform who wanted to join the all-Jewish outfit.[66] Eventually, the British Army brigade (approximately five thousand Jewish men) saw combat in Italy in March 1945.

The battlefields of Italy also provided an opportunity for some Canadian Jews to perform what could be considered the final acts of faith on behalf of their fallen comrades. Even some Jews who "weren't particularly religious," which is the way the family of the Montrealer Lawrence Melville Lipsey described him, carried out the mitzvah, or good deed. In September 1944, Lipsey was graveside in San Giovanni in Marignano, Italy, as the army buried Captain Sam Sheps, a lawyer and one of the first Winnipeg Jews to enlist in the army after Canada declared war on Germany.

Without a Jewish chaplain to conduct the religious rites, Lieutenant Lipsey stepped up to recite the traditional Hebrew burial prayers over Sheps's grave. "He certainly would have turned his hand to reading the service if he felt it would help poor Captain Sheps," said his son, Lord David Lipsey, a British journalist and politician.[67]

When David Devor and Toronto's Michael Bernstein were killed in Italy in December 1944, they had been sharing the same slit trench near the Senio River. After the Canadians captured Bagnacavallo, the senior Jewish non-commissioned officer in the Irish Regiment of Canada, Charlie Drubich, went back to help collect the boys' bodies. Drubich made sure the Protestant chaplain said all the right things when the two were buried side by side at the Canadian war cemetery in nearby Villanova. Then Sergeant Drubich let the boys' families know what had been done. "He was buried by Capt. Rowland, Protestant Padre, as a Jewish man should be buried, Star of David, etc.," Drubich wrote to Devor's mother, Kate.[68] A week later, the Canadian Jewish chaplain, Rabbi Isaac Rose, went to the cemetery to hold his own services for good measure.

They had already buried Captain Fred Pascal under a cross in a Normandy churchyard by the time his brother Arthur arrived two days later. Fred had been fatally wounded by friendly fire on August 8, 1944, during a major Allied offensive near Caen. Arthur Pascal says his brother probably hadn't heard the shells coming because his ears had been damaged during years of training on the artillery ranges. "While most of the people around were able to fall flat and able to escape with very minor injuries or no injuries at all, he was standing, and his insides received a very, very severe shock," Pascal said.

Arthur brought a Jewish chaplain with him to Fred's grave at St-Germain-la-Blanche-Herbe, northwest of Caen, in the community cemetery. The chaplain always carried a supply of wooden grave markers in the shape of the Star of David. Arthur wrote Fred's name on one and switched it for the cross. Then Jewish prayers were said. It meant a lot to Arthur then, and still did, years after the war. "It's hard to explain now but these things, it's all we could do."

13 Liberation

"He couldn't take them all"

After David Devor's funeral, Rabbi Isaac Rose also wrote to Devor's family, calling David a "very brave boy. Stating pure facts (no b.s.) he was very highly regarded by his comrades."[1] Then he told them that David had been part of an informal network of Canadian Jewish servicemen who helped rescue Holocaust survivors in Italy. The chaplain had asked all his men to be on the lookout for Jewish refugees and to pass their addresses on to him.

Unbeknownst to his family, just before he died, Devor discovered a Jewish refugee in need. He had dutifully sent the information in a letter to the chaplain. Unfortunately, probably due to his poor spelling, the letter went to the wrong address and arrived on the chaplain's desk only after he was killed. Rose nevertheless felt it would comfort the family to know about their son's noble gesture. "Well, help is being brought to this refugee. So you see David's good deeds live after him," Rose told them.

As the Allied forces pushed the Germans north through Italy and ousted them from other parts of Europe during 1944 and 1945, many Canadian Jewish servicemen and -women would come face to face with the truth about the fate of the continent's Jews. They found centuries-old synagogues that had been desecrated. They also found survivors of Nazi death camps. Some of the liberators responded by acting individually. Others took part in organized relief work, including measures spearheaded by the Canadian Jewish chaplains on the ground in Europe. For the Canadian Jews in uniform, liberation was an experience of exhilaration mixed with despair and a strong sense of responsibility.

Irving Schreiber, a Canadian signaller, didn't have much information to go on when his unit arrived in liberated Brussels in September 1944. All he had was a letter containing an old address where a Jewish family had been in hiding since the Nazi invasion of Belgium in 1940. He was looking for the Nussbaums, originally from Wanne-Eickel, in northwestern Germany. Their eldest son, Walter, had been sent to safety in Holland and then to England right after Kristallnacht in November 1938; he was later deported to Canada by the British as an enemy alien. Walter knew that his parents and two sisters had made it out of Germany to Brussels, but he hadn't heard from them in four years. Schreiber's younger brother, Bill, worked in the same suit factory as Walter on Pine Avenue in Montreal. The teenage Schreiber promised to write to Irving and ask him to search.

It took about a month for Irving to find them. Walter's parents, Yitzhak and Rose, and a younger sister, Edith, were still alive.[2] Right after Kristallnacht, they had made it across the German border thanks to secret arrangements involving a taxi ride into Belgium, a rendezvous at a restaurant, and a long journey by foot to Brussels. Edith, who was ten at the time, was tucked away in a monastery with the nuns.[3] Walter's older sister, Senta, however, was later caught in the streets in 1942 and deported to Auschwitz.[4]

When Irving Schreiber found the family, the Nussbaums were overjoyed to learn that their now twenty-year-old son, Walter, whom they had last seen when he was fourteen, was safe. Schreiber's unit spent five weeks in Brussels, and during that time he brought food and supplies to the Nussbaums, including gum and chocolates for Edith. He tucked their letters to Walter into his army mail home. "It was a righteous thing to do," said Bill Schreiber, a retired Montreal uniform manufacturer who was too young to enlist.

This search for the survivors is what the chaplain Rabbi Sam Cass would later describe as "the Great Hunt."[5] Canadian Jewish military personnel often took on these heartfelt unofficial missions to help desperate relatives look for traces of their families. Estelle Aspler's (née Tritt) mother used to send her names and addresses on behalf of people who knew that the Canadian Army nurse was serving overseas. What Aspler often found was absence and grief. She reconnected one Jewish girl in California with surviving family in Europe, tracking down a sister in unoccupied France. The father was missing, but she found the mother at a Salvation Army hostel in Amsterdam. "I went in to see the mother. When she came in I couldn't help thinking, 'There but for the grace of God, goes my mother.'"[6]

No one asked Hy Chud to comfort the Jewish survivors in Utrecht. Yet when the 7th Reconnaissance Regiment passed through the liberated Dutch city in May 1945, Chud swung into action. "The first thing all the Jewish guys did was ask, 'Are there any Jews around?' and 'Was there a synagogue?'" Chud said. He was told about a Jewish woman who was living with some nuns. He located the convent and met the Mother Superior, who agreed to introduce the Canadian Jewish soldier to her guest. Speaking to him in Yiddish, the survivor told him that her husband had been deported and she'd gone into hiding. The two embraced, then Chud asked if he could have her hated yellow Star of David badge.

Chud would have liked to help the woman more, but his unit was "moving fairly quickly" at the time. He left Utrecht, confident that she had enough to eat. Chud never did learn what happened to her. His army friends advised him to get rid of the woman's yellow badge, thinking it might be a dangerous souvenir to have, but he still has it.

Armbands figured prominently in the encounter that the Toronto soldier Reuben Cherry had with a family of Dutch Jewish survivors. In mid-April 1945, Cherry's unit, the 48th Highlanders, was clearing the way toward Apeldoorn. They went house to house searching for Germans. Cherry heard a noise in one of the rooms. "Come out," he called out in English. From behind the wall stepped a father, mother, and two children.

"He gave them food, and they were wearing those armbands," said Murray Jacobs, who came by later and met the family. "They were sharing whatever food we had with us. Like hard biscuits, you know, things [like] that; they were starving." When the family was ready to leave its hiding place and move elsewhere, Jacobs provided them with rations. Cherry urged them to remove their offensive armbands. The Dutch woman wrote down the story of what had happened to them and gave the document and one of the armbands to Cherry.

Sometimes the liberation involved a soldier's own family, as was the case for Max (Val) Rimer. The Winnipeg resident, who admits he initially enlisted in the army at 19 for adventure, saw action in Italy, Belgium, and Holland.[7] At the end of the war, Rimer went on his own "great hunt" for some lost relatives. Before he was shipped home in 1946, he made his way to the town of Valenciennes on the French–Belgian border where his father's sister had lived.[8] He found the town mostly destroyed, first by German bombs in 1940 and then by a fire. Over five hundred local Jews had been deported to Auschwitz in 1942.[9] Rimer's aunt had survived. She didn't know what to make of the young Canadian soldier. Rimer didn't speak French. She didn't speak English. He tried Yiddish. "I said to her in Jewish, 'I'm Jack's son,'" Rimer said. She started to cry. His aunt brought him into the kitchen and told him his uncle had been killed in the Holocaust. She was raising their five children, his cousins, alone. "I left everything I could for them," Rimer said. His family eventually brought them to live in Canada.[10]

Many of the survivors Herb Ludman encountered eventually went to Palestine. The Canadian airman was serving as a navigator with a Royal Air Force squadron in Foggia, Italy, and when he wasn't flying missions, Ludman teamed up with other Jewish service personnel, including some from the Jewish Brigade. They provided shelter for displaced Jewish persons who had nowhere to go. "We all got together with some American Jewish servicemen and bought several Italian farms where we brought all the children from the camps," Ludman reported.[11] On his days off, he would forage around the Italian countryside, collecting supplies for his charges. All the children would eventually be sent to live in Palestine.

The encounters with survivors could be traumatic for the Canadian liberators. Lorne Winer and his friend John Woodrow attended a Canadian-led memorial service for Allied Jewish soldiers who had been killed in Normandy. The event was being held near a Jewish cemetery in the ruins of Caen. Winer said that Rabbi David Monson gathered the men in the only building left standing. Memorial candles were lit and Winer and Woodrow joined a group of heavily armed American Jewish paratroopers in reciting the prayers. "Five minutes into the service we began to hear a moaning sound," Winer said, describing the noise coming from a "couple of dozen" Jewish survivors who had stepped out from behind a wall. They had been in hiding for five years and were stunned but also thrilled to see so many armed Jewish servicemen praying. "They looked like wraiths, ghosts standing against the wall. And they were moaning partly in elation."

Winer experienced "surreal" feelings at the service, but these certainly weren't the only emotions that Jewish Canadian personnel had in response to the liberation. Some reacted with anger. "I hated every German I saw, whether it was right or wrong," admitted Calgary's Mel Polsky, with the Royal Canadian Corps of Signals. "You can't shoot at them and be shot at by them for six years and then become friendly." He especially hated those Germans who said they didn't know what was happening to Jews.[12]

When Ruben Ostfield was shipped back to Canada from England for officers training in February 1943, a group of German prisoners of war was on board the same ship, en route to POW camps in Canada. "My father was required to do guard duty. He once told me that he was hard-pressed not to shoot some of them because of the plight of Jews in Europe," Michael Ostfield said.

Lawrence Levy's artillery unit were the first troops to enter liberated Elbeuf, France, in August 1944. He was thrilled with the welcome that the Canadians received but remembers seeing how the newly freed French heaped vengeance on those residents who had helped the Germans. "They were cutting the hair off the women collaborators," Levy said, adding that those who had slept with German soldiers were then forced to parade through the streets naked. The men who had collaborated were being shot. "Nobody stopped it," Levy said.

In Holland, Norman Gulko's unit would come across scores of retreating or captured German soldiers. Gulko yelled out at them. "'*Er komt de Herrenvolk!* Here come the Supermen!' I never felt so proud as a Jew, as a Canadian. Whether they heard it or cared, I just felt tremendous," Gulko said.[13] Trooper Val Rimer admitted doing something similar. He hurled his anger at the prisoners. Rimer recounted the episode for *War Story*, a documentary on the History Channel. "I was yelling at them. I didn't touch them, I knew better than that, but I was screaming," Rimer said. "I was shouting to them that 'I'm a *Jude*, I'm Jewish. I want you to know that there's a Jewish person here that helped end this war.'"[14]

Gerald Levenston, a Toronto jeweller, derived tremendous personal satisfaction from his unexpected role in the end of the war in Germany.[15] Although there was still sporadic fighting in Europe, by early May 1945 local German commanders in parts of Holland and also in northwest Germany were ready to surrender. In what Lieutenant Colonel Levenston would describe as "poetic justice" and the "culmination of my army career," he learned that his boss wanted him to represent the victors at a ceasefire ceremony on May 5, 1945, in Bad Zwischenahn, a lakeside resort near Oldenburg.

"I want a Jew to go tell those bastards what to do," Brigadier Darrell Laing told Levenston, who spent the next few days giving the defeated regional German troops "their marching orders." "I had the pleasure recently of conducting a conference with some senior German officers at their HQ and telling them curtly what they would and would not do," Levenston wrote to his mother.[16]

The official end of the war in Europe came on May 8, when the top Allied and German commanders met in Berlin to sign the formal articles of capitulation. German forces would have to remain where they were and surrender to the victors. After the end of hostilities, Irving Baron was posted to Cuxhaven, near Hamburg, with the Royal Canadian Air Force. The Montreal airman admits he took delight in watching the area's defeated Germans scrounging for scraps from the mess hall garbage bins. "They were desperate at the time. And we had cigarettes and we were trading cigarettes for cameras and jewellery and whatever."

Baron had already heard reports coming back from the concentration camps being liberated inside Germany, including Bergen-Belsen, which was about two hours away. Although he did not visit the site, he saw photos that a friend brought back. "It broke my heart," he said. "I was well aware of what was going on. How could you not [be]?"

Though Baron's involvement with Bergen-Belsen was peripheral—he supplied gas for the vehicles of soldiers who were making trips there—he was one of about a thousand Canadian military personnel who played some role in the aftermath of the liberation of Belsen. Some came just to bear witness. Others were involved in the rescue and rehabilitation of the sixty thousand survivors, and the proper burial for the tens of thousands of dead.[17] A Winnipeg physician, Maurice Victor, and his driver pulled in to Belsen after the British and Canadians liberated it on April 15, 1945. "The stench of the dead and dying was just overwhelming; cadaverous people were literally stacked up like cords of wood in rows, some of them still squirming," he wrote. "It had to be seen, it had to be smelled for anyone to grasp what the camps meant."[18]

Saul Laskin of Fort William, Ontario, spent forty-eight hours at the camp after Allies had burned most of the original site, including the incinerators, to stop the spread of typhus, tuberculosis, dysentery, and the infestation of lice and vermin. One smokestack had been left standing to serve as a monument to the fifty thousand mainly European Jews who had died there, including Anne Frank. Laskin, who served as a captain with the North Nova Scotia Highlanders, said what struck him hardest was the psychological devastation of the survivors. "Their many years of oppression in these concentration camps had left them broken wrecks, physically, and what is even worse, mentally," he said in 1946. After his visit, Laskin "openly wept."[19]

Monty Berger visited the camp on May 1, 1945, when his services weren't required at the Spitfire wing where he served as an intelligence officer. Berger's was an unofficial visit, yet as the son of a prominent Montreal rabbi, he felt he had a duty to go. "I was sick to my stomach, overcome with revulsion," Berger writes in his memoir. "Those images stay fresh in my mind. I am outraged and recall them vividly when I hear someone claim the Holocaust never happened."[20]

One Montreal soldier on guard duty at the site was so furious that he had to be restrained from killing the Belsen camp commandant on the spot. Jack Marcovitch had left his job as a plumber to enlist in the army in 1942. He served with the Régiment de la Chaudière but was attached to a British unit when it entered Belsen. Film footage taken on the day that commandant Josef Kramer was apprehended shows the twenty-two-year-old Canadian Jewish private raising his rifle as the liberators learned the true identity of the stocky German officer. Kramer had taken off the uniform with his real rank to try to hide who he was.[21] "Don't shoot, take him," a British officer cautioned Marcovitch.

Kramer was executed in December 1945, after a war crimes trial. Many years later, Marcovitch saw the film of the arrest for the first time. He said the images transported him back to April 16, 1945. "I smell it again," Marcovitch told the CBC. "The stench was something you cannot understand."[22]

While many Canadian Jewish troops followed their consciences in dealing with survivors, Canadian Jewish chaplains made sure to emphasize the sacred duty to act. Squadron Leader Jacob Eisen, the chaplain for Jewish RCAF personnel overseas, wrote a solemn pastoral letter to the airmen. He listed some of the assistance that the Tactical Air Force gave "in connection with the horror camps," such as donating food and cigarettes for inmates. They also put up stoves and provided washing facilities. Eisen celebrated the downfall of men like Belsen's commandant and Hitler's henchmen, whom he called "Germanic false Gods." His readers still had their work cut out for them because the "evil that they spread still mars our earth."[23]

One of the airmen whom Eisen may have inspired was Stan Winfield of Calgary. Winfield began to visit Belsen in May 1945.[24] He worked, mostly unofficially, as an aide to a non-Jewish Canadian RAF officer, Squadron Leader Ted Aplin.[25] Both men saw it as their mission to make life better for the survivors, who had by now been moved to a displaced persons camp nearby in order to inhibit any illness's advance.[26] The airmen found ways to get around the strict regulations barring access to the camp and barring the survivors from contact with the outside world except under the auspices of the British military. While Aplin spread the word to his fellow officers, Winfield, a sergeant, canvassed the lower ranks in the RCAF No. 8402 Disarmament Wing. Everyone asked their families to send care packages marked with a "B" for the Belsen survivors. "And have them send parcels, not necessarily food, but food of course, tinned food, but as well pretty things, combs, books, anything that might make life a little more pleasant and a little more humane for them," Winfield suggested.[27]

The pair also arranged picnics and outings for the children, and Canadian Jewish airmen went along, including Bernard Yale, an RCAF photographer from Toronto. The twenty-three-year-old had spent the war fixing the cameras attached to Spitfires. Now, he documented the liberation of the camp and the aftermath.[28] Winfield knew the top brass frowned on his activities, which took time away from the task of disarming the Luftwaffe. "Such flagrant abuse of duty time and misuse of military vehicles to transport this 'contraband' made our senior officers furious," admitted Winfield, but it didn't stop him or Aplin.[29]

One Hamilton soldier's unauthorized efforts on behalf of Belsen survivors nearly cost him his job. Solomon Goldberg, a former welder, wound up stationed in Celle, close to Belsen, running an army mobile field bath and laundry unit. Like Winfield and Aplin, Goldberg became frustrated with what he felt were the inadequate services being provided to the liberated prisoners. He would scavenge blankets and other supplies for them.[30] "He was caught on one occasion by a Canadian sergeant," said his granddaughter Adara Goldberg of Vancouver. Solomon was certain he would be severely punished after his superiors discovered he'd filled an entire Quonset hut with goods destined for the survivors. Instead, the sympathetic commanding officer not only rescinded his reprimand but added more supplies.

Although Bergen-Belsen received the most media attention,

Canadian Jewish military personnel were also active in the aftermath of the liberation of other European concentration and transit camps. In August 1945, Sam Boroditsky was posted at a military hospital located at the St. Ottilien Archabbey, a Benedictine monastery near Munich, about forty-five minutes west of the Dachau concentration camp. "One visit to Dachau where we saw what these people had been through was enough," Boroditsky writes in his memoir. He had no qualms about requisitioning clothing and supplies from the local German population. Boroditsky even took a large quantity of Masonite from a nearby factory to fashion partitions, which offered a modicum of privacy for the survivors and displaced persons.[31]

Catering to the physical needs of the liberated survivors was just the first level of help that the Canadian Jewish soldiers were able to provide. The chaplains also offered spiritual comfort, staging long-forbidden religious prayer services and sponsoring cultural events to mark Jewish holidays.

Just days after the Dutch city of Tilburg was liberated on October 27, 1944, Rabbi Sam Cass began planning for Chanukah, the upcoming Jewish festival of light. The rabbi approached his Jewish soldiers in the First Canadian Army, whom he likened to the Maccabees, to donate treats for the local children. "I am proud to say that our men contributed thousands of chocolate bars, bags of candy and other delicacies as Chanukah gifts to the children," Cass wrote to Rabbi Herman Abramowitz, of Montreal's Shaar Hashomayim synagogue. "I also purchased and scrounged all that we needed for parties and teas held in conjunction with the holiday."[32]

Chanukah parties were held in places such as Antwerp and Ghent in Belgium, and Breda and Tilburg in Holland. The Canadian Army recognized the significance of these celebrations, sending staff photographers to take pictures. One photo shows a beaming Cass as he helps a corporal identified only as M. Freedman (it was Mimi Hart of Montreal) present a gift to a young girl sporting a big bow in her hair.[33]

Another photo shows Eve Daniels (née Keller) at one such party in Belgium. Daniels holds a young girl of about two or three years old on her lap. The child, struggling to open her present, isn't smiling, but Daniels is. She felt the Chanukah party was extremely important not just for the traumatized children but also for the adults. It had symbolic value, she said, especially when a captured Nazi soldier was brought in to witness the festivities. "He didn't believe them when they said they were Jewish because he claimed Hitler said he got rid of all the Jews," said Daniels's daughter, Leslie Kinrys, referring not only to the children but also to the Jewish personnel in uniform. "They showed him how wrong Hitler was."

Rabbi Cass worked tirelessly to restore desecrated synagogues. On one occasion, he retrieved fragments of a torn Dutch Torah scroll from the window of a Belgian coffee shop that had been using it for insulation; he had the pieces buried in Tilburg.[34]

It would be another few months until the Canadian Army liberated Westerbork, the Nazi transit camp in Holland, on April 12, 1945. Cass arrived and held Sabbath services there for about five hundred surviving inmates. Participating in the Jewish prayer service had, Cass believed, given the survivors "the final evidence of their liberation." The clergyman called this Sabbath experience at Westerbork one of the most "dramatic memories I shall bring back" from the war.[35]

While the Jewish survivors were coming to terms with liberation, the end of the war in Europe also meant liberation for about eighty Jewish Canadian servicemen who had been held by the Germans as prisoners of war. Art Zaldin of Toronto was captured near Caen, France. The Americans freed him on April 12, 1945, from Oflag 79, known as Brunswick for its location near Braunschweig, in the north.[36] It housed over two thousand mainly British officers. His family had sent care packages via the Red Cross while he was a POW, but these never made it past his captors. "We got no food parcels from home, no clothing, nothing of any kind from the outside," Zaldin said. "The rations became increasingly less and less. During the nine-month period, I lost about 45 pounds, down to about 125 pounds."

Harry Hurwitz didn't lose any weight during his time as a POW. Prisoners in his camp shared their Red Cross packages, which included cigarettes and real coffee. They would sometimes use these valuable items to trade with the guards and local German farmers for better food. Hurwitz was liberated on April 28, 1945. He thinks he was the only Jewish POW in his part of the camp. When the British tanks rolled in around six o'clock in the morning, the sergeant major at the head of the tank column took charge. He immediately inquired whether there were any Jewish POWs. After keeping his religious identity a secret all this time out of fear, Hurwitz eagerly ran up and identified himself. The British liberator's name was Abramovich. "First thing I want to ask you—anybody commit any atrocities about you being a Jew?" the man demanded.

Hurwitz told him that all the guards were in their seventies and hadn't bothered him. "He believed me, because me being a Jew, telling another Jew," Hurwitz said. His first taste of freedom came in the form of some apples, a gift from one Jewish liberator to the other.

When Maxwell London was liberated from Stalag II-D prison camp at Stargard, then in Prussia, now Poland, he had been in German hands for close to three years, captured in the Dieppe Raid in August 1942, along with close to two thousand other Canadians. Once he got safely back to England, London met King George VI. He also went out and splurged on sweets.

"He always dreamt of eating a cake all by himself when he [got] out," his daughter Sandra London-Rakita said. But his long captivity made that wish impossible. "He went and bought a cake and he couldn't even eat a piece, because his stomach was so small."

Percy Gaum's stint as a POW was even longer than London's. The Nova Scotia airman, known as Pinky, survived thanks to a sympathetic German camp guard who sneaked extra bread to him. "The guard used to call him Pinkele—he knew he was Jewish," said Martin Chernin, a cousin, explaining how the guard figured it out. "He could see Pinky understood what the guards were yelling and screaming about [and how] he would warn the others, because he understood Yiddish." Gaum, whose Hebrew name was Pinchas, hence Pinky, begged the guard not to tell anyone. When Gaum arrived safely in England on April 23, 1945, "he looked like a skeleton," Chernin said. Pinky's brother David, a doctor serving with the Royal Canadian Army Medical Corps, was in London to greet him.[37] He put Pinky on a strict regimen to fatten him up, lest their mother see her son in that condition. "Steak and eggs and bacon and *treif* [unkosher food] and potatoes and beer. He made him put on ten to fifteen pounds."

One Toronto soldier who had spent six months in a German POW camp at Bathorn, on the German border with Holland, thinks he might have had a vastly different life after the war had he been permitted to date a particular woman who caught his eye just after his liberation. Louis Gelman, a Polish-born Jew, was recovering in a Birmingham hospital in April 1945 when he noticed the dark-haired girl wearing an Army Territorial Service uniform visiting the wards.

"A gorgeous girl goes by [saying], 'Get well, everybody. Get well, everybody,'" Gelman recalled. He asked his nurse how old the girl was. "I said, 'Well, maybe I can make a date with her?" The nurse quickly told Gelman to forget it, which infuriated him. "I says, 'What do you mean? I fought for your country, I nearly got killed, twice, you know? You're telling me I can't even go out with an English girl?'"

"No, you can't," the nurse patiently explained, although the reason she gave had nothing to do with his being a Jew and the girl an Anglican. "She's Princess Elizabeth."[38]

Some Canadians who had been on the front lines enjoyed the delights of the liberation in Europe. In London, on May 8, 1945, many joined the V-E Day crowds in front of Buckingham Palace to see the Royal Family while others lined the streets to hear Churchill speak at Whitehall; the party went on all night at Piccadilly Circus. David Croll was among them, having flown to England from Holland, to keep a promise to his friends that they would meet there when the war was over. "In Piccadilly Circus you met all the guys you ever knew," he recalled. "Hello! How are you? That sort of thing. The next morning, I flew to Canada."[39]

Herb Ludman's efforts to assist Jewish refugees in Italy had been cut short at the beginning of August 1944, when he was shot down over Hungary during a raid. The Lethbridge airman spent the rest of the war as a POW, including at Stalag Luft III in Poland, the site of the Great Escape.[40] After U.S. general George Patton's troops liberated his POW camp, the airman revelled in his newfound freedom. On arrival back in England in late May, he was quartered at the Royal Bath Hotel in Bournemouth, where he would seek out free Friday night dinners at a local Jewish-run hotel.[41] He did some sightseeing, including in liberated Paris, which he called "as gay as ever." Ludman also indulged at one of London's luxury hotels, the Savoy, where he enjoyed "a large, beautifully furnished room with bath for about 60 cents a day."[42]

Ludman's best friend, Manny Raber, was liberated from Stalag III-A at Luckenwalde, south of Berlin. He had survived the death march of prisoners from Stalag Luft III. Starting on January 27, 1945, the prisoners had been forced to make the journey west into Germany on foot during an unusually cold winter. While he was waiting for transportation, Raber and an American Jewish POW volunteered to go into the German countryside near their camp to forage for food supplies. "I could speak quite a lot of Jewish," Raber explained. They didn't find much food, since the Russians had already scavenged what the villagers had. But they did encounter two German officers and twenty fully armed enlisted men who stepped out of the bush, ready to surrender. Raber couldn't cooperate as he was a freed POW without enough food for himself, let alone the Germans.[43]

As the victory celebrations rolled out across Europe in May, Bill Zelikovitz was still flying military transport planes, but instead of carrying paratroopers into battle he was taking POWs to freedom. He once carried a group of German officers to Nuremburg to face war crimes trials, and also took Allied leaders into newly liberated Denmark. "We were amongst the first to enter Copenhagen, Denmark, and were certainly shown a wonderful time. Kids cling on to you, women hugging you (the part I like best) and people asking for your autograph. Boy, what a time we had," he writes. "They certainly make them tall and beautiful up there."[44]

Lawrence Levy found himself in Oldenburg, Germany, when the war ended. He wasn't a drinker, and the men were under orders to keep away from local girls, but Levy enjoyed some of liberation's other simple pleasures just as much. "We had showers. I hadn't had a shower for three to four months," he said. That wasn't the best part, though. "They gave us clean underwear."

Levy also had plenty of opportunities to find a warm bed and roll in the hay after his regiment began capturing territory from the Germans in the summer of 1944, but he couldn't bring himself to take advantage of his position as a liberator. The desperate circumstances that forced the girls into prostitution turned him off. A family of Polish refugees in Holland offered him their teenage daughter in payment for a bottle of liquor. "I had a drink and whatnot, and they said, 'You could go upstairs with our daughter,' and I said, 'No, she's only a baby,'" Levy recalled, adding that the girl was fifteen. "They wanted a fix-up [for her] with a nice soldier like me."

After VE-Day, Lorne Winer's unit was disbanded at Zeist, Holland. But like many thousands of servicemen and -women, he would have to wait months to return home. Ostensibly those who had enlisted earliest were to be sent home first, but there weren't enough ships to take everyone until Japan surrendered in August 1945. Furthermore, some military personnel were still needed in Europe.

While waiting his turn, Winer was sent to a new posting with the Canadian Occupation Force in Europe. When he reported for duty, he thought the building looked more like a brothel than a barracks. "I'm ducking brassieres and women's underpants and I think to myself, 'we're a highly disciplined outfit, now what the hell is this?'"

The senior officer, who was also bitter about not being sent home yet, had installed a lady in his quarters, and he didn't much care what his new soldiers did with their time. Winer could speak a bit of Dutch, so some of the other men sent him to The Hague, about an hour's drive away, so everyone could follow their major's example. "I went there with a driver and I went into two or three different cafés and asked the young ladies if they would be willing to join [a] sergeant on Sunday and stay with him for a week," Winer said. "And we would pick up whoever jumped first."

14 Coming Home

"I chased those five years my whole life"

Back in Canada, VE-Day parties were held across the country on May 8. In Vancouver, Esther Thorley watched the revellers take to the streets. "There was a lot of noise and a lot of yelling and screaming and drinking and confetti being thrown up into the air as if it were a marriage," she said.

She chose to avoid the whole scene. She and her uniformed friends went to a servicemen's centre and she also telephoned home to Toronto to hear some familiar voices. Her mother nearly had a heart attack. "She thought it was the army phoning to tell her bad news," Thorley said.

In Toronto, mayor Robert Saunders held a formal commemoration at the Cenotaph in front of City Hall. There were also plenty of unofficial parties. Dick Steele's widow, Esther, went out for a while to watch it all, but her heart wasn't in it. Just nine months had passed since Dick's death. She came home and wrote to Bill Walsh, who was still overseas: "While I was so happy that at last it was over, this day which we had been waiting for for such a long time, that it meant perhaps soon you will be back and others...too, yet inside of me I was crying that Dick and Muni [Erlick] aren't here to rejoice."[1]

Nowhere in Canada was May 8 marked as violently as it was in Halifax, where mass rioting and looting lasted for thirty-six hours. Three people died, and two hundred others were charged, both civilians and service personnel.[2] Manny Rubinoff, in the military police by then, was in the middle of it. He was wearing full battle dress, including a steel helmet, and had a bayonet mounted on his rifle. Passing the overturned cars and the ransacked liquor stores, Rubinoff and his squad "hammered a few legs" to try to stop the violence. He halted an assault on a fifteen-year-old girl who was being "horsed around" with by a man in the crowd. "I looked him in the eye and I said, 'I'm going to count to three and as soon as I count to three I'm gonna shove the bayonet right up your ass.' He was already running like hell fifty yards down the road."

Although hundreds of thousands of Canadian troops were celebrating the end of the war in Europe, many had also already signed up to put themselves back in harm's way. As early as April 1945, Canada had agreed to field a division for the war in the Pacific, with some sixty thousand volunteers needed to defeat the Japanese.[3] Those who volunteered were given speedy passes back to Canada from Europe, higher pay, and a month's leave at home before they had to report for duty.[4]

When Ruben Ostfield arrived back in Winnipeg at the end of July 1945, his wife was baffled. How had the Canadian officer managed to jump the queue to get home so quickly from England? His answer prompted Rose, his British war bride, to do something completely out of character for the well brought up young mother of two young children. "It was probably one of the few times in my life that I've used words that I've never used and I've never used them again. I screamed at your father, 'How could you do this to me?'" recounted their son, Michael Ostfield.

Esther Thorley thought about going to Japan, too, but not as part of the Canadian Army's Pacific Force. She was on leave from her base in Vancouver, having drinks at a service centre on the west coast of the United States. An older American officer took a shine to her. "He asked me what did I think of being sent to Japan. I said, 'Boy, that would be nice,'" Thorley recalled. He was being shipped out there soon. "So he proposed to me right away, that night, but I didn't know him, so of course I said no."

It would not be until after the two atomic bombs were dropped on Hiroshima and Nagasaki that the Canadian prisoners of war in Japanese-held territory were liberated. Japan capitulated in mid-August 1945, bringing to an end William Allister's three years and eight months of brutal treatment in forced-labour camps.

When Allister returned to Montreal, it took a few months before he felt ready to resume his acting career. In January 1946, Allister stepped back onto the stage as the lead in the play *The Skin of Their Teeth* at the Jewish Y. A reviewer in the *YMHA Beacon* found him fit and looking well, attributing it to Allister's having been able to steal food at his last Japanese work camp before liberation.[5]

Later, Allister expressed his psychological and physical trauma by painting and by writing several books about the war. In describing the experience of liberation, he wrote, "I was shrieking, waving, laughing, howling insane gibberish, freaking, weeping uncontrollably the tears sprouting up like an irrepressible orgasmic release. All the murders, tortures, all the Jews burning in Belsen, all the hellish years had gathered in a million voices bursting all bounds." With reference to the Allied airdrops of food to the newly liberated POWs, he recalled, "men ate as many as twenty chocolate bars a day, and vomited."[6]

Other Canadian Jewish POWs in Hong Kong weren't liberated as quickly as Allister. It would be September before Frederick Zaidman and Louis Brown were freed. David Golden didn't land in British Columbia until October 5.[7] Surprisingly, he decided not to blame an entire country for his lost years. "I have no animosity toward the Japanese people as such," Golden recalled. "They were caught up in something just as a lot of other people were.... I have grievances against individuals, not against the country."[8] Golden's hatred was reserved for his Japanese captors who murdered four of his men in Hong Kong. Golden also never forgave the prison camp officials who withheld Red Cross relief parcels, medicines, and letters.[9]

It would take months for the majority of the Canadian Jewish veterans to make it home. The timing of each repatriation depended on the individual's seniority, whether they were single, how many years of service they had, and other factors. Nathan Isaacs remembers his homebound journey fondly. "Coming home was fantastic," he said, referring to the ocean voyage. "[We] came on an American boat and all we did was line up for meals, because it was breaded veal cutlets, it was apple pie. It was [fantastic]. The Americans really took care of their [passengers]," he said.

For some of the returning Jewish Canadian veterans, their homecomings were a mixture of sadness and joy. Hong Kong POW George Harrison's arrival in Winnipeg started at the train station, where his brother Alf jumped on him, hugged him, then hurried him back to River Avenue to see his mother and the well-wishers who were waiting for them. "And we got out to my brother's place and hugging and kissing and so forth," Harrison said.[10] The hard part was telling the eager families of the other Winnipeg Grenadiers that their sons would not be coming back. His other brother, Robert, did not come back either; he was an RCAF airman who died in action.[11]

Manny Raber returned to Canada on the troopship *Île de France* and remembers playing cards—crown and anchor—the whole way home. After a long train ride from Halifax, he arrived in Medicine Hat. "My mother and sisters must have been baking for days," Raber recalled.[12]

Arthur Pascal's welcome home in Montreal was somewhat strained. Pascal's wife, Olga, and their two daughters, Paula and Susan, hadn't seen him in years since before he went overseas. Little Susan in particular was terrified. "Everybody had been telling her that she had no father or that he comes home full of mud, these crazy stories, so she hid under a bed and I had to pull her out," Pascal said.[13]

David Croll's three daughters were now young ladies. He hadn't realized how much time had passed since he left Windsor. "When I came home I remember one morning starting to walk into their room and my wife asked, 'Had you not better knock?' I said, 'What? Knock for the children?' She said, 'They are not children anymore.' Nothing else in the world struck me so hard. The time I had missed," Croll said.[14]

Croll's daughter Crystal Hawk still has a blanket her mother sewed from the kilt her father had worn in the Essex Scottish Regiment. Her mother, Sarah, had refused to allow her husband to return it to the army. Some veterans kept parts of their uniforms while others, like Jack Tweyman, didn't want reminders. "I was happy to get out of the army already, so when I got home I, right away, I threw the uniform away, and I even tore up my...discharge papers," he said. "I did not tear them up in anger, but it was finished. It was enough."

Leo Guttman didn't keep any of his Royal Canadian Air Force uniform and never wore the service medals he had earned. He refused to join the Royal Canadian Legion, and he dressed in civilian clothes for the annual Remembrance Day ceremonies held at his synagogue, Beth Ora, in Montreal. He also never talked about his service with his wife or three daughters. "I didn't really want to remember a lot of things. I wanted to get it behind me," he explained. The way he saw it, his hearing loss from years working on aircraft as a mechanic during the war was a minor price to pay. "I was lucky to get into the war and to get into the service and come out in one whole piece," he said, remembering his first trip to the Department of Veterans Affairs and seeing men with no arms and men who had lost eyes. "There were these guys and they can't write and they can't see and so I figured I was lucky."

Irving Friedlan returned to Montreal and didn't talk about his war experience serving in England and France. He told his wife, Ruth Friedlan (née Bogan), and two sons, that he'd been playing soccer and slept through the Blitz.

Mimi Freedman married a cousin, Bill Hart, also a veteran, and the couple moved to Long Island to work for a publishing company. She drove like a maniac, her relatives say, perhaps a habit retained from her days driving ambulances and staff cars for Canadian officers in wartime London.

She didn't talk about the war, about being a trailblazer, about her six and a half years in service, or her Mention in Dispatches. She didn't discuss surviving a V2 bomb that fell in the centre of Antwerp, and caused a great many casualties. "She was a very private person," said her niece, Ruth Elias.

Bill Walsh came home prepared to keep his promise to his best friend, Dick Steele, to look after his widow, Esther, and their twins. After Dick's death in France in 1944, Walsh and Esther began to correspond frequently. The tone of their letters moved from comradeship to companionship. "I'll make every effort to get back, consistent with doing the job that's got to be done," Walsh wrote. "My love is with you and for you. I must close now. We're leaving a little ahead of zero hour. XXX Bill."[15] Bill and Esther were married in 1946. They raised the twins and had a daughter of their own, Sherry Walsh. Bill picked up where he had left off with his union work and spent the rest of his career as a labour organizer in Southern Ontario.

Sue Jacobs called her two and a half years in the service "absorbing, amusing, sometimes uncomfortable, and never to be regretted." After she returned to the United States, the widow remarried, to an old flame, who was an American veteran. They had four children, while she pursued a career first as a social worker and then as a writer.

Max (Val) Rimer returned home to Winnipeg in the winter of 1946. His parents, sister, and fiancée, Doris, were waiting for him with a big Welcome Home banner strung across the entrance.[16] Doris fainted when he appeared. As he slung his kit bag off his shoulder, Rimer regretted not having souvenirs to show them. He'd thrown his cache of captured German weapons overboard before leaving Europe for fear they would be confiscated when he was repatriated to Canada.

Other returning Jewish veterans, however, managed to bring back tangible proof of their encounters with the enemy. Harry Hurwitz had an ornate silver sword with an eagle's head and red stones for eyes carved into the hilt, and engraved with a swastika. He'd taken it from the body of a dead German general near his POW camp after his liberation. Officials nearly confiscated the booty when he boarded the troopship. "They [the military] wouldn't allow me to [bring the German weapon] at first. But they said, 'Ah, he was a prisoner of war, the war is over,'" and waved the sword through.

It might have been a case of space limitations on board ship that prevented Selwyn (Shia) Campbell from bringing back a collection of souvenirs of war so large that he could have opened his own museum in Montreal. During his travels through the European theatre of war, the Black Watch sniper had collected enough booty to fill twenty-one duffel bags. When it was his turn to embark back to Canada, Campbell was told his extra luggage was not permitted.

"He could only have one bag," said his nephew Eric Campbell, which is why twenty bags of his uncle's meticulously gathered spoils were tossed into the sea. The one he kept included a prized Nazi pin.

Norm Gulko carried a piece of war crimes evidence around with him, one he'd taken out of a picture frame in a German home. The photograph showed a smiling soldier standing beside a pile of bodies. "That photo may have been taken in a concentration camp," Gulko said. He brought out the picture when "German civilians, mostly women...would always claim not to know anything about what the Nazis had done."[17]

The souvenir that Captain Isaac Rose brought back with him wasn't directly a Nazi symbol or evidence of a war crime, but his artifact was both a testament to the tragic fate of the Jews of Holland and a symbol of hope. A grateful Dutch Holocaust survivor had given a bronze Chanukah menorah to the Canadian chaplain as a "tribute to his services."[18]

Jack Marcovitch brought back two heirlooms from the Dutch Jewish community. He had found them when his unit liberated the Nazi concentration camp of Vught, near the city of 'sHertogenbosch (or Den Bosch), in southern Holland, in October 1944. One of the items was a tallit. The other was a black-and-gold-covered Hebrew–German prayer book that he'd found in one of the camp storerooms. "He wanted to save it, rescue it," explained his son Don Marcovitch, an Ottawa auto executive. "He couldn't take them all, so he took one."

The siddur and the prayer shawl haunted Jack all his life. After the war, he didn't feel worthy of wearing the tallit himself, and he kept the antique prayer book in his dresser. In 2016, his son learned the identity of the book's owner. Elise Cahn, a Dutch Jewish woman and her husband, Daniel, a butcher, had been rounded up from their home in Valkenburg, in Holland's southern tip, in 1943. They were transported first to Vught and then through the transit camp at Westerbork, in northeastern Holland, before perishing in the gas chambers of Sobibór, in eastern Poland, on May 14, 1943.[19] Three of the Cahns' adult children had also been murdered in the Holocaust—a daughter at Auschwitz and two sons at labour camps.

A fourth son, Louis, the oldest, had jumped off a transport train and survived the war, eventually making his way to Palestine. A daughter, Annette, had also survived by hiding in a monastery. Annette's children were stunned to learn that a Canadian Jewish liberator had saved their murdered grandparents' prayer book seventy years ago. "It brings my grandparents closer to me," said Elise Vrancken, of Elst, Holland, who bears her grandmother's name.

Although Marcovitch's story remained untold until now, many people in Cape Breton have long known about the sword that pathologist Isadore Gold of Glace Bay brought back from Japan. It belonged to General Hideki Tojo, the wartime Japanese prime minister and leader of the Japanese Imperial Army. Tojo had tried to commit suicide by shooting himself in the chest when officers came to his door to arrest him. Gold, who was serving as a doctor with the U.S. Army in the Pacific, supervised the blood transfusion when the general was brought into hospital in Yokohama. Tojo survived; he was put on trial for war crimes and hanged on December 23, 1948. The general's wife later presented Gold with the sword.

When Gold returned to his medical practice in Brooklyn, he brought the sword with him. Having seen so much death while serving in Nagasaki after the nuclear bomb fell, Gold only wanted to treat patients who were beginning their lives. He became an obstetrician and gynecologist.

Isadore Gold was not the only doctor who faced a dilemma about whether and how to care for the enemy. Many years after Nathan Levinne returned to Toronto, he recounted the story of his own test on the beaches of Walcheren Island, in southern Holland, in early November 1944. Levinne, who later became the head of family practice at Toronto's Mount Sinai Hospital, was a captain serving in the 17th Canadian Light Field Ambulance. His ambulance crew came to the rescue of some wounded Canadians when a teenage German soldier with an injured arm grabbed a gun and started shooting at him.

"So my batman said to me, 'Shall we let him have it?' and I must be honest and tell you I couldn't say yes," Levinne recalled during an interview for *No Greater Honour*. "So we picked him up and put him on the Jeep and dragged him back. So I guess the value of life, you never lose that...although maybe I didn't have the killer instinct." He returned to Canada with two bravery awards: a Mention in Dispatches and a medal from the Dutch government. Levinne, who had himself been wounded in Holland, called coming home to Toronto the "greatest thrill of my life."[20]

Like Levinne and Gold, plenty of demobilized Jewish medical personnel credit their years of battlefield experience with accelerating their post-war careers, as was the case with the Winnipeg dentist Jack Ludwig. After patching up the faces of so many wounded servicemen, Ludwig took a further medical degree in England and came home to practice as a dental surgeon.

A glowing letter of reference from a senior officer came in handy when Joseph Minden returned from the war. He completed his training in the United States and came home in 1949 to look for a position in Southern Ontario, where jobs had been closed to him and many other Jewish doctors before the war. His welcome back was quite different. He joined the staff at St. Joseph's Hospital in Hamilton and later was head of surgery at Joseph Brant Memorial Hospital in Burlington. He taught at McMaster University's medical school. He would often tell his six children that being a doctor was his personal way of "paying rent for being alive."[21]

Harry Winter of Toronto was one of the highest-profile Jewish physicians to capitalize on his wartime achievements, training in thoracic medicine in England. Winter had earned the title "the Hero of Coventry" for keeping the hospital running while German bombs all but destroyed the British city during an infamous raid on November 14, 1940, that killed more than five hundred people and injured hundreds more.[22] Winter, the son of a grocer, became an international celebrity when *Life* magazine reported on his bravery and Britain awarded him an Order of the British Empire. Sadly, he died of heart failure in 1949 at the age of thirty-six. He'd just moved home to Toronto to open an office.[23]

Jacob Markowitz was already a famous doctor in Toronto before the war. His reputation grew even greater after he returned as a hero from Asia in 1945, where Marko, as he was known, had spent three and a half years as a prisoner of war after being captured by the Japanese Imperial Army in Singapore. Transferred in May 1943 to the Chungkai POW camp north of Bangkok in Thailand, the surgeon improvised a style of jungle medicine credited with saving the lives of countless Allied POWs, particularly the men who were forced to build the infamous Railway of Death for the Japanese between Burma and Thailand.[24] Markowitz is said to have completed 115 amputations. He kept detailed case notes on his techniques, which he then buried inside bottles with the bodies of POWs who didn't survive. These notes would later be recovered and published.

In the summer of 1946, Markowitz was appointed a Member of the Order of the British Empire for improving the administration of transfusions using primitive equipment despite "great personal risk" and for his "gallant and distinguished services" while a prisoner of war."[25]

Shortly after receiving the award, Markowitz was invited to speak at the pro-British Empire Club in Toronto, where he described his life in captivity as "biblical" because it reminded him of the conditions that the Jewish people experienced during the days of Moses.[26] Markowitz told the crowd about the time an Australian POW was having surgery and stopped breathing. Without any medical equipment in the camp, Markowitz improvised a technique inspired by a story from the Hebrew Bible. "You remember how the widow came to Elijah and asked for help for her son? Elijah breathed into him face to face, and the child recovered," Markowitz said. So he scrounged a piece of rubber tubing to blow air into the man's lungs. Twenty minutes of artificial respiration later, the man revived. As the POW spat out the tube, he reportedly said to Markowitz, "I'm glad you guys don't eat onions."

After the Japanese surrender, Markowitz returned to England, married his second wife, Ruth, and then moved back to Toronto to resume his family practice from his home on Forest Hill Road. In the ensuing years, despite suffering from post-traumatic stress, he churned out scholarly research papers and continued his affiliation with the University of

Toronto's medical school, passing on his knowledge to generations of students.[27]

For his part, Louis Slotin didn't want anything more to do with the wartime work that had vaulted him, a Jewish scientist from Winnipeg, to prominence. Slotin had been part of the American team working on what was known as the Manhattan Project, which is credited with building the atomic bombs that were dropped on Japan. Before the war, Slotin's interest had been the use of nuclear material to cure disease. He might never have found himself working in a top-secret American military research lab in Los Alamos, New Mexico, during the war, had his application to work in Ottawa at the National Research Council been accepted. Slotin's family blames widespread prejudice in the federal government of prewar Canada. "There were some very strong antisemitic attitudes in those days, so there was no way they were going to let a Jewish guy get into that position," said his nephew Rael Ludwig.

Slotin went to work at the University of Chicago instead, and his research there with Enrico Fermi on nuclear reactions brought him to the attention of the American military. Slotin became an expert in assembling the business end of atomic bombs.[28] On August 6, 1945, "Little Boy" was dropped on Hiroshima; "Fat Man" destroyed Nagasaki three days later.[29] When the war in the Pacific ended, Slotin wanted to return to his preferred field of study and to academia at the University of Chicago. His conscience was troubled by the ethics of using nuclear energy to kill people.[30]

"There was a petition that went around," Ludwig said. "The scientists of Los Alamos were asking that this weapon not be used as part of the arsenal, and he was one of the scientists that signed that petition." But by May 1946, with the war already over for nine months, Slotin was still needed in Los Alamos as the resident expert. An accident during a routine lab experiment on some radioactive cores—some called this "tickling the dragon's tail"—on May 21 set off a nuclear reaction.[31] Slotin's screwdriver slipped while holding the two cores apart, and when they touched, a flash of blue light and heat burst out and burned Slotin. He reached down and grabbed one of the cores with his bare hands to separate them, ending the exposure.[32] By doing this, he likely saved the lives of the other six scientists in the room, but he absorbed a fatal amount of radiation, "possibly the highest dose of radiation anyone has ever taken."[33]

It would take nine agonizing days for Slotin to die in a New Mexico hospital. The U.S. Army flew his parents down to be with him. "It was a secret project, so they had no idea what he was working on or how dangerous it was," Ludwig said.

Even then, Slotin didn't tell them how sick he really was.[34] "Just a bit of a burn," he said, while soaking his blistered hands in ice buckets.

When he died, at the age of thirty-five, the army put his body into a specially lined lead coffin, draped with an American flag, and flew it and his parents back to Winnipeg. Three thousand people turned out for the funeral on the lawn of his home on Scotia Avenue. The Manhattan Project's director, Major General Leslie R. Groves, said the Canadian researcher should be credited for "ending the war without an invasion of Japan."[35] The kind of hands-on experiments that Slotin had been conducting were officially halted after the accident. Although he wore a lab coat and not an army uniform during the war, officials at the Canadian Jewish Congress gave his story the first four pages in their 1948 publication listing the 450 Canadian Jewish military casualties of World War II.[36]

As with many Canadian veterans in the scientific and medical fields who continued their careers, the end of the war also brought new opportunities for Jewish veterans in the arts and humanities. Milton Shulman was a Toronto lawyer when he enlisted in the army in 1941. He served in intelligence and earned the rank of major. He also received a Mention in Dispatches in 1945.[37] After the war, Shulman interviewed many of the top German generals, and his work became the basis for a book about Axis military tactics. Shulman later became a theatre critic and journalist in England.[38]

Monte Halparin (known better as Monty Hall) never got the chance to go overseas to entertain the Canadian troops, although the television host would have dearly loved to do so. He completed his science degree at the University of Manitoba, then moved to Toronto and entered show business. He credits entertaining the servicemen for helping him become an enormously successful post-war Hollywood celebrity. "Great training for my show business career that followed," Hall acknowledged.

When they returned from overseas, Frank Shuster and Johnny Wayne took advantage of the government's re-establishment credits for veterans: they bought a typewriter and used it to bang out the scripts for their peacetime show, *The Johnny Home Show.* The weekly radio sitcom helped explain government benefits to the returning veterans. The show ran on the CBC from July 1945 to the summer of 1946. "We wrote a series for fifty-two weeks about a soldier who comes back, and each week the Department of Veterans Affairs would send us a lot of information about, let's say, the use of the Veterans Land Act, how to explain it, what does it mean," Wayne said in a 1958 interview with the CBC. "And we wrote a comedy show actually around it but in the comedy show it contained the message."[39]

Scores of demobilized Canadian Jewish veterans took advantage of the benefits and went back to the classroom. After the war, Evelyn Miller studied commerce at the University of Alberta. She was one of eighteen women among 129 men in her 1950 graduating class. The university called her a trailblazer "in heels." Miller became an accountant and moved to California.[40] David Golden activated the Rhodes scholarship he had won before the war and studied in England. After a few years, he moved to Ottawa to work in the federal civil service.[41] Evelyn Bloom (née Bernstein) went to university to study art education and became a teacher and art professor in Montreal. Abe Ferstman studied for his commerce degree at McGill. He took three years' worth of courses in nineteen months.

Navy veteran David Hart went back to school to become an engineer, but it was the training that he received during the war that he credits for his success later in life. "In the service you run across a wide variety of people, some of whom you would never dream of associating with in normal life, and it was a real education," Hart said.[42] Bill Novick went to medical school at Queen's University.[43] Morris Polansky went to the University of Manitoba and became an electrical engineer.

Not all the Jewish veterans turned their backs on the military. Major Albert Mendelsohn of Ste-Agathe-des-Monts, Quebec, served for thirty-two years in the Canadian Army and rose to the rank of brigadier general.[44] Harold Fromstein, the Black Watch bravery medal winner, joined the U.S. military.[45]

Irving Kaplan was one of the first Canadian sailors to return home. Kaplan had volunteered for duty in Japan but was not called. After the war, he worked in the Merchant Marine, sometimes taking surplus Canadian warships to their final destinations to be scrapped. Eventually, in 1947, Kaplan, now a twenty-eight-year-old bachelor, came ashore for good, fastened his discharge pin onto his lapel, and started his own company in Montreal installing insulation. "The reception was good," he said. "As a young Jewish war veteran, I could tell that they [customers] wanted to give me a chance."[46]

Young Canadians from small towns and rural areas also had to restart their lives. Some returned home, including Manny Raber, who settled back in Medicine Hat and inherited the family clothing business, Raber's Department Store. More often, though, veterans from small towns settled in bigger cities, where they devoted their energy and leadership to new opportunities. As a consequence, the end of the war came at the same time as, or perhaps even accelerated, the demise of Jewish life in smaller communities. The author Bella Briansky Kalter watched this happen in her hometown of Ansonville, Ontario, which had lost three enlisted men—the Crotin brothers and David Abramson. "The Second World War came and began plucking up their sons and broke their homogeneity and spirit," she writes.[47]

In Kamsack, Saskatchewan, according to Harold Laimon, the older people began to retire, and the younger ones, many of whom had already left during the war, didn't come back. Eventually even Kamsack's rabbi, Yehuda Leib Olin, moved to Saskatoon.

Many veterans struggled with the readjustment to civilian life. Albert Glazer returned to Toronto with hopes of finding important work thanks to his war experience and his bravery medals from the King. But his homecoming turned out to be quite different from what he expected.[48]

"Here I came back as a hero in uniform, I was really riding the crest, and then to forget about all the honours, everyday life, now I'm back in Civvy Street looking for a job. It's quite a letdown," Glazer said.[49] Although he had graduated as an engineer from the University of Toronto before the war, Glazer reluctantly went back to his pre-war career in the movie theatre business and later, with a partner, opened a chain of hardware stores.[50]

Ben Dunkelman, a decorated war hero, quickly discovered that adulation was fleeting. "I found that the role was good only for a few days," he writes in his memoir, describing why he soon returned to his family company, Tip Top Tailors. "Nobody waited on you hand and foot and you were expected to get to work."[51]

To be sure, the returning veterans received public recognition in communities across Canada. Calgary's B'nai Brith Lodge No. 816 threw a welcome home banquet for the city's Jewish war veterans on May 19, 1946. Two hundred guests dined on roast chicken, blintzes, chopped liver, pickled herring, and other Jewish specialties.[52] In June of that year, the Council of Jewish Organizations in St. Catharines held a ceremony at the synagogue. The veterans all received specially engraved rings.[53] Saskatoon's B'nai Brith Lodge No. 379 held a reception on December 12 in honour of those servicemen who had returned, including Mickey Poplack, a survivor of Dieppe.[54]

A tribute dinner by Montreal's Jewish community in 1946 left David Lloyd Hart feeling used and unappreciated. The event was held at the Mount Royal Hotel. Hart was invited, as were several other decorated Jewish heroes, including Syd Shulemson and Bill Novick. When the evening was over, Hart had to find his own way home by streetcar. "It was in November, it was pretty cold," he said. "I was with Laz Peters who also got a DFC [Distinguished Flying Cross] and the two of us are waiting [but] nobody offered us a lift home.... Nobody interested."

David Croll came home to Canada as a war hero but also found it hard to get used to travelling without the entourage he'd had as a lieutenant colonel in the army. "He'd had a batman, a secretary, and a driver," his daughter said. Croll had served in the post-war reconstruction teams in Holland, helping restore some semblance of municipal government in the liberated towns and cities.

The former Windsor mayor characterized his army service as "the greatest adventure any person could have," and said that donning a Canadian uniform made him feel truly part of the Canadian social mosaic. "I can think of no greater honour than to serve your country in the time of need," Croll said. "I felt I belonged. It was my country. I had fought for it."[55]

Croll didn't wait long to jump right back into politics. Although he had wanted to go back to his law practice and make some real money, he was persuaded to run for the Liberals against the high-profile Labour-Progressive Party (formerly Communist) leader, Tim Buck, in the 1945 federal election in the riding of Toronto-Spadina. "The people of Spadina said, 'Oh no! After fighting against them all these years we are not going to have a communist represent us.' And since Spadina was a Jewish riding, it would not do to have a communist represent them," Croll said, explaining why he agreed to stand. He didn't campaign much, just put on his uniform. "It was a nice uniform," he quipped. He won the seat handily.

Croll wasn't the only Jewish veteran who tried the ballot box as a way to improve society in post-war Canada. Saul Cherniack had served in the intelligence corps during the war and became an expert in Japanese military communications. He returned home to Winnipeg and resumed his law career, where he later worked on behalf of Japanese who had been interned in Canadian prison camps during the war. He also entered politics, rising to the rank of Cabinet minister in several NDP governments in Manitoba.

Edwin Goodman, a veteran of the Fort Garry Horse Regiment, campaigned for a seat in the Ontario legislature in the summer of 1945, but lost to the communist stalwart J.B. Salsberg.[56] In the federal election of June 1945, Bert Sucharov, the decorated Dieppe engineer, campaigned as an independent in Winnipeg North, also unsuccessfully.[57]

After the war, the twice-wounded infantryman Harry Binder returned to Canada and settled in Montreal, where he resumed his work with the communist movement. He also entered politics, where he was a perennial candidate for the party in both Ottawa and Montreal. He served as a city councillor in Montreal from 1950 to 1952.[58]

Although Harry Binder had been able to recover from his battle injuries by war's end, it took some Jewish veterans a lot longer to do so. And for veterans who had suffered not only physical but also psychological trauma, the healing would take years. Some, like Moses Lutsky, chose to confront their medical issues away from the limelight. Lutsky, a corporal, was invalided home to Montreal after the fighting in Normandy. A tank driver with the Grenadier Guards, Lutsky lost both his feet while trapped in his burning tank on August 10, 1944. He would eventually have his legs amputated below the knee. After he was repatriated to Canada, Lutsky refused to visit his parents before starting rehabilitation. "My parents are not going to see me in a wheelchair," Lutsky vowed, according to his niece Phyllis Entis. "I won't go home until I can walk."[59] He was fitted with prosthetic legs and never looked back. He married, had three children, and worked as an elevator operator at Montreal's Queen Mary Veterans Hospital.

Lorne Winer's wounds were not visible. After his discharge, it took

Winer years to recover from what we now call post-traumatic stress disorder. "After I came back, there was some noise of a car firing or something, and I yelled, 'Get down! Get down!'" Winer said. Only much later did he understand his condition. "I chased those five years my whole life." After spending years in the service, Winer couldn't get used to seeing Toronto totally unscathed. "I kept looking around wondering why there was no destruction here. Because all I'd seen was destruction all the way through." It would take him another five years before he settled down in Toronto and found steady work.

Bill Zelikovitz came home in 1945. He went to work with a brother in the leather goods business and started his own family. Yet the Ottawa airman couldn't control his reactions to certain triggers. He would cry and scream at the television if he watched a documentary about the Holocaust. The war, said his son Joel, "encompassed every thought, every conversation he had with somebody."

After Barney Finestone of Montreal had a German 88 anti-tank shell land right beside him in Italy and tear him to pieces on May 30, 1944, he was repatriated to England and then to Canada.[60] He stayed in hospital until 1947. The malaria he had also contracted in Italy took seven years to disappear. His nightmares never fully went away. "When one of your tanks is hit and some of your men die...and you see them lying there... with his guts spilling out, you don't recover from that," Finestone told *The Memory Project*. "Never recover from that. And anybody who says they do is lying."[61]

Nineteen months in a German prison camp had left Nate Nathanson of Sydney, Nova Scotia, "moody" and uninterested in life. His family found the former RCAF rear air gunner a changed man. He wanted nothing to do with the service medals to which he was entitled, and the only thing he kept was his air force hat. His son Steven isn't sure you could call it PTSD, but says his father didn't talk about the war. "It was just too hard because of what he saw," he said. His father also had certain sights and sounds and smells that set him off, including when his mother served bread pudding one time, as a special treat. "He threw it at her."

Some veterans tried to cope with their psychological trauma by self-medicating with drugs or alcohol. Murray Steiner contracted tuberculosis while on active service in England and spent weeks in army hospitals in 1943 before he was shipped home. Although the army doctors recommended a lengthy stay in a sanitarium, the former Toronto druggist was discharged in September 1943. A year and a half after the end of hostilities, and still suffering from tuberculosis, Steiner died of alcohol poisoning and heart failure in Montreal.[62]

Lawrence Levy hadn't been a drinker while overseas. The young Toronto artillery private said he found the rum rations hard on his stomach. But once he was home, Levy turned to the bottle to cope with his memories of war. It took him two years to turn his life around. "I was lost when I came back. After the war, I started finding out that things were working on me and I started drinking," he said. "The experience I went through was unbelievable and I can't imagine I [went]...through that." Levy would find a job driving a cab, and eventually married and had three daughters. He became involved in the Jewish branch of the Royal Canadian Legion in Toronto, and was an eager volunteer to speak at local schools and on Remembrance Days until his death in April 2016.

When the Canadian veterans returned home after the war, they came back to a country that had been profoundly affected by the conflict. Over a million Canadians had put on a uniform and countless others had worked in vital industries. Many women had become accustomed to working in roles only men had previously held. Yet not everything had changed, including the widespread and systemic discrimination against Jews and other racial minorities. Restrictions were still in place in many provinces regarding land ownership, and access to some professions and to university training was still limited. This discovery came as a bitter disappointment to some Canadian Jewish veterans. It would take a few years before lobbying by the Jewish community, and by the wider human rights and labour union spheres, would move governments at many levels to bring in anti-discrimination legislation. A Jewish Canadian war veteran, Calgary lawyer Morris C. Shumiatcher, is credited with drafting the country's first bill of rights in 1947. Shumy, as he was called, served in the RCAF until 1945. After the war he became a well-known human rights lawyer in Saskatchewan, where he worked for Premier Tommy Douglas.[63]

At the individual level, however, the fact that so many Canadian Jews had worn a uniform likely made a difference in how post-war society began to treat Jews. Jewish military personnel had forged countless newfound friendships with their gentile comrades in the barracks, prison camps, wardrooms, and slit trenches. And with these relationships came tolerance.

Montrealers William Allister and Georges (Blackie) Verreault were thrown together as prisoners of war in Hong Kong in 1941. Verreault was a poor Catholic French Canadian who had held strong antisemitic views. The two would form a deep bond. His own change of heart came as a surprise even to him. "Strange. I used to despise Jews and now my best friend is a Jew," Verrault wrote in his diary. "It's regrettable to see the injustice shown to this race in the way we were raised, especially us French Canadians, in despising and even hating Jews. I'm closer to Allister than to Bruno [a fellow French Canadian], and I'm looking forward to meeting his family, as I am sure I will like them."[64]

Soon after the end of the war, several hundred Jewish veterans turned their attention to another battle. In 1948, they answered the call to fight for the soon-to-be-created State of Israel. Sydney Shulemson had gone back to work at an uncle's printing company in Montreal, but when the United Nations voted in 1947 to partition Palestine, Shulemson, the most highly decorated Canadian Jewish airman of World War II, found himself being asked to take on a new secret military mission.[65]

In the months leading up to the Israeli War of Independence, Shulemson agreed to work undercover in Canada for the Haganah, the unofficial army of the nascent Jewish state.[66] It was illegal to recruit for a foreign army inside Canada. Shulemson's job was to stay off the Canadian government's radar while persuading experienced servicemen to volunteer for Israel. They held invitation-only meetings in synagogues in Quebec and Ontario to find men with valuable military skills to build the Jewish air force, navy, and army and to prepare the Jewish country for the time when the Arab leaders in Palestine and Transjordan, among others, would declare war.[67] Although the majority of the Canadian volunteers, known in Hebrew as Machalniks, a short form of the Hebrew phrase *Mitnadvei Chutz L'Aretz* (volunteers from outside the country) were Jewish, Shulemson also recruited non-Jews, including Canada's top fighter pilot. George (Buzz) Beurling joined the cause, despite Shulemson's initial misgivings about the fundamentalist Christian hero's loyalties.[68]

Nearly three hundred Canadian Jews, including many veterans of World War II such as the former sailor Gerald Rosenberg, the pilot Bill Novick, and army veteran Jerry Gross of Montreal, became Machalniks. Among the highest profile was Ben Dunkelman, who helped arrange shipments of weapons for the Jewish forces before he, too, went to fight.

Dunkelman commanded the 7th Armored Brigade of the Haganah and captured the northern lands of the Galilee. Later, his refusal to expel the Arab residents of Nazareth despite orders from his superiors would become known and lauded, but only decades after the fact.[69] He died in 1997. Not until 2015, in a report in the *Toronto Star*, would Dunkelman's merciful actions in the biblical city during the War of Independence be confirmed.[70]

It would take even longer for Lorne Winer's contribution to the liberation of France to be specifically honoured by the French government. For decades, but especially after he retired, the artillery veteran devoted his time to telling young people about his war experiences, including about the way the corpses smelled in Normandy after D-Day, about being scared by German mortars called "Moaning Minnies"—they sounded like "ghosts from the grave"—and about the mosquitoes that plagued him in his slit trench during the breakout from Juno Beach in July 1944. When the government of France announced in 2014 that it would issue the country's highest honour, the Légion d'honneur, to all Allied veterans of the liberation of France, Winer put his name forward.

It took two years for the paperwork to be processed. Winer's Légion d'honneur—a green-and-white cross with a distinctive red ribbon—arrived in October 2016. He wore it on Remembrance Day the following month, when he and the handful of remaining Jewish war veterans from the Royal Canadian Legion Wingate Branch 256 marched on Spadina Avenue outside the Miles Nadal Jewish Community Centre in Toronto. After the November 11 ceremony, Winer and the guests went inside for refreshments and a short program. He was the main attraction.

"I felt honoured. I love the title that you get, *chevalier* [knight]," Winer said about being included as a member of l'Ordre nationale de la Légion d'honneur, then joking that his horse (*cheval* in French) was waiting outside. "It's quite an honour, but it's a long, long time [since the end of the war]."

Shortly after the medal arrived, Winer had an appointment for his rheumatism, and his doctor asked whether he was a veteran. He confirmed that he was. "For whatever reason, she just fell apart. Here was this stern doctor, she started to cry, and my wife started to cry. I mean, it was ridiculous!" Winer said the doctor's reaction made him realize, after such a long time, just what he had sacrificed and survived all those years ago.

15 Kaddish for D-Day

"She just should've lived"

Larry Rosenthal still remembers the day the telegram was delivered to their Hutchinson Street home in Montreal. It was a Saturday, August 14, 1943. His parents went to the front door. Rosenthal was six years old. He felt as if the whole street were watching.

DEEPLY REGRET D131028 GUNNER WILLIAM GUY ROSENTHAL OFFICIALLY REPORTED KILLED IN ACTION TWENTYFIFTH JULY 1943 STOP FURTHER INFORMATION FOLLOWS WHEN RECEIVED.[1]

Although more than seven decades have passed since his twenty-year-old brother was killed in Sicily while manning an anti-tank gun, Rosenthal's voice still quavers when he talks about Willie. "It was horrific. A stain in our heads. And nobody should ever be faced with that," Rosenthal said. "My late mother said, 'What I went through should be enough that no other mother should ever witness or feel what I feel today.'"

For years his parents, Saul and Molly Rosenthal, refused to accept that their oldest son wasn't coming back. They kept his letters, referred to as "Velvel's papers," in a grey hatbox tied with a frayed string. It would be another two years before they could bring themselves to apply for their son's war service gratuity. "I don't know if they ever changed their minds, but they stopped talking of him coming home," Rosenthal said.

Although more than sixteen thousand Canadian Jewish veterans of World War II did come home, the Rosenthals joined the ranks of the forty-four thousand Canadian families who faced the bitter reality of the loss of a father, a husband, an uncle, a cousin, a daughter, a son—in some cases, two or more family members. Nearly 450 Canadian Jewish men and one woman died in uniform in World War II. Their families had to begin the journey from private grieving to public remembrance. They took many different paths.

"When you see the guy coming up the street, you know it's bad news," Louis Schwartz said. The Montreal resident was eleven at the time, and the youngest of twelve children in a family of Romanian immigrants. The first born, Moses Schwartz, had served as a gunner with the Royal Air Force's 78 Squadron, based near Leeds. Moses was on his thirtieth mission, laying mines in the Kadet Channel between Germany and Denmark, when his Halifax bomber was lost.[2] "My mother couldn't read, [so] my brother Bill had to read it to her," Schwartz said. The telegram said that twenty-eight-year-old Moses was missing. "My mother just passed out."

After a few months, when the air force told the family that Moses was presumed dead, the Schwartzes observed the traditional Jewish seven days of mourning. The line of visitors to get into their second-storey flat stretched all the way up from Clark Street. "I could hear my father all night back and forth walking in the hallway and crying," Louis remembers.

Moses Schwartz's body was never found, so the family could not give him a Jewish burial. His name is engraved on the vast memorial arch at Runnymede Cemetery in England, which commemorates twenty thousand Allied airmen with no known grave. Without a grave or a tombstone to visit, the Schwartzes were left to find other ways to remember him. A sister, Toby, named her son Morton in her brother's honour. For years, another brother placed a memoriam notice in the Montreal *Gazette* on Remembrance Day:

SCHWARTZ, Moses (Moe). Pilot Officer Moe Schwartz. Royal Canadian Air Force. February 15, 1945. Death can fall upon your door like rain. You must live each moment, each day as though it was your last. We remember you with pride and love. Missing you, Abie, Jake, Louis, Rachel and Bettie.[3]

Louis, now in his eighties, remembers Moe as "a great guy" who came home with a Christmas tree one time when Louis was eight, to keep his little brother happy. "I said, 'All my friends had a Christmas tree! Why can't we have a Christmas tree?'" He paid twenty-five cents for the tree at the Rachel Street market, and then carried it past the synagogue and put it up in the house.

"My God! With the lights flashing!"

Now, Schwartz finds solace by visiting the Jewish war memorial monument at the historic Baron de Hirsch Cemetery in Montreal each fall, around the time of the Jewish New Year. Moses Schwartz's name is engraved on it, as are the names of two cousins who also served and died, brothers Donald and Hyman Gaskin. "It gives me comfort," he says.

For Larry Rosenthal, a business trip to Sicily in 1972, during which he took a side trip to visit his brother's grave, gave him a profound sense of purpose for the rest of his life. It was dark when the driver got to the Canadian War Cemetery in Agira. By the light of the caretaker's lantern, Rosenthal found Willie's tombstone. It bore a Star of David, but the space below it, where the next of kin should have been and perhaps also a lasting epitaph, was blank. Rosenthal doesn't blame his parents for this oversight, understanding that they had just lost a son when the paperwork arrived three decades earlier. He decided the stone needed redoing and persuaded the Commonwealth War Graves Commission to make it happen. "They said, 'We can't, I don't know.' I said, 'Yes you can, yes you can.'" Rosenthal related. The new stone was inscribed with the Hebrew lettering that Rosenthal sent in. "Here lies Velvel, son of the worthy Simon Zelig." It gives the date of 22 Tamuz 5704, the date on the Jewish calendar corresponding to Rosenthal's death on July 25, 1943. "May his soul be bound up in the bonds of eternal life."[4]

That same tenacity and dedication led Rosenthal to undertake a much more ambitious project to commemorate all the Jews who have died fighting for Canada. In 2014, he spoke at the dedication ceremony for the expanded Jewish war cenotaph at Baron de Hirsch Cemetery, which now displays the names of 579 fallen Jewish Canadians, including soldiers from World War I and the Korean War. Rosenthal collected the names. He organizes two community-wide services there each year. The monument is the largest of its kind in Canada. "We have to speak for them because they can't. I don't say that lightly. I mean this with every part of me. Sometimes it's not easy, because people say, 'Spend your time with the living.'"

Framed photos of Willie in uniform are prominently displayed in

Rosenthal's Montreal den, where he also keeps the former journalist's large collection of favourite books, including Jack London's *The Call of the Wild*, Shakespeare's *Twelfth Night*, and Wickham Steed's *The Press*. However, it is his own brother's words that Rosenthal carries around with him on a laminated card. The passage comes from one of Willie's letters home.

And when the air is once again clear from the smoky dust of fire, and when the blood of the dead and wounded is dry and the stench of the bodies is pure, the men who are alive after victory is achieved with God's aid will return, for they, the dead, shall not have fallen in vain. Not in a world where our holy sanctuaries are safe and unmolested. In a world where organizations, institutions of culture and learning and education, are respected and upheld and supported. No price is too great to pay, no life is too precious to enforce our beliefs and ideals.[5]

Rosenthal believes his brother meant for him not only to put up monuments to the dead but also to honour them by doing the work that they can no longer do. That means carrying out good deeds, being kind to others, giving charity, and fighting injustice, duties now fuelled by Rosenthal's embrace of Orthodox Judaism. His latest project is printing and distributing a special edition of the Hebrew Bible with the 579 names on the inside covers.

"My objective is to make sure they didn't die in vain. And we do the mitzvahs, that's for us to do, to make this a better place," Rosenthal explains, adding that people today should take life seriously and appreciate what they have. "Also if you see something that's not right, stand up, say something, do something."

Larry Rosenthal commemorated his brother through personal action in his community, but many bereaved families followed the more private Jewish custom of naming the next child born in the family after the deceased. Fred Pascal's niece Susan Levine named one of her sons Fred. Fred Harris's brother Jack named a son Fred. William Nelson's sisters named their children after him. Michael Steele named a son after Dick. Joe Gertel's sister Ruth Lande named a daughter after him. There are several Clifford Shniers. Ten Silverstein cousins are named after Jacob. There are three Johns in the family of John Lazarus, the Montreal merchant mariner who went down with the SS *City of Benares* in 1940. Sylvia Hoffman, his sister, continues to faithfully honour her brother's memory in other traditional ways, including lighting a yahrzeit (memorial) candle on the anniversary of his death each year. Her parents paid to plant trees in Israel in her brother's memory. Now in her nineties, the California woman would like to fulfill one last duty to him: to read a novel about the September 1940 tragedy that killed her brother. The children's book *September 17* was published in 2013, but Hoffman hasn't made much headway with it because thinking about John's death, even after seventy-five years, is too hard. "I've made my mind up that before I die I should read the book, and I've started, but I haven't picked up because I just…I haven't read the whole book," she said.

It wasn't only family members who named their children after the Jewish men lost in the war. In November 1945, Jack Sills and his wife, Louise, named their second child Robert in memory of his father's childhood best friend from Montreal, Sergeant Robert Macklin, who died in a Hong Kong prison camp in 1942. Macklin's widow, Girlie (Ursula), and two-year-old daughter Bonita would stay with the Sillses in New York for a while after their liberation from the Stanley internment camp in 1943. Patricia Matthews, the oldest Sills daughter, was about four or five at the time. She remembers the traumatized survivors in her house. "My mother kept saying, 'Whatever she does it's all right because she's been having a terrible time,'" Matthews said.

She said that Robert Sills always knew why he bore the name of his father's best friend. "[Our father] said [Macklin] was a prince and he loved him," she remembered. "[Robert] was glad he was named after someone [our father] loved." Robert Allan Sills died in 2006. His oldest son, Todd Sills, married a woman named Benita. Todd says he wasn't aware until now that Macklin's daughter was named Bonita. "But that's not weird, it makes sense to me," Todd said. When the couple had their first child in 2010 they named him Robert (Bobby). "There was a lot of love being passed down through this name."

Todd Sills made a special pilgrimage with young Bobby in 2015 to see Macklin's grave at the Sai Wan War Cemetery on the northeastern side of Hong Kong Island. The cemetery is the final resting place for fifteen hundred Allied servicemen who died after the Japanese invasion of 1941. In the photos, the boy's fine blond hair appears plastered to his sweaty cheeks, and his red backpack—one with ears that make it look like a fox's face—seems to be weighing him down. "It was hot as blazes and I didn't want Bobby to get sunburnt, so we didn't dawdle," said Sills, a documentary filmmaker. "We walked straight to [Macklin's] tombstone, spent about ten minutes talking about my grandfather, my dad, how I missed them, how important it is to have best friends, and lastly, how special his name is to me." Then, solemnly, the boy took a potato-size rock they had found outside the cemetery and placed it on top of the gravestone. Sills did the same. Theirs were the only two stones. The child bent down and gently touched the letter "R" on the tombstone. Then they walked out of the cemetery and found an ice-cream shop to have a snack.

It shouldn't be surprising that it took the Sillses so long to visit Macklin's grave. Right after the war, it would have been very difficult for grieving Canadian families to visit the places where their loved ones had been killed. Some casualties had no known graves, while others were located in far-flung places including Khartoum, Sudan, where John Lewis Michaels is buried, and Gambia, where Joseph Shulman was killed in a plane crash in January 1943.[6]

It would be 1979, thirty-five years after Jacob Mandel's death, before Jackie Adler of San Diego, California, made it to Normandy to see the grave of the uncle after whom she had been named. The doctor from Estevan, Saskatchewan, was killed in August 1944, and buried at the Bény-sur-Mer Canadian war cemetery near Juno Beach. Just before Jackie got there, Omar Bradley, the retired five-star U.S. Army general who had led the American troops on D-Day, had also visited, and he placed a wreath at Mandel's grave. Mandel had been killed while taking a shift for his friend, another Jewish Canadian doctor in uniform, Eliot Corday, who happened to be Bradley's cardiologist. At the time of Bradley's visit to Mandel's grave in 1979, the American general was eighty-six and in a wheelchair, but he asked to be taken to see Mandel's grave so he could thank him for sparing Corday. "He wanted to find the grave of the man who died in [Corday's] place," said Dr. Stephen Corday, Eliot's son.

If they couldn't visit the actual cemetery, some families established memorials of a different sort, closer to home, where the names of their departed might be more easily remembered—not just by themselves but also by the general public.

Herbert Wolf's relatives set up a scholarship at Carleton University in the airman's memory. Michael Bernstein's brothers donated money to open a prayer chapel that bears his name in the Miles Nadal Jewish Community Centre in Toronto. Lawrence Abelson's parents, Molly and Jess, established a basketball trophy for senior Ottawa high school students in 1945. Abelson's younger brother Alan won the trophy in 1947.[7] Philip Meyer Davis's family donated a new plane to the British Air Force in his memory. He was the adopted son of the wealthy Montreal tobacco magnate Sir Mortimer Davis and his wife, Lady Henrietta Davis. Philip, with the RAF, was killed in 1942 in a plane crash near the British capital.

In 2007, Meyer Greenstein's parents set up a Meyer (Mike) Greenstein prize for writing excellence through the University of Toronto. It took that long because his family refused to accept that he was not coming back, which is why they would also not permit his name to be inscribed on the university's Soldiers' Memorial Tower until the 1960s. "The government sent the medals, the government sent the telegram, the government sends the letters, the government can do whatever the government wants to do. It doesn't mean they have to agree with it and they never did and they never accepted it [his death]," said Hersh Gross, Meyer's nephew. Gross named his son after the downed airman.

Other families chose to give to Jewish organizations and to the State of Israel in their loved ones' memories. Some families planted groves of trees in Israel or asked that donations go toward this cause. In 1966, Kate Devor paid for the planting of a thousand trees in Israel through the Jewish National Fund. She did it in memory of her son David, and also in memory of the relative for whom he had been named: her brother, David Tuvya Risidore, killed in action during World War I.[8]

The wider Jewish community responded with public commemorations and tributes. Ottawa's B'nai Jacob Synagogue held a memorial service for the three young men in its congregation who were killed. Flying Officer Philip Bosloy was killed in 1942 in a plane crash off Nova Scotia.[9] His body was never found. Corporal Mike Litwack died of wounds five days after landing in France in July 1944.[10] His truck was carrying ammunition to the front when a bomb hit it. He is buried in Normandy.[11] The third casualty was Warrant Officer Jack Cooper, killed on a bombing mission to Wuppertal, in western Germany, in May 1944.[12] His grave is in Belgium.[13] Their names were inscribed on a marble tablet, along with the names of forty-two other members of the synagogue who had enlisted.

“The record of the members of this congregation in the war that just ended is truly a remarkable one,” Ottawa mayor J.E. Stanley Lewis, who attended as a special guest, was quoted as saying.[14]

In the months after the war, similar ceremonies were held across Canada. In Toronto, the Jewish National Fund held a Servicemen’s Memorial Dinner at the Royal York Hotel to dedicate a scroll of honour.[15] That list had eighty-three names on it, although the final total would be closer to one hundred. When Calgary’s B’nai Brith lodge had a ceremony at the House of Israel Community Building at 18th Avenue and Centre Street, former Royal Canadian Air Force prisoner of war David (Pappy) Rosenthal carried the wreath in memory of the local men who had been killed.[16]

Saint John’s Shaarey Zedek Synagogue unveiled a scroll of honour designed by the Group of Seven artist A.J. Casson.[17] In Edmonton, the community paid tribute to the eleven Jewish casualties from the region. Rabbi Jacob Eisen, who had been the spiritual leader of Beth Shalom Synagogue before serving as the RCAF chaplain overseas, attended the ceremony in uniform.[18]

Jewish charities and service organizations named local chapters after some of the casualties. There was a Moe Hurwitz Jewish war veterans’ group in Montreal. In London, Ontario, the Aleph Zadik Aleph young men’s association renamed their chapter the Hyman Bonder–Nathan Tafler Branch after two local men who died during the war: Bonder died of cancer back home in Canada after being diagnosed while serving with the RCAF, and Rifleman Tafler was killed in a deadly battle on June 8, 1944, at Putot-en-Bessin, France, about a half hour’s drive from the beaches where he landed with the Royal Winnipeg Rifles just two days earlier.[19]

Cenotaphs were also put up in cemeteries such as Winnipeg’s Shaarey Zedek and also at the community’s Hebrew Sick Benefit location. Calgary’s Jewish war memorial is in the Erlton Cemetery. The Tiferes Israel Synagogue in Moncton collected the names of all the Jewish men from Atlantic Canada who served and engraved them on a plaque in the lobby. Both of Toronto’s main Jewish veterans groups put up memorials: one in 1984, in the shape of a split artillery shell at the Mount Sinai Memorial Park cemetery and, more recently, in 2014, the Jewish War Veterans of Canada, Toronto Post, unveiled a monument on the grounds of the Sherman campus of the Jewish Community Centre recording more than five hundred names of Jewish Canadians who fought in both world wars and Korea.[20]

The Jewish fallen were also included when various governments in Canada carried out commemorative projects. Beginning in the 1950s, the provinces of Manitoba and Saskatchewan named geographical landmarks after the deceased. Approximately five thousand lakes, bays, and islands in Manitoba bear the names of Canadians killed in World War II. There is a Mandel Island in northern Saskatchewan in memory of Captain Jacob Mandel.

Families received an official laminated certificate with the landmark's geographical coordinates. Few actually made the trips, as the locations are remote, although Jackie Adler said her father visited Mandel Island several years ago. Brownstone Lake, more than seven hours flying time north of Winnipeg, west of Churchill in northern Manitoba, was named after Yude Brownstone, killed at Carpiquet, France, in early July 1944.[21] It was too far for Brownstone's surviving older brother, Benny, also a war veteran. But just seeing the photos of the official plaque that the Manitoba government installed at the site was deeply satisfying. "[The] plaque states that 'Brownstone Lake is named after Rifleman Yude Brownstone, RWR, born February 19, 1924, forever remembered by brother Ben and family,'" said Ellen Brownstone, Ben's daughter.

The people of Flin Flon, Manitoba, turned out to a memorial service at the Northminster United Church in honour of Squadron Leader Phil Foster, who was killed in May 1942. In July 1950, thanks to a bequest in his will, the community was able to open a new children's wading pool and change facilities and named the facility in his memory.[22]

Some Jewish families weren't content just to see their sons' names displayed on a monument or a plaque here in Canada; they wanted their sons' bodies brought home for burial. Abraham Chizy, the father of Sick Berth Attendant Harold Chizy, begged the navy to honour his request. "You no doubt know how badly I feel about my son's death, and bringing him here would be such a consolation as only a father can feel," he wrote from Montreal.[23] But Canadian policy required casualties to be buried near where they died outside of North America. Chizy's father was informed Harold's body would stay in Scotland, where he'd been buried after his aircraft carrier, HMS *Nabob*, was torpedoed. In 1949, Abraham Chizy visited his son's grave for himself at Dunfermline, north of Edinburgh.[24]

The U.S. Army Air Force operated under a different set of repatriation procedures, which led to a happier outcome for the family of Aaron Cummings of Glace Bay, Nova Scotia. Cummings (born Archie Cohen) was a bombardier with an American unit based in China; he was killed in a plane crash in September 1944. His body was brought back to Canada and buried in the Sons of Israel Synagogue cemetery in Sydney. The headstone inscription reads, "CANADA GAVE UP ITS BEST FOR FREEDOM."[25]

"His mother wanted the body back," said Steve Nathanson, who used to cut the grass at the cemetery. "When Mummy wants you, I guess the U.S. government did it!" Cummings is one of only about thirty Jewish Canadians who died in uniform in World War II—whether in action, due to an accident, or of natural causes—and are buried at home. Lieutenant Henry Goody, who served as a U.S. Army chaplain but was killed in October 1943 in a traffic accident near Washington DC, is interred at the Dawes Road cemetery in Toronto.

Section Officer Rose Goodman's grave lies on the slopes of Montreal's Mount Royal, in a plot her family had purchased earlier. She was the first woman officer in the RCAF to die in uniform. According to *Discovery: The Journal of the Jewish Historical Society of South Alberta*,

> *Rose Goodman was buried with full military honors and full Jewish ritual on February 2, 1943 at the Cemetery of the Spanish and Portuguese Congregation in Montreal. Her casket was carried on a flower-bedecked gun carriage, accompanied by RCAF colleagues of both sexes. Her parents, sisters, and many friends from New Glasgow and Halifax were present.*[26]

After the funeral, Solomon Goodman wrote a formal thank-you letter to the chief of the Air Staff in Ottawa. He described the death of his daughter as a sacrifice that his family had made to Canada for the war effort.

> *Dear Sir,*
>
> *On behalf of Mrs. Goodman and myself I wish to thank you for the sympathetic letter of Jan. 28th. The loss is a heavy one and is keenly felt and bears out again that the price of liberty is not money but* Blood Tears and Sweat.[27]

Rose's parents were devastated by her death. "Apparently, my grandmother, after that, only wore black," said Darrel Pink, Rose's nephew. "It was just tragic and apparently my grandmother never recovered. My grandfather, as I understand it, decided to retire and they moved to Halifax." Eventually, the Goodmans turned their grief into a permanent physical memorial to their daughter, buying a beach and campground east of New Glasgow. The site at Egerton had been the Girl Guide camp where Rose had spent many summers, and the family donated it to the organization in her name.

Rose's mother eventually received the Silver Cross medal, which the Canadian government awards to all bereaved war mothers and widows. She, or someone in the family, sent it to a jeweller to have a few modifications made. Discarding the original purple ribbon, she added a Star of David on top of the cross in yellow gold, and also turned it into a broach, which Darrel Pink and his wife, Elizabeth, now have.

"I'm sure parents always feel, when they get a daughter who they've taught to get in there and stand up for what she wants, and that's how you've raised her, then you have to live with the fact that that's what she's going to do with her life," Elizabeth Pink said.

Rose's sister Anetta Chernin still feels the pain of losing her. "I think she was a dedicated free spirit. And she would've had very high principles, even though she was a fun person," Chernin said. "She just should've lived."

When the initial seven-day official Jewish mourning period ends, relatives of the deceased are encouraged to resume their lives. Some, such as Larry Rosenthal, turned their grief into action. After Flight Sergeant Jack Tritt, a navigator in the RCAF posted to the No. 425 "Alouette" Squadron, in Dishforth, England, died in a crash in England in 1942, his mother, Sarah, agreed to head Montreal's branch of the Next of Kin League, a Jewish group created to provide comfort and welfare to families like her own.[28]

However, grief proved too much for the father of Alex Balinson to bear. The Hamilton airman was killed during an air raid on Malta in April 1942.[29] His father, Henry, had expected Alex to take over his popular Yiddish-language newspaper, the *Voice of Hamilton* when the war ended. Henry, an immigrant from Odessa, wrote a eulogy and published it in the paper. It was a cry of despair from a man who had lost too much. "Who do you think I am? Job?" Balinson wrote, comparing himself to the biblical character. "Why have you brought me to this land of milk and honey, and now you have taken my children." Henry started drinking. He stopped publishing the paper, stopped speaking, at least publicly, and "lived the rest of his days in sorrow."[30]

For the family of Mitchell Sterlin, killed in Italy in December 1943, their public statements to the Montreal *Gazette* belied the private grieving that went on for a long time after. "We have lost a good son, but we are proud that he gave his life in the service of his country," the Sterlins told the paper in May 1944.[31] Yet his younger brother, Martin Sterlin, who was eighteen and studying engineering at McGill, remembers the family reacting less stoically when the reporters were gone. "My mother turned grey overnight. Or maybe she stopped dying her hair, I don't know. It's quite possible. You can imagine the shock," he said, adding that his mother had predicted she would never see Mitchell again when he went overseas.

Martin couldn't handle talking about his brother with well-meaning friends and neighbours, "If I saw someone coming, I'd go to the other the side of the street," he recalled, saying losing a brother "leaves you frozen...and you never get over it."

His loss also left him furious with some of his brother's friends from McGill who chose to defer their military service and finish their medical degrees. Mitchell had been accepted to medical school, too, but enlisted right after his final undergraduate exams.

With the war's end, it became easier to find out what had happened to sons who had been reported as missing, although some families still had to wait years for the answers. The Allies mobilized teams of military forensic experts and investigators to locate the remains of those who had died in action overseas. In some cases, the interment had been carried out hastily by locals or by the Germans. Sometimes the men had been buried by their own, near where they fell, as happened with Yude Brownstone, along with many of the Canadian casualties of the attack on Carpiquet airport. His body lay in a temporary grave in a copse two hundred metres south of an elegant French mansion named Château de Marcelet.[32]

After the bodies were located, the remains were usually exhumed and reburied in official war cemeteries. Other times, the bodies were left where they had been buried, particularly if they were in mass graves, as was the case with the body of the RCAF air gunner Alan Rodd (who enlisted as Abraham Rodnunsky) of Edmonton. He died during a bombing mission outside Paris on June 11, 1944, shortly after D-Day.[33] Investigators found his grave in September 1945, buried with his entire Lancaster crew, opposite a church in the village of Berou-la-Mulotière.[34] They remain there to this day.

Protocol was to send the families a form letter with the coordinates and a map. Photos of the new graves were usually included, and most families were eager to see these, especially after permanent headstones were installed bearing the inscriptions that the next of kin had requested.

Although Israel Pavelow had changed his name to the less-Jewish-sounding name Ervin Povol when he enlisted in the Canadian Army in Regina, that didn't prevent a German soldier from murdering him in France after D-Day. The Regina Rifles fought their way inland for eleven kilometres toward the German-occupied village of Bretteville-l'Orgueilleuse. Povol fell, wounded, along the Caen–Bayeux highway. A German soldier saw the injured Jewish man on the ground and shot him through the forehead. Povol was one of a dozen Canadian POWs executed there by the Germans.[35]

After the Canadians discovered Povol's body, his family was officially notified. His father, Hyman, wrote to the Imperial War Graves Commission, as it was called then, in May 1947, pleading with them for an update about his son's final resting place in the Bény-sur-Mer Canadian War Cemetery. The letter was even more poignant because Ervin and his father had had a falling-out in 1934; the younger Povol had "run away" from home and cut all ties with his father. While overseas, he'd refused to answer any of his father's letters.

"I would thank you very much if possible to send me a PHOTOGRAPH of my son's grave," Hyman Pavelow wrote, after sending instructions about what should be written on the tombstone. "It would be, to me, to the rest of my life the only memory left of my son."[36] The photographs were sent just one month later.

Unfortunately, sometimes the photos of these graves caused further grief to the bereaved families when they discovered that their loved ones had been buried under a cross. This was the case for the family of Hymie Steinberg of Winnipeg, who was nineteen when his plane crashed into a mountainside outside Reykjavik, Iceland, in December 1944. The air force determined that Steinberg's pilot was at fault for taking a shortcut in poor weather; all the aircrews in Reykjavik knew they were to avoid the mountain beside the landing strip.[37] Eight crewmen were buried on Christmas Eve in the cemetery at Fossvogur. Although an American Jewish chaplain conducted the service, Steinberg's grave was adorned with a cross with the word "Hebrew" on it.

Their father wrote to the air force to have Hymie's headstone changed to the correct religious symbol; the military apologized for its mistake. "The additional distress which you were caused by the erection of the cross on your son's grave is indeed regretted," replied the RCAF casualty officer in 1945.

"The whole family just fell apart, and my mother stayed in her room for almost a whole year, it seemed like, to me," said his brother David Steinberg, who was four years old at the time. Their mother, Ruth, had been so furious with Hymie for enlisting that she had refused to speak to him for the day or two before he left home. Steinberg remembers his family sitting shiva, although nobody told him that his eldest brother had died. "I would just stay on the street," he said. "I found it unbearable."

At times when he was young, David would think his brother was still alive. Now, Steinberg has only vague memories of his brother, who was fifteen years older, but the comedian treasures a wartime portrait of the four siblings showing Hymie, in uniform, holding David's hand. In 2012, the television host and producer was floored to discover a long-suppressed memory that it was actually he who had delivered the telegram with the bad news, although his sister insists it couldn't have happened that way. When a therapist offered an explanation, it was a revelation. "Did you ever think that someone who would bring a telegram that would make people unhappy might devote his whole life to making people laugh with comedy?" Steinberg was told. "So somewhere in there, there's something primal that happened to me."

Sister Tammy Lazar turned seventy-five in 2004, and that year the Los Angeles woman was able to fulfill her lifelong dream to visit Hymie's grave in Iceland. "I went because there had been no one from my family who had been to my brother's gravesite, and I wanted to say Kaddish [a Jewish prayer of mourning]," said Lazar. The Canadian ambassador to Iceland and a local pastor accompanied her to the cemetery, where they held a short service. They read some of Hymie's favourite poems out loud, including "Elegy Written in a Country Courtyard," by Thomas Gray: "Here rests his head upon the lap of Earth / A youth to Fortune and to Fame unknown."[38]

Around the same time Norman Shnier, the brother of Clifford Shnier, was making his own first trip to his brother's grave in Germany. Clifford had been a flamboyant pilot who resembled movie idol Errol Flynn. The Manitoba airman was also a bit of a romantic and was close to his sisters: he sent home a gold African necklace when one of them became engaged. Shnier's Lancaster was shot down at the end of July 1943, one of over seven hundred planes to go out that night as part of the Allied destruction of Hamburg, code-named Operation Gomorrah.[39] The crew's bodies were located in 1946 in a German cemetery. All seven were reinterred in the Commonwealth War Cemetery at Becklingen, south of Hamburg.

Norman had himself been an RCAF navigator during the war and was shot down a month after his brother's death. In his eighties, Norman began having vivid dreams of his brother asking him to come and visit his grave. When they approached the row of graves, Norman noticed all the headstones had crosses. "My parents were not particularly religious; we didn't keep kosher," said John Shnier, who accompanied his parents to the cemetery. Yet the family would appeal to the administrators for a new tombstone with the Star of David. Sadly, Norman wouldn't live to see it. He died in July 2007; the installation was done on July 30, 2009, the sixty-sixth anniversary of Clifford's death.

"We were just so happy we could do this for the family," said nephew Mitchell Shnier, who took the headstone project on. The Toronto man runs a website in memory of his uncle Clifford and about the members of the extended Shnier clan. Mitchell went to Germany in 2010, bringing pebbles from the family's cottage in Muskoka, north of Toronto, to place on top of the headstone. Despite the family's lingering doubts that Clifford's body is actually beneath the new tombstone—wartime dental records were inconclusive—Mitchell said that displaying the Jewish symbol sends an important message about why his uncles joined up during World War II. "It's for Canada. Some people were Jewish."

Harry Hurwitz would undoubtedly have liked to pay one last visit to Holland to see the grave of his brother, Moe, who died of his wounds in October 1944. After the war, Hurwitz's family was shocked to learn that the twice-decorated Canadian Jewish tank commander was resting under a cross in a Commonwealth War Cemetery in Holland. The Canadian Jewish Congress intervened in July 1947 to try to minimize anguish for the Hurwitzes, and insisted the mistake be corrected:

Lieutenant-Colonel H.M. Jackson,
Director of Records
Department of National Defence
Ottawa, Ontario
July 9, 1947
Dear Sir:
Re: Photographs of Hurwitz Grave

Please do not mail these photographs as members of the family are upset and would rather wait for the corrected snaps. I have informed the family that your office is taking all steps to remedy this error. Sincerely,
M. Levitt
Canadian Jewish Congress[40]

The new tombstone at Bergen-op-Zoom Canadian War Cemetery has the Star of David, as well as information in Hebrew about Moe's next of kin and the Jewish date of his death. Moe, who was only twenty-five when he died, is never far from his family's thoughts. "I know my father misses his brother every day," said Harry's daughter, Debbie Cooper, who paid her own tribute to her famous uncle by naming her son Michael after him. "This man deserved to be honoured as long as people care to remember him. He was totally, totally selfless and fearless, and he just wanted to help his fellow Jews. He wanted to see justice. He wanted to see people treated well."

Despite the passage of nearly seventy-five years, the message of Moe Hurwitz's wartime service continues to resonate, as people outside his immediate family discover his story. For Remembrance Day in 2015, the popular international genealogy website Ancestry.ca picked three Canadian war heroes of World War II to showcase. Two were Victoria Cross recipients; the third was Samuel Moses Hurwitz.[41] He even appears as a character in the novels and stories of the New York crime writer Shelly Reuben, a Hurwitz relative. "He was the counter-Jewish-weakling myth," she said, comparing her uncle to a Golem, but with a "beautiful soul." In Jewish folklore, Golems are giant creatures without souls who can be created out of soil to protect people from danger.

The legacy and the challenge of Moe Hurwitz's life are also being passed on to new generations of Canadian military personnel. The Hurwitz Cup is awarded each August to the army cadet with the highest score in marksmanship at the Connaught Ranges, near Ottawa. In 2014, Moe's family donated his bravery medals and his mother's Silver Cross to the Grenadier Guards Museum in Montreal.

Municipalities also paid tribute to the Jewish men who died in the war. Sarnia named a road after Max Berger, who was killed in Hong Kong.[42] In 2013, the city of Toronto unveiled a new street sign in the former Jewish neighbourhood west of Spadina Avenue now known as Harbord Village. The eighty-seven-metre-long paved lane, which gives access to the backs of homes on Major Street, was officially named Boys of Major Lane. The city wanted to honour the unusually high number of young Jewish men—at least thirty—from the short street who had gone off to war. Half a dozen did not come back.[43] Joe Greenberg, the veteran who grew up at 98 Major Street, helped push the project forward. He'd known them all. "Goddammit, I don't think there's any other street in this country that had that kind of casualties," he said, referring to the boys he'd played ball and walked to school with. "These are real people and they all lived on Major Street and they all didn't come home." Greenberg felt there was something special about where he grew up, calling it "the Street of Collective Goodness."[44]

Although most of the Canadian Jews who died in uniform in World War II were single men, a significant number were married, and plenty of children grew up without their fathers. Alvin Schrage was four and a half when his father, David, died on board his troopship en route to Hong Kong in 1941. Alvin remains bitter about the futility of the doomed Canadian mission, and angry with the army doctors who let his diabetic father enlist. "You know how many times I wanted to hire a lawyer and sue them?" said Schrage, who named his own son after a man he really doesn't remember. "They really screwed up my life. I meet so many guys who say, 'My father stayed behind, he went into the scrap metal business.' I had this whole thing in my life torn away. We had no money, no Yiddishkeit [Jewish culture]. No nothing." He still can't understand what motivated his father's decision to enlist. "They always call them a volunteer. I hate that word," Schrage said. "He was a mensch. I don't know what he was. I either think he was a great man or a fool."

Schrage's conflicted feelings about his father haven't prevented him from honouring the man's memory in traditional ways, including going to synagogue on the anniversary of his death and giving to charity. York University now offers two scholarships for needy students in the name of Schrage's parents, and in 2003, he paid a visit to the Sai Wan War Cemetery in Hong Kong. His father's name is on the memorial wall for those Canadian and Allied soldiers with no known grave.[45] "I couldn't cry," said Schrage.

Michael Steele was also four when his father was killed in Normandy in August 1944, after his tank was hit. He and his brother asked their mother, "Why didn't he jump out of the tank?"[46] It was a question she would ask herself for years, but after she married Dick's best friend, Bill Walsh, in 1946, she didn't talk so much about the boys' father. And while Steele heard snippets about his father from the people in Canada's labour and social justice circles, it is only recently that the retired Toronto engineer was able to confront the ghost who still speaks to him across time. In the summer of 2015, Steele finally went through the box containing his late mother's files, including hundreds of much-handled blue wartime airmail letters from his father. In early 2017 Steele donated the box to the Ontario Jewish Archives. He thinks he understands why many bereaved families didn't talk about those they lost during the war. "It's hard on the parents who are trying to spare their children from the tragedies and pain they went through," Steele said. "In the end it produces its own pain and tragedy in a different way because there are just gaps you don't know."

Other widows also kept their memories of their first marriage locked away. Out of respect to her second husband, Maurice, Ruth Selby of Winnipeg stored the wedding photos from her earlier life with her sister, for safekeeping. "I think my father was particularly sensitive," said Mindy Selby, one of the couple's two daughters.

Ruth had married Hector Rubin, the RCAF navigator from Kamsack, Saskatchewan, when she was twenty-one. She was a widow by twenty-four. She and her second husband would eventually divorce. Near the end of her life, the photos of Hector reappeared and were placed in a prominent spot on her piano. "My mother never looked as happy in the years that I knew her as she did in those pictures," said Mindy. "He was absolutely the love of her life."

Ruth visited Hector's grave in Germany, where his tombstone reads:

A son of Israel
Who gave their life
That others
Might cherish freedom.[47]

She remained sad there was nothing like it here in Canada. A year after her death, daughters Mindy and Karyn placed a footstone at her grave in Winnipeg's Shaarey Zedek Cemetery, just for Hector, a "Beloved First Husband." "My mother felt like it was her fault, that if she hadn't been pushing him to come home, that he wouldn't have gone out with that crew that night," Selby said, referring to the requirement for an airman to fly a certain number of missions before he was eligible for leave. "I think she always felt a little guilty about it."

William Henry Nelson's widow, Marjorie, did not display guilt or anger after her husband's death in November 1940. Nelson was the first Canadian Jew to win a medal for flying in the Battle of Britain, a task that likely meant even more to him because his wife and infant son were British residents. "It is different, because the war was closer to us here," said their son Bill McAlister, who was two months old when Nelson died.

McAlister bears his father's first name and his stepfather's last name: after Nelson's death Marjorie moved to Canada to stay with her in-laws. She met her second husband while acting in a play. The couple had five children of their own before moving back to England in the late 1950s. There, McAlister enjoyed the benefits that came with being the son of a fallen Battle of Britain hero. The Royal Air Force paid for a private boarding school education and Nelson's name is on oversize sculptures and memorials to the men whom a grateful Churchill had christened "the Few." But it was only when McAlister was thirty-seven and raising his own family in London that his mother drank a little too much sherry one evening and revealed a secret about his birth. "She just looked at me and then she started to cry and she said, 'Your father was a Jew.'"

She hadn't told him partly in order to protect him; she had had a bad experience with an antisemitic landlord in Canada. Since that revelation, McAlister has reached out to his father's Jewish relatives and their descendants, from whom he learned that Nelson's birth name was

Katznelson. Nowadays, when the seventy-seven-year-old McAlister wants to feel close to his war-hero father, he goes fishing in a particular spot in the English Channel near Dover.

Louis Slotin's family has had to live with the publicity surrounding their famous relative's war service. The legacy of the Canadian Jewish nuclear scientist has been somewhat complicated for his Winnipeg next of kin. During the 1960s, his work would be considered shameful by the peace movement, and by his niece Beth Shore's own two children, including her son who was named after Louis. "'Ban the bomb' became the word in our house," which stung, Shore admitted, although she remained "very proud of who I was."

Her uncle's groundbreaking work on the Manhattan Project and the accident that killed him sparked critical books, magazine articles, and a 1989 Hollywood movie called *Fat Man and Little Boy*.[48] It would take a trip to Los Alamos in 1993 to see where their uncle had died to put Beth Shore and her cousin Rael Ludwig's minds at ease. There they met with a scientist who had been in the room when the accident happened. They also looked through reams of declassified documents. Shore has since been to Japan to the memorials for the victims of the 1945 bombings, and both she and Ludwig have worked to maintain a positive public image of their uncle's contribution to world history. "His early stuff that we received from Los Alamos showed that he was one of the forerunners in what has become radio-chemotherapy today," she said.

The passage of time has softened the criticism of their uncle's reputation. He has had an asteroid named after him, and his photo is part of a heritage mural in the lobby of Winnipeg's Asper Jewish Community Centre. In 2010, the city named a park in his honour.[49]

Thelma Shapiro died on November 15, 2016, just a few days after Remembrance Day. She had worked in the communications department of the Montreal Jewish YM-YWHA on Westbury Avenue, and for years she helped arrange the institution's annual Remembrance Day service and Jewish veterans' march.

"They all come in their blue blazers and their berets and their chests filled with medals," she recalled in a 2015 interview. She admitted that until she experienced the colour parade with the flags and met the veterans, especially the late Barney Finestone and Sam Gordon, she had little personal connection to the war. She was, however, aware of the Y's original stained-glass window, installed in 1953, which honoured the one thousand Montreal Y members who served in World War II, including 150 who were killed. Shapiro felt that with the passing of time and a series of expansions to the building, most members simply rushed past the window on their way to fitness classes, and she was inspired to build a newer war memorial there. It was unveiled in 2005 or 2006.

"I feel the subject is important and the people who played a role in it need to be remembered and need to be respected," she said, adding that the project took on a whole new meaning for her when her son Logan joined the Canadian Forces and served in both Afghanistan and Ukraine.

The new memorial takes the form of an exhibit with five panels. Some contain photos of the Y members in uniform during wartime. There is also an explanation of the historic stained-glass window and an expanded honour roll. A portrait of Nathan Dlusy stands out at the top of the display. Its prominence is no accident; Dlusy's younger brother Jon came forward with a donation toward the cost of the memorial. Jon also commemorates his brother each November 11 by placing a memoriam notice in the Montreal *Gazette*. The text always contains a hint of bitterness. That is intentional.

"His application for Canadian citizenship while in the service was never finalized. Always remembered and loved," the notice reads, below a brief summary of the twenty-three-year-old's wartime service.[50] The Dlusy family had escaped Hitler's Germany in 1938, and Nat Dlusy handed in his naturalization application while he was in Scotland in the air force. He was killed before the paperwork was put through.

Jon Dlusy feels the citizenship for his brother is more than seventy years overdue. "He served Canada but not as a Canadian citizen, and by right he should be considered posthumously and given that honour," Dlusy said. "He applied and they gave him the runaround, claiming that Canada is only a Dominion and it's a part of the British Empire and it takes a lot of consideration and so forth, and it's not usually the custom to do this, and whatever it was."

Dlusy's feelings are familiar to those of Martin Saslove of Ottawa. Ever since his brother Eddie's death in Germany in January 1945, he has been seeking to have Canada acknowledge the act of bravery that cost Eddie his life. Saslove wants nothing less than a Victoria Cross for him, although the government stopped awarding them posthumously years ago. "I just feel as long as I keep on trying, he never died," Martin said.

Piloting a Lancaster bomber was the culmination of Eddie Saslove's boyhood dreams to fly. When they were attacked returning from a raid on Munich, he ordered the crew to jump. He would have bailed out himself but saw that the two rear gunners were too badly wounded to move. Saslove remained at the controls and attempted to crash-land. All three men were killed.[51] The rest of the crew survived, and the navigator, Max Chisick from Winnipeg, later named one of his sons after his pilot.

Martin Saslove has made Eddie a tangible part of the lives of his own daughters and grandchildren. Everyone in the family uses Eddie's ring and his Hebrew Bible at their weddings. The ring was a gift from a trio of childhood friends. The Hebrew Bible was the one Eddie received for his bar mitzvah ceremony in 1934. "I think it's important to tell the story of anybody who did something a little bit out of the ordinary," Saslove said.

As in the cases of Larry Rosenthal, Martin Saslove, and others, there are usually one or two relatives of a deceased Canadian Jewish serviceman who are the family history buffs. They're the ones who take a special interest in collecting the war records and medals. They're the ones who often create online family trees, and who post information about their war hero on social media and websites.

Larry Donen of Vancouver and his three siblings have their uncle Samuel Jacob Donen's wartime flying goggles, an African knife he collected, and a bullet. When they were growing up in Winnipeg, the downed Ferry Command airman's effects were kept in a locked box. "There was a bit of a Harry Potter area beneath the stairs that was locked up and every once in a while [brother] Shane and I would crawl in there and that's where my dad kept his memories of Sammy," Larry Donen said.

The boys would touch the war medals and the RCAF sergeant's stripes and imagine the man whom Shane was named for, who had been killed in a crash in Accra, Ghana in 1943. "I feel that he suffered great depression from the loss of his brother and it affected him throughout his whole life," Larry says of his father, Norman.

Larry's memorabilia collection got a huge boost in December 2015. While researching this book, I discovered Samuel Donen's flight logbook in the Library and Archives Canada's storage box containing his military records. It had been there for more than seventy years. The air force had tried to deliver the blue hardcover back in 1948, but the parcel was returned to Ottawa.[52]

The archives policy is to repatriate anything that would have come home with the veteran had he or she survived the war. When Larry Donen received his uncle's logbook in early 2016, he was stunned. "It's in great condition for something as old," said Donen, a Vancouver marketing executive. Now, thanks to the logbook, the Donens are able to piece together where their uncle flew, such as Belem in Brazil, and Bathurst, in Gambia. Seeing his uncle's handwriting is also very comforting. "He writes Donen the same way I do," Larry said.

Larry feels that his uncle's logbook was a learning opportunity. "We can continue to remind our own children and our grandchildren about the critical historic events that happened in World War I and World War II because we're almost at the end of it, as far as any survivors of that time frame," he said. "As that actually occurs we are doing a bit of a disservice to all these people who preceded us if we fail to appreciate the freedoms that we have."

Ruth Lande has been sharing stories about her brother Joe Gertel with her children and grandchildren. The Chicago woman, now in her eighties, has also started writing about him. He was killed in July 1944 in France, leaving behind a grieving fiancée in England and a heartbroken family in Montreal. "He was the most remarkable brother a kid could have," said Lande. "I was small and he was tall, and sometimes...I'd be at the bus stop and he would put me on his shoulders and march me down the street to my house. So there I was, like a queen!"

Lande has been to visit Joe's grave in France. She keeps a photo of his grave, his medals, and his bar mitzvah picture on a dresser in her den. Her grandchildren call it "Joe's Shrine." Lande admits to being traumatized by her brother's death, especially because her parents had lied to her when the telegram came. "They didn't know how to tell me," she said, recalling being in a rented summer home in St-Jérôme, north of Montreal, at the time. She was told that Joe was wounded and was getting better. "They weren't psychologists, you know, they didn't want to see me cry, they didn't realize that in a way they made the pain worse."

Eventually, thanks to some caring schoolteachers, Lande was able to come to terms with Joe's death. Now she sees his service as the fulfillment of his support for Zionism because he helped get rid of Hitler, and then the State of Israel was created four years later. "I certainly didn't want to lose a brother, but if I had to lose one I'm really proud," she said. "He followed his love, he followed his instinct, he followed his honour. He really put his life on the line for what he believed, and to me that's a hero."

After the war, Gertel's wartime fiancée, Hedy Neumann, married and settled with her American husband, James Reeds, in the United States. She told their children about Gertel, whose letters and photos she's kept in a special green box. One of her grandchildren is named in Gertel's honour.

"He was just a great man. Just a very devoted, beautiful human being, this is all I can say about him," said Hedy Reeds, who is now in her nineties. "And I was so fortunate to have met him because it was the best thing in my life."

George Meltz's nineteen-year-old widow, Trudy, must have felt that way, too. She lived the rest of her days in her parents' house in London. The army sent her George's war medals and his personal effects, including a Hebrew Bible and her signet ring.[53] Trudy did visit Canada briefly, in the summer of 1946, to stay with one of Meltz's siblings in Toronto.[54]

"She didn't work. My mother said, 'We would all come home from work and she would be painting her nails,'" Isabella Meltz, George's niece, was told. The young widow remained in Canada long enough to get George's survivor's pension—$752.65—and then returned to England. She never remarried. Isabella said Trudy became a recluse, and died in 1982 at the age of fifty-six. "She kept things of his, like his razor, forever and always, and that's very, very sad. She was a young woman."

It was Trudy's epitaph on Meltz's tombstone—"He Died So Jewry Shall Suffer No More"—that leaped out at me in 2011 and set me on the journey that led to this book. After my stories about his grave were published, people began to pay attention to Meltz's story.

During the celebrations leading up to the seventieth anniversary of D-Day in 2014, Isabella Meltz was touched when the Toronto Jewish community asked her to participate in the annual Holocaust Remembrance Day ceremony. Two thousand people saw her light a memorial candle in honour of the liberators from the Allied armed forces. The symbolism of the event was not lost on her. "We think of the Holocaust, the victims, the survivors and then somewhere in another box in your mind are the soldiers who went over. But to put it together as Jewish soldiers, I thought it was really wonderful because it was acknowledging this… part of a Jewish story," Meltz said.

Meltz's epitaph also became a powerful symbol for Toronto's United Jewish Appeal fundraising campaign in 2015. Its message was that all is not yet well for the world's Jews. "Anti-Semitism remains and is rearing its ugly head ever more frequently and in more places," wrote David Matlow, a Toronto lawyer who co-chaired that campaign. According to Matlow, it is incumbent on Canadian Jews to improve the lives of the ten thousand elderly Holocaust survivors who live in Toronto. "We may never achieve George Meltz's objective to end all Jewish suffering. But we should keep trying," he said.[55]

Isabella Meltz's own journey of remembrance started out with a few vague family stories and a couple of cousins who bear her uncle's name. Her father, Jake, and eight older brothers and sisters were left to mourn, their parents having died before the war started.

"He was the youngest. They must have been just heartbroken," Isabella said, who was born after the war and did not have much information about her uncle until recently. "They didn't talk about it," she said.

Now, Meltz attends Remembrance Day ceremonies every year in her uncle's honour. She has taken to lighting a yahrzeit candle each July on the anniversary of his death. She lights a second one on the same day for the Jews in her family's small Lithuanian town of Sesik, who were murdered in the summer of 1941 during the German occupation.[56] The Allies, including her uncle George, landed too late to save them.

"You think, 'You know, that could've been me,'" she says.

Notes

ABBREVIATIONS

ADCJA: Alex Dworkin Canadian Jewish Archives, Montreal, https://www.cjarchives.ca/en/ (formerly the Canadian Jewish Congress Charities Committee National Archives)

CJC: Canadian Jewish Congress

CJWWII: David Rome, ed., *Canadian Jews in World War II, Part II: Casualties* (Montreal: Canadian Jewish Congress, 1948); *CJWWII, Part I: Decorations* (Montreal: Canadian Jewish Congress, 1947) cited separately

LAC: Library and Archives Canada, Ottawa

LAC Service Files: Service Files of the Second World War—War Dead, 1939–1947, http://www.bac-lac.gc.ca/eng/discover/military-heritage/second-world-war/second-world-war-dead-1939-1947/Pages/files-second-war-dead.aspx

OJA: Ontario Jewish Archives, UJA Federation of Greater Toronto, http://ontariojewisharchives.org

INTRODUCTION

1 George Meltz's family in Canada was told that he was taking a smoke break when a German sniper shot him. There is no mention of the specifics of his death in his military file, only that he was hospitalized on July 8 and died of wounds he sustained in action. His in-laws' family in England remembers being told that George had stepped on a mine, and that is what killed him. See also LAC Service Files, series RG 24 vol. 26600, George Meltz, Medical Report.

2 *CJWWII, Part I: Decorations*, foreword.

1 FIGHTING AMALEK

1 "Prime Minister Mackenzie King Outlines Canada's Duty in War," *Globe and Mail*, September 5, 1939, in *Democracy at War: Canadian Newspapers and the Second World War*, Canadian War Museum, http://www.warmuseum.ca/cwm/exhibitions/newspapers/canadawar/wlmking_e.shtml.

2 "Issue Is Clear for Jews, Avers Rabbi Feldman," *Hamilton Spectator*, September 14, 1939, in *Democracy at War*, Canadian War Museum, http://collections.warmuseum.ca/warclip/objects/common/webmedia.php?irn=5052795.

3 "Britain's Fight Is Jews' Fight, Rabbi Declares," *Globe and Mail*, September 14, 1939, in *Democracy at War*, Canadian War Museum, http://collections.civilisations.ca/warclip/objects/common/webmedia.php?irn=5052796.

4 William Abrams, "A Report on the Formation and Development of the War Efforts Committee of the Canadian Jewish Congress," December 31, 1941, OJA, Harry R. Moscoe fonds 69, file 9, WEC General 1941–1944.

5 Minutes of the National Dominion Council, Canadian Jewish Congress, War Efforts Committee, March 21, 1943, Montreal, Agenda, Item 3. Furniture for Huts of the Army, Navy and Air Force, Harry R. Moscoe fonds 69, box 1, file 18, Jewish Chaplains 1942–1943, OJA.

6 Max Beer, "What Else Could We Have Done? The Montreal Jewish Community, the Canadian Jewish Congress, the Jewish Press, and the Holocaust." MA thesis, Department of History, Concordia University, 2006, 53-54. https://spectrum.library.concordia.ca/8974/1/MR14193.pdf

7 "Memo on Points to Be Remembered in Connection with Talks Given to Organizations throughout the Country on Behalf of the War Efforts Committee," Talking Points for a Speakers' Bureau, 1941, ADCJA.

8 S. Gershon Levi, *Breaking New Ground: The Struggle for a Jewish Chaplaincy in Canada*, ed. David Golinkin (Montreal: National Archives Canadian Jewish Congress, 1994), 4.

9 Derek J. Penslar, *Jews in the Military: A History* (Princeton, NJ: Princeton University Press, 2013), 2.

10 Irving Abella, *A Coat of Many Colours: Two Centuries of Jewish Life in Canada* (Toronto: Lester & Orpen Dennys, 1990), 13, 25.

11 Cynthia Toman, *An Officer and a Lady: Canadian Military Nursing and the Second World War* (Vancouver: UBC Press, 2008), 47.

12 Hyman Sokolov, "Battling Bias in Manitoba: The Exposure of Discrimination in Methods of Selection of Students to the Medical College Brings Important Gains," *Jewish Post* (Winnipeg), March 22, 1945, 3; Chief Justice Samuel Freedman, "Student Days at the University of Manitoba," *Manitoba Law Journal* (special edition, 2014) 37, chap. 2: 23.

13 Sokolov, "Battling Bias in Manitoba."

14 Abella, *A Coat of Many Colours*, 180, 251.

15 Louis Rosenberg, "Jews in Canada," *Contemporary Jewish Record*, March–April 1939, 2, no. 2: 37.

16 Saul Cherniack, "Personal Perspective," in Daniel Stone, ed., *Jewish Life and Times*, vol. 3, *Jewish Radicalism in Winnipeg 1905–1960* (Winnipeg: Jewish Heritage Centre of Western Canada, 2003), 206.

17 Cy Gonick, *A Very Red Life: The Story of Bill Walsh* (St. John's: Canadian Committee on Labour History, 2001), 76.

18 Helen Feinstein diary, unpublished, Tel Aviv, courtesy of Louis Devor.

19 Gerald Tulchinsky, *Canada's Jews: A Peoples Journey* (Toronto, University of Toronto Press, 2008), 376.

20 Penslar, *Jews in the Military*, 252.

21 Alexandra Stelzer, "Winnipeg Jews in the Canadian Army in World War II," 1987, Jewish Heritage Centre, of Western Canada, Winnipeg, Z971.2STE, 13.

22 LAC Service Files, series RG (record group) 24, vol. 25215, Nat Dlusy, RCAF Interview Report, July 27, 1942, No. 13 Recruiting Centre, note by Flying Officer J.C. Laffoley.

23 LAC Service Files, series RG 24, vol. 25950, Joe Gertel, Personnel Selection Board, April 1, 1943.

24 Arthur Pascal interview with his grandchildren, tape 2a, unpublished, courtesy of Kathy Cohen.

25 Jewish War Veterans of Canada, *No Greater Honour: A Record of Canadian Jewish Military Service*, 1987, video documentary, OJA, http://search.ontariojewisharchives.org/Permalink/accessions24504.

26 "Letter from David, June 5, 1944," Devor Family file 1990 6/1, OJA.

2 SIGNING UP

1 Levi, *Breaking New Ground*, 31; Morton Weinfeld, "Louis Rosenberg and the Origins of the Socio-Demographic Study of Jews in Canada," *Jewish Population Studies (Papers in Jewish Demography)* (1993): 31, https://www.bjpa.org/search-results/publication/131.

2 C.P. Stacey, *Official History of the Canadian Army in the Second World War, vol. 1, Six Years of War: The Army in Canada, Britain and the Pacific* (Ottawa: Department of National Defence, Directorate of History and Heritage, and Queen's Printer, 1955), 57–58. http://www.cmp-cpm.forces.gc.ca/dhh-dhp/his/docs/Sixyrs_e.pdf.

3 J.L. Granatstein, *The Best Little Army in the World* (Toronto: HarperCollins, 2015), 260.

4 Ben Dunkelman, *Dual Allegiance: An Autobiography* (Toronto: Macmillan, 1972), 55, 56.
5 Robert Farquharson, *For Your Tomorrow: Canadians and the Burma Campaign* (Victoria: Trafford Publishing, 2004), 126.
6 "Physician Dies," *Ottawa Journal*, May 15, 1940, 4.
7 Stacey, *Six Years of War*, 115.
8 Ruth A. Frager, *Sweatshop Strife: Class, Ethnicity, and Gender in the Jewish Labour Movement of Toronto 1900–1939*, appendix, part A, Statistical Information on the Jewish Population of Canada, tables 1 and 2 (Toronto: University of Toronto Press, 1992), 219.
9 Jacob Markowitz biography, 20, unpublished, courtesy of Jane Markowitz.
10 Penslar, *Jews in the Military*, 208–209.
11 Mathias Joost, "Racism and Enlistment: The Second World War Policies of the Royal Canadian Air Force," *Canadian Military History* 2, no. 1: 17, 27.
12 LAC Service Files, series RG 24, vol. 25076, Samuel Cohen, RCAF Interview Report, Flying Officer Henri Geoffrion, 14–10–1940.
13 Canadian Jewish Congress War Efforts Committee, OJA, RG 297, MG 8, box 2, file Mrs. H. Allen Memos, 1941, Report, War Efforts Committee, CJC Central Division, 9.
14 Honourable David Croll, Senator, *Oral History Project,* transcript of interview by Tom Earle, Library of Parliament, 1983, 20.
15 Canadian Jewish Congress brochure, 1940, courtesy of Ferne Phillips collection.
16 Max Bookman, "Canadian Jews in Uniform," in Eli Gottesman, ed., *Canadian Jewish Reference Book and Directory* (Toronto: Jewish Institute of Higher Research of the Central Rabbinical Seminary of Canada, 1963), 111.
17 Herb Wolf letter to Sam Ages, July 3, 1941, courtesy of Elaine Schwartz. Wolf volunteered to fly in a special Royal Air Force squadron in North Africa, No. 109. It was testing experimental radar jamming equipment. Wolf, a co-pilot the night his plane was shot down, November 21, 1941, is buried in Egypt, near the Libyan border.
18 *CJWWII*, 36.
19 LAC Service Files, series RG 24, vol. 28724, Hymie Steinberg, Attestation Papers.
20 LAC Service Files, Hymie Steinberg, interview report.
21 W.R. Feasby, *Official History of the Canadian Medical Services, 1939–1945*, vol. 2, *Clinical Subjects* (Ottawa: Queen's Printer, 1953), 412.
22 Leo Heaps, *The Grey Goose of Arnhem* (London: Weidenfeld and Nicolson, 1976), 30–31.
23 Dunkelman, *Dual Allegiance*, 7.

24 Michael Brown, "Rose Dunkelman," *Jewish Women: A Comprehensive Historical Encyclopedia*, March 1, 2009, Jewish Women's Archive; https://jwa.org/encyclopedia/article/dunkelman-rose.
25 Dunkelman, *Dual Allegiance*, 54, 55.
26 *CJWWII*, 38.
27 "Mimi Freedman, Woman Veteran Overseas Six and a Half Years," *Gazette* (Montreal), September 20, 1946, 4.
28 "Ashore and Afloat," clipping from a Halifax newspaper, OJA, Harry R. Moscoe fonds 69, box 1, file 19, Newspaper Clippings 1943.
29 "Ottawa Rabbi Has Seven Sons Serving in Canada's Forces," *Ottawa Journal*, July 4, 1942, 19; "Military Theme at Wedding of Dorothy Maser," *Ottawa Journal*, August 4, 1942, 7.
30 Howard Fluxgold, "Shining a Light on a Painful Loss," *Globe and Mail*, November 10, 2008, http://www.theglobeandmail.com/life/shining-a-light-on-a-painful-loss/article1065438.
31 LAC Service Files, series RG 24, vol. 30620, Sydney Brown, Attestation Papers; OJA, box 2009, files 1–4, Sydney and Zave Brown, 83–85, letter to Zave, November 10, 1941.
32 *CJWWII*, 10.
33 Canadian Jewish Congress War Efforts Committee, OJA, RG 297, MG 8, box 2, file Mrs. H. Allen Memos, 1941, Report, War Efforts Committee, CJC Central Division, 10.
34 List of Jewish men who attested under non-Jewish religion, ADCJA, CJC DA 18.1, box 16, file 2/12.
35 LAC Service Files, series RG 24, vol. 27515, Edmond David Fleishman, Occupational History Form. November 4, 1939.
36 Cyril Crain, memoir, http://www.freewebs.com/keithstevenson/dday6thjune.htm.
37 Russell Alexander Souchen, "Beyond D-Day: Maintaining Morale in the 3rd Canadian Infantry Division June–July 1944," MA thesis, Faculty of History, University of Ottawa, 2010, 19, 32, http://www.collectionscanada.gc.ca/obj/thesescanada/vol2/002/MR73778.PDF.
38 LAC Service Files, series RG 24, vol. 26062, Fred Harris, List of Personal Effects from 1st Canadian Kit Storage Depot, Acknowledgement Form, and Soldier's Pay Book, 8.
39 LAC Service Files, series R 112, vol. 30511, David Harold Bindman, Attestation Papers, September 5, 1939.
40 WWII Service Files of War Dead, 1939–1947, online database, ancestry.ca, examples: files of Frank Adams, R 13640, and Frederick Adams, R 54373.

41 LAC Service Files, series RG 24, vol. 28173, Charles Males, Personal Record, October 27, 1942.

42 LAC Service Files, series RG 24, vol. 28411, Jacob Silverstein, Medical Form in Attestation Papers.

43 LAC Service Files, series RG 24, vol. 24793, Alex Balinson, RCAF Interview Report, Special Reserve, April 4, 1940, RCAF Recruiting Centre, Hamilton.

44 Gary Barwin, "Jewish Voice of Hamilton Exhibit Opening," *Hamilton Jewish News*, September 2015, https://hamiltonjewishnews.com/arts-culture/jewish-voice-of-hamilton-exhibit-opening.

45 LAC Service Files, series RG 24, vol. 30827, George Holidenke, Field Medical Card and Attestation Papers.

46 "Veteran Stories: Nathan 'Sonny' Isaacs, Air Force," The Memory Project, http://www.thememoryproject.com/stories/1023:nathan-sonny-isaacs.

47 LAC Service Files, series RG 24, vol. 25950, Joe Gertel, letter from Israel Gertel to Department of National Defence.

48 Hymie Greenberg letter to his mother in Spedden, Alberta, January 8, 1941, Provincial Archives of Alberta, PR 1988.0242/28 (box 2).

49 Daniel Byers, *Zombie Army: The Canadian Army and Conscription in the Second World War* (Vancouver: UBC Press, 2016), 6.

50 Byers, *Zombie Army*, 135–36, including table.

51 Jack Granatstein, "Ethnic and Religious Enlistment in Canada during the Second World War," Essays in Honour of Gerald Tulchinsky, *Canadian Jewish Studies* 21 (2013): 178.

52 Byers, *Zombie Army*, 136.

53 "Memo from Cpt. G.S. Allen, 154 Aylmer Annex, Ottawa, to Miss B. Wollow, November 18, 1944, on Jewish Army enlistments and NRMA," ADCJA DA 18.1, box 18, file 6/b.

54 Feasby, *Clinical Subjects*, 413–14.

55 "The Honour Roll," *Canadian Jewish Chronicle*, November 24, 1944, 14.

56 Irving Kaplan letter to Corporal A. Goldbloom, December 12, 1944, 3, courtesy of Sadie Kaplan.

57 Letter dated February 24, 1941, ADCJA, War Efforts Committee, CJC ZA 1941, box 13, file 137.

58 Tulchinsky, *Canada's Jews*, 375.

59 H. Wolofsky, "S.O.S.," *Jewish Daily Eagle*, July 11, 1941 (free translation, author unknown), War Efforts Committee, ADCJA, CJC ZA 1941, box 13.

60 *Daily Hebrew Journal*, June 19, 1941, ADCJA, War Efforts Committee, CJC ZA 1941, box 13, file 137.

61 Sam Abrahamson letter to Major Cox, HQ Military District #1, London, Ontario, October 29, 1941, ADCJA CJC ZA 1941, box 13, file 137.

62 "Jewish Honour Roll Is Unveiled," *Winnipeg Free Press*, June 24, 1942, 16.

63 "Approaching a Decade," War Efforts Committee Report, 9th Annual Regional Conference, Canadian Jewish Congress Central Division, War Efforts Committee 1942–1943, OJA, Harry R. Moscoe fonds 69, file 11.

64 Tulchinsky, *Canada's Jews*, 379.

65 Saul Hayes, "Jews in the Forces," Letters to the Editor, *Ottawa Citizen*, May 4, 1943, 8.

66 "Estimate of Jewish Males of Military age 18–40 in Canada, by Province and Cities, 1939," War Efforts Committee Supplementary, ADCJA, CJC DA 18.1, box 22, file 1.

67 Levi, *Breaking New Ground*, 24; *CJWWII*, inside front cover illustration.

68 Tulchinsky, *Canada's Jews*, 380.

69 Levi, *Breaking New Ground*, 77 (notes).

70 Tulchinsky, *Canada's Jews*, 115; "Pechet, Simon," Canadian Jewish Heritage Network, Canadian Jewish Archives (Jewish Colonization Archives), http://www.cjhn.ca/en/permalink/genealogy2718.

71 "S. Pechet Marks 81st Birthday," *Winnipeg Tribune*, April 1, 1942, 5.

72 Mitch Pechet, Canadian Military Oral History Collection, University of Victoria, March 13, 2007, audio file, http://contentdm.library.uvic.ca/cdm/compoundobject/collection/collection13/id/1953/rec/1; Tom Hawthorn, "Mitch Pechet, Hockey Player 1918–2009," Tom Hawthorn's Blog, http://tomhawthorn.blogspot.ca/2010/02/mitch-pechet-hockey-player-1918-2009.html.

73 Grant Grams, "Enemies within Our Bosoms: Nazi Sabotage in Canada," *Journal of Military and Strategic Studies* 14, no. 3 and 4 (2012): 7.

74 LAC Service Files, series RG 24, vol. 26145, Jack Faibish, Soldier's Qualification Card, p. 2.

75 Joseph B. Glass, "Isolation and Alienation: Factors in the Growth of Zionism in the Canadian Prairies 1917–1939," *Canadian Jewish Studies* 9 (2001): 101–106.

76 Cherie Smith, *Mendel's Children: A Family Chronicle* (Calgary: University of Calgary Press, 1997), 6.

77 Glass, "Isolation and Alienation," 103.

78 "Well Done, Kamsack Jewry," *Canadian Jewish Chronicle,* August 22, 1941, 2. http://bit.ly/2yThsQ8.

79 News release, August 11, 1941, War Efforts Committee, Canadian Jewish Congress Eastern Division, Canadian Jewish Congress, OJA, RG 297 Canadian Jewish Congress War Efforts Committee, box 4, M68 A11, 1941.

80 "Fine Service Record of Small Community," *Ottawa Journal*, July 15, 1941, 9.
81 Rosenberg, "Report of the Executive Director," 16.
82 Iroquois Falls and District Chamber of Commerce, "History" (1972), http://iroquoisfallschamber.com/page/history; Henry Abramson, "Just Different: The Last Jewish Family of Ansonville, Ontario," *Canadian Jewish Studies* 9, no. 1 (2003): 154.
83 LAC Service Files, series RG 112; vol. 30790, David Abramson, Attestation Papers for Active Service.
84 Report delivered by H.M. Caiserman at the Maritime Convention, Saint John, NB, August 18, 1943, OJA, Harry R. Moscoe fonds 69, file 7, War Efforts Committee.
85 Tulchinsky, *Branching Out*, 28.
86 Ben Rose, "From Belarus to Cape Breton and Beyond," *Canadian Jewish News*, May 15, 1997, http://www.billgladstone.ca/?p=8008.

3 JEWISH COMMUNISTS IN UNIFORM

1 M.J. Scott, "War Diary of the 21st Armoured Regiment (Governor General's Foot Guards), July 1944–August 1944," RG 24 C-3, vol. 14255, microfilm reel T-12722, Department of National Defence fonds, Laurier Military History Archive, http://lmharchive.ca/wp-content/uploads/2014/03/21st-Armoured-Regiment.pdf.
2 Dick Steele letter to Esther Steele, August 12, 1944, courtesy of Michael Steele.
3 Gonick, *A Very Red Life*, 26; Bill Walsh and Esther Steele Walsh, tape 5, audio interview with family members, 2004, unpublished, tapes 3–5 courtesy of Michael Steele.
4 Tulchinsky, *Branching Out*, 123. Erlick said he attended Baron Byng, although by the time he arrived in Canada in 1927 he was already twenty-two, which makes it doubtful.
5 Gonick, *A Very Red Life*, 36.
6 Moishe Kosowatsky and Moishe Wolofsky, "From the Land of Despair to the Land of Promise," 30, courtesy of Michael Steele.
7 Walsh family interview, tape 3, side A.
8 Michelle McBride, "From Indifference to Internment: An Examination of RCMP Responses to Nazism and Fascism in Canada from 1934 to 1941," MA thesis, Department of History, Memorial University of Newfoundland, May 1997, http://www.collectionscanada.gc.ca/obj/s4/f2/dsk2/ftp04/mq23157.pdf, 288.
9 "Muni Erlick and Dick Steele Killed in Battle for Freedom," *Canadian Jewish Weekly* 4, no. 201 (August 31, 1944): 1.
10 Walsh family interview, tape 3, side B.

11 Walsh family interview, tape 3, sides A and B.
12 Victor Howard, "*We Were the Salt of the Earth!*": *The On-to-Ottawa Trek and the Regina Riot* (Regina: University of Regina, 1985), 67.
13 Gonick, *A Very Red Life*, 107.
14 Irving Abella, *Nationalism, Communism, and Canadian Labour: The CIO, the Communist Party, and the Canadian Congress of Labour, 1935–1956* (Toronto: University of Toronto Press, 1973), 55.
15 J.B. Salsberg,"Tribute to a Fallen Hero," *Canadian Tribune* (Toronto), September 9, 1944, 7.
16 Walsh family interview, tape 3, side B.
17 Byers, *Zombie Army*, 107–108.
18 Esther Steele letter to Louis St. Laurent, April 20, 1942, courtesy of Michael Steele.
19 "Our Fight for Freedom," pamphlet produced by the National Front for Democratic Rights, October 1941, Toronto, 21, http://collections.mun.ca/PDFs/radical/OurFightForFreedom.pdf.
20 LAC Service Files, series RG 24, vol. 27113, Richard Steele, Attestation Papers.
21 Dick Steele letter to Esther Steele, August 12, 1943.
22 LAC Service Files, series RG 24, vol. 25830, Muni Erlick, Attestation Papers, and Personnel Selection documents, September 6, 1943; Ben Swankey, *What's New? Memoirs of a Socialist Idealist* (Victoria: Trafford Publishing, 2008), 112.
23 Dick Steele letter to Esther Steele, n.d., but he embarked June 10, 1943, and disembarked June 18, 1943.
24 *CJWWII*, 29; LAC Service Files, series RG 24, vol. 25984, Reuben Gorodetsky, Attestation Papers.
25 Dick Steele letter to Esther Steele, January 3, 1943.
26 Dick Steele letter to comrades in London, Jane, Sally, Aida, Bill, Nelly, Fred, April 12, 1944.
27 Chris Frazer, "From Pariahs to Patriots: Canadian Communists and the Second World War," *Past Imperfect*, vol. 5, 1996. http://dx.doi.org/10.21971/P7NK5Z.
28 *CJWWII*, 87; Henry Srebnick, "Changing an Illusion: The Canadian Communist Movement," in Matthew B. Hoffman and Henry F. Srebnick, eds., *A Vanished Ideology: Essays on the Jewish Communist Movement in the English Speaking World in the Twentieth Century* (Albany: State University of New York Press, 2016), 110; "Innocence Pleaded at Sedition Trial," *Gazette* (Montreal), May 11, 1940, 5, http://bit.ly/2zSk2pY.
29 "Veteran Stories: Hyman 'Chud' Chudnovsky, Army," The Memory Project, Http://www.thememoryproject.com/stories/1368:hyman-Chudnovsky/.
30 M.J. Scott, "War Diary," 12.

31 A.R. Jessup, The Regimental History of the Governor General's Foot Guards (Ottawa: Mortimer, 1948), 135–136.
32 *CJWWII, Part I: Decorations*, 53.
33 Dick Steele letter to Esther Steele, August 12, 1944.
34 David J. Bercuson, *Our Finest Hour: Canada Fights the Second World War* (Toronto: HarperCollins, 2015), 394.
35 Mark Zuehlke, *Breakout from Juno: First Canadian Army and the Normandy Campaign, July 4–August 21, 1944* (Vancouver: Douglas & McIntyre, 2011), 380–381.
36 Scott, "War Diary," 31.
37 Guardsman Joe Levitt letter to Esther Steele published as "How Dick Steele Died," *Canadian Tribune* (Toronto), October 7, 1944, 8.
38 Walsh family interview, tape 5.
39 LAC Service Files, series RG 24, vol. 25984, Reuben Gorodetsky, Testimony of P. Hanson, witness, Court of Inquiry into the Death of Acting Corporal Reuben Gorodetsky, Lieutenant Colonel F.M. Mitchell, September 4, 1944.
40 LAC Service Files, Reuben Gorodetsky. Major General H.F.G. Letson, Adjutant General, letter to Rita Gorodetsky, September 30, 1944.
41 "Muni Erlick and Dick Steele Killed in Battle for Freedom," *Canadian Jewish Weekly* 4 (Toronto), no. 201 (August 31, 1944): 1.
42 Sergeant Bill Walsh letter to Esther Steele published as "The Quota Has Gone Up," *Canadian Tribune* (Toronto), October 7, 1944, 8.
43 Douglas Umaron, "Heroes of Calcar," February 22, 1945, courtesy of Michael Steele.
44 Original news clipping, April 1, 1945, courtesy of Michael Steele; see also William Walsh fonds, LAC, MG 31, B 27.

4 THE BATTLE OF HONG KONG

1 Ross Savage, "Dick Steele Asks Assurances He Won't Be Interned If He Seeks to Enlist," *Canadian Tribune*, Toronto, undated clipping, Esther Steele Walsh collection of letters and files, courtesy of Michael Steele.
2 Nathan M. Greenfield, *The Damned: The Canadians at the Battle of Hong Kong and the POW Experience 1941–45* (Toronto: HarperCollins, 2010), 13.
3 Brereton Greenhous, *"C" Force to Hong Kong: A Canadian Catastrophe 1941–1945* (Toronto: Dundurn, 1997).
4 *Brown and Gold, 1941*, University of Manitoba Yearbook, 148.
5 Tom Slater, *The City of Sarnia War Remembrance Project, A Record of Sarnia's Sacrifices and Contributions Made During War* (Sarnia: Haines Printing, 2014), 197–198.
6 LAC Service Files, series RG 24, vol. 25440, Max Berger, Record of Service.

7 Bureau of War Records, Canadian Jewish Congress, Jewish War Casualties 1943–1944, Wounded, Missing, Dead. OJA, Harry R. Moscoe fonds 69, file 15.

8 "Robert Macklin [1909–1942]," Gwulo: Old Hong Kong, http://gwulo.com/node/17458.

9 Tony Banham, *We Shall Suffer There: Hong Kong's Defenders Imprisoned, 1942–1945* (Hong Kong: Hong Kong University Press, 2009), 74.

10 LAC Service Files, series RG 24, vol. 26997, David Schrage, Medical Files.

11 Penslar, *Jews in the Military*, 28.

12 LAC Service Files, David Schrage, Attestation Papers.

13 Hymie Greenberg letter to his mother in Spedden, Alberta, January 1, 1941, Provincial Archives of Alberta, PR 1988.0242/28, box 2.

14 LAC Service Files, series RG 24, vol. 25734, Hymie Greenberg, Attestation Papers.

15 Moses Jampolsky letter from Spedden, Alberta, to his stepson, Hymie Greenberg, September 22, 1941, Provincial Archives of Alberta, PR 1988.0242/28, box 2.

16 D. Burke Penny, *Beyond the Call: Royal Canadian Corps of Signals, Brigade Headquarters, "C" Force, Hong Kong and Japan, 1941–1945* (Nepean, ON: Hong Kong Veterans Commemorative Association, 2009), 34.

17 Tom Hawthorn, "William Allister, PoW and Painter (1919–2008)," *Globe and Mail*, November 29, 2008, http://tomhawthorn.blogspot.ca/2008/11/william-allister-pow-and-painter-1919.html.

18 Greenhous, *"C" Force to Hong Kong*, 27.

19 *CJWWII*, 119.

20 Penny, *Beyond the Call*, 36.

21 Greenhous, *"C" Force to Hong Kong*, 21.

22 David Golden, "I Was Poorly Trained!," Heroes Remember video series, Veterans Affairs Canada, http://www.veterans.gc.ca/eng/video-gallery/video/10284.

23 Stacey, *Six Years of War*, 445, http://www.cmp-cpm.forces.gc.ca/dhh-dhp/his/docs/Sixyrs_e.pdf.

24 Quoted in Greenhous, *"C" Force to Hong Kong*, 27.

25 Penny, *Beyond the Call*, 38.

26 Hymie Greenberg postcard from Debert, Nova Scotia, to his stepfather, Moses Jampolsky, in Spedden, Alberta, October 19, 1941, Provincial Archives of Alberta, PR 1988.0242/28, box 2.

27 Historical Section, Canadian Military Headqurters, "Canadian Participation in the Defence of Hong Kong," Report No. 163, December 1941. http://publications.gc.ca/collections/collection_2016/mdn-dnd/D63-4-163-1946-eng.pdf.

28 Hymie Greenberg postcard from Vancouver to Moses Jampolsky, in Spedden, Alberta, October 28, 1941, Provincial Archives of Alberta, PR 1988.0242/28, box 2.

29 Greenhous, *"C" Force to Hong Kong*, 16.

30 "Individual Report: H6375 George Harrison, 1st Bn The Winnipeg Grenadiers," Hong Kong Veterans Commemorative Association, http://www.hkvca.ca/cforcedata/indivreport/indivdetailed.php?regtno=H6375.

31 George Harrison, "The Awatea Mutiny," Heroes Remember video series, Veterans Affairs Canada, http://www.veterans.gc.ca/eng/video-gallery/video/10716.

32 Vince Lopata, *From Heaven to Hell Part One: The Story of the Winnipeg Grenadiers as Part of "Y" Force and "C" Force during World War II* (Winnipeg: McNally Robinson, 2013), http://www.mcnallyrobinson.com/9781927533468/vince-lopata/from-heaven-to-hell-part-one#.

33 Harrison, "The Awatea Mutiny," http://www.veterans.gc.ca/eng/video-gallery/video/10716.

34 Greenhous, *"C" Force to Hong Kong*, 29.

35 Greenfield, *The Damned*, 16.

36 Hawthorn, "William Allister," http://tomhawthorn.blogspot.ca/2008/11/william-allister-pow-and-painter-1919.html.

37 Greenfield, *The Damned*, 16.

38 LAC Service Files, David Schrage, Medical Officer's Report.

39 "Individual Report: B38365 David Schrage, 1st Bn The Royal Rifles of Canada," Hong Kong Veterans Commemorative Association, http://www.hkvca.ca/cforcedata/indivreport/indivdetailed.php?regtno=B38365.

40 Arch Dale, "A Canadian Surprise," *Winnipeg Free Press*, November 18, 1941, ink on paper, in Charles Hou, "World War Two in Cartoons," McCord Museum, 2005, http://collection.mccord.mcgill.ca/ObjView/PERS-17.jpg.

41 Greenhous, *"C" Force to Hong Kong*, 35.

42 André de la Varre, *Hong Kong: Gateway to China*, A Screen Traveler Picture, May 15, 1938, http://bit.ly/2yUw81z.

43 Lyman Jampolsky letter from Spedden, Alberta, to Hymie Greenberg, November 26, 1941, Provincial Archives of Alberta, PR 1988.0242/28, box 2.

44 Brian McKenna, *Savage Christmas: Hong Kong 1941*, National Film Board of Canada, 1991.

45 Greenhous, *"C" Force to Hong Kong*, 16.

46 Greenfield, *The Damned*, 27, 28.

47 David Golden, "An Uninformed Intelligence Officer," Heroes Remember video series, Veterans Affairs Canada, http://www.veterans.gc.ca/eng/video-gallery/video/10285.

48 Greenhous, *"C" Force to Hong Kong*, 47.

49 Greenfield, *The Damned*, 124.

50 Greenfield, *The Damned*, 125.

51 Harrison, "Escape from High Ground," http://www.veterans.gc.ca/eng/video-gallery/video/10721.

52 Banham, *We Shall Suffer There*, 166.

53 "Berger, Max," Sarnia Historical Society, http://www.sarniahistoricalsociety.com/warmemorialproject/berger-max-a56551/.

54 John Grehan and Martin Mace, *Disaster in the Far East, 1940–1942* (Barnsley, UK: Pen and Sword Books, 2015), 128.

55 Harrison, "Final Battle," http://www.veterans.gc.ca/eng/video-gallery/video/10722.

56 *CJWWII*,120.

57 Greenfield, *The Damned*, 277.

58 *CJWWII*, 133.

59 Robert Macklin, Colonial Office, Register of Deaths, Register No. H.K. 1, folio no. 51, 26, RG 33/11, serial number 301, ancestry.co.uk.

60 Banham, *We Shall Suffer There*, 74.

61 "Macklin, Ursula Teresa," Gwulo: Old Hong Kong, http://gwulo.com/node/15051.

62 LAC Service Files, Hymie Greenberg, Moses Jampolsky letter to National Defence.

63 "Canadian Jews in the News," *Canadian Jewish Review*, December 18, 1942, 6.

64 Hawthorn, "William Allister," http://tomhawthorn.blogspot.ca/2008/11/william-allister-pow-and-painter-1919.html.

65 David Golden, "Poor Rations," Heroes Remember video series, Veterans Affairs Canada, http://www.veterans.gc.ca/eng/video-gallery/video/10288.

66 Penny, *Beyond the Call*, 120, 216.

67 "Paintings from a POW Camp," Veterans Affairs Canada, http://www.veterans.gc.ca/eng/remembrance/those-who-served/diaries-letters-stories/second-world-war/camp-painting.

68 LAC Service Files, Hymie Greenberg, Lieutenant Colonel F.W. Clarke letter to Mrs. Sonya Jampolsky, August 12, 1942.

69 Hawthorn, "William Allister," http://tomhawthorn.blogspot.ca/2008/11/william-allister-pow-and-painter-1919.html.

70 Penny, *Beyond the Call*, 184.

71 *CJWWII*, 133; "Individual Report: B40578 Frederick Zaidman, 1st Bn The Royal Rifles of Canada," Hong Kong Veterans Commemorative Association, http://www.hkvca.ca/cforcedata/indivreport/indivdetailed.php?regtno=B40578.

72 Harrison, "Kai Tak Airport," http://www.veterans.gc.ca/eng/video-gallery/video/10725.

73 Harrison, "Kai Tak Airport," "Garlic Therapy," "Beri Beri," "Sudden Blindness," "Avoiding Amputation," http://www.veterans.gc.ca/eng/video-gallery/search/people/768.

5 DIEPPE

1 "Feared Her Son Was Dead When Cheque Didn't Come," clipping from unidentified Toronto newspaper, September 30, 1942, courtesy of Sandra London-Rakita.
2 Bercuson, *Our Finest Hour*, 91, 95.
3 *CJWWII*, 47.
4 "The Dieppe Raid," Canada in the Second World War, Juno Beach Centre, https://www.junobeach.org/canada-in-wwii/articles/the-dieppe-raid.
5 LAC Service Files, series RG 24, vol. 25271, Meyer Bubis, Attestation Papers; LAC Service Files, series RG 24, vol. 26006, Simon Green, Attestation Papers.
6 *CJWWII*, 98, 33.
7 "Captain Poag, R.H.L.I. Adjutant, Died of Wounds at Dieppe," *Toronto Daily Star*, December 8, 1942.
8 Martin Sugarman, "World War II: Canadian and Allied Jews at the Raid on Dieppe," Jewish Virtual Library, August 1942, http://www.jewishvirtuallibrary.org/jsource/ww2/sugar7.html.
9 Hugh G. Henry, "The Calgary Tanks at Dieppe," *Canadian Military History* 4, no. 1 (1995): 61.
10 Charles G. Roland, "On the Beach and in the Bag: The Fate of Dieppe Casualties Left Behind," *Canadian Military History* 9, no. 4 (Autumn 2000): 6–25.
11 LAC Service Files, series RG 24, vol. 25339, Abram Arbour, Soldier's Qualification Card.
12 "Mentioned for Dieppe Gallantry," *Jewish Chronicle* (London), October 30, 1942, 5; Sugarman, "World War II," http://www.jewishvirtuallibrary.org/jsource/ww2/sugar7.html; "Rumsey Boys Serve in Two Wars," *Discovery: The Journal of the Jewish Historical Society of Southern Alberta* 5, no. 4 (Spring 1995): 3.
13 David O'Keefe, *One Day in August: The Untold Story behind Canada's Tragedy at Dieppe* (Toronto: Knopf, 2013), 273.
14 LAC Service Files, series RG 24, vol. 26090, Leizer Heifetz, Attestation Papers.
15 LAC Service Files, series RG 24, vol. 26538, Leon Paul Magner, Permission to Marry Form.
16 "Canadian Jews in Dieppe Raid," *Jewish Chronicle* (London), October 9, 1942, 1.
17 "Operation Chariot, St. Nazaire — 28th Mar 1942," Combined Operations, http://www.combinedops.com/St%20Nazaire.htm.
18 *CJWWII*, 8.
19 *CJWWII, Part I: Decorations*, 10.

20 Mark Zuehlke, *Tragedy at Dieppe: Operation Jubilee, August 19, 1942* (Vancouver: Douglas & McIntyre, 2013), 268; *CJWWII*, 33.
21 *CJWWII*, 14; Sugarman, "World War II," http://www.jewishvirtuallibrary.org/jsource/ww2/sugar7.html.
22 "The Dieppe Raid," https://www.junobeach.org/canada-in-wwii/articles/the-dieppe-raid/.
23 *CJWWII*, 127.
24 Jonathan Vance, *Objects of Concern: Canadian Prisoners of War in the Twentieth Century* (Vancouver: UBC Press, 1994), 142, 134–135.
25 Sugarman, "World War Two," Http://www.jewishvirtuallibrary.org/jsource/ww2/sugar7.html.
26 *CJWWII*, 133.
27 Roland, "On the Beach and in the Bag," 6–25.
28 "Mentioned for Dieppe Gallantry," *Jewish Chronicle* (London), October 30, 1942, 5; The Mention in Dispatches, or MiD as it was also sometimes written, was a bravery award that didn't result in a medal but rather entitled a person to wear an oak leaf on the uniform and receive a certificate from the King describing the gallant or brave act that had prompted senior commanders to mention their name in reports.
29 *CJWWII*, 5.
30 Laura Beauchamp, "My Soldiers of Dieppe," *Canadian Battlefields* blogpost, 2009, http://www.canadianbattlefields.ca/?p=149.
31 "Operation Jubilee," The Royal Hamilton Light Infantry (Wentworth Regiment), http://kgarlano.wix.com/royal-hamilton#!operation-jubilee/c7zj.
32 Zuehlke, *Tragedy at Dieppe*, http://zuehlke.ca/excerpt-from-tragedy-at-dieppe/.
33 LAC Service Files, Jack Gralick, "Details of Information Received from Echelon, January 15, 1943."
34 LAC Service Files, Leizer Heifetz, Information Concerning Missing Soldiers, Statement Made by Private McCleery, D. POW No. 26597, April 18, 1943.
35 "Veterans Interview — Fred Englebrecht — 19 August 2003," Royal Hamilton Light Infantry, http://www.rhli.ca/dieppe/dieppeenglebrecht.html.
36 LAC Service Files, Murray Irving Bleeman, Hospital Discharge Notification, August 21, 1942.
37 Zuehlke, *Tragedy at Dieppe*, 289–290.
38 Email from Barbara Fitchette to Lamsdorf website, http://www.lamsdorf.com/names.html (look for Sandy Chesterman [Saul Shusterman]).
39 Helen Shusterman interview, CBC Radio, *Morningside*, August 19, 1993, http://www.cbc.ca/archives/entry/wives-of-dieppe-prisoners-of-war.
40 "Dieppe Hero Recounts His Role on That Fateful Day," Canadian Army, August

19, 2013, Project no. 13-0068 (archived), http://www.army-armee.forces.gc.ca/en/news-publications/national-news-details-no-menu.page?doc=dieppe-hero-recounts-his-role-on-that-fateful-day/hkjeedfw.

41 *CJWWII, Part I: Decorations*, 54; letter to his family, *Gazette* (Montreal), October 14, 1942.

42 Lionel Shapiro, "Dieppe," in George E. Nelson, ed., *Cavalcade of the North: An Entertaining Collection of Distinguished Writing by Selected Canadian Authors* (New York: Doubleday, 1958), 423.

43 *CJWWII*, 11; "Timmins Soldier Buried at Brookwood," *Ottawa Journal*, August 25, 1942, 5.

44 *CJWWII, Part I: Decorations*, 54.

45 "David Hart, MM, 'Y' War Hero and Veteran of Dieppe, Addresses Large Gathering of Senior Membership," *MHA Beacon*, 18, no. 22 (December 29, 1943): 4.

6 JEWS IN THE AIR FORCE

1 LAC Service Files, series RG 24, vol. 24714, Lawrence Abelson, RCAF Record of Service.

2 Abelson Family fonds, Duke Abelson, Ottawa Jewish Archives, box 2, file: Canadian Correspondence, November 1942–December 1942; L.B. Abelson letter to parents, November 30, 1942.

3 Pierre Lagacé, "A Real Survivor: P/O Eli Ross," January 14, 2015, https://athabaskang07.wordpress.com/2015/01/14/a-real-survivor-po-eli-ross/.

4 Usher, "Jews in the Royal Canadian Air Force," 93–114; Tulchinsky, *Canada's Jews*, 380.

5 Allan Douglas English, *The Cream of the Crop: Canadian Aircrew, 1939–1945* (Montreal and Kingston: McGill-Queen's University Press, 1996), 5.

6 English, *Cream of the Crop*, 5.

7 "William (Bill) Novick (BBHS '40)," Baron Byng High School Museum, including video, http://www.baronbynghighschool.ca/alumni/william-novick.

8 LAC Service Files, series RG 24, vol. 27889, Norman Kendall, Attestation Papers, Record of Service Airmen, General Medical and Surgical Examination.

9 Wayne Ralph, *Aces, Warriors and Wingmen: Firsthand Accounts of Canada's Fighter Pilots in the Second World War* (Toronto: Wiley, 2005), 152.

10 Monty Berger and Brian Jeffrey Street, *Invasions without Tears: The Story of Canada's Top-Scoring Spitfire Wing in Europe during the Second World War* (Toronto: Random House of Canada, 1994), ix.

11 LAC Service Files, series RG 24, vol. 27515, Edward David Fleishman, Evidence of Education, RCAF Special Reserve.

12 *CJWWII*, 74.

13 Feasby, *Official History*, 459–460.

14 "The British Commonwealth Air Training Plan," Veterans Affairs Canada, http://www.veterans.gc.ca/eng/remembrance/history/second-world-war/british-commonwealth-air-training-plan.

15 Usher, "Jews in the Royal Canadian Air Force," 96.

16 Mathias Joost, "Racism and Enlistment: The Second World War Policies of the Royal Canadian Air Force," *Canadian Military History* 2, no. 1: 17, 23.

17 L. Ray Silver, *Last of the Gladiators: A World War II Bomber Navigator's Story* (Shrewsbury, UK: Airlife, 1995), 14–15.

18 "Helped in Glorious Victory over Nazis: The Epic of Dunkirk," *Canadian Jewish Chronicle*, October 11, 1940, 2.

19 *CJWWII*, 25.

20 "Eulogy for Philip Foster," handwritten notes by George W. Evans, former Flin Flon mayor, courtesy of Doug Evans.

21 Freeda Baron, "Memories of a Farmer's Daughter," ed. Bruce Sarbit, unpublished, 144–145, courtesy of Ricki J. Miles.

22 Usher, "Jews in the Royal Canadian Air Force," 107.

23 Silver, *Last of the Gladiators*, 39.

24 Tyler Trafford, *Memories on the March: Personal Stories of the Jewish Military Veterans of Southern Alberta* (Jewish War Veterans of Canada, Post Number 2, Calgary, 2001), 32.

25 Jewish Historical Society of Southern Alberta, *Land of Promise: The Jewish Experience in Southern Alberta, 1889–1945* (Calgary: Jewish Historical Society of Southern Alberta, 1996), 162, book and exhibition, http://www.jhssa.org/book/1.html.

26 Trafford, *Memories on the March*, 109.

27 LAC Service Files, Lawrence Abelson, Report on Pupil Air Observer.

28 Jean Martin, "The Great Canadian Air Battle: The British Commonwealth Air Training Plan and the RCAF Fatalities during the Second World War," *Forces Magazine* 3, no. 1 (2002): 69.

29 Acker, Sidney; Axler, David; Bosloy, Philip; Cohen, Syd; Endelman, Saul; Herman, Donald; Kendall, Norman; Kirsch, Lionel Abraham (Abie); Kugelmass, Jack; Levine, Harry E.; Levine, Sam Meyer; Levy, Daniel; Levy, Henry; Marshall, Tommy; Morris, Lionel Joseph; Revzen, Hyman (Hymie); Schwartz, Albert Abraham; Schwartz, Frank; Stromberg, Bennie. All names taken from *CJWWII*; Les Allison and Harry Hayward, *They Shall Grow Not Old* (Brandon, MB: Commonwealth Air Training Plan Museum, 1992); Commonwealth War Graves Commission (https://www.cwgc.org); Ancestry.ca.

30 F.J. Hatch, *The Aerodrome of Democracy: Canada and the British Commonwealth Air Training Program, 1939–1945* (Ottawa: Directorate of History, Department of National Defence, 1983), 151.

31 LAC Service Files, Norman Kendall, Royal Canadian Air Force, Officer or Airman, Report on Accidental or Self-Inflicted Injuries or Immediate Death Therefrom.

32 Abelson, Lawrence; Abrams, Hyman; Ash, Joe; Brovender, Jack; Charton, Moses; Cherkinsky, Joseph; Cornfield, Joseph Samuel; Dlusy, Nat; Goldberg, Louis; Goldman, Arthur Jacob; Green, Charles; Jacobs, Daniel Lewis; Jacobs, Michael Stein; Kahn, Melvin; Klatman, Joseph; Levine, David; Marcus, John Joseph: Nagley, Arthur, Padveen, Issie; Pullen, Cy. All names taken from *CJWWII, They Shall Grow Not Old, Commonwealth War Graves Commission*, Ancestry.ca.

33 "Jewish Personnel Enlisted and Taken on Strength at No. 1 Manning Depot RCAF Toronto," 13. ADCJA, CJC DA 18.1, box 18, file 2/13; LAC Service Files, series RG 24, vol. 25253, Jack Brovender, Attestation Papers, and Royal Air Force, Officer or Airman—Report on Accident Death or Self-Inflicted Injuries or Immediate Death Therefrom.

34 Abelson Family fonds, Ottawa Jewish Archives, box 2, file: Canadian Correspondence, November 1942 to December 1942; Thom Thorne email to Dawn Logan re Duke Abelson inquiry, October 13, 2007.

35 LAC Service Files, Lawrence Abelson, Report on Flying Accident Not Attributable to Enemy Action, 4;

36 Abelson Family fonds, Ottawa Jewish Archives, box 2, file: Canadian Correspondence, Duke Abelson letter to parents, December 28, 1942.

37 "Archive Report: Allied Forces," Aircrew Remembered, http://aircrewremebered.com/carpenter-leonard.html.

38 Murray Peden, quoted in "Bomber Command's Losses," Bomber Command Museum of Canada, http://www.bombercommandmuseum.ca/commandlosses.html.

39 Allison and Hayward, *They Shall Grow Not Old*; Usher, "Jews in the Royal Canadian Air Force," 93.

40 Charles Foster, "Dambuster of the Day No. 53: Albert Garshowitz," Dambustersblog, https://dambustersblog.com/2013/11/16/dambuster-of-the-day-no-53-albert-garshowitz/.

41 LAC Service Files, series RG 24, vol. 27642, Meyer Greenstein.

42 Richard Foot, "WW2 Navigator Too Busy to Be Scared," CanWest News Service and Historica Canada, Stories of Remembrance, 2005, http://www.dominion.ca/Downloads/sor_ArthurHiller.pdf.

43 *CJWWII*, inside cover, plus author's counting of the POW mentions in the book.

44 Ruth Pike, "Lives Lived: Joseph Sonshine," *Globe and Mail* (Toronto), September 27, 2006, A18, http://v1.theglobeandmail.com/servlet/story/LAC.20060927.LIVES27/BDAStory/BDA/deaths.
45 Buchenwald Memorial website, http://www.buchenwald.de/en/72/.
46 "POW Reports," Leslie Faircloth website, Http://lesfaircloth.co.uk/index.php?p=1_11_POW-Reports.
47 Pike, "Lives Lived: Joseph Sonshine."
48 RAF Flight Engineer Fred Shaw Maltas, interview with the Imperial War Museum, catalogue no. 33043, reel three, http://www.iwm.org.uk/collections/item/object/80033259; John Jay, *Facing Fearful Odds: My Father's Story of Escape, Capture and Resistance, 1940–1945* (Barnsley, UK: Pen and Sword Books, 2014), 132; Daniel Nolan, "Shapiro Helped Dig Tunnels for 'Great Escape'," *Hamilton Spectator*, January 23, 2014, http://www.thespec.com/news-story/4329366-shapiro-helped-dig-tunnels-for-great-escape-/.
49 Manny Raber, *Manny Goes to War*, self-published (Medicine Hat, AB), 1999, 88–97, 106, 110; Trafford, *Memories on the March*, 114.
50 Jewish Historical Society of Southern Alberta, *Land of Promise*, 263, http://www.jhssa.org/book/263.html.
51 *CJWWII, Part I: Casualties*, 123.
52 "David Goldberg," *Hamilton Jewish News*, July 19, 2010, https://vimeo.com/13467130.
53 Bill Zelikovitz letter to Laura and Butch Zelikovitz, November 16, 1994, courtesy of Joel Zelikovitz, 1–5.
54 Louis N. Ridenour, "Birds on Ascension Island Were Comical, But Not to the Army," Wideawake Engineers: Americans on Ascension Island in World War II, June 18, 2011, originally published in the *Birmingham News*, February 4, 1947, http://ascensionislandwideawakes.blogspot.ca/2011/06/birds-on-ascension-island-were-comical.html.
55 RCAF Logbook of William Zelikovitz, courtesy of Joel Zelikovitz.
56 William Zelikovitz, draft notes for a letter to then Canadian defence minister David Collenette, outlining his military service, undated but likely early 1990s, courtesy of Joel Zelikovitz.
57 "Novick, William," Database of awards, RCAF Association, http://rcafassociation.ca/heritage/search-awards/?search=novick&searchfield=field_all&type=all.
58 "Henry William Novick DFC," Wartime Memories Project — The Second World War, http://www.wartimememoriesproject.com/ww2/view.php?uid=212468
59 "Halifax MZ603 at East Moor Airfield," Aircraft Accidents in Yorkshire website, http://www.yorkshire-aircraft.co.uk/aircraft/yorkshire/york44/mz603b.html;

Clarence Simonsen, "Where's the Original Halifax 'A' Serial NA337," in *Lest We Forget*, Blog Run by Pierre Legacé, November 30, 2014, Https://Athabaskang07.Wordpress.Com/2014/11/30/Wheres-the-Original-Halifax-a-Serial-Na337/.

60 *CJWWII, Part I: Decorations*, 43.

7 THE NAVY AND THE MERCHANT NAVY

1 Alan Hustak, "Remembrance Day Is Every Day," *Gazette* (Montreal), November 11, 2003, A3, courtesy of Joyce Kaplan.

2 Bill Berger, "The Y Bugle," *YMHA. Beacon*, December 19, 1945, 6.

3 "HMCS *Valleyfield*," Naval Museum of Manitoba, http://www.naval-museum.mb.ca/battle_atlantic/valleyfield/; Michael L. Hadley, *U-Boats against Canada: German Submarines in Canadian Waters* (Montreal and Kingston: McGill-Queen's University Press, 1985), 217.

4 James B. Lamb, *On the Triangle Run: The Fighting Spirit of Canada's Navy*, 2nd ed. (Toronto: Stoddart, 2000), 199.

5 Hustak, "Remembrance Day Is Every Day."

6 Irving Kaplan, memoir, unpublished, 2007, courtesy of Joyce Kaplan, 65.

7 F.J. Blatherwick, "Royal Canadian Navy Citations," *Canadian Orders, Decorations, and Medals*, 6th ed., List of names beginning with K, p. 2, http://www.blatherwick.net/documents/Royal%20Canadian%20Navy%20Citations/K%20-%20RCN%20-%20WW2.pdf.

8 Kaplan letter to Corporal Abe Goldbloom, July 16, 1944, courtesy of Sadie Kaplan.

9 Kaplan, memoir, 70.

10 "The War at Sea," Veterans Affairs Canada, http://www.veterans.gc.ca/eng/remembrance/history/second-world-war/canada-and-the-second-world-war/warsea; Tulchinsky, *Canada's Jews*, 380.

11 *CJWWII, Part I: Decorations*, inside cover.

12 "Second World War," Veterans Affairs Canada, http://www.veterans.gc.ca/eng/remembrance/history/canadian-armed-forces/royal-canadian-navy/sww.

13 J.L. Granatstein, "The Problem of Religion in Canadian Forces Postings: Liebmann vs the Minister of National Defence et al.," *Canadian Military History* 19, no. 4 (2015): 69.

14 Jewish Historical Society of Southern Alberta, *Land of Promise*, 56.

15 Tulchinsky, *Canada's Jews*, 380, 383.

16 Paul Jackson, "Quiet Courage," *Calgary Sun*, November 11, 1993, page unknown, clipping on display at the Jewish Community Centre, Calgary, in the Veterans' Hall.

17 Peter Lester, "Four Cents to Sea: 16 mm, the Royal Canadian Naval Film Society and the Mobilization of Entertainment," *Film History* 25, no. 4 (2013): 62–81.

18 E. David Hart interview, *The Memory Project*, oral history, June 9, 2010, OJA AC 375.

19 Simon James Theobald, "A False Sense of Equality: The Black Canadian Experience of the Second World War," MA thesis, Department of History, University of Ottawa, 2008, 45–46.

20 LAC Service Files, series RG 24, vol. 29037, Harold Chizy, Attestation Papers, and Acting Lieutenant Commander M.R. Campbell, RCNVR, HMCS *Montreal*, letter to the Officer Commanding, RCMP Montreal, January 4, 1943, and Memo from Superintendent Gagnon to the RCMP commissioner in Ottawa, January 18, 1943.

21 Stephen Rybak, "The Canadian Naval Reserve: From War to War," Nauticapedia website, 2011, http://www.nauticapedia.ca/Articles/Rybak3_From_War_to_War.php.

22 Israel Glassman interviewed as part of Oral History Military Veterans project, Scott Masters, director, Crestwood Academy, February 2016, http://www.crestwood.on.ca/ohp/glassman-israel.

23 Gordon Mumford, "Convoy ONS," http://www.gordonmumford.com/m-navy/ons154-0.htm; Tony German, "Preserving the Atlantic Lifeline," *Legion Magazine*, May–June, 1998, https://legionmagazine.com/en/1998/05/preserving-the-atlantic-lifeline/; "Argentine Jew Comes to Canada to Join Canadian Navy," *Jewish Telegraphic Agency*, October 29, 1941.

24 Lamb, *On the Triangle Run*, 5.

25 "U-356," uboat.net, http://uboat.net/boats/u356.htm.

26 "Veteran Stories: Gerald Rosenberg, Navy," The Memory Project, http://www.thememoryproject.com/stories/1032:gerald-rosenberg/

27 Shelley Lipke, "HMCS Esquimalt Remembered," *Lookout*, April 22, 2013, http://www.lookoutnewspaper.com/hmcs-esquimalt-remembered/.

28 Michael Whitby, "The Case of the Phantom MTB and the Loss of HMCS *Athabaskan*," *Canadian Military History* 11, no. 3 (Summer 2002): 5–14.

29 Irwin Block, "Remembrance Day: The Captain Yelled Out, 'Abandon ship!' " *Senior Times* (Montreal), November 11, 2013, http://www.theseniortimes.com/remembrance-day-the-captain-yelled-out-abandon-ship/.

30 Whitby, "The Case of the Phantom MTB," 5.

31 Brian Ferstman, "Notes from an Interview with Maurice Novek, March 20, 2005, and April 18, 2005," unpublished.

32 Maurice Novek, "War Story," unpublished memoir, 4, 5, courtesy of Brian Ferstman.

33 Novek was later involved in rescuing forty-five survivors of an American military tug, USS *Partridge*, which the Germans torpedoed in the English Channel on June 11. He won a Mention in Dispatches for this.

34 John Lazarus letter to Sylvia Lazarus, July 25, 1940, courtesy Sylvia Hoffman.
35 Martin Sugarman, "'Full Ahead Both!': Jewish Service in the British, Commonwealth and Israeli Merchant Navies in WW2; A Record of Honour," unpublished draft of research paper, courtesy of Martin Sugarman, Association of Jewish Ex-Servicemen and Women of the UK-AJEX Museum, May 17, 2016; *CJWWII*, 51.
36 John Lazarus letter to Charles Lazarus, July 21, 1940, courtesy of Sylvia Hoffman.
37 "OB-213," uboat.net, http://uboat.net/ops/convoys/convoys.php?convoy=OB-213.
38 Ian Kikuchi, "The Story of Child Evacuee Beryl Myatt and the Sinking of the SS *City of Benares*," Imperial War Museums, 2016, http://www.iwm.org.uk/history/the-story-of-child-evacuee-beryl-myatt-and-the-sinking-of-the-ss-city-of-benares.
39 "21 Local Seamen Reported as Lost," *Gazette* (Montreal), April 15, 1944,13–14, http://bit.ly/2iKjtoH.
40 Untitled article from the *Montreal Standard*, September 28, 1940, ADCJA, CJC DA 18.1, box 18, file 2.
41 Sugarman, "'Full Ahead Both!'"
42 *CJWWII*, 34, 67.
43 Ayah McKhail, "Somer James, Sailor and Numismatist: 1921–2005," *Globe and Mail* (Toronto), May 4, 2005, S7.
44 "Somer Oscar James," Passages, *Winnipeg Free Press*, January 19, 2005, http://passages.winnipegfreepress.com/passage-details/id-92106/Somer_James; "'B.E.M. Is Awarded to Somer O. James," *Toronto Daily Star*, February 1, 1945, 10.

8 JEWISH WOMEN IN UNIFORM

1 Sue Ransohoff, "A Yank in the RCAF," unpublished memoir, May 2015, 2, courtesy of Sue Ransohoff.
2 Tulchinsky, *Canada's Jews*, 376.
3 Ghita Reuben Olitt, "Chronology," unpublished memoir, courtesy of Shelly Reuben, March 13, 2015.
4 Jewish War Veterans of Canada, *No Greater Honour*.
5 "Polish Girl Joins R.C.A.F., Hopes to Reach Berlin," *Ottawa Journal*, October 15, 1942, 10.
6 "Israel Miller and Daughter Ethel Allman: A Jewish Family's Life as Alberta Pioneers," *Discovery: The Journal of the Jewish Historical Society of Southern Alberta* 19, no. 1 (February 2009): 2.
7 LAC Service Files, Evelyn Fainer, Department of National Defence, Army, Personnel Selection Record, CWAC, signed by Lieutenant H.T. Douglass, January 19, 1943, courtesy of Shirley Ellis.

8 "Veteran Stories: Esther Mager, Air Force," The Memory Project, http://www.thememoryproject.com/stories/1119:esther-mager/.
9 Martin Sugarman, "World War II: Jewish Personnel at Bletchley Park," Jewish Virtual Library, http://www.jewishvirtuallibrary.org/jewish-personnel-at-bletchley-park-in-world-war-ii, originally published in "Breaking the Codes: Jewish Personnel at Bletchley Park in WW2," *Journal of the Jewish Historical Society of England*, November 2005.
10 "T.H. Schatz," Roll of Honour, Bletchley Park, https://bletchleypark.org.uk/roll-of-honour/8112.
11 "Mimi Freedman, Woman Veteran, Overseas Six and a Half Years," *Gazette* (Montreal), September 20, 1946, 4. http://bit.ly/2A3Rk5t.
12 *CJWWII, Part I: Decorations*, 69.
13 "Mimi Freedman," (Montreal Gazette).
14 "Potential 'Policemen,'" *Winnipeg Tribune*, August 17, 1942, 1.
15 "Ottawa Girl in Military Police Learns Use of Pistol and Jujitsu," *Ottawa Journal*, December 1, 1942, 1, 7.
16 Evelyn Fainer, Department of Pensions and National Health, Service Interview Summary, Further Information and Follow up, Remarks Captain Patricia Blair, S.P. Officer, CWAC, London, England, October 25, 1944, courtesy of Shirley Ellis.
17 LAC Service Files, Rose Jette Goodman, CWAAF Selection Board Report, Halifax, September 26, 1941.
18 Esther Nobleman audio interview, part 1, Jewish Historical Society of British Columbia, Jewish Museum and Archives of British Columbia, February 24, 2014, https://archives.jewishmuseum.ca/esther-nobleman-part-1.
19 Letter from Petty Officer Irv Kaplan to Corporal A. Goldbloom, September 12, 1943, courtesy of Sadie Kaplan.
20 Ransohoff, "A Yank in the RCAF," 8, 10.
21 Esther Nobleman audio interview, Jewish Historical Society of British Columbia.
22 LAC Service Files, Rose Jette Goodman, Record of Service, Airwomen; "Confidential Personal Assessment," Recommendation for Promotion as Acting Section Officer, Rank ASO Administrative (WD), January 11, 1943, December 7, 1942, No. 15 STFT, Claresholm, Alberta.
23 "#15 Service Flying Training School," Bomber Command Museum of Canada, http://www.bombercommandmuseum.ca/bcatpclaresholm.html.

9 LIFE IN THE BARRACKS

1 "Windsor Mayor Private in Essex Scottish," *Ottawa Journal*, September 29, 1939, 1.
2 Jerry Grafstein, "The Life and Times of the Late Senator David A. Croll," Beth Tzedec Congregation of Toronto, June 25, 2006, http://bit.ly/2zuIjmH.

3 LAC Service Files, series RG 24, vol. 25674, Walter Joseph Crotin, Attestation Papers.
4 LAC Service Files, Walter Joseph Crotin, Doctor's Report on Walter Crotin, January 1943.
5 "Crash of a Short S.25 Sunderland III near Lothbeg: 15 Killed," Bureau of Aircraft Accidents Archives, http://www.baaa-acro.com/1944/archives/crash-of-a-short-s-25-sunderland-iii-near-lothbeg-15-killed/.
6 "Veteran Stories: Irvin Lorne Winter, Army," The Memory Project, http://www.thememoryproject.com/stories/2701:irvin-lorne-winer/.
7 Arthur Pascal interview with his grandchildren, tape 2a, courtesy of Kathy Cohen.
8 Laurel Halladay, "Ladies and Gentlemen, Soldiers and Artists: Canadian Military Entertainers 1939–1946," MA thesis, University of Calgary, 2000, 103.
9 Harry R. Moscoe fonds 69, file 6, OJA, News Releases, 1943 Sapper Herbert Reiter, Winnipeg, letter to Canadian Jewish Congress, Winnipeg Section.
10 Harry R. Moscoe fonds 69, file 11, OJA, Canadian Jewish Congress News Releases, 1943–1944, Report.
11 Montreal War Efforts Committee pamphlets, RG 297, MG 8, A11, box 4, OJA, War Efforts Committee, Canadian Jewish Congress, 1941.
12 "Women Pack Comfort Boxes for Jewish Men Overseas," *Winnipeg Tribune*, September 7, 1944.
13 "Approaching a Decade," 9th Annual Regional Congress program, Canadian Jewish Congress Central Division, Harry R. Moscoe fonds 69, file 11, OJA, RG 297, War Efforts Committee, 1942–H1943.
14 Harry R. Moscoe fonds 69, file 12, OJA, Canadian Jewish Congress News Releases, 1943–1944, W.G. Rosenthal letter, March 1, 1943, to Chairman, War Efforts Committee, Canadian Jewish Congress, Montreal.
15 Canadian Jewish Congress War Efforts Committee, OJA, RG 297, MG 8, box 2, file Mrs. H. Allen Memos, 1941, Report, War Efforts Committee, CJC Central Division, 9.
16 Tulchinsky, *Canada's Jews*, 382; Allan Levine, *Coming of Age: The Jews of Manitoba* (Winnipeg: Heartland Associates, 2009), 280.
17 Transcript of an interview by Ian Hodson with Ron Barkley and Bert Hovey, April 2, 1992, for a project commemorating the 50th anniversary of the Royal Canadian Regiment's action near Ortona, and specifically Sterlin Castle, courtesy of Sergeant Major Jack O'Brien (Retd), Kingston, Ontario, 1.
18 Tulchinsky, *Canada's Jews*, 384.

19 Dunkelman, *Dual Allegiance*, 63–64.

20 LAC Service Files, series R 112, vol. 30871, Harry Niznick, Supplement to Personnel Selection Record.

21 LAC Service Files, Harry Niznick, Supplement to Personnel Selection Record.

22 Nearly seven hundred Canadian officers went to join British Army regiments under the CANLOAN program between D-Day and V-E day. Wilfred I. Smith, *Code Word CANLOAN* (Toronto: Dundurn, 1992), xii.

23 LAC Service Files, Jacob Silverstein, Solemn Declaration Form, February 13, 1941.

24 Stephen Franklin, *A Time of Heroes, 1940–1950* (Toronto: Natural Science of Canada, 1977), 74.

25 LAC Service Files, Jacob Silverstein, correspondence from Group Captain L.E. Wray AFC, Commanding Officer, Gander.

26 "LChaim Earl Braemer," Passages, *Winnipeg Free Press*, December 31, 1969, http://passages.winnipegfreepress.com/passage-details/id-76141/name-Lchaim_Braemer/.

27 Levine, *Coming of Age*, 280.

28 Joe King, "Sydney's Beaufighter," *Montreal Jewish Magazine*, undated, http://montrealjewishmagazine.com/sydneys-beaufighter; Steve Mertl, "Ace Aviator Honed Technique for Rocket Attacks," Canadian Press, February 5, 2007, https://www.thestar.com/news/2007/02/05/ace_aviator_honed_technique_for_rocket_attacks.html.

29 Ralph, *Aces, Warriors and Wingmen*, 156.

30 Levi, *Breaking New Ground*, 37.

31 "Former Mayor Croll Becomes an Officer," *Detroit Free Press*, January 8, 1941, 1.

32 "David A. Croll Writes Despatch Rider's Primer and Alphabet of Map Reading for British Forces," *Detroit Jewish Chronicle and the Legal Chronicle*, September 19, 1941, 14.

33 "David Croll on Map Reading," *Ottawa Journal*, September 13, 1941, 21.

34 Jonathan V. Plaut, *The Jews of Windsor, 1790–1990: A Chronicle* (Toronto: Dundurn, 2007), 106.

35 "Jewish Contributions to Canadian Society," Centre for Israel and Jewish Affairs, http://www.cija.ca/resource/canadian-jewry/jewish-contributions-to-canada.

36 Sheldon Kirshner, "Robert Rothschild: Canada's First Jewish General," *Canadian Jewish News*, November 12, 1981, 5.

37 *CJWWII, Part I: Decorations*, 9.

38 David Novek, "Around and About," *Canadian Jewish Chronicle*, August 14, 1964, 9; *CJWWII, Part I: Decorations*, 44.

39 "Commander Edward Ryan, RCN, in uniform (Kingston, ON)," OJA, Item 3952, accession no. 1986-3-5, http://search.ontariojewisharchives.org/Permalink/descriptions19554.

40 *Queen's University Yearbook*, 1928, 165, courtesy of Heather Home, Public Services and Private Records Archivist, Queen's University Archives, Kingston, Ontario, in an email July 11, 2016.

41 LAC Service Files, series R 112, vol. 30727, Tim Pervin, Medical Interview, Attestation Papers.

42 Sam Boroditsky, "Sam Boroditsky's War," unpublished memoir, 1989, 18–19, courtesy of Manny Borod.

10 OFF-DUTY ACTIVITIES

1 War Efforts Committee 1943–1944, Harry R. Moscoe fonds 69, file 10, OJA, photograph of 36th Res. Brigade Group Coy, RCASC, Concert Party, Staff Sergeant Roy. S. Cooper, director, and news clipping from *The Evening Mail*, Halifax.

2 Parks Canada news release, "Backgrounder, Pier 21 Halifax," last modified September 26, 2013, http://bit.ly/2hMVd4j.

3 Religious Calendar for the Jewish Men and Women in the Canadian Armed Forces, Religious Welfare Committee Canadian Jewish Congress 1944–45/5705, courtesy of Joel Zelikovitz, p. 9; Tristan Stewart-Robertson, "History: The Jewish Community of Moncton," Tiferes Israel Synagogue, http://www.tiferesisrael.com/history.html; ADCJA, "What's Doing in the Congress Servicemen's Centres?" *Congress Bulletin*, March 1943, 8; Tulchinsky, *Branching Out*, 205.

4 Richard B. Goldbloom, *A Lucky Life* (Halifax: Formac, 2013), 29.

5 ADCJA, CJC PC 01, box 01, files 034A, 034 B, and 034C; "Yehudi Menuhin at Congress Centre," *Congress Bulletin*, March 1943, 8.

6 Visitors Registration Books to Montreal Servicemen's Centre, June 10, 1945, 1, ADCJA CJC DA 18.1, box 18, 27B.

7 "Turn Over House to Armed Forces," *Globe and Mail* (Toronto), September 30, 1942, ADCJA, CJC DA 18.1, box 18/25; *Toronto Daily Star*, March 9, 1944, ADCJA, CJC DA 18.1, box 1, file 23.

8 "My Wartime Experiences," interview with Mitch Pechet, University of Victoria, March 19, 2017, http://contentdm.library.uvic.ca/cdm/compoundobject/collection/collection13/id/1953/rec/1.

9 "Service Club Three Years Old," *Evening Telegram* (Toronto), June 6, 1945, ADCJA CJC DA 18.1, box 18, file 3.

10 "600,000 Guests Is Club's Record in Three Years," *Globe and Mail* (Toronto), December 3, 1945, ADCJA, CJC DA 18.1, box 18, file 23.

11 Louis Rosenberg, Western Division, Canadian Jewish Congress, "Report of the Executive Director to the Fifth Biennial Session of the Canadian Jewish Congress, Winnipeg, Manitoba, December 31, 1941," 21, A.I. Shumiatcher fonds, Canadian Jewish Congress, box M1107, file 54, Glenbow Museum Archives, Calgary.
12 "The Soldiers' Corner," *YMHA Beacon*, September 20, 1940, 6.
13 "Y Intensifies War Effort," *YMHA Beacon*, August 2, 1940, 1.
14 Pechet, "My Wartime Experiences."
15 "Esther Mager," photographs, OJA, http://search.ontariojewisharchives.org/Permalink/accessions24435.
16 Irving Kaplan letter to Harry Abelson, November 3, 1942, courtesy of Sadie Kaplan.
17 LAC Service Files, series RG 24, vol. 25266, Yude Brownstone, Service Record.
18 Cy Torontow letter to Willie Zelikovitz, sent July 23, 1943 to Nassau, Bahamas, courtesy of Joel Zelikovitz.
19 LAC Service Files, Michael Jacobs, General Conduct Sheet, October 21, 1940.
20 "General Conduct Page," Clifford Shnier website, http://clifford.shniers.com/WebFiles/LargeImagesPNG/19410602GeneralConductSheet.png.
21 "1941," Clifford Schnier website, June 21, 1941, http://clifford.shniers.com.
22 Boroditsky, "Sam Boroditsky's War," 10–11.
23 Esther Nobleman audio interview, Jewish Historical Society of British Columbia.
24 "Two Waynes and a Shuster," *The Sunday Edition with Michael Enright*, CBC Radio One, April 29, 2016, interview with Brian and Michael Wayne and Rosie Shuster.
25 Steve Pitt, "Laughing Matters," *Legion Magazine*, November 1, 2013, https://legionmagazine.com/en/2003/11/laughing-matters/.
26 "Wayne and Shuster on Readjusting to Civilian Life," *Assignment*, CBC Radio, February 24, 1958, http://www.cbc.ca/archives/entry/wayne-and-shuster-on-readjusting-to-civilian-life.
27 Dick Sanburn, "Canadian Troops Enjoy Timely Invasion Review," *Winnipeg Free Press*, August 1, 1944, 4.
28 Halladay, "Ladies and Gentlemen," 69.
29 Photo p010871 in PhotosNormandie, edited by Patrick Peccatte and Michel Le Querrec, https://flic.kr/p/eePLLD.
30 Photo p010872 in PhotosNormandie, https://flic.kr/p/eeVxqJ; Photo p010876, PhotosNormandie, https://flic.kr/p/eeVwuU.
31 Halladay, "Ladies and Gentlemen," 95.
32 Program, November 7, 1942, Leeds Greyhound Stadium, Abelson Family fonds, Ottawa Jewish Archives.
33 "Jack Kahane Blowing the Y Bugle," *YMHA Beacon*, February 17, 1943, 4.

34 "Overseas Mail," *YMHA Beacon*, April 5, 1940, 1.

35 David Devor letter to mother, November 4, 1944, OJA Devor Family file 89-2/5.

36 Jack Kahane, "The Y Bugle," *YMHA Beacon*, February 29, 1944, 4.

37 Servicemen/Palestine snapshots, ADCJA, CJC PC 01, box 08, 041E.3.

38 LAC Service Files, Alex Balinson, Royal Air Force, Airman's Record Sheet.

39 Alex Balinson letter to his parents, October 21, 1941, courtesy of his nephew Alex Balinson.

40 *CJWWII, Part I: Decorations*, 67.

41 "427 SquadronWartime Log — October 1943," 427 Squadron Association, http://www.427squadron.com/history/wartime_logs/oct_1943.html.

42 John G. Armstrong, "RCAF Identity in Bomber Command Squadron Names and Sponsors," *Canadian Military History* 8, no. 2 (Spring 1999): 43–52.

43 *"Lions" Adopt Lion Cub*, British Pathé, 1943, http://www.britishpathe.com/video/lions-adopt-lion-cub.

44 "Canadian War Brides," Veterans Affairs Canada, October 23, 2014, http://www.veterans.gc.ca/eng/remembrance/history/second-world-war/canadian-war-brides#a08.

45 Gay Abbate and John Ibbitson, "Wounded in the Battle of Normandy, Soldier Returned Still Wanting to Serve," *Globe and Mail* (Toronto), October 20, 2011, https://tgam.ca/2A2ndLQ.

46 Barney Danson and Curtis Fahey, *Not Bad for a Sergeant* (Toronto: Dundurn, 2002). 40.

47 Joe Gertel letter to Hedy Neumann, February 26, 1944, courtesy of Susan Ellman.

48 LAC Service Files, Joe Gertel, Attestation Papers.

49 Joe Gertel letter to Hedy Neumann, April 17, 1944.

50 Joe Gertel letter to Hedy Neumann, June 6, 1944.

51 Murray Bleeman letter to sister Diana, May 19, 1941, courtesy of Ferne Phillips.

52 LAC Service Files, Murray Irving Bleeman, Record of Service.

53 Feasby, *Official History*, 444, 472, 446.

54 LAC Service Files, series R 112, vol. 30807, David Charles Cramer, Attestation Papers, and Soldier's Pay Book, and Field Medical Card, March 1, 1944.

55 LAC Service Files, Jack Faibish, Attestation Papers and Medical Exam.

56 Jeffrey Keshen, *Saints, Sinners and Soldiers* (Vancouver: UBC Press, 2007), 126.

57 Bercuson, *Our Finest Hour*, 91.

58 LAC Service Files, series RG 24, vol. 25974, Louis Goldin, Company Conduct Sheet.

59 LAC Service Files, series RG 24, vol. 25908, Israel Freedman, Company Conduct Sheet.

60 LAC Service Files, series RG 24, vol. 27116, Murray Steiner, Attestation Papers, Court Martial Reports, Petition from Maidstone Prison, Private Murray Steiner, January 16, 1941.

61 David Devor letter to Kate Devor, August 28, 1944, Devor Family files, 89, 2–5, OJA.

62 Feasby, *Official History*, 426, 508, 404.

63 LAC Service Files, series RG 24, vol. 26618, Morris Miller, Statement of the Service of Morris Miller, H 37472, and Proceedings of a Court of Inquiry, February 6, 1945, Testimony of Corporal K. E. Slade, 2, and Testimony of Corporal D.T. McKnight, 1, and Testimony of Lieutenant Corporal R. Barnabe, 8th Platoon, RCASC, 2.

64 LAC Service Files, Morris Miller, Office of the Jewish Chaplain, Read HQ 1 Canadian Corps, letter to Mrs. M. Miller, April 17, 1945.

65 "Starry Y Basketballer Reported Casualty," *YMHA Beacon*, October 22, 1942, 3.

66 Charles P. Abelson, "Circumstances Beyond Our Control," unpublished manuscript, 99.

67 LAC Service Files, series RG 24, vol. 27971, Solomon Lavine, Attestation Papers.

68 Andrew Hibbert, "Remembering the Olga," *Lake Erie Beacon*, June 20, 2014, 1, 5.

69 Delaney Leitch, "Panic in Port Stanley: The Loss of the 'Olga,' 1944," Tyrconnell Heritage Society, April 8, 2015, http://tyrconnellheritagesociety.blogspot.ca/2015/04/world-war-wednesdays-panic-in-port.html.

70 Frank Rasky, "Newfoundland's Furious Fire by Sabotage: The Knights of Columbus Hostel Disaster of 1942," *Liberty*, October 1959, reproduced at http://ngb.chebucto.org/Articles/dis-knights-of-columbus-1942.shtml; "Soldiers in Hostel Fire Died to Save Girls," *Ottawa Journal*, December 14, 1942, 1, 3; Sir Brian Dunfield, *Destruction by Fire of Knights of Columbus Hostel, St. John's, December 12th, 1942, with Loss of 99 Lives* (St. John's: Robinson, 1943), 23, 25; "Jewish Sailor Loses Life in Newfoundland Fire," news release, Canadian Jewish Congress, Montreal, December 1942, OJA Harry R. Moscoe fonds 69, file 6.

71 LAC, series RG 24-C-3, vol. 14394, "War Diary, 5th Canadian Medium Regiment, RCA, July 1942," image 765, http://heritage.canadiana.ca/view/oocihm.lac_reel_t15911/765?r=0&s=1.

72 LAC Service Files, series RG 24, vol. 26731, Solomon Shia Offman, Court of Inquiry, August 11, 1942, Testimony of Witness Joseph Henry Stocks, Lorry Driver, 114 Congreve Road, and Testimony of Witness Private A. Williams, Royal Montreal Regiment, and Testimony of 4th witness, PC Coombs, and Opinion of the C.O.; *CJWWII*, 55.

73 LAC Service Files, series RG 24, vol. 28483, Harry Ratner, Attestation Papers, Movements and Casualties Form.

74 Peter Coupland, *Straight and True: A History of RAF Leeming* (London: Leo Cooper, 1997), 144.

75 LAC Service Files, series RG 24, vol. 28483, Harry Ratner, Royal Air Force, Report on Accidental or Self-Inflicted Injuries or Immediate Death Thereof, May 28, 1944.

76 "Rainsforth-Broad Wed," *Claresholm Local Press*, January 28, 1043, 3.

77 Station Chaplain J.M. Roe letter to Mr. and Mrs. Solomon Goodman, January 27, 1943, Darrel Pink collection.

78 LAC Service Files, Rose Jette Goodman, Testimony of Pilot Officer Peter Douglas Meyers, contained in RCMP Report, K Division, Lethbridge, Claresholm Detachment, January 30, 1943, Corporal F.J. Brailsford, includes witness and expert statements and final conclusion.

79 LAC Service Files, Rose Jette Goodman, RCMP Report, K Division, Lethbridge, Claresholm Detachment.

80 Roe letter to Mr. and Mrs. Goodman.

81 LAC Service Files, Rose Jette Goodman, Statement of Hector Rose, and Statement of Squadron Leader G. A. Lawson, and Proceedings of Court of Inquiry Flying Accident, January 27, 1943, at No. 15 SFTS Claresholm, and Testimony of Pilot Officer Peter Douglas Meyers, and Group Captain W.E. Kennedy telex to AFHQ Casualty Branch, received January 28, 1943, and Corporal F.J. Brailsford, final conclusion.

82 "Air Force Woman Officer Victim of Crash Tues. Night," *Claresholm Local Press*, January 28, 1943, 1, http://www.ourfutureourpast.ca/newspapr/np_page2.asp?code=1g2p0194.jpg

83 LAC Service Files, series RG 24, vol. 25911, Carl M. Fried, Record of Service.

84 Carl Fried letter to Nina Cohen, August 31, 1942, courtesy of Bruce Baff.

85 LAC Service Files, Carl M. Fried, Miss Iris Emery letter to Canadian Forces personnel regarding missing property of Carl Fried, July 10, 1944.

86 Carl Fried letter to Nina Cohen, undated, courtesy of Kathy Cohen.

87 LAC Service Files, Carl M. Fried, Record of All Casualties, etc., and Appeal for Reconsideration of Sentence of F.G.C.M., and Proceedings of a Court of Inquiry into the escape of D-82925 Private Fried, C.M., June 19, 1944.

88 "Breaking the Hitler Line: May 23, 1944," Seaforth Highlanders of Canada, June 12, 2014, http://www.seaforthhighlanders.ca/seaforthnews/breaking-the-hitler-line-may-23rd-1944.

89 LAC Service Files, Carl M. Fried, Government letter to Mrs. Harry Cohen, 4881 Mira Road, Montreal, Fall 1977, and Records Management Branch, and typewritten note signed by Vokes.

11 JEWISH HEROES

1 Brad Mackay, "Inductee: Iron Man," CBC Arts and Entertainment, May 9, 2005, https://archive.li/obBtC; Sean Tepper, "Heroes of the Canadian Golden Age of Comics," *Toronto Star*, October 11, 2013, https://www.thestar.com/entertainment/2013/10/11/heroes_of_the_canadian_golden_age_of_comics.html.

2 Hope Nicholson, "Nelvana of the Northern Lights," 2017, https://hopenicholson.com/projects/nelvana-of-the-northern-lights

3 Rachel Richey, "Vernon Miller," The Joe Shuster Awards, https://joeshusterawards.com/hof/miller-vernon/.

4 John Bell, *Invaders from the North: How Canada Conquered the Comic Book Universe* (Toronto: Dundurn, 2006), 67–68.

5 John Bell, "Johnny Canuck," *Guardians of the North: The National Superhero in Canadian Comic-book Art*, Library and Archives Canada, 2009, http://epe.lac-bac.gc.ca/100/200/301/lac-bac/guardians_north-ef/2009/www.collectionscanada.gc.ca/superheroes/index-e.html.

6 *Canadian Heroes*, Canada's Own Comics, http://canadasowncomics.com/comic/canadian-heroes-2/; *Adventures of Canada Jack*, Canada's Own Comics, http://canadasowncomics.com/comic/canada-jack-nn/.

7 Sarah B. Hood, "Rare 'Jewish War Heroes' Comic from 1944 Found in Box of Donated Used Books," *National Post*, October 31, 2014, http://news.nationalpost.com/news/canada/rare-jewish-war-heroes-comic-from-1944-found-in-box-of-donated-used-books.

8 Renee Ghert-Zand, "Rare Canadian Jewish Comic Book Turns Up in Toronto," *Times of Israel* (Jerusalem), November 11, 2014, http://www.timesofisrael.com/rare-canadian-jewish-comic-book-turns-up-in-toronto/.

9 Hugh A. Halliday, "Plucked from the Sea: Air Force, Part 45," *Legion Magazine*, June 25, 2011, https://legionmagazine.com/en/2011/06/plucked-from-the-sea-air-force-part-45/.

10 "Gen. Morrice Abraham Cohen," *Jewish War Heroes*, Canadian Jewish Congress, February 1944, 8, https://digitalcomicmuseum.com/preview/index.php?did=12218&page=8.

11 Paula Simmons, "Peace River Jim and Two-Gun Cohen Were an Unlikely Duo," *Edmonton Journal*, August 9, 2014, http://ww1.canada.com/faces-of-war/peace-river-jim-and-two-gun-cohen-were-an-unlikely-duo; Ruth Wright Millar, *Saskatchewan Heroes and Rogues* (Regina: Coteau Books, 2004), 82.

12 "Three Enemy Planes Shot Down by Canadians on British Patrols," *Lethbridge Herald*, September 29, 1943, 7.

13 Phineas J. Biron, "Strictly Confidential," *Wisconsin Jewish Chronicle* (Milwaukee), March 31, 1944, 1.

14 "Shulemson, Samuel," Database of awards, RCAF Association, http://rcafassociation.ca/heritage/search-awards/?search=shulemson&searchfield=field_all&type=all.

15 "Squadron Leader Sydney Simon Shulemson, DSO, DFC," video, Air Force Museum of Alberta, Calgary, http://www.digitalheritage.ca/airforce/shulemson/shulemson.htm.

16 Ralph, *Aces, Warriors and Wingmen*, 156; "Shulemson, Samuel," Database of Awards, RCAF Association.

17 Martin Middlebrook and Chris Everitt, *The Bomber Command War Diaries: An Operational Reference Book, 1939–1945* (Harmondsworth: Penguin, 1990), 362–363.

18 An aircraft is coned when a group of searchlights focuses on it individually, lighting it up as an easier target for ground defenders; see Royal Canadian Air Force, *The RCAF Overseas: The Fifth Year* (Toronto: Oxford University Press, 1945), xvi.

19 *CJWWII*, 74.

20 Middlebrook and Everitt, *The Bomber Command War Diaries*, 401.

21 Vernon White, *Four Years and a Bit*, 427th Squadron Association, 2002, http://www.427squadron.com/book_file/white/four_years_leeming.html.

22 James Rusk, "Student Soldiers' Statute Gets Ready for Action," *Globe and Mail* (Toronto), May 5, 2007, http://www.theglobeandmail.com/news/national/student-soldiers-statue-gets-ready-for-action/article18138698/.

23 Coupland, *Straight and True*, 121; "Somers, Lou Warren," Commonwealth War Graves Commission, http://www.cwgc.org/find-war-dead/casualty/2964960/SOMERS,%20LOU%20WARREN#carousel3.

24 Robert C. Fisher, "Tactics, Training, Technology: The RCN's Summer of Success, July–September 1942," *Canadian Military History* 6, no. 2 (Autumn 1997): 7–20.

25 "HMCS St. Croix—A Tragic Saga," Naval Museum of Manitoba, http://www.naval-museum.mb.ca/battle_atlantic/st.croix/tragic-saga.htm.

26 Fisher, "Tactics, Training, Technology," 8.

27 "U-90," uboat.net, http://uboat.net/boats/u90.htm.

28 David Bercuson and Holger H. Herwig, *Deadly Seas: The Duel between the St. Croix and the U305 in the Battle of the Atlantic* (Toronto: Vintage Canada, 1977), 160.

29 "26 Canadian Navy Men Win Awards for Skill," *Globe and Mail*, November 27, 1942; http://collections.civilisations.ca/warclip/objects/common/webmedia.php?irn=5056208; Bercuson and Herwig, *Deadly Seas*, 161.

30 *CJWWII, Part I: Decorations*, 64.

31 Dunkelman, *Dual Allegiance*, 85.

32 *CJWWII, Part I: Decorations*, 3.

33 Martin Sugarman, "World War II: Jewish Pilots and Aircrews in the Battle of Britain," Jewish Virtual Library, http://www.jewishvirtuallibrary.org/jsource/ww2/sugar4.html#_ftnref28; author email correspondence with Martin Sugarman, June 2, 2016; Hugh Halliday, "CAN/RAF: The Canadians in the Royal Air Force," *Royal Canadian Air Force Journal* 4, no. 2 (Spring 2015): 22.

34 *CJWWII, Part I: Decorations*, 29.

35 Hugh Halliday, "F/L W. Henry Nelson, Man of Many Talents," *Journal of the Canadian Aviation Historical Society* 8, no. 2 (Summer 1970): 35–36.

36 Supplement to the London Gazette, May 31, 1940, https://www.thegazette.co.uk/London/issue/34860/supplement/3256/data.pdf.

37 Jay Bennett, "7 of the Greatest Flying Aces throughout History," *Popular Mechanics*, November 29, 2015, http://www.popularmechanics.com/flight/g2323/greatest-flying-aces/.

38 Hugh Halliday, "Battle of Britain: Canadians in the Royal Air Force," Royal Canadian Air Force website, September 7, 2016, http://www.rcaf-arc.forces.gc.ca/en/news-template-standard.page?doc=battle-of-britain-canadians-in-the-royal-air-force/iekdm9qc.

39 *CJWWII, Part I: Decorations*, 29.

40 Author unknown, "Some Never Die," ADCLA, CJC ZA 1946-7-124 (1946), CJC Publications, Pamphlets and Ephemera, box 1/2, files 01-08.

41 *CJWWII, Part I: Decorations*, 46–52.

42 Ghita Reuben Olit, memoir, unpublished, courtesy of Shelly Rubin, March 13, 2015, via email.

43 "Ice Hockey Wiki 1939–40 PSHL," http://icehockey.wikia.com/wiki/1939-40_PSHL.

44 LAC Service Files, series RG 24, vol. 26164, Samuel Moses Hurwitz, Soldier's Qualification Card.

45 I.P. Phelan, "Some Never Die: A Tribute to Sgt. Samuel Moses Hurwitz D.C.M., M.M. of Montreal, Canadian Grenadier Guards," 52 *Natural*, Canadian Grenadier Guards Official Publication Overseas, 1945, 1–8.

46 *CJWWII, Part I: Decorations*, 47–52.

47 LAC Service Files, Samuel Moses Hurwitz, Statement on Questionnaire of Missing Soldiers, Major G.R. Hale, November 2, 1944.

48 LAC Service Files, Samuel Moses Hurwitz, Bella Hurwitz letter to Captain Gordon, March 11, 1945.

49 Phelan, "Some Never Die."

50 Canadian Army Film Unit, *Canadian Army Newsreel*, Issue No. 1, November 1942, LAC, https://www.youtube.com/watch?v=ai2ROCamGzU.

51 *CJWWII, Part I: Decorations*, 52.

52 "Two Decorated Brothers: Leo and David Heaps at the OJA," OJA Blog, Ontario Jewish Archives, February 9, 2015, http://www.ontariojewisharchives.org/Blog/Two-Decorated-Brothers-Leo-and-David-Heaps.

53 Jeffrey Williams, *The Long Left Flank: The Hard Fought Way to the Reich, 1944–1945* (London: Leo Cooper, 1988), 220.

54 "Heaps, David, Lieutenant—Military Cross," Royal Hamilton Light Infantry—Individual Honours and Awards, http://www.rhli.ca/honourslist/heaps.html.

55 Heaps, *The Grey Goose of Arnhem*, 31.

56 "The Road to the Netherlands," Canada – Netherlands, Veterans Affairs Canada, Http://www.veterans.gc.ca/eng/remembrance/history/second-world-war/canada-netherlands#liberation.

57 Martin Sugarman, "World War II: Jews at the Battle of Arnhem," *Jewish Virtual Library*, September 1994, http://www.jewishvirtuallibrary.org/jews-at-the-battle-of-arnhem.

58 "Ottawa Veterans Get Awards at Rideau Hall Investiture," *Ottawa Journal*, December 3, 1946, 3.

59 "Dr. Maxwell Lerner," obituary, *Jewish Post and News* (Winnipeg), October 27, 1993, 18.

60 Barry Broadfoot, *Ten Lost Years, 1929–1939: Memories of Canadians Who Survived the Depression* (Toronto: McClelland & Stewart, 1973), 103–105.

61 *CJWWII, Part I: Decorations*, 20.

62 Ben Miller, "War Story as Told by Joe Minden," unpublished, courtesy of Sarah Minden, 4–5.

63 Lieutenant Colonel Byron B. Cochrane, Headquarters, Seventh Infantry Division, Office of the Division Surgeon, Letter of Recommendation for Captain Joseph Minden, July 31, 1945, courtesy of Mark Minden; Joe Minden, "War Diary," 25–27, courtesy of Mark Minden.

64 Ron Charles, "Special Honours Were Given to the Last Surviving Veterans of an Extraordinary WW II Regiment Known as the Kangaroo," *The National,* CBC News, September 10, 2011, https://youtu.be/_zrrrPBS9Do.

65 John R. Grodzinsky, "Kangaroos at War: The History of the 1st Canadian Armoured Personnel Carrier Regiment," *Canadian Military History* 4, no. 2 (January 2012): 2–3.

66 "Victoria Cross Recipients," Veterans Affairs Canada, http://www.veterans.gc.ca/eng/remembrance/history/second-world-war/canada-and-the-second-world-war/victoricr.

67 Farley Mowat, *And No Birds Sang* (Vancouver: Douglas & McIntyre, 2012 [1975]), 210.

68 Mowat, *And No Birds Sang,* 223.

69 Mark Zuehlke, *Ortona: Canada's Epic World War II Battle* (Vancouver: Douglas & McIntyre, 1999), 274.

70 *CJWWII, Part I: Decorations*, 56.

71 "U-1225," uboat.net, http://uboat.net/boats/u1225.htm.

72 "Bodnoff, Israel Joseph," Database of awards, RCAF Association, http://rcafassociation.ca/heritage/search-awards/?search=Bodnoff&searchfield=field_all&type=all.

73 "David Ernest Hornell," Victoria Cross — Second World War, 1939–1945, National Defence and the Canadian Forces," http://www.cmp-cpm.forces.gc.ca/dhh-dhp/gal/vcg-gcv/bio/hornell-de-eng.asp.

74 LAC Service Files, series RG 24, vol. 30594, Mitchell Sterlin, Record of Service.

75 Zuehlke, *Ortona*, 152.

76 Zuehlke, *Ortona*, 152, 153.

77 J.L. Granatstein, *Canada's Army: Waging War and Keeping the Peace*, 2nd ed. (Toronto: University of Toronto Press, 2011), 234.

78 Terry Copp, "Overcoming the Moro: Army, Part 67," *Legion Magazine*, November 1, 2006, https://legionmagazine.com/en/2006/11/overcoming-the-moro/.

79 Captain Philip J. Dagnall, Royal Canadian Regiment, letter to Mrs. Sterlin, January 18, 1944, McGill Remembers, http://www.archives.mcgill.ca/public/exhibits/mcgillremembers/war_records/0000-0481.01.2.e2615.jpg.

80 Granatstein, *Canada's Army*, 495n27.

81 LAC Service Files, Jacob Silverstein, Recommendation for Honours and Awards, Immediate, March 31, 1943. Silverstein had by this point flown 1089.35 hours, of which 809.35 were on operations, and completed 114 sorties.

82 LAC Service Files, Jacob Silverstein, Recommendation for Honours and Awards, reply by Station Commander, January 17, 1944.

83 "Silverstein, Jacob (Jack)," Canadian Jewish Heritage Network, Canadian Jewish Archives (Jewish Colonization Archives), http://www.cjhn.ca/en/permalink/genealogy469.

84 Michael A. Dorosh, "Bourguébus Ridge," 2009, www.canadiansoldiers.com, http://www.canadiansoldiers.com/history/battlehonours/northwesteurope/bourguebusridge.htm.

85 Terry Copp, "The Approach to Verrières Ridge, Army: Part 25," *Legion Magazine*, March 1, 1999, https://legionmagazine.com/en/1999/03/the-approach-to-verrieres-ridge/.

86 J.A.M. Cook, "Rubin Bider, Winnipeg Soldier, Can Take It and Dish It Out," *Winnipeg Free Press*, July 24, 1944, 5.

87 Trafford, *Memories on the March*, 21.
88 Bercuson, *Our Finest Hour*, 371.
89 *CJWWII, Part I: Decorations*, 55.
90 LAC Service Files, Harold Fromstein, Canadian Army Supplementary Declaration of Service in Pacific Theatre form, signed May 25, 1945, courtesy of Judy Neinstein; Terry Copp, *The Brigade: The Fifth Canadian Infantry Brigade in World War II* (Harrisburg, PA: Stackpole Books, 1992), 187.
91 *CJWWII, Part 1, Decorations*, 55; Bernie Farber, "Angels of the Battlefield," *National Post*, November 11, 2016, http://nationalpost.com/opinion/bernie-m-farber-angels-of-the-battlefield.

12 KEEPING THE FAITH

1 Cy Torontow, *There I Was: A Collection of Reminiscences by Members of the Ottawa Jewish Community Who Served in World War II* (Ottawa: Ottawa Post of the Jewish War Veterans and Ottawa Jewish Historical Society, 1999), 61.
2 LAC Service Files, series RG 24, vol. 26177, Simon Isenstein, Field Medical Card.
3 Torontow, *There I Was*, 61.
4 Ira Robinson, "A Letter from the Sabbath Queen: Rabbi Yudel Rosenberg Addresses Montreal Jewry," in *The Canadian Jewish Studies Reader*, ed. Richard Menkis and Norman Ravvin (Markham, ON: Red Deer Press, 2004), 127.
5 "Home for Passover Holidays," *Canadian Jewish Chronicle*, April 24, 1942, Harry R. Moscoe fonds, OJA, Canadian Jewish Congress War Efforts Committee, file 18, Jewish Chaplains, 1942–1943.
6 "Letter from Lottie Levinson to Harry R. Moscoe, May 13, 1943," ADCJA, CJC DA 18.1, box 18, file 18/26.
7 "Dr. Joe Greenberg — 18 Oct. 2013," interview with Dara Solomon, AC 412, OJA, http://search.ontariojewisharchives.org/Permalink/oralhistoriesoralid-145.
8 Melanie Buddle, "You Have to Think Like a Man and Act Like a Lady: Businesswomen in British Columbia, 1920–1980," *BC Studies* no. 151 (Autumn 2006): 81.
9 Sydney Brown letter to his parents, April 10, 1943, box 2009, files–1–4, Sydney and Zave Brown, 83-5, Ottawa Jewish Archives.
10 "Winnipeg Servicemen at a Seder," *Jewish Post and News*, April 15, 1992, A3; author email interview with Sheila Baslaw, June 7, 2016.
11 "1966: Muhammad Ali Tucks into a Chicken at Isow's Restaurant in Brewer Street, Soho, London," May 21, 1966, http://flashbak.com/1966-muhammad-ali-tucks-into-a-chicken-at-isow%C2%92s-restaurant-in-brewer-street-soho-london-3013/; Wikipedia contributors, "Isow's," Wikipedia, The Free Encyclopedia, https://en.wikipedia.org/wiki/Isow%27s.

12 "Weekly Report," January 29, 1943, War Efforts Committee, Harry R. Moscoe fonds 69, file 12, OJA.

13 Jewish War Veterans of Canada, *No Greater Honour*.

14 Lieutenant Barney J. Gloster, Department of National Defence, LAC PA-174315, MIKAN no. 3241238.

15 Samuel Cass, "A Passover Seder in Kleve, Germany, March 1945," in *Battle Lines: Eyewitness Accounts from Canada's Military History*, eds. J.L. Granatstein and Norman Hillmer (Toronto: Thomas Allen, 2004), 366–367.

16 "For King and Country: The Jewish Canadian Military Experience," online exhibition, Ontario Jewish Archives, http://www.ontariojewisharchives.org/cms_uploads/flash/military/identity/lg/jcmm_p3_12_lg.jpg; author email from Al Rubin, curator of the Jewish Canadian Military Museum collection, July 20, 2016.

17 Cass, "A Passover Seder."

18 Levi, Breaking New Ground, 72.

19 Cass, "A Passover Seder."

20 Danson and Fahey, *Not Bad for a Sergeant*, 39.

21 Louis Devor, "Devor, Devore, Dorfman, D'wor, Dwor, Sandler First Family Reunion," July 29, 1983, Toronto, 4.

22 John Devor letter to mother, January 30, 1945, Devor file 89- 2/5, OJA.

23 Syd Devor, letter to mother, 59 Havelock Street, Toronto, September 18, 1944, Devor file, OJA.

24 David Devor letter to mother, November 4, 1944, Devor file OJA.

25 David Devor letter to mother, April 1943, Devor file, OJA.

26 "Religious Identity," in "For King and Country," http://wwwontariojewisharchives.org/Exhibitions/Online/For-King-and-Country/Religious-Identity.

27 Levi, *Breaking New Ground*, 4–5, 6, 13–14.

28 Wilfred Shuchat, *The Gate of Heaven: The Story of Shaar Hashomayim in Montreal* (Montreal and Kingston: McGill-Queen's University Press, 2000),133.

29 "The Chaplaincy Service," briefing note, p. 5, ADCJA, CJA DA 18.

30 Levi, *Breaking New Ground*, x.

31 Mrs. Lazarus Phillips, "We Support Our Soldiers," *Canadian Jewish Chronicle*, June 6, 1944, 7; "Revised Tentative Budget for War Efforts Committee for 1942," War Efforts Committee Agenda for Dominion Council Meeting of Congress, September 7, 1941, ADCJA.

32 Halladay, "Ladies and Gentlemen," 42.

33 Dick Steele letter to Esther Steele, February 3, 1943, courtesy of Michael Steele.

34 "Services in the Aleutians," *Israelite Press* (Winnipeg), November 19, 1943, 1.

35 "Kiska, Alaska," Canadian Heroes website, http://canadianheroes.org/henri/henri2.htm.

36 LAC Service Files, Hymie Steinberg, Mr. J. Steinberg letter to Commanding Officer, No. 2 Bombing and Gunnery School, Calgary, March 21, 1944.

37 Vilhjálmur Örn Vilhjálmsson, "Iceland, the Jews, and Anti-Semitism, 1625–2004," in *Behind the Humanitarian Mask: The Nordic Countries, Israel and the Jews*, ed. Manfred Gerstenfeld (Jerusalem Centre for Public Affairs, 2008), 226–227; author email correspondence with Vilhjálmsson, June 9, 2015.

38 Vilhjálmur Örn Vilhjálmsson, "Remembering Lionel Cohen and Meyer Bubis," June 11, 2015, http://fornleifur.blog.is/blog/fornleifur/entry/1791178/.

39 Vilhjálmsson, "Iceland, the Jews, and Anti-Semitism," 227.

40 "Meyer Bubis [graphic material, textual record] – 12 Oct. 1940," Ontario Jewish Archives, http://search.ontariojewisharchives.org/List?q=bubis&p=1&ps=50.

41 "Why Is This Night Different Than All Other Nights?" March 31, 2015, http://www.ontariojewisharchives.org/Blog/Celebrating-Passover-at-the-Ontario-Jewish-Archives.

42 "Allied Forces Celebrate Jewish New Year: Religious Celebrations at the Balfour Service Club, London, UK, 1943," D16282, Ministry of Information Second World War Official Collection, Imperial War Museums London, http://www.iwm.org.uk/collections/item/object/205200390.

43 "Allied Forces Celebrate Jewish New Year," D16288, http://www.iwm.org.uk/collections/item/object/205200391.

44 Murray Bleeman letter to Diana Bleeman, March 28, 1941, courtesy Ferne Phillips.

45 Boroditsky, "Sam Boroditsky's War," 23.

46 Danson and Fahey, *Not Bad for a Sergeant*, 57.

47 LAC Service Files, series RG 24, vol. 25042, Arthur Cherkinsky, Personal Effects Inventory, March 29,1943.

48 LAC Service Files, series R 112, vol. 30576, Fred Pascal, Estates Branch Inventory.

49 LAC Service Files, series RG 24, vol. 24874, Harry Bloch, Department of National Defence Inventory, Ottawa, February 27, 1946.

50 LAC Service Files, Mitch Sterlin, Estates Branch Inventory.

51 LAC Service Files, series RG 24, vol. 28755, Mortimer Sam Sucharov, List of Personal Effects.

52 LAC Service Files, series RG 24, vol. 26709, Samuel Nichols, List of Personal Effects.

53 Levi, *Breaking New Ground*, 46.

54 *Prayer Book for Jewish Members of H.M. Forces,* new edition, H.M. Stationery Office, 1940, 5, courtesy of Michael Ostfield.

55 Gershon Levi note, June 21, 1942, ADCJA, DA 18.1, box 16, file 2/15.

56 Flight Lieutenant J.M. Roe letter to Gershon Levi, August 12, 1942, ADCJA, CJC DA 18, file 3/3.
57 *Book of Jewish Thoughts/Calendar*, 1944, ADCJA, CJC DA 18.1, box 14, file 6.
58 Tulchinsky, *Branching Out*, 219.
59 *The Quad '35: The Yearbook of the University of Bishop's College* (Lennoxville, QC: Beck Press, 1935), 24.
60 *CJWWII*, 50.
61 Louis Scully, "Roll of Honour — Palestine 1938–1939 — Worcestershire Regiment," Worcestershire Regiment website, http://www.worcestershireregiment.com/roll_honour_palestine.php; Louis Scully, "1st Battalion Worcestershire Regiment—Sudan and Eritrea (1939–1941)," Worcestershire Regiment website, http://www.worcestershireregiment.com/h_eritrea_1941.php; Robert Palmer, "British Troops in the Sudan, History and Personnel," British Military History.co.uk.com, 2011, http://www.britishmilitaryhistory.co.uk/webeasycms/hold/uploads/bmh_document_pdf/British-Troops-in-The-Sudan-History-Personnel.pdf.
62 LAC Service Files, series RG 24, vol. 27915, Ira Irwin Kliman, RCAF interview report, February 1941, Hospital or Sick List Record Card, July (unreadable).
63 *CJWWII*, 41.
64 LAC Service Files, series RG 24, vol. 28724, Gordon Steinberg, Record of Service.
65 *CJWWII*, 76.
66 Tulchinsky, *Canada's Jews*, 359.
67 "Tributes Paid Capt. S. Sheps," *Winnipeg Tribune*, October 18, 1944, 2.
68 Charlie Drubich letter to Mrs. Kate Devor, January 3, 1945, courtesy of Louis Devor family collection.

13 LIBERATION

1 Captain Isaac Rose letter to John Devor, February 4, 1945, courtesy of Louis Devor.
2 Sebastian Engelbrecht, "Wiedersehen mit der alten Fußball-Liebe," ARD-Hörfunkstudio Tel Aviv, http://web.archive.org/web/20101104233234/http://www.tagesschau.de/ausland/schalkechampionsleague100.html.
3 Notes from Gita Guttman Berman interview with Edith Nussbaum Brichta, October 30, 2016, Tel Aviv.
4 "Testimony of Walter Naftali Nussbaum, born in Wanne Eickel, Germany, 1924, regarding his experiences in Amsterdam, Arnhem, Huyton camp in Britain and New Braunswick and Fort Lenox camps in Canada," filmed in 1999, from the collection of Yad Vashem, Google Cultural Institute, 2015, https://www.google.com/culturalinstitute/beta/asset/testimony-of-walter-naftali-nussbaum-born-in-

wanne-eickel-germany-1924-regarding-his-experiences-in-amsterdam-arnhem-huyton-camp-in-britain-and-new-braunswick-and-fort-lenox-camps-in-canada/jgHEjNDspFO66w.

5 Richard Menkis, "'But You Can't See the Fear That People Lived Through': Canadian Jewish Chaplains and Canadian Encounters with Dutch Survivors, 1944–1945," *American Jewish Archives Journal* 60, no. 1–2 (2008): 31, http://americanjewisharchives.org/publications/journal/PDF/2008_60_01_02_menkis.pdf.

6 Rod Mickleburgh with Rudyard Griffiths, *Rare Courage: Veterans of the Second World War Remember* (Toronto: McClelland & Stewart, 2005), 179.

7 Max (Val) Rimer letter to his mother, December 15, 1943, Canadian Letters and Images Project, Department of History, Vancouver Island University, 2016.

8 Trafford, *Memories on the March*, 127–128.

9 "Valenciennes en 1939–1945," Anonymes, Justes et persécutés durant la période nazie website, http://www.ajpn.org/commune-Valenciennes-en-1939-1945-59606.html.

10 Trafford, *Memories on the March*, 127–128.

11 "Lethbridge Flyer Aids Jewish Refugees in Italy," *Discovery: The Journal of the Jewish Historical Society of Southern Alberta* 5, no. 4 (Spring 1995): 7.

12 Trafford, *Memories on the March*, 17.

13 Norman Gulko, "A Toronto Boy Goes to War," unpublished memoir, 2003, 10, Norman Gulko fonds, OJA, accession number 24469, http://search.ontariojewisharchives.org/Permalink/accessions24469.

14 Val Rimer interview, "Liberation," episode 3024 of *War Story*, executive producers Barry Stevens and David York, 52 Media and War Torn Productions, History Channel, Shaw Media, 2012–2016, http://www.warstory.ca/assets/pdf/rimer_val_transcript.pdf.

15 *CJWWII, Part I: Decorations,* 9; Fred Langan, "Veteran Took Great Pride in Allied Victory," *Globe and Mail* (Toronto), January 18, 2011, http://v1.theglobeandmail.com/servlet/story/LAC.20110118.OBLEVENSTONATL/BDAStory/BDA/deaths.

16 Michael Levenston, ed., *My Darling Mom: Gerald Levenston's WWII Letters Home to Canada*, Kindle ebook, Amazon Digital Services LLC, 2012, iv.

17 "Bergen-Belsen," United States Holocaust Memorial Museum, July 2016, https://www.ushmm.org/wlc/en/article.php?ModuleId=10005224.

18 Franklin Bialystok, *Delayed Impact: The Holocaust and the Canadian Jewish Community* (Montreal and Kingston: McGill-Queen's University Press, 2010), 14.

19 "Saul Laskin Describes Belsen Camp," *Fort William Daily Times Journal*, March 26, 1946, courtesy of Mark Celinscak.

20 Berger and Street, *Invasions without Tears*, 208–209.

21 Sergeant Michael Lewis, 35 mm footage, "Belsen at Liberation, Kramer, Women Jeer at SS," story RG-60.0062, film ID 10, Steven Spielberg Film and Video Archives, United States Holocaust Memorial Museum, copyright by the Imperial War Museums, A700/304/1-2, 1991, https://collections.ushmm.org/search/catalog/irn1000208.

22 Eric Sorenson, interview with Jack Marcovitch, CBC TV news report from the 1980s, https://www.youtube.com/watch?v=1mXVpVwx59g.

23 Squadron Leader Jacob Eisen, *Your RCAF News Digest* 2, no. 6 (June 15, 1945): 1, courtesy of Joel Zelikovitz.

24 Stanley Winfield, "Bergen-Belsen Liberated, Canadians Help Camp Survivors," *Zachor: The Journal of Vancouver Holocaust Education Centre Society*, reprinted in *Discovery: The Journal of the Jewish Historical Society of Southern Alberta* 5, no. 4 (Spring 1995): 7.

25 Mark Celinscak, *Distance from the Belsen Heap: Allied Forces and the Liberation of a Nazi Concentration Camp* (Toronto: University of Toronto Press, 2015), 92.

26 "Bergen-Belsen Displaced Persons Camp," *Holocaust Encyclopedia*, United States Holocaust Memorial Musuem, https://www.ushmm.org/wlc/en/article.php?ModuleId=10007066; *Land of Promise*, 166.

27 Interview with Stan Winfield, June 16, 2014, Winfield Collection, Vancouver Holocaust Education Centre. The video clip is part of the PowerPoint for *Canadian Soldiers Encounter the Holocaust* in *Canada Responds*, an online exhibition, https://web.archive.org/web/20170302104614/http://www.canadaresponds.ca/download.html.

28 Bernard Yale Donation, OJA, Accession 2010-5/15, part of an exhibition called *Traces of War*, Lipa Green Building, http://www.ontariojewisharchives.org/cms_uploads/images/albums/Traces-of-War/2010-5-15.jpg.

29 Winfield, "Bergen-Belsen Liberated," 7.

30 Goldberg, "Witnessing Bergen-Belsen."

31 Boroditsky, "Sam Boroditsky's War," 38–41.

32 Menkis, "'But You Can't See the Fear,'" 32.

33 LAC, photo by Lieutenant Ken Bell, Department of National Defence, "Corporal M. Freeman, Canadian Women's Army Corps (C.W.A.C.), and H/Captain Samuel Cass, Jewish chaplain, presenting a gift to a Belgian girl during a Hanukkah celebration, Tilburg, Netherlands, 17 December 1944", PA-188717. Series R112-536-X-E, Online Mikan No. 3514333, http://bit.ly/2tJchwL.

34 Levi, *Breaking New Ground*, 66.

35 Mark Zuehlke, *On to Victory: The Canadian Liberation of the Netherlands, March 23–May 5, 1945* (Vancouver: Douglas & McIntyre, 2010), 251.

36 *CJWWII*, 133.

37 Nova Scotia Legislature, "Debates and Proceedings," April 27, 2005, http://nslegislature.ca/index.php/proceedings/hansard/C50/59_1_house_05apr27/.

38 "Veteran Stories: Louis "Billy the Kid" Gelman, Army," The Memory Project, http://www.thememoryproject.com/stories/1018:louis-billy-the-kid-gelman/. Despite Gelman's story, the Royal Archives at Windsor Castle found no record of such a visit, but officials say that if it did happen, it could have been an unofficial visit. Author email interview with Julie Crocker, Archivist, Royal Archives, Windsor Castle, Windsor, June 7, 2016.

39 Tom Earle, Library of Parliament, Ottawa, *Oral History Project*, interview with the Hon. David Croll, Senator, 29.

40 *CJWWII*, 126.

41 Raber, *Manny Goes to War*, 277.

42 "Yanks, Britons Ranked Canadian Red Cross POW Parcels 'Tops,'" *Lethbridge Herald*, August 9, 1945, 6.

43 Raber, *Manny Goes to War*, 245.

44 William Zelikovitz letter to his brother Butch and Laura, May 11, 1945, courtesy of Joel Zelikovitz.

14 COMING HOME

1 Esther Steele letter to Bill Walsh, May 8, 1945, courtesy of Michael Steele.

2 "Two Are Dead, Shops Looted, Liquor Stolen," Canadian Press, *Globe and Mail* (Toronto), May 9, 1945.

3 C.P. Stacey, *The Canadian Army, 1939–1945: An Official Historical Summary* (Ottawa: Department of National Defence and King's Printer), 308, http://www.cmp-cpm.forces.gc.ca/dhh-dhp/his/docs/CDN_ARMY_39-45_E.pdf; "Canada and the War in the Far East," Veterans Affairs Canada, October 23, 2014, http://www.veterans.gc.ca/eng/remembrance/history/second-world-war/southeast-asia/vfe-back.

4 Captain M.B. Huffman, RCAPC, Report No. 77, Directorate of History, Department of National Defence, "The Repatriation of the Canadian Military Forces Overseas 1945–1947," Ottawa, 1986, 13.

5 Bill Berger, "The Y Bugle," *YMHA Beacon*, January 9, 1946, 6.

6 William Allister, *Where Life and Death Hold Hands* (Delta, BC: Retsila, 2000), 285–286.

7 Hong Kong Veterans Association, "C" Force Personnel Summary, David Golden, 15, courtesy of Vince Lopata, association historian.

8 David Golden, "Thoughts on Japan," Heroes Remember video series, Veterans Affairs Canada, http://www.veterans.gc.ca/eng/video-gallery/video/10290.
9 The four Canadian POWs escaped from Sham Shui Po barracks on August 19, 1942, and were subsequently caught and executed. Vance, *Objects of Concern*, 206.
10 George Harrison, "Avoiding Amputation," Heroes Remember video series, Veterans Affairs Canada, http://www.veterans.gc.ca/eng/video-gallery/video/10739.
11 *CJWWII*, 35.
12 Raber, *Manny Goes to War*, 358.
13 Arthur Pascal interview with grandchildren, unpublished audiotape, tape 2c, courtesy of Kathy Cohen.
14 Tom Earle interview with Hon. David Croll, *Oral History Project*, 25.
15 Sergeant Bill Walsh letter to Esther Steele, October 23–24, 1944, courtesy of Michael Steele.
16 Trafford, *Memories on the March*, 128.
17 Gulko, "A Toronto Boy Goes to War," 14.
18 "Fighting for Freedom: Special Exhibition Marking VE Day," Yad Vashem online exhibition, 2016, http://www.yadvashem.org/yv/en/exhibitions/jewish_fighters/rose.asp.
19 Jan Diederen, "Gezin Cahn, het meest Valkenburgs alle joden," *Kijk op Valkenburg*, May–June–July 2012, 21–23.
20 Captain Nathan Levinne in *No Greater Honour*.
21 Unpublished speech by Sarah Minden from the ceremony at Hamilton's Delta High School in 2012 honouring Joseph Minden on the school's Wall of Excellence, courtesy of Sarah Minden.
22 Harry Winter, "Coventry: English Men in White Perform Surgical Miracles Under a Hail of German Bullets," *Life*, January 20, 1941, 39–41; Martin Gilbert, "Coventry: What Really Happened," International Churchill Society, http://www.winstonchurchill.org/resources/myths/1561-coventry-what-really-happened.
23 "Harry Winter," Geni website, https://www.geni.com/people/Harry-Winter/6000000006566836210.
24 Farquharson, *For Your Tomorrow*, 126.
25 "Empire Order Awarded Capt. Jacob Markowitz," *Globe and Mail* (Toronto), June 8, 1946.
26 Jacob Markowitz, "Some Experiences as a Medical Officer with the Royal Army Medical Corps," Empire Club of Canada, October 17, 1946, http://speeches.empireclub.org/60822/data?n=17. Markowitz may indeed have been referring to the story of Elisha, not Elijah, who revived a dead boy by putting his mouth on the boy's mouth. 2 Kings: 4, 34–35. The Elijah story is 1 Kings: 17, 21–22.

27 Victor Johnson, "Obituary, Jacob Markowitz," *Canadian Family Physician*, March 1969, 15, https://www.ncbi.nlm.nih.gov/pmc/articles/PMC2281325/?page=1.
28 "Louis Slotin, Scientist Los Alamos, NM," Atomic Heritage Foundation, 2016, http://www.mphpa.org/profile/louis-slotin.
29 "Little Boy and Fat Man," Atomic Heritage Foundation, 2016, http://www.atomicheritage.org/history/little-boy-and-fat-man; Kyle Hill, "Tickling the Dragon's Tail: The Story of the 'Demon Core,'" Nerdist.com, December 11, 2014, http://nerdist.com/tickling-the-dragons-tail-the-story-of-the-demon-core/.
30 Martin Zelig, "Louis Slotin and 'The Invisible Killer,'" *Beaver* 75, no. 4 (August–September 1995): 20–27.
31 Bryan Hubbard, "A Critical Accident: 'Tickling the Dragon's Tail,'" *Military.com,* 2016, http://www.military.com/Content/MoreContent1/?file=cw_nuclear_slotin; "Remembering a Winnipeg Jewish Hero," Editorial Comment, *Jewish Post and News* (Winnipeg), August 16, 1995, 4.
32 Barbara Moon, "The Nuclear Death of a Nuclear Scientist," *Maclean's*, republished in *The Jewish Post*, November 30, 1961, 15, Jewish Heritage Centre of Western Canada, Martin Zelig Collection, box no. JHC 367, file 14.
33 Hill, "Tickling the Dragon's Tail."
34 Moon, "The Nuclear Death," 38.
35 Major General L.R. Groves, War Department, Washington DC, letter to Mr. and Mrs. Albert Slotin, 125 Scotia, Winnipeg, Manitoba, Canada, June 1, 1946, *CJWWII*, 2.
36 *CJWWII*, 1–4.
37 *CJWWII, Part I: Decorations*, 82.
38 Milton Shulman wrote *Defeat in the West,* published in 1947 (London: Orion/Cassell Military Paperbacks, 2004 [1947]).
39 Gerry Quinney, "Wayne and Shuster on Readjusting to Civilian Life," *Assignment*, February 24, 1958, CBC Archives, http://www.cbc.ca/archives/entry/wayne-and-shuster-on-readjusting-to-civilian-life.
40 "Evelyn Miller," *Edmonton Journal*, November 3, 2011, http://www.legacy.com/obituaries/edmontonjournal/obituary.aspx?pid=154446858; Monica Wegner, "Dancing Backwards in Heels," *U of A Business Alumni Magazine*, Fall–Winter 2011–2012, 9.
41 Hugh Grant, "The Remarkable Career of David Golden," *Manitoba History*, no. 67 (Winter 2012), republished on RadioAlumni.ca, http://radioalumni.ca/x_Golden-David.htm.
42 Hart, The Memory Project, http://www.thememoryproject.com/stories/2121:e.-david-hart/.

43 Novick, Baron Byng High School Museum and Hall of Honour, http://www.baronbynghighschool.ca/alumni/william-novick/.

44 Murray C. Johnston, *Canada's Craftsmen at 50!: The Story of Electrical and Mechanical Engineering in the Canadian Armed Forces Up to and Including the 50th Anniversary of the Formation of the Corps of Royal Canadian Electrical and Mechanical Engineers* (Borden, Ontario: EME Officers' Fund, 1997), 509.

45 LAC Service Files, Harold Fromstein, Statement of War Service Gratuity, February 1, 1946.

46 Kaplan, memoir, 73, 94.

47 Bella Briansky Kalter, "Ansonville: A Jewish Community That Was," *American Jewish Archives* 30, no. 2 (November 1978): 107–125.

48 Albert Glazer, "WWII Biography of Albert Glazer," unpublished memoir, 1997, 6, courtesy of Steven Glazer.

49 Albert Glazer, *No Greater Honour* video.

50 James McCready, "A Hero of the Siege of Malta," *Globe and Mail* (Toronto), September 7, 2004.

51 Dunkelman, *Dual Allegiance*, 151.

52 Trafford, *Memories on the March*, 19; "JHSSA 21st Annual General Meeting," *Discovery: The Journal of the Jewish Historical Society of Southern Alberta* 21, no. 3 (Fall 2011): 1.

53 "St. Catharines: Military Service," Ontario Jewish Archives, http://ontariojewisharchives.org/exhibits/osjc/communities/stcatharines/community/military.html.

54 *Heritage and History: The Saskatoon Jewish Community* (Saskatoon: Congregation Agudas Israel, 1998), 105.

55 David Croll, *No Greater Honour.*

56 Sandra Martin, "Eddie Goodman—Lawyer," *Globe and Mail* (Toronto), August 25, 2006, S11.

57 "965 Nominated for Federal Election of June 11," *Ottawa Journal*, May 15, 1945, 13.

58 David Levy, *Stalin's Man in Canada: Fred Rose and Soviet Espionage* (Enigma Books, 2011), chap. 9; Archives Montreal, Dossier D1322, Harry Binder, Conseiller, 1950–1952, VM94-Z1340-02.

59 Phyllis Entis, "Remembering Uncle Moshe," Prompt Prose, May 26, 2013, http://promptprose.blogspot.ca/2013/05/remembering-uncle-moshe.html.

60 *CJWWII*, 94.

61 "Veterans Stories: Bernard J. Finestone, Army," The Memory Project, http://www.thememoryproject.com/stories/64:bernard-j.-finestone/.

62 LAC, War Graves Registers: Circumstances of Death, series RG 150, 1992–93/314, vols. 239–302, box 301.

63 Dariah Coneghan, "Morris Cyril Shumiatcher, 1917–2004," *Encyclopedia of Saskatchewan* (Regina: Canadian Plains Research Centre, University of Regina, 2006), https://web.archive.org/web/20171002022027/http://esask.uregina.ca/entry/shumiatcher_morris_cyril_1917-_2004.html.

64 Greenfield, *The Damned*, 251.

65 Ralph, *Aces, Warriors and Wingmen*, 158.

66 Brian Nolan, *Hero: The Buzz Beurling Story* (Toronto: Lester & Orpen Dennys, 1981), 138.

67 Background and Overview, Israeli War of Independence, Jewish Virtual Library, http://www.jewishvirtuallibrary.org/background-and-overview-israel-war-of-independence.

68 "Overseas Volunteers in Israel's War of Independence, 1947–1949: A Brief Summary," *World Machal*, http://www.machal.org.il/index.php?option=com_content&view=article&id=302&Itemid=357&lang=en; Nolan, *Hero*, 140–142.

69 Penslar, *Jews in the Military*, 234–235.

70 Mitch Potter, "The Toronto Man Who Saved Nazareth," *Toronto Star*, December 20, 2015, https://www.thestar.com/news/insight/2015/12/20/the-toronto-man-who-saved-nazareth.html.

15 KADDISH FOR D-DAY

1 LAC Service Files, series RG 24, vol. 26935, William Guy Rosenthal, Telegram August 14, 1943.

2 LAC Service Files, series RG 24, vol. 28602, Moses Schwartz, Record of Service, and L. Breadner, RCAF casualty officer, letter to Mr. B. Schwartz, February 23, 1945.

3 "Moses Schwartz," Nécrologie, http://necrologie.genealogiequebec.com/avis-de-deces/327266-SCHWARTZ-Moses.

4 "Canadian Virtual War Memorial: William Guy Rosenthal," Veterans Affairs Canada, http://www.veterans.gc.ca/eng/remembrance/memorials/canadian-virtual-war-memorial/detail/2202790?William%20Guy%20Rosenthal.

5 *CJWWII*, 62.

6 LAC Service Files, series RG 24, vol. 28643, Joseph Shulman.

7 "Duke Abelson Memorial Trophy," *Ottawa Citizen*, February 9, 1945, 19.

8 Devor Family files 89 2-5, OJA, Kate Devor certificate, December 1966, Jewish National Fund.

9 LAC Service Files, series RG 24, vol. 24887, Philip Bosloy.

10 LAC Service Files, series RG 24, vol. 26381, Mike Litwack.

11 *CJWWII*, 45.

12 LAC Service Files, series RG 24, vol. 25102, Jack Cooper.

13 "Cooper, Jack," Commonwealth War Graves Commission, http://www.cwgc.org/find-war-dead/casualty/2777368/COOPER,%20JACK.

14 "Marble Plaque Unveiled in Honour of Jewish War Dead," *Ottawa Journal*, November 19, 1945.

15 *Canadian Jewish Review*, January 31, 1947, 9.

16 Photo of ceremony, Jewish Heritage Society of Southern Alberta #606.

17 "World War II Roll of Honour," St. James the Assiniboine Anglican Church, Winnipeg, http://www.stjamesanglicanchurch.ca/WW_II_Roll_of_Honour.html.

18 "Memorial Service Held for Jewish Members of the Armed Forces Held in Edmonton in 1946," *In Defence of Alberta*, Archives Society of Alberta, 2006 Virtual Exhibition, http://www.archivesalberta.org/2006exhibit/jahsena4.htm.

19 *CJWWII*, 77; LAC, War Graves Registers: Circumstances of Death, box 288, Hyman Bonder.

20 David Horowitz, "Monument Honours Jews Who Died for Their Country While Serving in Canadian," Jewish Toronto, June 13, 2014, https://jewishtoronto.com/news-media/monument-honours-jews-who-died-for-their-country-while-serving-in-canadian-forces.

21 "Brownstone Outpost," Excellent Adventures and Cat Island Lodge, http://exc-adventures.com/fly-in-fishing-outpost-cabins/brownstone-outpost/.

22 Stephanie Jarvis, Lois Burke, and Joyce Henderson, *Flin Flon: A Visual History, 1933–1983* (Flin Flon Jubilee Committee, 1983), 88; *CJWWII*, 25.

23 LAC Service Files, Harold Chizy, Abraham Chizy letter to Department of National Defence, Ottawa, October 17, 1944.

24 LAC Service Files, Harold Chizy, Secretary, Naval Board, letter to Abraham Chizy, October 30, 1944.

25 Applications for Headstones for U.S. Military Veterans, 1925–1941, microfilm publication M1916, 134 rolls, ARC ID 596118, Records of the Office of the Quartermaster General, Record Group 92, National Archives, Washington DC.

26 "Jewish Airwoman Dies in 1943 Alberta Air Crash," *Discovery: The Journal of the Jewish Historical Society of Southern Alberta*," June 2004, p. 3, http://jhssa.org/wp-content/uploads/2012/08/JHSSA-June-2004-4.0.pdf.

27 LAC Service Files, Rose Jette Goodman, S. Goodman letter to L.S. Breadner, chief of air staff, Ottawa, February 9, 1943.

28 "Next of Kin Members Hear Y.M. Minstrels," *Canadian Jewish Chronicle*, April 21, 1944, 12. Tritt's crew had not yet been sent to conduct any operational bombing raids. Nephew Joseph Aspler says they were on a final training mission, which he calls a Bullseye Cruise, and which they were required to complete before

being cleared to go operational. Http://www.canveyisland.org/page_id__863.aspx?path=0p2p288p26p185p.

29 Allison and Hayward, *They Shall Grow Not Old*, 29.

30 Exhibit on Henry Balinson, Rose and Phil Rosenshein Museum, Beth Jacob Synagogue, Hamilton, Ontario, opened September 20, 2015.

31 "Lt. Sterlin, ex-Gazette Carrier, Praised by Former Fellow Officer," *Gazette* (Montreal), May 8, 1944, in McGill Remembers, McGill University War Records, File Folder (recto), McGill University Archives, 0000-0481.01.2.e2614, http://www.archives.mcgill.ca/public/exhibits/mcgillremembers/results.asp?id=269.

32 LAC Service Files, Yude Brownstone, Reburial Card.

33 LAC Service Files, series RG 24, vol. 28544, Alan Rodd, Copy Report from No. 1 Missing Research and Enquiry Unit, Royal Air Force, British Forces in France, June 7, 1946.

34 Cemetery Details, Bérou-la-Mulotière Communal Cemetery, Commonwealth War Graves Commission, https://www.cwgc.org/find-a-cemetery/cemetery/2031890/berou-la-mulotiere-communal-cemetery/.

35 Howard Margolian, *Conduct Unbecoming: The Story of the Murder of Canadian Prisoners of War in Normandy* (Toronto: University of Toronto Press 1998), 105–106, 30.

36 LAC Service Files, series RG, vol. 30891, Israel Pavelow, Hyman Pavelow letter to Imperial War Graves Commission, May 19, 1947, and details of Estate Form sent by Hyman Pavelow to Department of National Defence, Estates Branch, July 22, 1944.

37 LAC Service Files, Hymie Steinberg, J.K. Bully, wing commander, RCAF Reykjavik, letter to Mrs. Ruth Steinberg, December 30, 1944.

38 LAC Service Files, Hymie Steinberg, Flying Officer Orton letter to Mrs. J.D. Steinberg, July 16, 1945.

39 "Aircrew Losses: Captain Shnier," 97 Squadron at Bourn website, https://web.archive.org/web/20130716135707/Http://www.97squadron.co.uk/Crew%20Shnier.html; Middlebrook and Everitt, *The Bomber Command War Diaries,* 414.

40 LAC Service Files, Samuel Moses Hurwitz, M. Levitt, Canadian Jewish Congress, letter to Lieutenant-Colonel H.M. Jackson, Director of Records, Department of National Defence, Ottawa, July 9, 1947, and photos of the grave.

41 "In Memory: Ancestry Launches Historic WWII Collection," ancestry.ca news release, November 5, 2015, http://www.newswire.ca/news-releases/in-memory-ancestry-launches-historic-wwii-collection-540777021.html.

42 Tom St. Amand, "Street Names Tell the Story of Sarnia," *Sarnia Journal*, August 4, 2016.

43 Four of the six men who died were in the RCAF and one each in the army and navy. Irving (Porky) Lindzon lived at 80 Major Street. Solomon (Solly) Kay—"the milkman's son"—lived at 3 Major Street. Kay's neighbour Harold Sobel, lived at number 5. Charles (Chucky) Males lived at 35 Major. Art Gold (born Goldenthal) lived at number 144 Major Street. Bernard Webber was the only one of "the boys" who did not grow up on Major Street. He was from Fort William, but moved to 125 Major Street after he married. Webber left behind a wife, Dinah, and two small boys, Herbert and Sheldon.

44 Joe Greenberg interview, OJA.

45 "Sai Wan War Cemetery," Commonwealth War Graves Commission, http://www.cwgc.org/find-a-cemetery/cemetery/2000320/SAI%20WAN%20WAR%20CEMETERY#.

46 Walsh family interview, tape 5.

47 "Rubin, Hector Bernard," Commonwealth War Graves Commission, http://www.cwgc.org/find-war-dead/casualty/2200851/RUBIN,%20HECTOR%20BERNARD#carousel5.

48 *Fat Man and Little Boy*, directed by Roland Joffé, 1989, http://www.imdb.com/title/tt0097336/.

49 Martin Zelig, "Dr. Louis Slotin Recognized for 1946 Sacrifice: Hero Receives Honor with Naming of Park," *Winnipeg Free Press*, October 23, 1993.

50 "In Memoriam, Nathan (Nat) Dlusy," *Gazette* (Montreal), November 11, 2014, http://www.legacy.com/obituaries/montrealgazette/obituary.aspx?pid=173125467.

51 Martin Saslove, "Flying Officer Edward L. Saslove, Pilot," RAF Fiskerton website, http://www.fiskertonairfield.org.uk/photo3_3.html.

52 LAC Service Files, Samuel Jacob Donen, original mailed envelope with R stamped on front addressed to Mr. Jacob Donen on Luxton Avenue, Winnipeg.

53 LAC Service Files, George Meltz, Personal Effects List.

54 LAC Service Files, George Meltz, Gertrude Meltz letter to Estates Branch, received June 22, 1946.

55 David Matlow, "He Died So Jewry Shall Suffer No More," Centre for Israel and Jewish Affairs, October 15, 2014, http://www.cija.ca/he-died-so-jewry-shall-suffer-no-more/#.VEVy4VhQ_Y4.email.

56 Josef Rosin, "Siesikiai," translated from *Pinkas Hakehillot Lita* by Shimon Joffe, http://www.jewishgen.org/Yizkor/Pinkas_lita/lit_00437.html.

References

ESSENTIAL STATE PAPERS AND GOVERNMENT RECORDS

Library and Archives Canada, Militia and Defence Headquarters Central Registry (HQ 593-1-77), Department of the Secretary of State, Courtesy of Paul Marsden, Senior Military Archivist, Government Records. (Enlistment numbers in the First World War by religion.)

Library and Archives Canada, Ottawa, Service Files of the Second World War—War Dead, 1939–1947

ARCHIVAL SOURCES

Alex Dworkin Canadian Jewish Archives, Montreal

Canadian War Museum, Ottawa

Crestwood Academy, Toronto

Glenbow Museum Archives, Calgary

Jewish Archives and Historical Society of Edmonton and Northern Alberta, Edmonton.

Jewish Canadian Military Museum, Toronto

Jewish Heritage Centre of Western Canada, Winnipeg

Jewish Historical Society of Southern Alberta, Calgary

Jewish Museum and Archives of British Columbia, Vancouver

Jewish Public Library Archives, Montreal

Montreal Aviation Museum, Ste-Anne-de-Bellevue, Quebec

Ontario Jewish Archives, Blankenstein Family Heritage Centre, UJA Federation of Greater Toronto

Provincial Archives of Alberta

Queen's University Archives, Kingston

Royal Canadian Legion, Wingate Branch 256, Toronto
Saint John Jewish Historical Museum, Saint John, New Brunswick
University of Victoria
Vancouver Holocaust Education Centre
Vancouver Island University
Veterans Affairs Canada, Ottawa, Canadian Virtual War Memorial
Wilfrid Laurier Military History Archive

IMPORTANT RESEARCH WEBSITES

AirCrew Remembered
    http://www.aircrewremembered.com
AJEX
    http://www.ajex.org.uk
Ancestry.ca
    http://www.ancestry.ca
Bishops Remembers
    http://www.buremembers.ubishops.ca
Canadian Jewish Military Museum
    http://www.jcmm.ca
Commonwealth War Graves Commission
    http://www.cwgc.org
Forces War Records
    http://www.forces-war-records.co.uk
Geni.com
    https://www.geni.com
Hong Kong Veterans Commemorative Association C Force Data
    http://hkvca.ca
Juno Beach Centre
    http://www.junobeach.org
McGill Remembers
    http://mcgillremembers.mcgill.ca
The Memory Project (Historica Canada)
    http://www.thememoryproject.com
Myheritage.com
    http://www.myheritage.com
Newspapers.com
    http://www.newspapers.com
Flying Officer Clifford Shnier, RCAF Pilot J17452
    http://clifford.shniers.com

Uboat.net
http://uboat.net
Democracy at War Canadian Newspapers and the Second World War, Canadian War Museum
http://www.warmuseum.ca/cwm/exhibitions/newspapers/intro_e.shtml
World Machal
http://www.machal.org.il

INTERVIEWS BY THE AUTHOR

Charles P. Abelson, July 1, 2016
Kandi Abelson and Sari Abelson, July 1, 2016
Ethel Abramson, November 9, 2015
Myrna Adessky, August 2014
Jackie Adler, July 23, 2015
Oscar Adler, September 27, 2015
Brian Allen, August 21, 2015
Oscar Antel, October 6, 2015
Alex Balinson, March 15, 2016
Joan and Morley Balinson, February 6, 2016
Freeda Baron, October 8, 2015
Irving Baron, February 10, 2016
Ted Barris, August 2014
Sheila Baslaw, June 7, 2016
Beryl (Bunny) Bergstein, July 29, 2015
Coleman Bernstein, August 31, 2015
Katherine Biggs-Craft, February 6, 2015
Bea Bindman, July 7, 2015
Morley Blankstein, December 7, 2014
Gerry Bloch, November 15, 2015
Evelyn Bloom, May 22, 2016
Manny Borod, April 28, 2016
Edna Brinker, August 25, 2014
Jerome Brookler, June 10, 2016
Sharon Brown, November 17, 2015
Ellen Brownstone, October 25, 2015
Meyer Brownstone, October 30, 2015
Bert Bruser, September 7, 2014
Hal Burns, December 8, 2015
Eric Campbell, June 6, 2016
Saul Cherniack, October 6, 2015, and January 7, 2016
Anetta Chernin, June 6, 2015
Janet Chernin, February 14, 2015
Martin Chernin, April 13, 2016
David Chochinov, October 6, 2015
Hy Chud, October 9, 2015
June Claman, December 17, 2015
Gary Clement, May 9, 2016
Kathy Cohen, May 3, 2015
Lynda Cohen, November 1, 2015
Norman Cohen, September and October 2014
Esther Cole, November 7, 2014
Karen and Howard Conter, June 5, 2015
Robin Conway, November 3, 2015
Debbie Cooper, May 2, 2015
Steve Corday, July 4, 2016
Abraham Crotin, August 25, 2014
Louis Crotin, September 13, 2014
Nicola Davies, August 2015
Evelyn and Hal Davis, January 29, 2016
Louis Devor, Zipporah Eidlitz Kogut, and Katharine Williams, August 24, 2015

Jon Dlusy, September 3, 2015
Deena Dolgoy, January 4, 2017
Larry Donen, March 9, 2016
Shane Donen, August 18, 2015
Arthur Donin, September 8, 2015
Melany Eli, July 24, 2016
Ruth Elias, January 8, 2017
Shirley Ellis, June 4, 2016
Susan Ellman, July 29, 2014
Howard Erdunast, January 7, 2017
Davida Feder, January 26, 2016
Marjorie Feldman, August 20, 2015
Jack Feldman, March 19, 2015
Miriam Fenster, October 2, 2015
Brian Ferstman, October 4, 2015
Naomi Finkelstein, October 6, 2015
Barbara Fitchette, May 17, 2016
Steven Friedman, January 18, 2017
Harold Fromstein, March 26, 2016
Eby Gale, November 3, 2015
David Garshowitz, January 10, 2016
Bill Gladstone, November 25, 2014
Sharon Glass, October 21, 2015
Helen and Stephen Glazer, August 24, 2015
Mark Golden, January 19, 2016
Raymond Goldman, April 15, 2016
Julie Domb Gonik, January 15, 2015
Meyer Gordon, November 8, 2015
Jerry Grafstein, March 1, 2016
Joe Greenberg, August 1, 2014, and January 26, 2016
Hersh Gross, January 23, 2015
Prissy Guberman, October 8, 2015
Norman Gulko, March 19, 2015
Leo Guttman, August 11, 2014
Monty Hall (Monte Halparin), January 14, 2016
Jim Handman, June 13, 2016
Marion Harris, October 22, 2015
Robert Harris, November 2, 2015
David Hart, May 21, 2016
Crystal Hawk, August 4, 2016, and January 23, 2017
Yude Henteleff, October 23, 2015
Sylvia Hoffman, March 6, 2016
Harry Hurwitz, May 2, 2015
Nathan Isaacs, March 2, 2016
Millie Jacobs, December 29, 2014
Murray Jacobs, December 29, 2014
Doreen Jampolsky, November 1, 2015
Rayna Jolley, August 14, 2016
Joyce Kaplan, June 22, 2016
Sadie Kaplan and Bonnie Kaplan, June 26, 2016
Harry Kaushansky, May 25, 2015
Leslie Kemp, November 3, 2015
Sherry King, March 12, 2016
Leslie Kinrys, July 24, 2016
Monte Kwinter, September 18, 2015
Harold Laimon, May 1, 2016
Ruth Lande, July 27, 2014
Thelma (Tammy) Lazar, September 28, 2015
Ruth Lazare, April 7, 2016
Lawrence and Betty Levy, April 4, 2016
Julia Libby, April 29, 2016
Dorothy Lieff, August 15, 2014
Gordon Lindsay, January 22, 2015
David Lipsey, April 21, 2016
Steve Liss, May 18, 2016
Sandra London-Rakita, January 31, 2016
Robert Longworth, June 22, 2014
Maylene Ludwig, October 8, 2015

Rael Ludwig, October 8, 2015, and February 18, 2016
Danielle Markert, August 6, 2016
Morris Macklin, October 1, 2015
Mark Mager, March 30, 2016
Don Marcovitch, July 20, 2016
Danielle Markecht, August 7, 2016
Thomas Markowitz, July 28, 2017
David Matlow, October 17, 2014
Patricia Matthews, October 1, 2015
Martin Maxwell, September 21, 2014
Laurence Mayrans, June 26, 2016
Bill McAlister, October 19 and 26, 2015
George Meltz (nephew), July 2011
Fay Mendelsohn, August 13, 2016
Sarah Minden, March 5, 2016
Isabella Mintz, July 2011, November 2014, and August 2015
Henry Molot, September 7, 2015
John Molot, June 10, 2016
Matthew Moore, November 13, 2014
George Nashen, August 12, 2014
Steve Nathanson, April 29, 2016
Judy Neinstein, June 15, 2017
Melville Neuman, October 6, 2015
Hersh Nichols, August 25, 2015
Richard Nosov, March 22, 2016
Bill Novick, email, July 28, 2016
Jack O'Brien, February 7, 2017
Michael Ostfield, September 12, 2014
Jim Parks, November 3, 2015
Casey Pechet, March 9, 2016
Judy Pechet, March 13, 2016
D. Burke Penny, October 23, 2015
Tim Pervin, September 29, 2014
Ferne Phillips, August 7, 2015, and November 16, 2015
Elizabeth and Darrel Pink, June 7, 2015
Morris Polansky, March 13, 2015
Mayer Rabkin, October 6, 2015
Sue Ransohoff, April 11, 2015
Ed Rasky, July 1, 2016
Hedy Reeds, July 29, 2014
James A. Reeds III, July 28, 2014
Shelly Reuben, March 12, 2015
Jerry Richmond, August 17, 2015
Shom Roitenberg, October 6, 2015
Gerald Rosenberg, May 2016
Larry Rosenthal, September 3, 2015
Martin and Ricky Saslove, June 1, 2015
Alvin Schrage, November 5, 2015
Marilyn and Bill Schreiber, June 26, 2016
Elaine Schwartz, June 2, 2015
Louis Schwartz, October 14, 2015
Mindy Selby, December 16, 2015
Riva Selchin, October 6, 2015
Barbara Shafran, January 7, 2017
Thelma Shapiro, May 2, 2015
Roberta Sheps, April 30, 2016
Hal Sher, November 15, 2015
Eleanor Sherman, June 11, 2016
Karen Shiller, November 17, 2015
Clifford Franklin Shnier, January 20 and 21, 2016
John Shnier, August 11, 2016
Max Shnier, August 13, 2015
Mitchell Shnier, August 9, 2016
Beth and Norm Shore, October 7, 2015
Lorne Shusterman, June 4, 2016
Todd Sills, September 7, 2015
David Silver, October 6, 2015
Belva Spiel, May 1, 2016
Michael Steele, April 27, 2015

David Steinberg, December 14, 2015
Lawrence Steinberg, August 26, 2015
Martin Sterlin, August 14, 2014
Denise Stallman, March 27 and 30, 2016
Carole Stoffman, March 14, 2016
Max Sucharov, September 22, 2014
Howard Tenenbaum, May 26, 2015
Lee Thompson, January 13, 2016
Esther Thorley, June 2, 2016
Jack Tweyman, June 18, 2014
Elyse Vrancken, July 26, 2016 and May 31, 2017
Shirley Wagner, September 28, 2014
Francis Weil, August 12, 2016
Terry Whitty, August 28, 2015
Lorne Winer, December 31, 2014
Myra Wolch, October 6, 2015
Merle Wolofsky, July 28, 2014
Israel Yamron, October 6, 2015
Kitty Yaros, May 28, 2016
Clinton Young, May 3, 2016
Esther Zadjeman, Oct 21, 2015
Judi and Joel Zelikovitz, March 28, 2016
Chezi Zionce, August 10, 2016
Frank Zipursky, June 2014

BOOKS

Abella, Irving. *A Coat of Many Colours: Two Centuries of Jewish Life in Canada.* Toronto: Lester & Orpen Dennys, 1990.

———. *Nationalism, Communism, and Canadian Labour: The CIO, the Communist Party, and the Canadian Congress of Labour, 1935–1956.* Toronto: University of Toronto Press, 1973.

Allison, Les, and Harry Hayward. *They Shall Grow Not Old.* Brandon, MB: Commonwealth Air Training Plan Museum, 1992.

Allister, William. *Where Life and Death Hold Hands.* Delta, BC: Retsila, 2000.

Banham, Tony. *We Shall Suffer There: Hong Kong's Defenders Imprisoned, 1942–1945.* Hong Kong: Hong Kong University Press, 2009.

Barris, Ted. *Days of Victory 1939–1945.* Toronto: Thomas Allen, 2005.

———. *The Great Escape: A Canadian Story.* Toronto: Thomas Allen, 2013.

Bell, John. *Invaders from the North: How Canada Conquered the Comic Book Universe.* Toronto: Dundurn, 2006.

Bercuson, David J. *Our Finest Hour: Canada Fights the Second World War.* Toronto: HarperCollins, 2015.

Bercuson, David J., and Holger H. Herwig. *Deadly Seas: The Story of the St. Croix, the U305 and the Battle of the Atlantic.* Toronto: Random House of Canada, 1997.

Berger, Monty, and Brian Jeffrey Street. *Invasions without Tears: The Story of Canada's Top-Scoring Spitfire Wing in Europe during the Second World War.* Toronto: Random House of Canada, 1994.

Bialystok, Franklin. *Delayed Impact: The Holocaust and the Canadian Jewish Community.* Montreal and Kingston: McGill-Queen's University Press, 2010.

Bishop, Arthur. *Unsung Courage: 20 Stories of Canadian Valour and Sacrifice.* Toronto: HarperCollins, 2001.

Bracken, Robert. *Spitfire II: The Canadians.* Erin Mills, ON: Boston Mills Press, 1999.

Broadfoot, Barry. *Ten Lost Years, 1929–1939: Memories of Canadians Who Survived the Depression.* Toronto: McClelland & Stewart, 1973.

Byers, Daniel. *Zombie Army: The Canadian Army and Conscription in the Second World War.* Vancouver: UBC Press, 2016.

Celinscak, Mark. *Distance from the Belsen Heap: Allied Forces and the Liberation of a Nazi Concentration Camp.* Toronto: University of Toronto Press, 2015.

Chartrand, René. *Canadian Forces in World War Two.* Illustrated by Ron Volstad. Oxford: Osprey Publishing, 2001.

Christie, Carl A., with Fred Hatch. *Ocean Bridge: The History of RAF Ferry Command.* Toronto: University of Toronto Press, 1995.

Cook, Tim. *Fight to the Finish.* Toronto: Allen Lane/Penguin Canada, 2015.

———. *The Necessary War.* Toronto: Allen Lane, 2014.

Copp, Terry. *Fields of Fire: The Canadians in Normandy.* Toronto: University of Toronto Press, 2004.

———. The Brigade: *The Fifth Canadian Infantry Brigade in World War II.* Harrisburg, PA: Stackpole Books, 1992.

Copp, Terry, with Richard Nielsen. *No Price Too High: Canadians and the Second World War.* Toronto: McGraw-Hill Ryerson, 1996.

Coupland, Peter. *Straight and True: A History of RAF Leeming.* London: Leo Cooper, 1997.

Dalhousie University. *Pharos: Dalhousie University Yearbook 1941.* Halifax: Dalhousie University, c. 1941.

Danson, Barney, and Curtis Fahey. *Not Bad for a Sergeant.* Toronto: Dundurn, 2002.

Dunfield, Sir Brian. *Destruction by Fire of Knights of Columbus Hostel, St. John's, December 12th, 1942, with Loss of 99 Lives.* St. John's: Robinson, 1943.

Dunkelman, Ben. *Dual Allegiance: An Autobiography.* Toronto: Macmillan Canada, 1972.

English, Allan Douglas. *The Cream of the Crop: Canadian Aircrew, 1939–1945.* Montreal and Kingston: McGill-Queen's University Press, 1996.

Farquharson, Robert H. *For Your Tomorrow: Canadians and the Burma Campaign, 1941–1945.* Victoria: Trafford Publishing, 2004.

Feasby, W.R. *Official History of the Canadian Medical Services, 1939–1945*, vol. 2: *Clinical Subjects*. Ottawa: Queen's Printer, 1953.
Finestone, Colonel B. J., with K. David Brody. *An Honour to Serve: A Memoir by Colonel B.J. Finestone*. Montreal: Transcréation, 2013.
Frager, Ruth A. *Sweatshop Strife: Class, Ethnicity, and Gender in the Jewish Labour Movement of Toronto 1900–1939*. Toronto: University of Toronto Press, 1992.
Franklin, Stephen. *A Time of Heroes, 1940–1950*. Toronto: Natural Science of Canada, 1977.
Gaum, Lawrence. *From Belarus to Cape Breton and Beyond: My Family, My Roots*. Toronto: Rainbow Recording and Publications, 1996.
Goldbloom, Richard B. *A Lucky Life*. Halifax: Formac Publishing, 2013.
Gonick, Cy. *A Very Red Life: The Story of Bill Walsh*. St. John's: Canadian Committee on Labour History, 2001.
Gossage, Carolyn. *Greatcoats and Glamour Boots: Canadian Women at War (1939–1945)*. Toronto: Dundurn, 2001.
Granatstein, J.L. *The Best Little Army in the World*. Toronto: HarperCollins, 2015.
———. *Canada's Army: Waging War and Keeping the Peace*, 2nd ed. Toronto: University of Toronto Press, 2011.
Granatstein, J.L., and Norman Hillmer. *Battle Lines: Eyewitness Accounts from Canada's Military History*. Toronto: Thomas Allen, 2010.
Greenfield, Nathan. *The Damned: The Canadians at the Battle of Hong Kong and the POW Experience, 1941–45*. Toronto: HarperCollins, 2010.
———. *The Forgotten: Canadian POWs, Escapers and Evaders in Europe, 1935–1945*. Toronto: HarperCollins, 2014.
Greenhous, Brereton. *"C" Force to Hong Kong: A Canadian Catastrophe, 1941–1945*. Toronto: Dundurn, 1997.
Grehan, John, and Martin Mace. *Disaster in the Far East, 1940–1942*. Barnsley, UK: Pen and Sword Books, 2015.
Hadley, Michael L. *U-Boats Against Canada: German Submarines in Canadian Waters*. Montreal and Kingston: McGill-Queen's University Press, 1985.
Hatch, F.J. *The Aerodrome of Democracy: Canada and the British Commonwealth Air Training Program, 1939–1945*. Ottawa: Directorate of History, Department of National Defence, 1983.
Heaps, Leo. *The Grey Goose of Arnhem*. London: Weidenfeld & Nicolson, 1976.
Heritage and History: The Saskatoon Jewish Community. Saskatoon: Congregation Agudas Israel, 1998.
Historical Section of the Royal Canadian Air Force. *The RCAF Overseas: The Sixth Year*. Toronto: Oxford University Press, 1949.

How, Douglas. *Night of the Caribou.* Hantsport, NS: Lancelot Press, 1988.

Howard, Victor. *"We Were the Salt of the Earth! The On-to-Ottawa Trek and the Regina Riot.* Regina: University of Regina Press, 1985.

Jay, John. *Facing Fearful Odds: My Father's Story of Escape, Capture and Resistance, 1940–1945.* Barnsley, UK: Pen and Sword Books, 2014.

Jessup, A.R. *The Regimental History of the Governor General's Foot Guards.* Ottawa: Mortimer, 1948.

Jewish Historical Society of Southern Alberta. *Land of Promise: The Jewish Experience in Southern Alberta, 1889–1945.* Calgary: Jewish Historical Society of Southern Alberta, 1996. http://www.jhssa.org/book.

Johnston, Murray C. *Canada's Craftsmen at 50!: The Story of Electrical and Mechanical Engineering in the Canadian Armed Forces Up to and Including the 50th Anniversary of the Formation of the Corps of Royal Canadian Electrical and Mechanical Engineers.* Borden, Ontario: EME Officers' Fund, 1997.

Keshen, Jeffrey. *Saints, Sinners and Soldiers: Canada's Second World War.* Vancouver: UBC Press, 2007.

Lake, Deborah. *Tartan Air Force: Scotland and Century of Military Aviation 1907–2007.* Edinburgh: Birlinn, 2009.

Lamb, James B. *On the Triangle Run: The Fighting Spirit of Canada's Navy*, 2nd ed. Toronto: Stoddart, 2000.

Levenston, Michael. *My Darling Mom: Gerald Levenston's WWII Letters Home to Canada.* Amazon Digital Services, 2012.

Levi, S. Gershon. *Breaking New Ground: The Struggle for a Jewish Chaplaincy in Canada.* Edited by David Golinkin. Montreal: Canadian Jewish Congress Archives, 1994.

Levine, Allan. *Coming of Age: The Jews of Manitoba.* Winnipeg: Heartland Associates, 2009.

Levy, David. *Stalin's Man in Canada: Fred Rose and Soviet Espionage.* Enigma Books, 2011.

Lewis, Amanda West. *September 17: A Novel.* Markham, ON: Red Deer Press, 2013.

Lopata, Vince. *From Heaven to Hell Part One: The Story of the Winnipeg Grenadiers as Part of "Y" Force and "C" Force during World War II.* Winnipeg: McNally Robinson, 2013. http://www.mcnallyrobinson.com/9781927533468/vince-lopata/from-heaven-to-hell-part-one#.

Ludwig, Sidura. *Holding My Breath.* Toronto: Key Porter, 2007.

MacLaren, Roy. *Canadians behind Enemy Lines, 1939–1945.* Vancouver: University of British Columbia Press, 1981.

Margolian, Howard. *Conduct Unbecoming: The Story of the Murder of Canadian Prisoners of War in Normandy.* Toronto: University of Toronto Press, 1998.

Marshall, Eliot. *Once upon a Story.* Renfrew, ON: General Store Publishing House, 2008.

Menkis, Richard, and Norman Ravvin, eds. *The Canadian Jewish Studies Reader.* Markham, ON: Red Deer Press, 2004.

Mickleburgh, Rod, with Rudyard Griffiths. *Rare Courage: Veterans of the Second World War Remember.* Toronto: McClelland & Stewart, 2005.

Middlebrook, Martin, and Chris Everitt. *The Bomber Command War Diaries: An Operational Reference Book, 1939–1945.* Harmondsworth: Penguin, 1990.

Millar, Ruth Wright. *Saskatchewan Heroes and Rogues.* Regina: Coteau Books, 2004.

Mowat, Farley. *And No Birds Sang.* Vancouver: Douglas and McIntyre, 2012 [1975].

Nolan, Brian. *Hero: The Buzz Beurling Story.* Harmondsworth: Penguin, 1982.

O'Keefe, David. *One Day in August: The Untold Story Behind Canada's Tragedy at Dieppe.* Toronto: Knopf Canada, 2013.

Peden, Murray. *A Thousand Shall Fall: The True Story of a Canadian Bomber Pilot in World War Two.* Toronto: Dundurn, 2003.

Penny, D. Burke. *Beyond the Call: Royal Canadian Corps of Signals, Brigade Headquarters, "C" Force, Hong Kong and Japan, 1941–1945.* Nepean, ON: Hong Kong Veterans Commemorative Association, 2009.

Penslar, Derek J. *Jews in the Military: A History.* Princeton, NJ: Princeton University Press, 2013.

Petrou, Michael. *Renegades: Canadians in the Spanish Civil War.* Vancouver: UBC Press, 2008.

Plaut, Jonathan V. *The Jews of Windsor, 1790–1990: A Chronicle.* Toronto: Dundurn, 2007.

Raber, Manny. *Manny Goes to War.* Medicine Hat, AB: self-published, 1999.

Ralph, Wayne. *Aces, Warriors and Wingmen: Firsthand Accounts of Canada's Fighter Pilots in the Second World War.* Toronto: Wiley, 2005.

Roland, Charles G. *Long Night's Journey into Day: Prisoners of War in Hong Kong and Japan.* Waterloo, ON: Wilfrid Laurier University Press, 2001.

Rome, David, ed. *Canadian Jews in World War II, Part I: Decorations.* Montreal: Canadian Jewish Congress, 1947.

Rome, David, ed. *Canadian Jews in World War II, Part II: Casualties.* Montreal: Canadian Jewish Congress, 1948.

Rosenberg, Louis. *Canada's Jews: A Social and Economic Study of Jews in Canada in the 1930s.* Edited by Morton Weinfeld. Montreal and Kingston: McGill-Queen's University Press, 1993.

Royal Canadian Air Force. *The RCAF Overseas: The Fifth Year.* Toronto: Oxford University Press, 1945.

Sarty, Roger. *War in the St. Lawrence: The Forgotten U-boat Battles on Canada's Shores.* Toronto: Penguin Canada, 2012.

Shaw, Susan Evans. *Canadians at War, vol. 2: A Guide to the Battlefields and Memorials of World War II.* Fredericton, NB: Goose Lane, 2014.

Shuchat, Wilfred. *The Gate of Heaven: The Story of Shaar Hashomayim in Montreal.* Montreal and Kingston: McGill-Queen's University Press, 2000.

Silver, L. Ray. *Last of the Gladiators: A World War II Bomber Navigator's Story.* Shrewsbury, UK: Airlife, 1995.

Slater, Tom. *The City of Sarnia War Remembrance Project: A Record of Sarnia's Sacrifices and Contributions Made During the War.* Sarnia: Haines Printing, 2014.

Smith, Cherie. *Mendel's Children: A Family Chronicle.* Calgary: University of Calgary Press, 1997.

Smith, Ken. *War at Sea: Canada and the Battle of the Atlantic.* Halifax, NS: Nimbus Publishing, 2015.

Smith, Wilfred I. *Code Word CANLOAN.* Toronto: Dundurn, 1992.

Stacey, C.P. *The Canadian Army 1939–1945: An Official Historical Summary.* Ottawa: Department of National Defence and King's Printer, 1948. http://www.cmp-cpm.forces.gc.ca/dhh-dhp/his/docs/CDN_ARMY_39-45_E.pdf.

———. *Official History of the Canadian Army in the Second World War, vol. 1, Six Years of War: The Army in Canada, Britain and the Pacific.* Ottawa: Department of National Defence, Directorate of History and Heritage, and Queen's Printer, 1955. http://www.cmp-cpm.forces.gc.ca/dhh-dhp/his/docs/Sixyrs_e.pdf.

Swankey, Ben. *What's New? Memoirs of a Socialist Idealist.* Victoria: Trafford Publishing, 2008.

Toman, Cynthia. An Officer and a Lady: Canadian Military Nursing and the Second World War. Vancouver: UBC Press, 2007.

Torontow, Cy. *There I Was: A Collection of Reminiscences by Members of the Ottawa Jewish Community Who Served in World War II.* Ottawa: Ottawa Post of the Jewish War Veterans and Ottawa Jewish Historical Society, 1999.

Trafford, Tyler. *Memories on the March: Personal Stories of the Jewish Military Veterans of Southern Alberta.* Calgary: Jewish War Veterans of Canada, Post Number 2, 2001.

Tulchinsky, Gerald. *Branching Out: The Transformation of the Canadian Jewish Community.* Toronto: Stoddart, 1998.

———. *Canada's Jews: A People's Journey.* Toronto: University of Toronto Press, 2008.

Vance, Jonathan. *Objects of Concern: Canadian Prisoners of War in the Twentieth Century.* Vancouver: UBC Press.

Vincent, Carl. *No Reason Why: The Canadian Hong Kong Tragedy; An Examination.* Stittsville, ON: Canada's Wings, 1981.

Williams, Jeffrey. *The Long Left Flank: The Hard Fought Way to the Reich, 1944–1945.* London: Leo Cooper, 1988.

Zuehlke, Mark. *Assault on Juno.* Victoria: Raven Books, 2012.

———. *Breakout from Juno: First Canadian Army and the Normandy Campaign, July 4–August 21, 1944.* Vancouver: Douglas & McIntyre, 2011.

———. *Forgotten Victory: First Canadian Army and the Cruel Winter of 1944–45.* Vancouver: Douglas & McIntyre, 2014.

———. *Holding Juno: Canada's Heroic Defence of the D-Day Beaches: June 7–12, 1944.* Vancouver: Douglas & McIntyre, 2005.

———. *On to Victory: The Canadian Liberation of the Netherlands, March 23–May 5, 1945.* Vancouver: Douglas & McIntyre, 2010.

———. *Ortona: Canada's Epic World War II Battle.* Vancouver: Douglas & McIntyre, 1999.

———. *Tragedy at Dieppe: Operation Jubilee, August 19, 1942.* Vancouver: Douglas & McIntyre, 2013.

ARTICLES AND THESES

Abramson, Henry. "Just Different: The Last Jewish Family of Ansonville, Ontario." *Canadian Jewish Studies* 9, no. 1 (2003).

Armstrong, John G. "RCAF Identity in Bomber Command Squadron Names and Sponsors." *Canadian Military History* 8, no. 2 (Spring 1999): 43–52.

Arnold, Abraham. "Welcoming the Jews." In *Visions of the New Jerusalem, Religious Settlement on the Prairies.* Edited by Benjamin G. Smillie. Edmonton: NeWest, 1983.

Beer, Max, "What Else Could We Have Done? The Montreal Jewish Community, the Canadian Jewish Congress, the Jewish Press, and the Holocaust." MA thesis, Department of History, Concordia University, April 2006.

Bookman, Max. "Canadian Jews in Uniform." In *Canadian Jewish Reference Book and Directory*, 111–128. Edited by Eli Gottesman. Toronto: Jewish Institute of Higher Research of the Central Rabbinical Seminary of Canada, 1963.

Buddle, Melanie. "You Have to Think like a Man and Act Like a Lady: Businesswomen in British Columbia, 1920–1980." *BC Studies*, no. 151 (Autumn 2006).

Byers, Daniel. "Canada's Zombies: A Portrait of Canadian Conscripts and Their Experiences during the Second World War." In *Forging a Nation: Perspectives on the Canadian Military Experience*. Edited by Bernd Horn. St. Catharines, ON: Vanwell Publishing, 2002.

———. "Mobilizing Canada: The National Resources Mobilization Act, Department of National Defence and Compulsory Military Service in Canada." PhD thesis, McGill University, August 2000.

Cafferky, Sean. "Battle Honours Won HMS Nabob, 1944." *Canadian Military History* 19, no. 3 (Summer 2010).

Cherniack, Saul. "Personal Perspective: Saul Cherniack." In *Jewish Life and Times*, vol. 3: *Jewish Radicalism in Winnipeg 1905–1960*. Edited by Daniel Stone. Winnipeg: Jewish Heritage Centre of Western Canada, 2003.

Dickson, Paul. "Crerar and the Decision to Garrison Hong Kong." *Canadian Military History* 3, no. 1 (January 23, 2012).

Fisher, Robert C. "Tactics, Training, Technology: The RCN's Summer of Success, July–September 1942." *Canadian Military History* 6, no. 2 (Autumn 1997): 7–20.

Frazer, Chris. "From Pariahs to Patriots: Canadian Communists and the Second World War," *Past Imperfect*, vol. 5: 3–36, 1996. http://dx.doi.org/10.21971/P7NK5Z.

Freedman, Chief Justice Samuel. "Student Days at the University of Manitoba." *Manitoba Law Journal* 37 (special issue), chap. 2, 2014.

Glass, Joseph B. "Isolation and Alienation: Factors in the Growth of Zionism in the Canadian Prairies, 1917–1939." *Canadian Jewish Studies* 9 (2001).

Grams, Grant. "Enemies within Our Bosoms: Nazi Sabotage in Canada." *Journal of Military and Strategic Studies* 14, no. 3 and 4 (2012).

Granatstein, J.L. "The Problem of Religion in Canadian Forces Postings: Liebmann vs the Minister of National Defence et al.," *Canadian Military History*, 19, no. 4 (Autumn 2010): 68–74.

———. "Ethnic and Religious Enlistment in Canada during the Second World War." Essays in Honour of Gerald Tulchinsky. *Canadian Jewish Studies* 21 (2013): 174–180.

Grodzinsky, John R. "Kangaroos at War: The History of the 1st Canadian Armoured Personnel Carrier Regiment." *Canadian Military History* 4, no. 2 (January 2012): 2–3.

Halladay, Laurel. "Ladies and Gentlemen, Soldiers and Artists: Canadian Military Entertainers 1939–1946." MA thesis, Department of History, University of Calgary, 2000.

Halliday, Hugh. "F/L W. Henry Nelson, Man of Many Talents." *Journal of the Canadian Aviation Historical Society* 8, no. 2 (Summer 1970): 35–36.

———. "CAN/RAF: The Canadians in the Royal Air Force." *Royal Canadian Air Force Journal* 4, no. 2 (Spring 2015).

Henry, Hugh G. "The Calgary Tanks at Dieppe," *Canadian Military History* 4, no. 1 (1995).

Hill, Kyle. "Tickling the Dragon's Tail: The Story of the 'Demon Core.'" Nerdist.com, December 11, 2014, http//nerdist.com/tickling-the-dragons-tail-the-story-of-the-demon-core.

Jessup, Pat. "Kriegsgefangenenlager: A POW's Account of the Loss of Athabaskan in 1944." *Canadian Naval Review* 5, no. 2 (Summer 2009).

Jones, Edgar. "LMF: The Use of Psychiatric Stigma in the Royal Air Force During the Second World War." *Journal of Military History* 70 (April 2006).

Joost, Matthias. "Racism and Enlistment: The Second World War Policies of the Royal Canadian Air Force." *Canadian Military History* 21, no. 1.

Kabeary, Jennifer. "The Field of Play: Military and Sport in Southern Alberta Communities during the Second World War," MA thesis, Kinesiology and Physical Education, University of Lethbridge, 2009.

Kalter, Bella Briansky. "Ansonville: A Jewish Community That Was." *American Jewish Archives*, November 1978, 107–125.

Lester, Peter. "Four Cents to Sea: 16mm, the Royal Canadian Naval Film Society and the Mobilization of Entertainment." *Film History* 25, no. 4 (2013): 62–81.

Margolis, Rebecca. "A Tempest in Three Teapots: Yom Kippur Balls in London, New York and Montreal." In *The Canadian Jewish Studies Reader*. Edited by Richard Menkis and Norman Ravvin. Markham, ON: Red Deer Press, 2004.

Martin, Jean. "The Great Canadian Air Battle: The British Commonwealth Air Training Plan and the RCAF Fatalities during the Second World War." *Forces Magazine* 3, no. 1 (2002).

McBride, Michelle. "From Indifference to Internment: An Examination of RCMP Responses to Nazism and Fascism in Canada from 1934 to 1941." MA thesis, Department of History, Memorial University of Newfoundland, May 1997. http:/www.collectionscanada.gc.ca/obj/s4/f2/dsk2/ftp04/mq23157.pdf.

McGeer, Eric. "Words of Valediction and Remembrance: The Bény-sur-Mer Canadian War Cemetery, Normandy, France." *Canadian Military History* 13, no. 3 (2004).

Menkis, Richard. "Canadian Jewish Chaplains and Canadian Encounters with Dutch Survivors 1944–1945." *American Jewish Archives Journal* 60, no. 1–2 (2008).

Moon, Barbara. "The Nuclear Death of a Nuclear Scientist." *Maclean's*, republished in *The Jewish Post*, November 30, 1961.

Rasky, Frank. "Newfoundland's Furious Fire by Sabotage: The Knights of Columbus Hostel Disaster of 1942." *Liberty*, October 1959, http://ngb.chebucto.org/Articles/dis-knights-of-columbus-1942.shtml.

Robinson, Ira. "A Letter from the Sabbath Queen: Rabbi Yudel Rosenberg Addresses Montreal Jewry." In Richard Menkis and Norman Ravvin, eds., *The Canadian Jewish Studies Reader.* Markham, ON: Red Deer Press, 2004

Roland, Charles G. "On the Beach and in the Bag: The Fate of Dieppe Casualties Left Behind." *Canadian Military History* 9, no. 4 (Autumn 2000): 6–25.

Rosenberg, Louis. "Jews in Canada." *Contemporary Jewish Record* 2, no. 2 (March–April 1939).

Shapiro, Lionel. "Dieppe." In *Cavalcade of the North: An Entertaining Collection of Distinguished Writing by Selected Canadian Authors.* Edited by George E. Nelson. New York: Doubleday, 1958.

Sokolov, Hyman. "Battling Bias in Manitoba: The Exposure of Discrimination in Methods of Selection of Students to the Medical College Brings Important Gains," *Jewish Post* (Winnipeg), March 22, 1945.

Souchen, Russell Alexander. "Beyond D-Day: Maintaining Morale in the 3rd Canadian Infantry Division June–July 1944." Thesis, Faculty of History, University of Ottawa, 2010.

Srebnick, Henry. "Changing an Illusion: The Canadian Communist Movement." In *A Vanished Ideology: Essays on the Jewish Communist Movement in the English-Speaking World in the Twentieth Century.* Edited by Matthew B. Hoffman and Henry F. Srebnick. Albany: State University of New York Press, 2016.

Stelzer, Alexandra. "Winnipeg Jews in the Canadian Army in World War II." Winnipeg Jewish Archives, 1987, Jewish Heritage Centre of Western Canada.

Theobald, Simon James. "A False Sense of Equality: The Black Canadian Experience of the Second World War." MA thesis, Department of History, University of Ottawa, 2008.

Usher, Peter J. "Jews in the Royal Canadian Air Force." *Canadian Jewish Studies* 20 (2012): 93–114. http://cjs.journals.yorku.ca/index.php/cjs/article/viewFile/36059/34618

———. "Removing the Stain: A Jewish Volunteer's Perspective in World War II." *Canadian Jewish Studies* 23 (2015): 37–67.

Vilhjálmsson, Vilhjálmur Örn. "Iceland, the Jews, and Anti-Semitism, 1625–2004." In *Behind the Humanitarian Mask: The Nordic Countries, Israel and the Jews.* Edited by Manfred Gerstenfeld. Jerusalem: Jerusalem Centre for Public Affairs, 2008.

Weinfeld, Morton. "Louis Rosenberg and the Origins of the Socio-Demographic

Study of Jews in Canada." Jewish Population Studies (Papers in Jewish Demography). Avraham Harman Institute of Contemporary Jewry, 1993: 39–53. https://www.bjpa.org/search-results/publication/131.
Whitby, Michael. "The Case of the Phantom MTB and the Loss of HMCS *Athabaskan*." *Canadian Military History* 11, no. 3 (Summer 2002).
Zelig, Martin. "Louis Slotin and 'The Invisible Killer.'" *Beaver* 75, no. 4 (August–September 1995): 20–27.

UNPUBLISHED MANUSCRIPTS

Abelson, Charles P. "Circumstances Beyond Our Control." Montreal. Manuscript about the life of his namesake and uncle, Charles Abelson, killed on SS *Caribou* off Newfoundland in October 1942.
Baron, Freeda."Memories of a Farmer's Daughter." Edited by Bruce Sarbit. Courtesy of Ricki J. Miles.
Boroditsky, Sam. "Sam Boroditsky's War," unpublished memoir, 1989, courtesy of Manny Borod.
Devor, Louis. "Devor, Devore, Dorfman, D'Wor, Dwor, Sandler: First Family Reunion, July 29, 1983."
Feinstein, Helen. "Diary of Helen Feinstein." Tel Aviv. Courtesy of Louis Devor.
Freedman, Samuel. "Memoir." Courtesy of David Freeman.
Glazer, Albert. "WWII Biography of Albert Glazer," 1997. Courtesy of Steven Glazer.
Hollinger, Sophie. "Reminiscences: A Romanian Heritage." Courtesy of John Hoffman.
Kaplan, Irving. "Kaplan Memoir," 2007. Courtesy of Joyce Kaplan.
Kosowatsky, Moishe, and Moishe Wolofsky. "From the Land of Despair to the Land of Promise." Travel journals of Dick Steele and Bill Walsh, early 1930s. Courtesy of Michael Steele.
Markowitz, Thomas. Excerpt from "Jacob Markowitz biography."
Miller, Ben. "War Story as Told by Joe Minden." Courtesy of Sarah Minden.
Minden, Sarah. Speech at Delta High School, Hamilton, in 2012 at the ceremony honouring Joseph Minden on the school's Wall of Excellence.
Novek, Maurice. "War Story," unpublished memoir. Courtesy of Brian Ferstman.
Olitt, Ghita Reuben. Chronology in "Memoir." Courtesy of Shelly Reuben, March 13, 2015.
Ransohoff, Sue. "A Yank in the RCAF," unpublished memoir, May 2015, 2.
Sugarman, Martin. "'Full Ahead Both!' Jewish Service in the British, Commonwealth and Israeli Merchant Navies in WW2—Record of Honour." Draft of

research paper. Courtesy of Martin Sugarman, Association of Jewish Ex-Servicemen and Women of the UK–AJEX Museum, May 17, 2016.
White, Vernon. *Four Years and a Bit.* 427 Squadron Association, 2002. http//www.427squadron.com/book_file/white/four_years_leeming.html.

PRIVATE PAPERS AND DIARIES

Abelson, Charles P. Draft notes for a speech to the 2010 YM-YWHA Alex Dworkin Sports Hall of Fame Induction Ceremony, by Charles P. Abelson. Courtesy of Charles P. Abelson.
Balinson, Alex. Letters. Courtesy of Alex Balinson and Morley and Joan Balinson.
Barris, Ted. Diary notes, "Interview with Peter Desjardins," May 6, 2005.
Bleeman, Murray. Letters. Courtesy of Ferne Phillips.
Canadian Jewish Congress Brochure, 1940. Courtesy of Ferne Phillips.
Devor, David. Letters from Charlie Drubich and to Devor family. Courtesy of Louis Devor family collection.
Evans, George W, "Eulogy for Philip Foster," handwritten notes by the former Flin Flon, Manitoba, mayor. Courtesy of Doug Evans.
Ferstman, Brian, "Notes from an Interview with Maurice Novek, March 20, 2005, and April 18, 2005."
Fried, Carl M. Letters. Courtesy of Kathy Cohen and Bruce Baff.
Gertel, Joe. Letters to Hedy Neumann. Courtesy of Susan Ellman.
Goodman, Mr. and Mrs. Solomon. Letter from Station Chaplain I.M. Roe, January 27, 1943. Darrel Pink collection.
Greenstein, Meyer. Letters. Courtesy of Hersh Gross.
Kaplan, Irving. Letters to various people during WWII. Courtesy of Sadie Kaplan.
Lazarus, John. Letters. Courtesy of Sylvia Hoffman.
Minden, Joseph. Diary and letters. Courtesy of Sarah Minden and Mark Minden.
Pascal, Fred. Letters. Courtesy of Kathy Cohen.
Rosenthal, William. Letters. Courtesy of Larry Rosenthal.
Steele, Dick. Letters to Esther Steele, and Esther to Dick, 1940–1944, including clippings from newspapers, cards, telegrams, and photos; also miscellaneous letters from Bill Walsh, Muni Erlick, J.B. Salsberg, and others, and letters from Dick Steele to individuals in the labour movement in Canada and United Kingdom. Michael Steele collection (since donated to OJA).
Wolf, Herb. Letters. Courtesy of Elaine Schwartz.
Zelikovitz, William. Letters. Courtesy of Joel Zelikovitz, and Flight Logbook, and *Religious Calendar for the Jewish Men and Women in the Canadian Armed Forces*, Religious Welfare Committee Canadian Jewish Congress 1944–45/5705.

VIDEO AND AUDIO

Belsen, Kramer; Corpses. Steven Spielberg Film and Video Archive, United States Holocaust Memorial Museum, RG-60.4358, Film ID: 2805, April 16, 1945. https://collections.ushmm.org/search/catalog/irn1003822.

Canadian Army Film Unit, *Canadian Army Newsreel,* Issue No. 1, November 1942, Library and Archives Canada.

de la Varre, André, director. *Hong Kong: Gateway to China*, A Screen Traveler Picture, May 15, 1938, http://bit.ly/2yUw81z.

Heroes Remember series, Veterans Affairs Canada, http//www.veterans.gc.ca/eng/video-gallery/. Interviews with David Golden, George Harrison, and Bernard J. Finestone.

"Lions" Adopt Lion Cub, British Pathé, 1943, b&w, 1 min. Members of the RCAF "Lion" Squadron adopt as their mascot a lion from the London Zoo, http://www.britishpathe.com/video/lions-adopt-lion-cub.

Marcovitch, Jack. Interviewed by Eric Sorensen in a CBC TV news report from the 1980s, https://www.youtube.com/watch?v=1mXVpVwx59g.

McKenna, Brian, director. *Savage Christmas: Hong Kong 1941*, National Film Board, 1991, from "The Valour and the Horror" series.

Nobleman, Esther. Audio interview, part 1, Jewish Historical Society of British Columbia, Jewish Museum and Archives of British Columbia, February 24, 2014, https://archives.jewishmuseum.ca/esther-nobleman-part-1.

No Greater Honour: A Record of Canadian Jewish Military Service. Jewish War Veterans of Canada and Triune Productions, 1987, held at Ontario Jewish Archives, http://search.ontariojewisharchives.org/Permalink/accessions24504.

Olin, Chuck, director, producer, writer. *In Our Own Hands: The Hidden Story of the Jewish Brigade in World War II*, 1998, video, produced in cooperation with the Spertus Institute of Jewish Studies, Chicago, http//www.mediaburn.org/video/in-our-own-hands-the-hidden-story-of-the-jewish-brigade-in-world-war-ii.

Pascal, Arthur. Interview with his grandchildren, three audiotapes. Courtesy of Kathy Cohen.

Pechet, Mitch. "My Wartime Experiences," interview, University of Victoria, March 19, 2017, http://contentdm.library.uvic.ca/cdm/compoundobject/collection/collection13/id/1953/rec/1.

"Squadron Leader Sydney Simon Shulemson, DSO, DFC," video, Air Force Museum of Alberta, Calgary, http://www.digitalheritage.ca/airforce/shulemson/shulemson.htm.

Tribute to Hamilton's Jewish Veterans, video, Hamilton Hebrew Academy, May 2010.

VE Day London, British Pathé, 1945, http//www.britishpathe.com/video/ve-day-london-3.

"Veteran Stories," The Memory Project (Historica Canada). Interviews with Nathan Isaacs, Hy Chud(novsky), E. David Hart, Esther Mager, Irvin Lorne Winer, Estelle Aspler, Louis Gelman, Bernard J. Finestone. Used with permission. http://www.thememoryproject.com.

Walsh, Bill, and Esther Steele Walsh. Interview with family, audiotapes 3–5, 2004. Courtesy of Michael Steele (since donated to OJA).

Photographs

1

2

1 Tombstone of Bombardier George Meltz, in Bény-sur-Mer Canadian War Cemetery, Normandy, France. "He died so Jewry shall suffer no more." (John Friedlan photo.)

2 Gertrude and George Meltz, wedding portrait, England, October 1943. (Photo courtesy Isabella Meltz.)

1

2

1 Nathan Isaacs, originally from Winnipeg, flew Halifax bombers for the RCAF, and survived more than 30 missions over Europe. (Ellin Bessner photo.)

2 Morris Polansky, originally of Oxbow, Saskatchewan, on Remembrance Day 2016 in Toronto. Polansky served in England, Italy, Belgium, and Holland. (Ellin Bessner photo.)

1

2

1 Pilot Officer Hymie Steinberg of Winnipeg served as an RCAF wireless operator and air gunner. Killed in Iceland, December 1944. His brother David Steinberg is a Hollywood comedian. (Photo courtesy Library and Archives Canada, Department of National Defence fonds/Vol. 28724, item no. 33973.)

2 Lt. Col. Norman Cohen (left), with Lorne Winer, both of Toronto. Cohen served with the RCAF in Europe and Burma. Winer served with Royal Canadian Artillery in Europe. (Ellin Bessner photo.)

1

2

1 Toronto's Ben Dunkelman, (left) in Europe in 1944. Rejected by the Royal Canadian Navy because of his religion, Dunkelman later won a Distinguished Service Order medal for bravery in battle in Germany. Dunkelman later volunteered with the Machal fighters in Israel's War of Independence in 1948. (Courtesy Ontario Jewish Archives. Fonds 2, Series 4 File 11.)

2 David Croll was a two-time mayor of Windsor when he enlisted, as a private, in 1939. (Photo courtesy Crystal Hawk.)

1

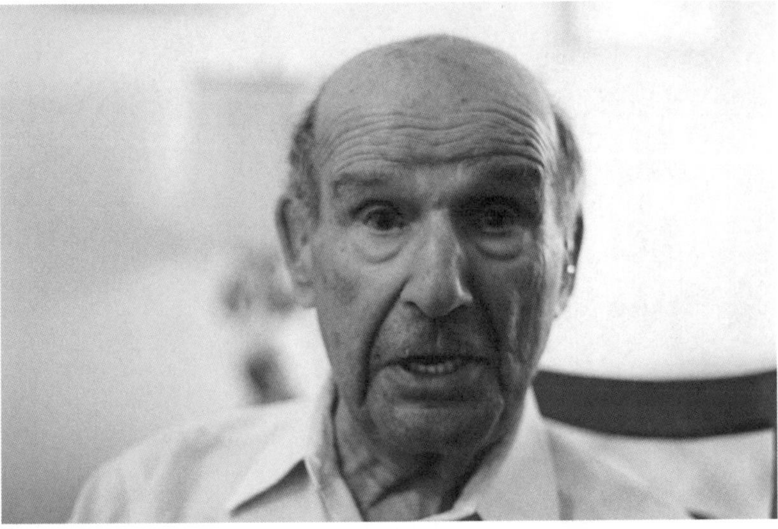
2

1 Sue Ransohoff (on the left) served in Newfoundland with the RCAF Women's Division. An American, she enlisted in 1943 after her first husband, RCAF Pilot Officer Michael Jacobs of Montreal, was killed. (Photo courtesy Sue Ransohoff.)

2 Col. (Hon.) David Lloyd Hart of Montreal won the Military Medal for saving 100 Canadian troops at Dieppe in August 1942. (Ellin Bessner photo.)

1

2

1 Montreal's Sydney Shulemson became the most highly decorated Canadian Jewish airman in World War II, winning a Distinguished Service Order and a Distinguished Flying Cross. (Photo courtesy Alex Dworkin Canadian Jewish Archives.)

2 Miriam "Mimi" Hart (née Freedman) of Montreal was awarded a Mention in Dispatches, the only Canadian Jewish servicewoman decorated in the war. Shown here with Toronto's Rabbi Samuel Cass distributing Chanukah gifts to Jewish Holocaust survivors, Belgium 1944. (Photo courtesy Library and Archives Canada/Department of National Defence fonds/a188717)

1

2

1 Five Olfman brothers from Kamsack, Saskatchewan. Left to right: Abe, Royal Canadian Dental Corps; Jack, RCAF; Solomon "Shia" (killed 1942) with the artillery; Maurice and Hymie, both RCAF. (Photo courtesy Ontario Jewish Archives.)

2 The seven Maser brothers of Ottawa at their sister's wedding in July 1942. (Photo courtesy Ottawa Jewish Archives.)

1

2

1 Dick Steele (born Moishe Kosowatsky) was a labour leader and communist before his arrest in Toronto in 1940. He later enlisted in the army and fought in France, where he was killed in 1944. (Photo courtesy Michael Steele.)

2 Montreal-born Hy Chud (left), brother Ben Chudnovsky (right), with Oscar Antel of Winnipeg (bottom), on leave in England. (Photo courtesy Hy Chud.)

1

2

1 Toronto comedians Frank Shuster (left) and Johnny Wayne (centre) enlisted in the Canadian Army in 1941, and performed at home and overseas. (Photo courtesy Library and Archives Canada/Department of National Defence fonds/ a132839)

2 Harry Hurwitz of Montreal was a POW in April 1944 after his ship HMCS *Athabaskan* was torpedoed off the coast of France. Hurwitz took the sword he is holding from a dead German officer after liberation. (Ellin Bessner photo.)

1

2

1 Sgt. Samuel Moses "Moe" Hurwitz won the Distinguished Conduct Medal and the Military Medal. The Montrealer was killed in Holland in 1944. (Photo courtesy Alex Dworkin Canadian Jewish Archives.)

2 Hurwitz played professional hockey with the Lachine Rapides in Montreal. He turned down a tryout with the Boston Bruins to enlist in 1940. (Photo courtesy Shelly Reuben.)

1

2

1 Section Officer Rose Goodman of New Glasgow, Nova Scotia, with the RCAF Women's Division, killed in January 1943. She was the only serving Canadian Jewish woman to die in the war. (Courtesy Claresholm and District Museum G. 997.-012.129A)

2 Canadian Jewish soldiers attend the first ever Yom Kippur service held in Iceland, 1940. Left side, top row, second from left, Maxwell London. Left side, middle row, extreme left, Lionel Cohen. Bottom row, left, wearing prayer shawl, Abe Conway, a British soldier. Right side, middle row, second from end, Meyer Bubis. Right side, top row, second from left, Harry Yaros, a British-born soldier from Toronto. (Photo courtesy Sandra London-Rakita.)

1

2

1 Rabbi Samuel Cass holds services for Canadian troops in Cleve, Germany in March 1945. Among the troops were brothers Lionel and Gerald Mernick, and Hy Chud. (Photo courtesy Library and Archives Canada/Department of National Defence e010753348)

2 Canadian Jewish airmen attend a Passover seder at Isow's restaurant in London, March 1945. Back row: Sid Slonim, Jack Hershfield, Oscar Nerman from Winnipeg, unknown, George Nashen and Gil Mogil of Montreal. Bottom left: Nathan Isaacs of Toronto, Archie Levine. (Photo courtesy Joel Zelikovitz.)

Index